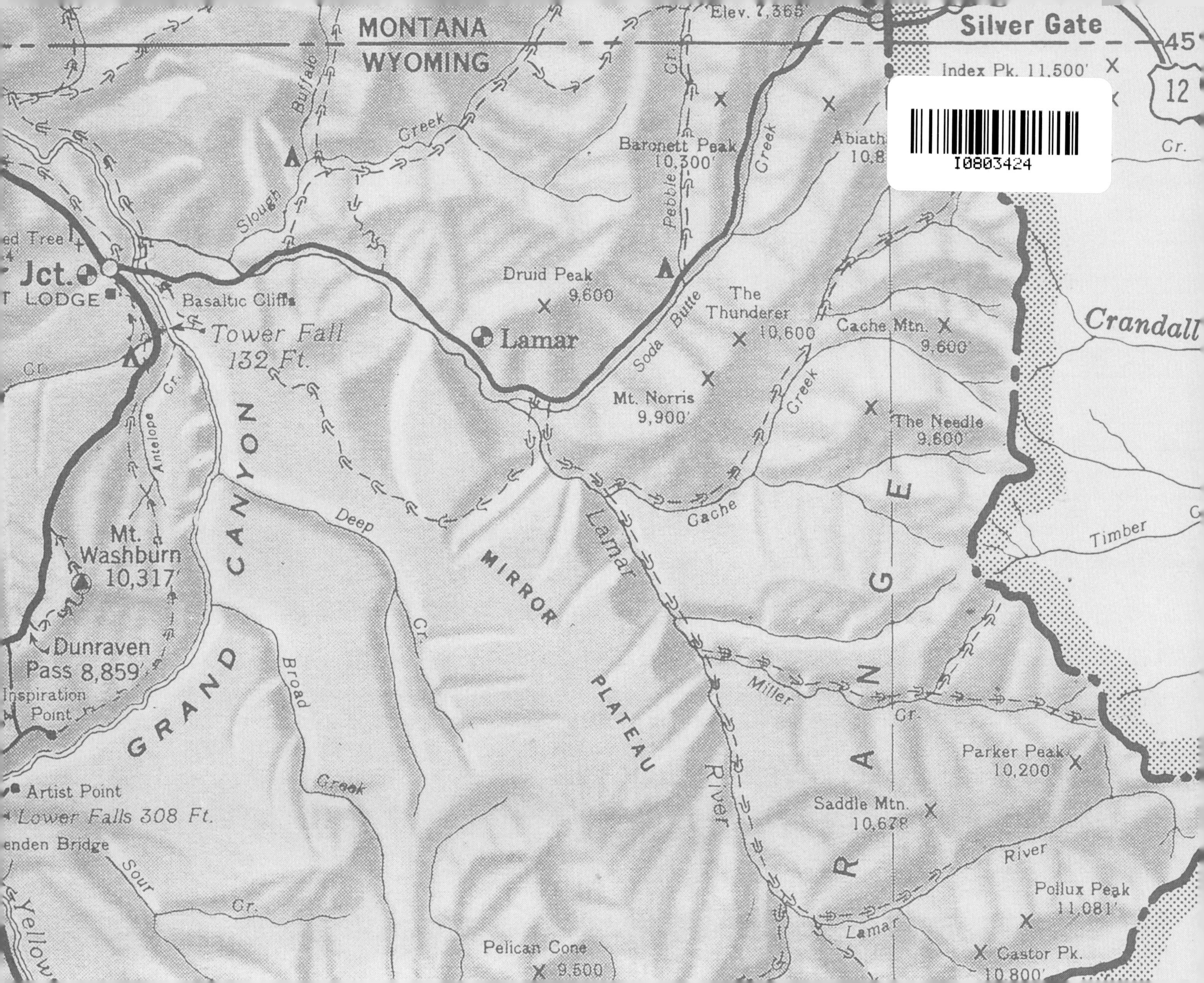
MONTANA
WYOMING
Silver Gate
Elev. 7,365'
Index Pk. 11,500'
Baronett Peak
10,300'
Abiath
Druid Peak
9,600
Lamar
The Thunderer
10,600
Cache Mtn.
9,600'
Mt. Norris
9,900'
The Needle
9,600
Crandall
Jct.
LODGE
Basaltic Cliffs
Tower Fall
132 Ft.
Mt. Washburn
10,317'
Dunraven
Pass 8,859'
Inspiration
Point
GRAND CANYON
MIRROR PLATEAU
RANGE
Artist Point
Lower Falls 308 Ft.
Parker Peak
10,200
Saddle Mtn.
10,678
Pollux Peak
11,081'
Castor Pk.
10,800'
Pelican Cone
9,500
Buffalo
Slough
Creek
Pebble Cr.
Soda Butte Creek
Cache Creek
Deep Cr.
Broad Creek
Lamar River
Miller Cr.
Timber
Sour Cr.
Antelope Cr.
Yellow
45
12

YELLOWSTONE NATIONAL PARK

PAST AND PRESENT

Suzanne Silverthorn & I-Ting Chiang

Schiffer Publishing Ltd®

4880 Lower Valley Road • Atglen, PA 19310

Other Schiffer Books by the Author:
Glacier National Park: Past and Present, 978-0-7643-3857-1, $24.99
Rocky Mountain Tour, 978-0-7643-2848-0, $24.95
Cabin Style: Decorating with Rustic, Adirondack, and Western Collectibles, 0-7643-2019-X, $29.95

Copyright © 2012 by
Suzanne Silverthorn & I-Ting Chiang

Library of Congress Control Number: 2012944029

All rights reserved. No part of this work may be reproduced or used in any form or by any means—graphic, electronic, or mechanical, including photocopying or information storage and retrieval systems—without written permission from the publisher.

The scanning, uploading and distribution of this book or any part thereof via the Internet or via any other means without the permission of the publisher is illegal and punishable by law. Please purchase only authorized editions and do not participate in or encourage the electronic piracy of copyrighted materials.

"Schiffer," "Schiffer Publishing, Ltd. & Design," and the "Design of pen and inkwell" are registered trademarks of Schiffer Publishing, Ltd.

Designed by Justin Watkinson
Type set in Castellar/Humanst 521 BT

ISBN: 978-0-7643-4175-5
Printed in China

Published by Schiffer Publishing, Ltd.
4880 Lower Valley Road
Atglen, PA 19310
Phone: (610) 593-1777; Fax: (610) 593-2002
E-mail: Info@schifferbooks.com

For the largest selection of fine reference books on this and related subjects, please visit our website at:
www.schifferbooks.com.
You may also write for a free catalog.

This book may be purchased from the publisher. Please try your bookstore first.

We are always looking for people to write books on new and related subjects. If you have an idea for a book, please contact us at:
proposals@schifferbooks.com

Schiffer Books are available at special discounts for bulk purchases for sales promotions or premiums. Special editions, including personalized covers, corporate imprints, and excerpts can be created in large quantities for special needs. For more information contact the publisher.

In Europe, Schiffer books are distributed by:
Bushwood Books
6 Marksbury Ave.
Kew Gardens
Surrey TW9 4JF England
Phone: 44 (0) 20 8392 8585
Fax: 44 (0) 20 8392 9876
E-mail: info@bushwoodbooks.co.uk
Website: www.bushwoodbooks.co.uk

Unless otherwise noted, all images are the property of the authors. Grateful acknowledgment is made to the original producers of the materials included in the book. The copyright has been identified for each item whenever possible. If any omission or incorrect information is found, please notify the authors or publisher and it will be amended in any future edition of the book.

Cover: Sylvan Lake. Back Cover: Grand Canyon of the Yellowstone from Artists Point, and vintage souvenir train decal from West Yellowstone Entrance.

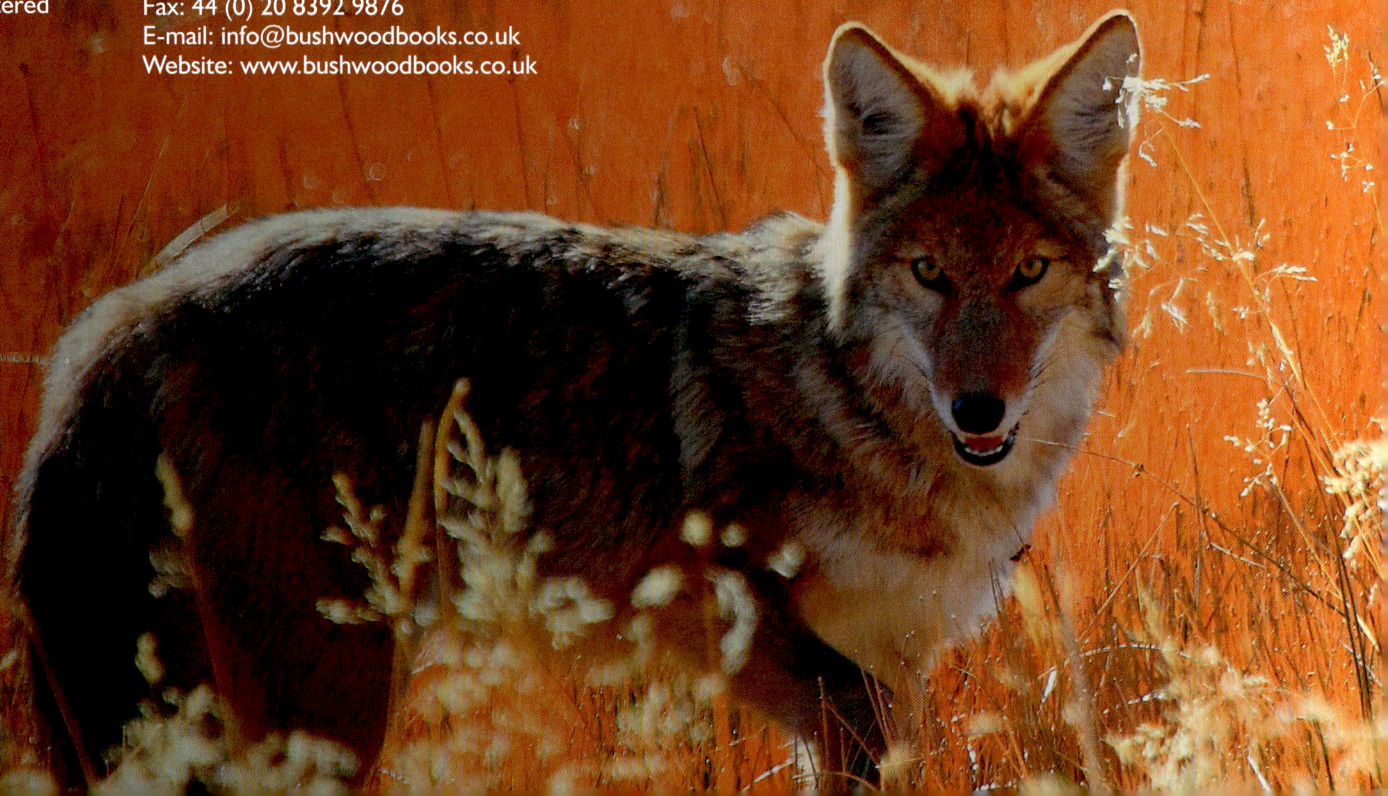

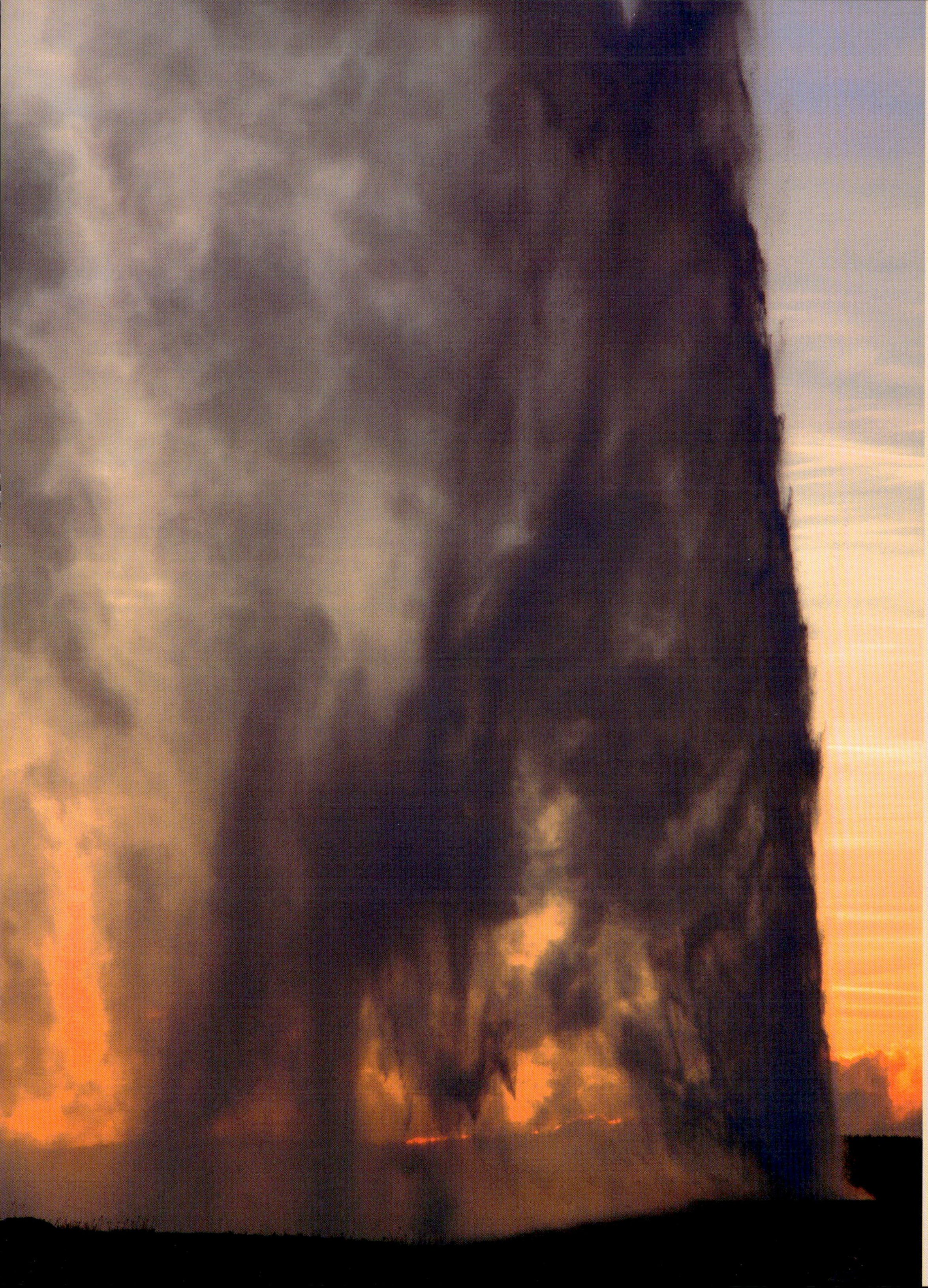

CONTENTS

FOREWORD

The talents of three individuals have come together to present an illustrated tour of the wonders of Yellowstone National Park that not only serves as a remembrance for past visitors, but also a resource to help plan a first-ever trip to the nation's oldest national park.

Featured here are postcard images by Frank Jay Haynes (1853-1921), the official photographer of Yellowstone National Park. Who better to illustrate the early history of Yellowstone? Historian Suzanne Silverthorn has skillfully selected and annotated the vintage postcards, photographs, and ephemera while award-winning photographer I-Ting Chiang's contemporary photographs complete the visual tour of the park.

The only constant is change. Change has been constant in Yellowstone and these striking "then and now" illustrations document both natural and man-made changes in the park. Violent natural events, including relatively new earthquakes and wildfires, have created these wonders.

The arrival of the railroad brought tourists to Yellowstone's gateways, resulting in the construction of in-park lodges that catered to the wealthy and a primitive road system that connected the park's major natural features.

The "Good Roads" and "See America First" movements resulted in the admission of automobiles into Yellowstone in 1915. The immediate invasion of "sagebrushers," or motorists who brought their own camping equipment, resulted in major upgrades to the road system and the proliferation of auto camps. The 140-mile-long Grand Loop Road — that narrow, dusty, counterclockwise one-way road used by stagecoaches — was slowly improved for safe automobile use. Yellowstone's Publicity Director, Harry W. Frantz, credited in 1923 for naming this road-with-a-view, noted: "The Grand Loop Road of Yellowstone Park is becoming a great national highway . . . the path of pilgrims seeking the God of the Open Air."

National Park Service policy changes, such as restrictions on the feeding of wildlife, including the elimination of established bear feeding grounds, protection of near-extinct bison herds, and the reintroduction of the wolf, have modified tourists' wildlife viewing habits.

Also altering the current look of Yellowstone was Mission 66, the National Park Service's largest parks improvement program. From 1956 to 1966, use of modern construction material was a deliberate departure from the rustic buildings previously associated with the park. In hindsight, perhaps not all change is progress.

The release of this book comes at a perfect time, as we approach the centennial celebrations of the arrival of the automobile in Yellowstone and the establishment of the National Park Service.

. The reintroduction of vintage White touring buses, updated museums and interpretive centers, and the continued popularity of the remaining rustic lodges, all demonstrate our interest in history and "retro" Yellowstone National Park.

-- Lee Whiteley, Centennial, Colorado, author of *The Yellowstone Highway: Denver to the Park, Past and Present*; *The Playground Trail, The National Park-to-Park Highway: To and Through the National Parks of the West in 1920*; and *The Cherokee Trail: Bent's Old Fort to Fort Bridger*

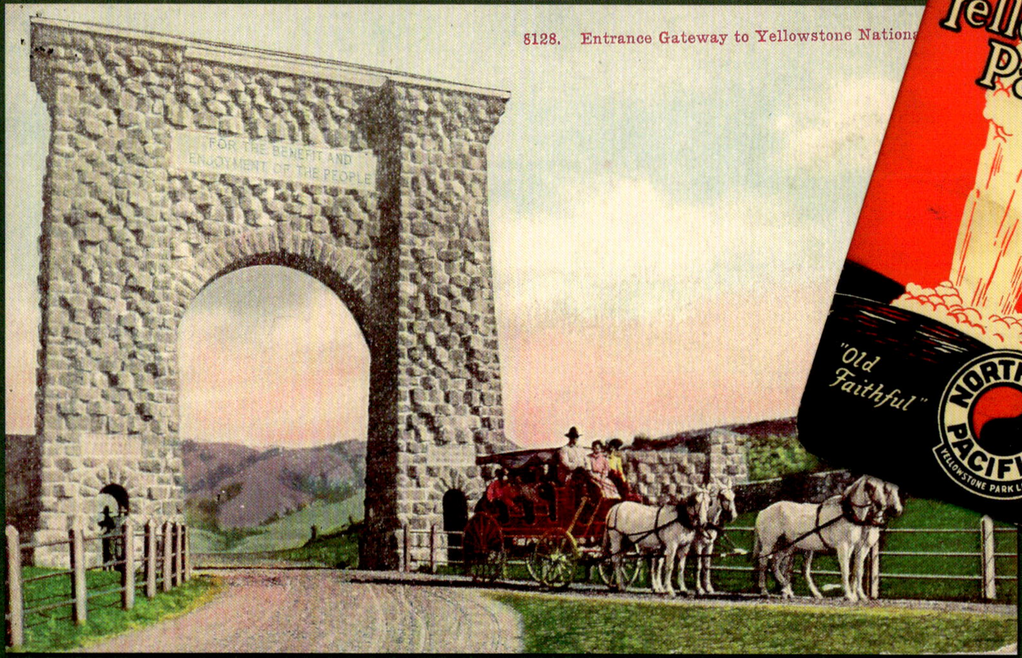

Stagecoach passengers pass through the arch at the North Entrance in this unmarked postcard circa 1905.

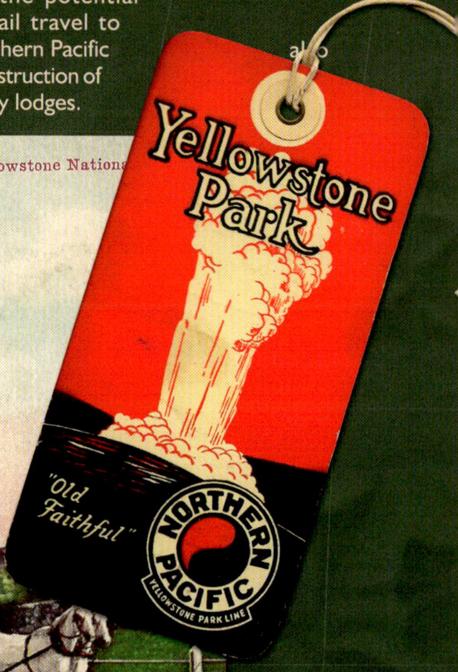

Baggage label for the North Coast Limited which brought train travelers to Yellowstone's North Entrance. Recognizing the potential to increase rail travel to the area, Northern Pacific invested in construction of the park's early lodges.

INTRODUCTION

The early explorers of the land that would become Yellowstone National Park had experienced nothing quite like it before as they came upon steaming rivers, boiling mud, spitting water, lush forests, abundant wildlife, and so much more. What is most remarkable about their discovery all those years ago is how insightful they were in identifying a place like nowhere else. Established in 1872 as the first national park in the world, Yellowstone is timeless in its ability to create wonder and awe.

In the beginning, Yellowstone was enjoyed mostly by wealthy sightseers who were lured to the park by the railroads. Luxurious hotels were built within the park to serve as a peaceful respite following a dusty and primitive stagecoach ride through the wilderness. As word spread about the park's fascination, its popularity increased – and so did its vulnerability. Poaching and vandalism soon overtook the park, which, in 1886, was turned over to the U.S. Army for protection. This arrangement would last more than thirty years.

By 1915, private automobiles were allowed into the park, a milestone that made access easier and more affordable. The opening of camps and lodges soon followed to serve the growing number of visitors, many of whom enjoyed the now-outlawed practice of feeding bears. Accommodations and services were modernized in the 1950s and '60s along with renewed protection of the park's wildlife.

Today, Yellowstone continues its legacy as the world's oldest national park. It attracts more than three million visitors a year with its iconic natural features, historic architecture, and groundbreaking scientific research. In the pages that follow, the history of the park, its amazing sights, and captivating wildlife are brought to life through the award-winning photography of I-Ting Chiang, whose works have been paired with postcard scenes by the park's first photographer, Frank J. Haynes, and his son Jack Haynes.

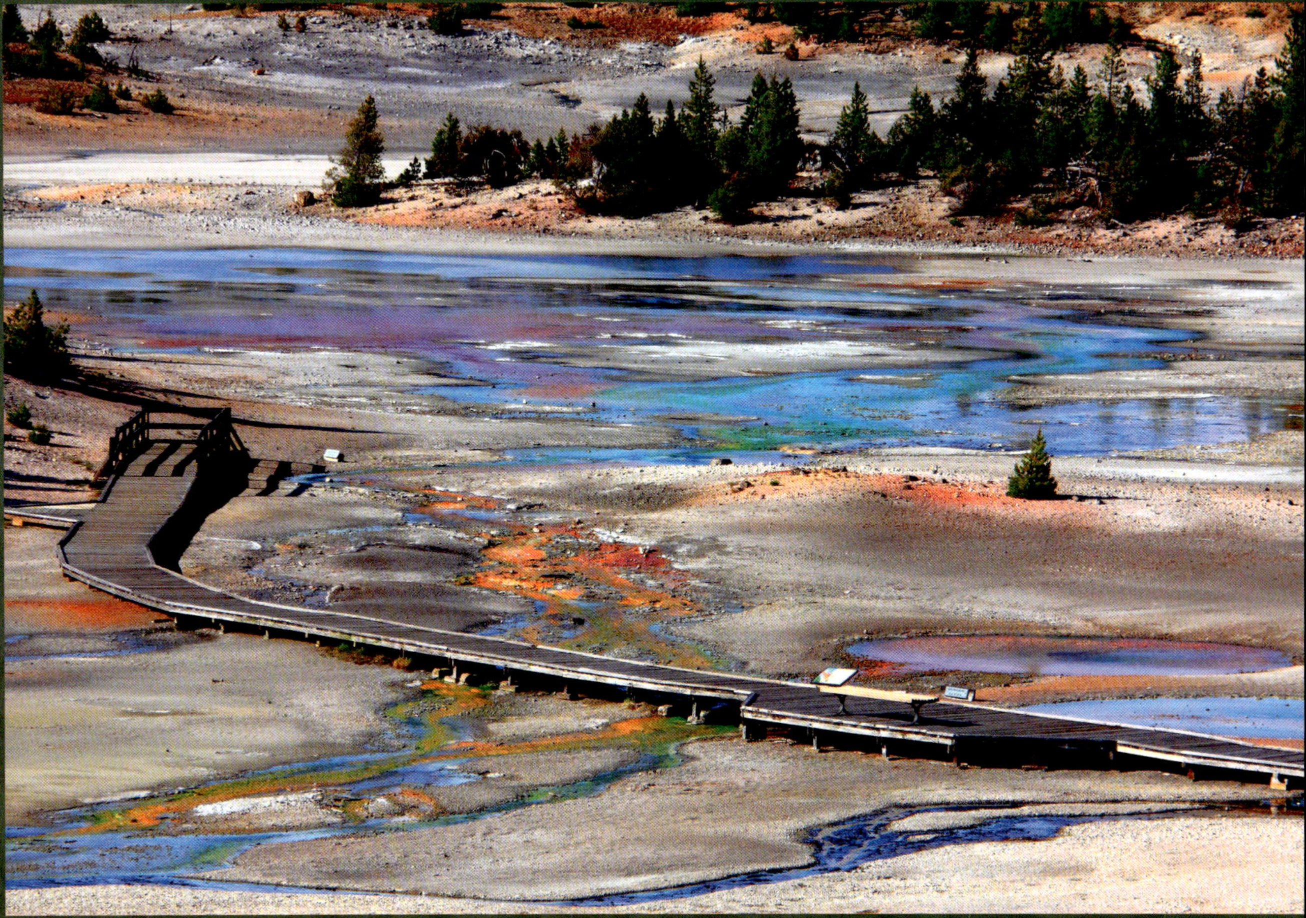

Norris Geyser Basin.

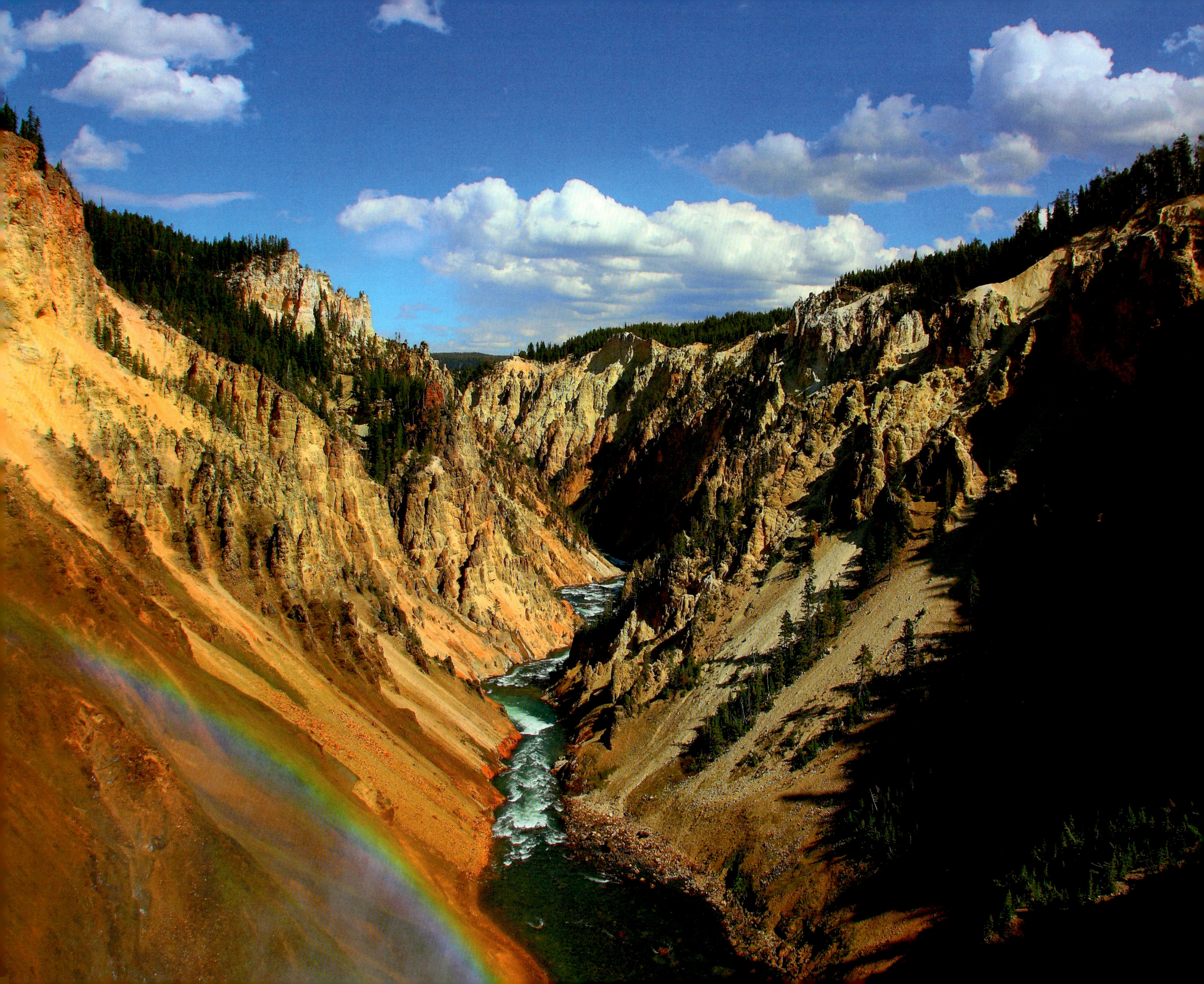

YELLOWSTONE NATIONAL PARK: THE HISTORY

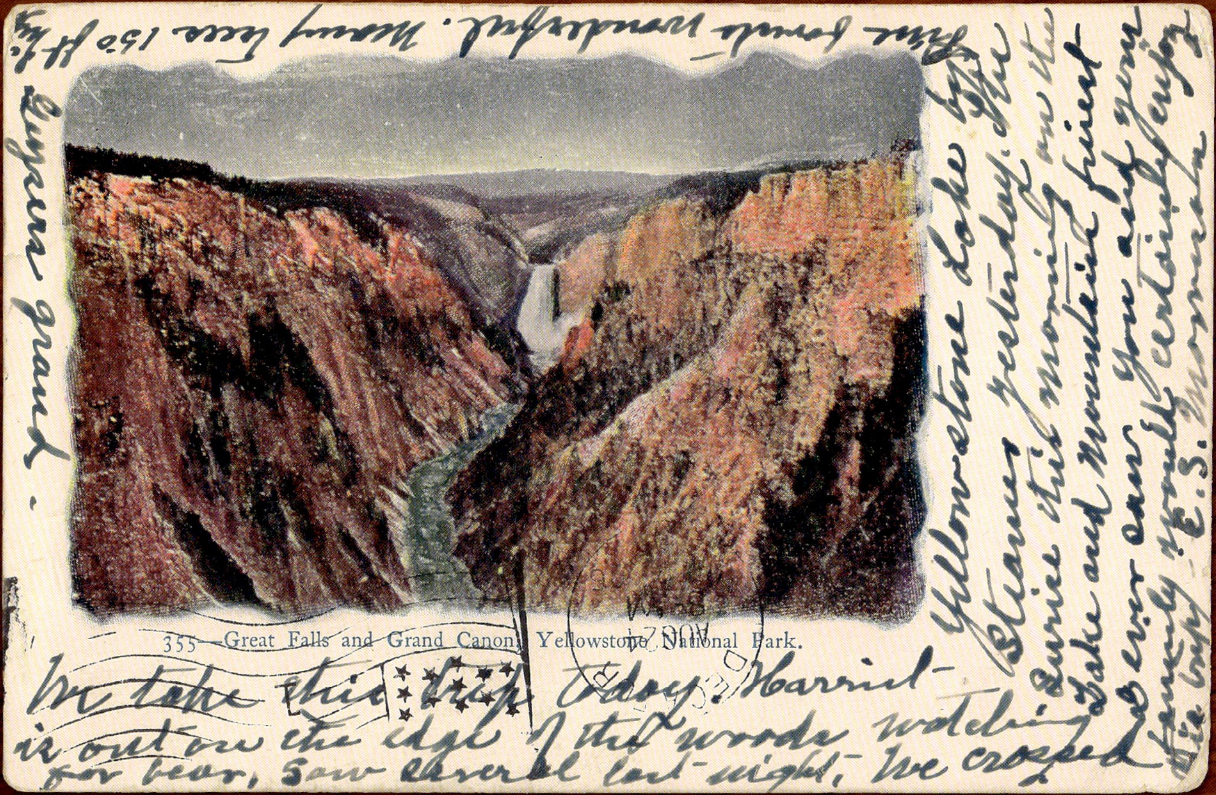

The message on this unmarked postcard dated August 21, 1906, describes a visitor's appreciation of the park all those years ago. It reads, "We take this trip today (Great Falls and Grand Canyon of Yellowstone). Harriet is out on the edge of the woods watching for bears. Saw several last night. We crossed Yellowstone Lake by Steamer yesterday. The sunrise this morning on the lake and mountain finest I ever saw. You and your family would certainly enjoy this trip. The forests wonderful. Many trees 150 feet high. Geysers grand." Opposite page: More than one hundred years later, the beauty of the Grand Canyon of the Yellowstone is shown as it looks today.

Yellowstone National Park was formed by fire and finished by ice, wind, and water. The result is a landscape of glaciers, canyons, mountains, and geysers, as well as lakes, rivers, and forests.

The park covers more than 2.2 million acres, has over 10,000 thermal features, thousands of miles of waterways, and is home to a wide variety of flora and fauna. Created in 1872, it is the world's first national park, a proud distinction that will never disappoint.

HISTORIC DATES

The following information is from the U.S. Department of Interior.

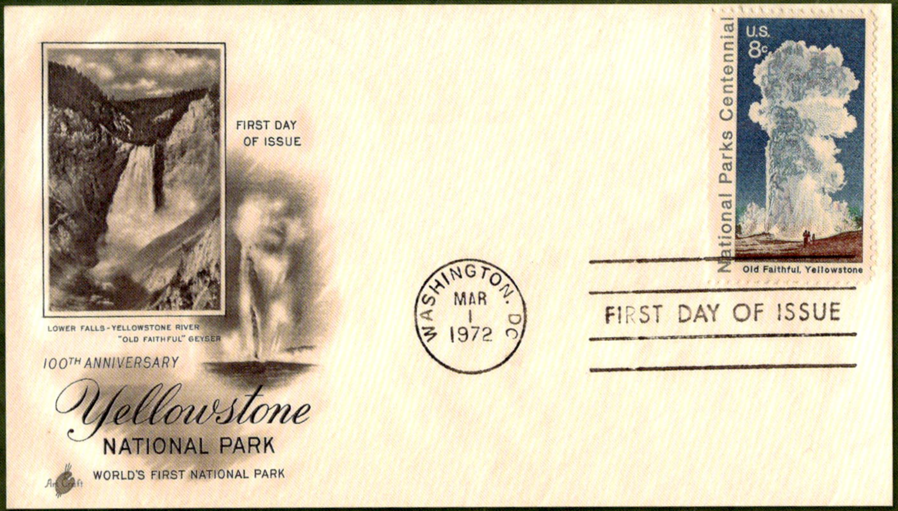

The 100th anniversary of Yellowstone National Park was celebrated in 1972 and included this first-day of issue cover from the United States Postal Service.

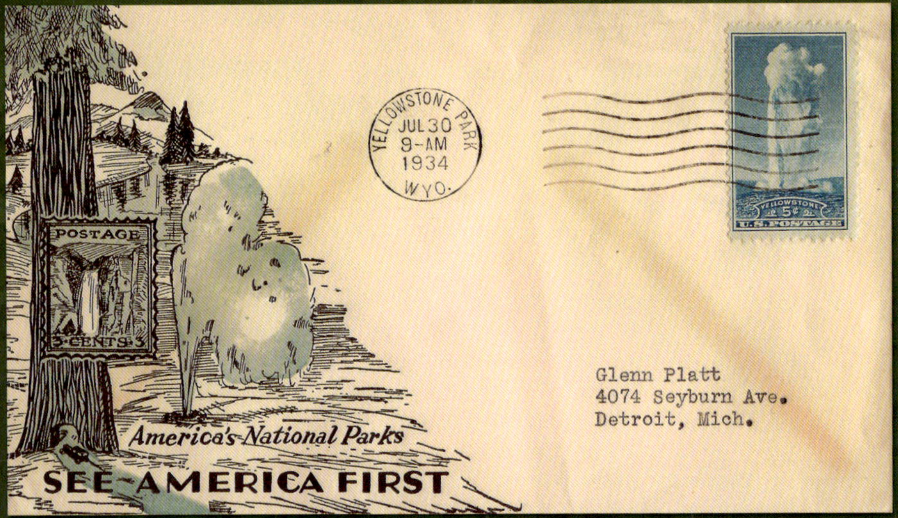

In 1934 the U.S. Postal Service issued a series of ten postage stamps featuring scenic views from the national parks during the observance of "National Parks Year." Fittingly, Old Faithful Geyser, one of the foremost scenic wonders of the park, was selected to represent Yellowstone in the series.

1807

John Colter, a member of the earlier Lewis and Clark Expedition, is the first explorer of European descent to discover region.

1869

Cook-Folsom-Peterson Expedition

1870

Washburn-Langford-Doane Expedition

1871

The Hayden Geological Survey report is used to suggest land that should become public parks.

1872

Congress and President Ulysses S. Grant authorize creation of Yellowstone National Park on March 1st.

Nathaniel P. Langford is named first park superintendent.

1883

Northern Pacific Railway builds a railroad spur line from Livingston, Montana, to Cinnabar near the park's North Entrance.

1886

Administration of the park is turned over to the United States Army.

1894

The Lacey Act is passed by Congress to protect birds and animals in the park and to establish violations for crimes that occur in the park.

1904
Old Faithful Inn opens.

1908
Union Pacific train service at West Yellowstone begins.

1915
First automobiles allowed in the park.

1916
President Woodrow Wilson signs Act of Congress, creating the National Park Service as a bureau of the Department of the Interior.

1916-1918
Guardianship of park transfers from the Army to the Department of Interior.

1919
Civilian, Horace M. Albright, is named superintendent.

1930
The Norris Geyser Basin museum opens.

1943
Because of World War II, most park facilities are closed until war's end.

1959
Earthquake hits park and nearby areas.

1961
All rail service to the park had ended.

1956-1966
Mission 66 initiative takes place with development of Canyon Village and Grant Village.

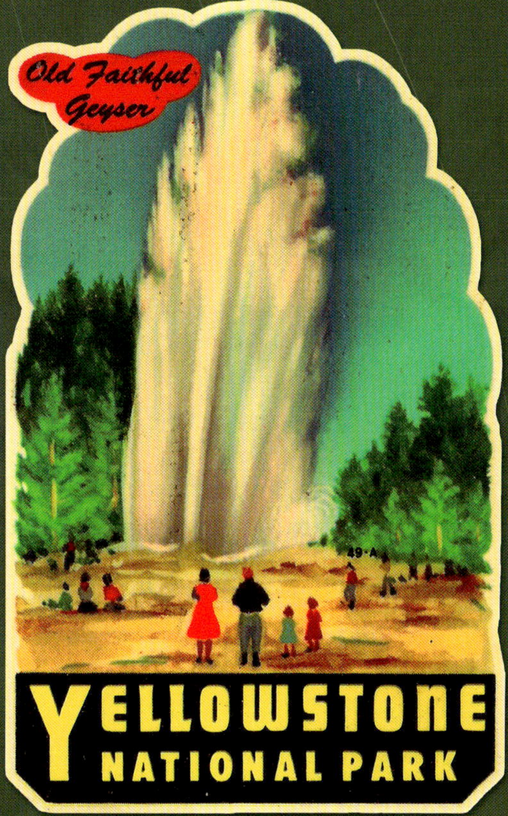

Vintage decal of Old Faithful Geyser produced by the Meyercord Company of Chicago.

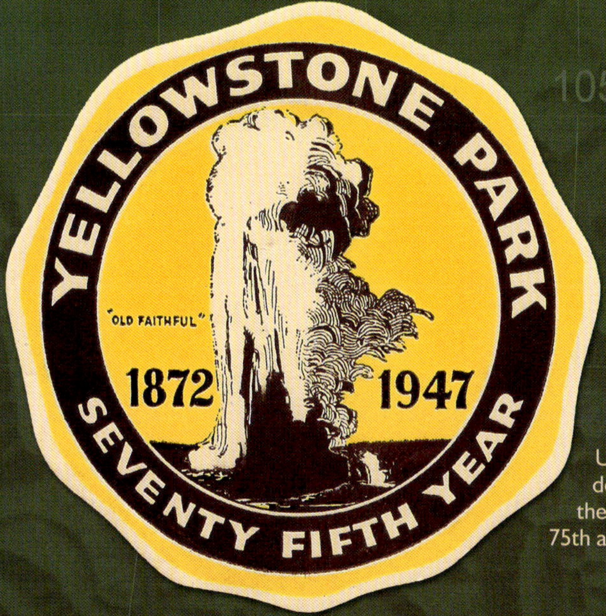

Unmarked decal celebrating the park's 75th anniversary.

1972
Yellowstone celebrates 100th anniversary.

1976
International Biosphere Reserve designation

1978
Named a United Nations World Heritage Site

1988
Summer of wildfires, including "Black Saturday" on August 20th

1995
Reintroduction of wolves in the park

2004
Old Faithful Inn, the park's oldest hotel, celebrates its 100th anniversary.

2010
Old Faithful Visitor Education Center opens.

PARK DISCOVERY

Although Native Americans had hunted, fished, and even lived in the Yellowstone Park area for hundreds of years, explorers of European descent brought new attention to the land. The first of these explorers was John Colter, who had taken part in the Lewis and Clark Expedition from 1804-1806. Accounts indicate Colter independently explored the area around Yellowstone Lake, the Grand Canyon, Mount Washburn, and Tower Fall circa 1807. He shared details about this trip when he returned to St. Louis in 1810.

By 1869, fur traders and gold seekers were describing their adventures in the park. One of these was Jim Bridger, who was said to have exaggerated his tales of the area. More truthful stories were told by members of the 1870 Washburn-Langford-Doane Expedition. This group was led by General Henry Washburn, Surveyor-General of Montana, Nathaniel P. Langford, and Lt. Gustavus Doane of the U.S. Army, plus additional men making a total of nineteen in the party. This group named Old Faithful and other landmarks during their trip.

In 1871, another important expedition was made to the Yellowstone area when Ferdinand V. Hayden headed a scientific and military expedition. Painter Thomas Moran and photographer William H. Jackson joined the group and provided documentation so people could see the wonders of the proposed park and to offer support for its preservation.

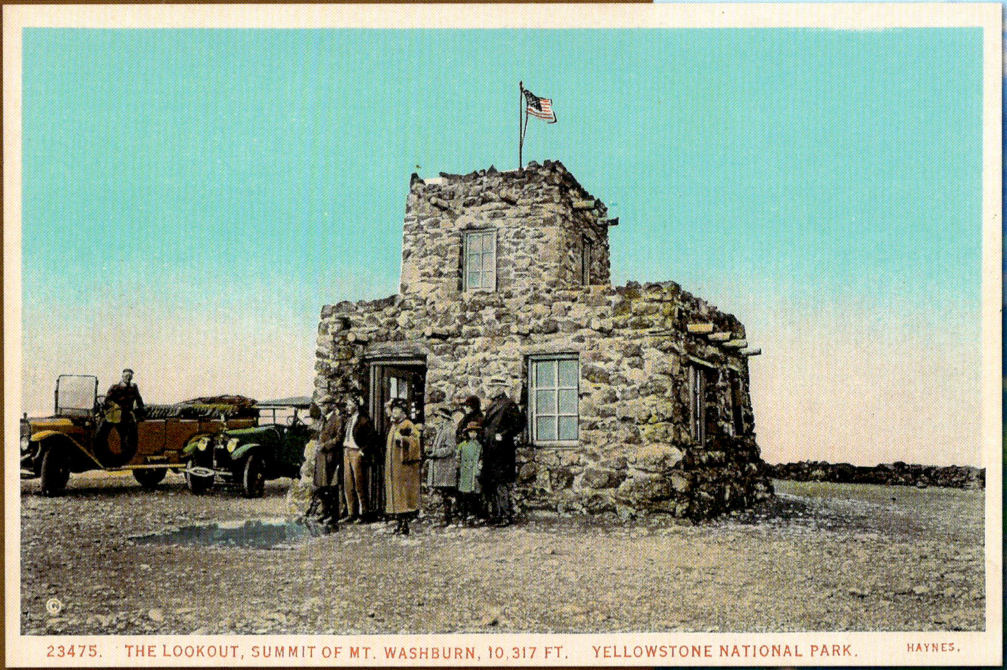

The lookout at the summit of Mount Washburn is pictured on this early 1920s postcard by Haynes Picture Shops, Inc. It was built by the National Park Service as a fire lookout and as a resting place for guests. Fire lookout operations continue to be manned at the summit, albeit in a newer structure, and serves as one of three active lookouts in the park.

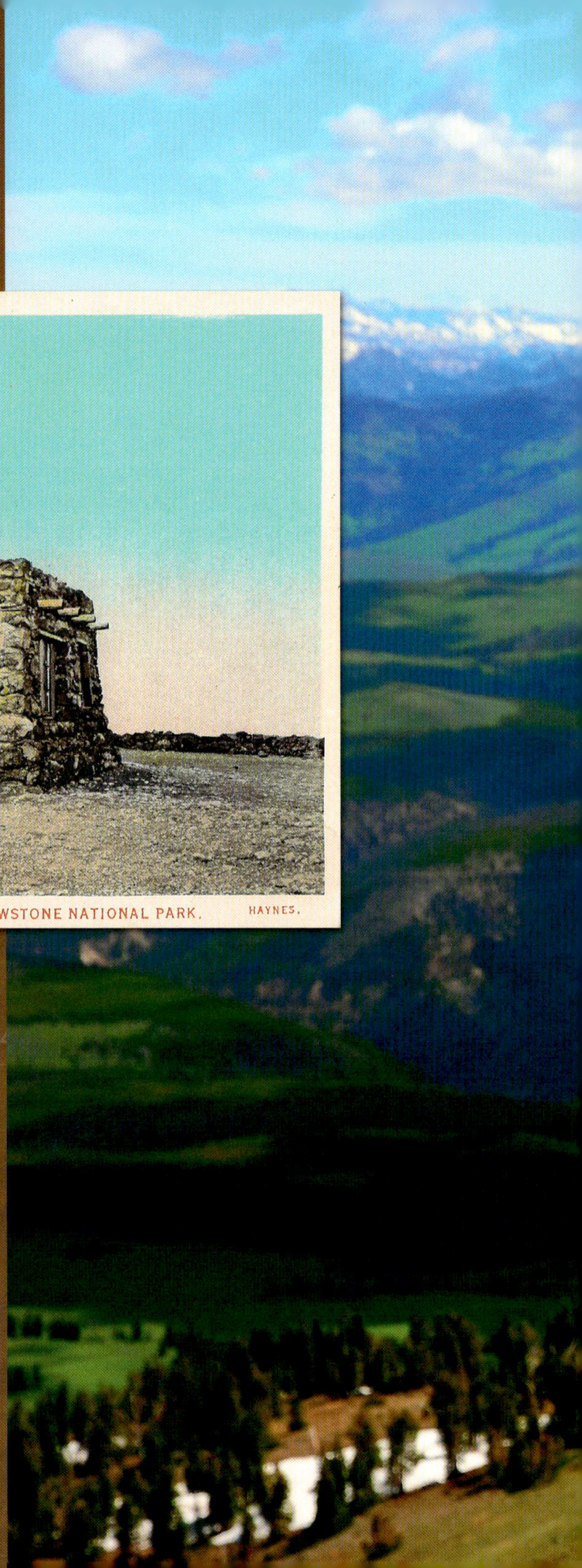

Mount Washburn bears the name of General Henry Washburn who was one of the leaders of the 1870 Washburn-Langford-Doane Expedition. Today, a three-mile hike to the summit is the park's single most recommended trail due to its expansive views, sightings of bighorn sheep, and numerous species of wildflowers.

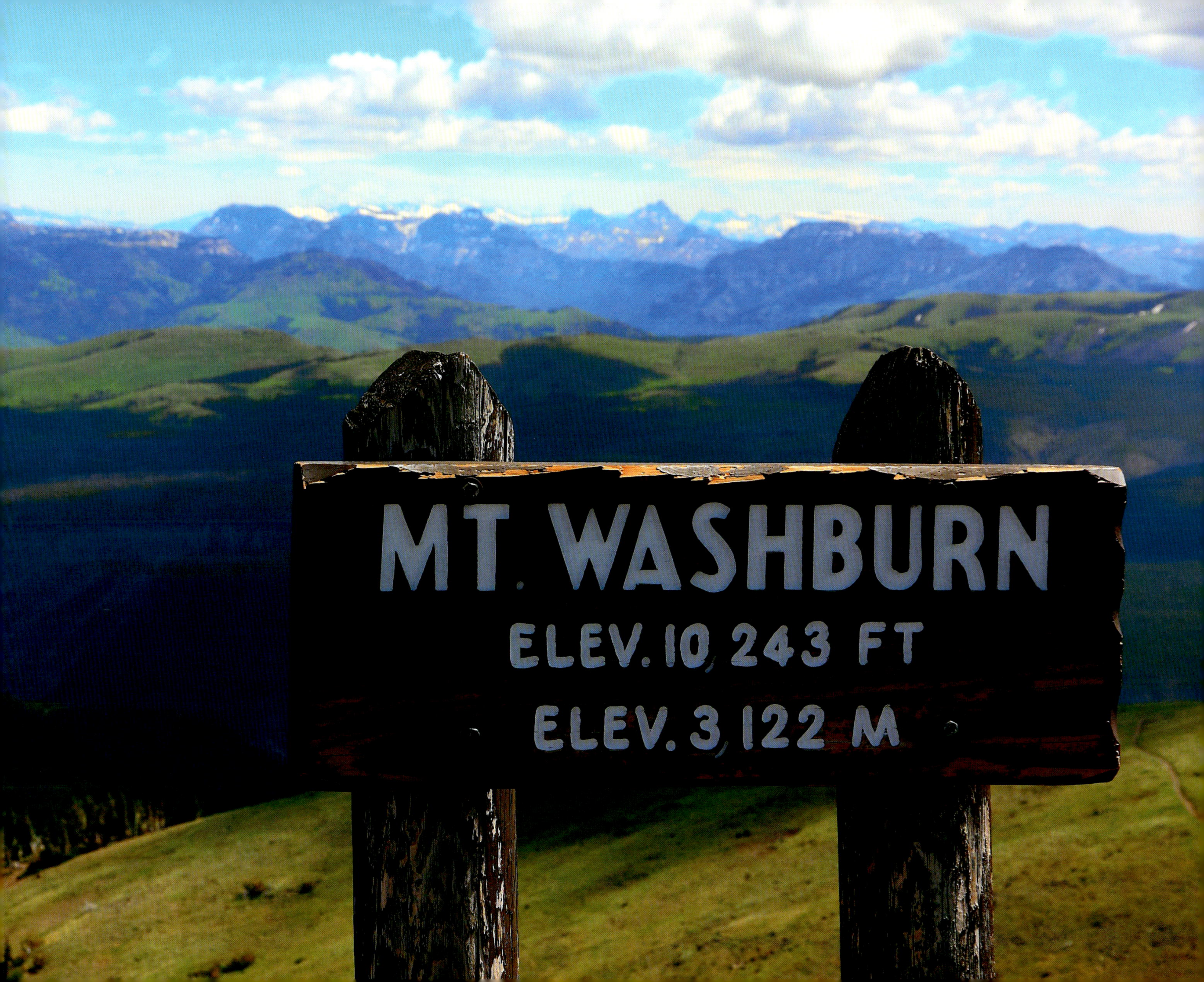
MT. WASHBURN
ELEV. 10,243 FT
ELEV. 3,122 M

EARLY BEGINNINGS

The congressional bill to make Yellowstone the first-ever national park was signed by President Ulysses S. Grant on March 1, 1872. This action made it "a public park of pleasuring ground for the benefit and enjoyment of the people" and "for the preservation. . .of all timber, mineral deposits, natural curiosities, and wonders. . ."

Because of problems caused by poachers and vandalism in the early days of the park, the Secretary of the Interior asked the Secretary of War to take over the administration of the park in 1886 to restore order and to protect its natural resources. The military arrived on August 17, 1886, and set up a tent camp that became Camp Sheridan. It was located at the foot of the Mammoth Hot Spring Terraces. A permanent camp, Fort Yellowstone, was soon established where the U.S. Calvary would continue its assignment for nearly three decades until a new government branch was created, the National Park Service, in 1916.

Fort Yellowstone was established at Mammoth Hot Springs on May 11, 1891, to replace the earlier Camp Sheridan, and by the end of the year, twelve buildings had been built, which included an administration building as well as a barracks, commissary, bakery, stable, and other necessary establishments. This Haynes Fort Yellowstone postcard was postmarked in 1912.

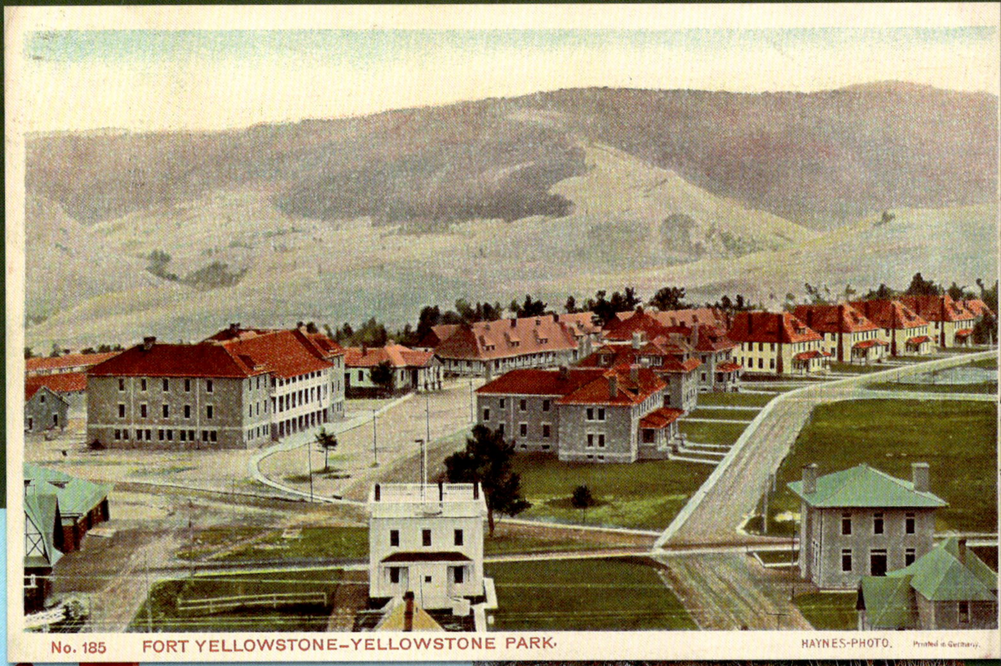

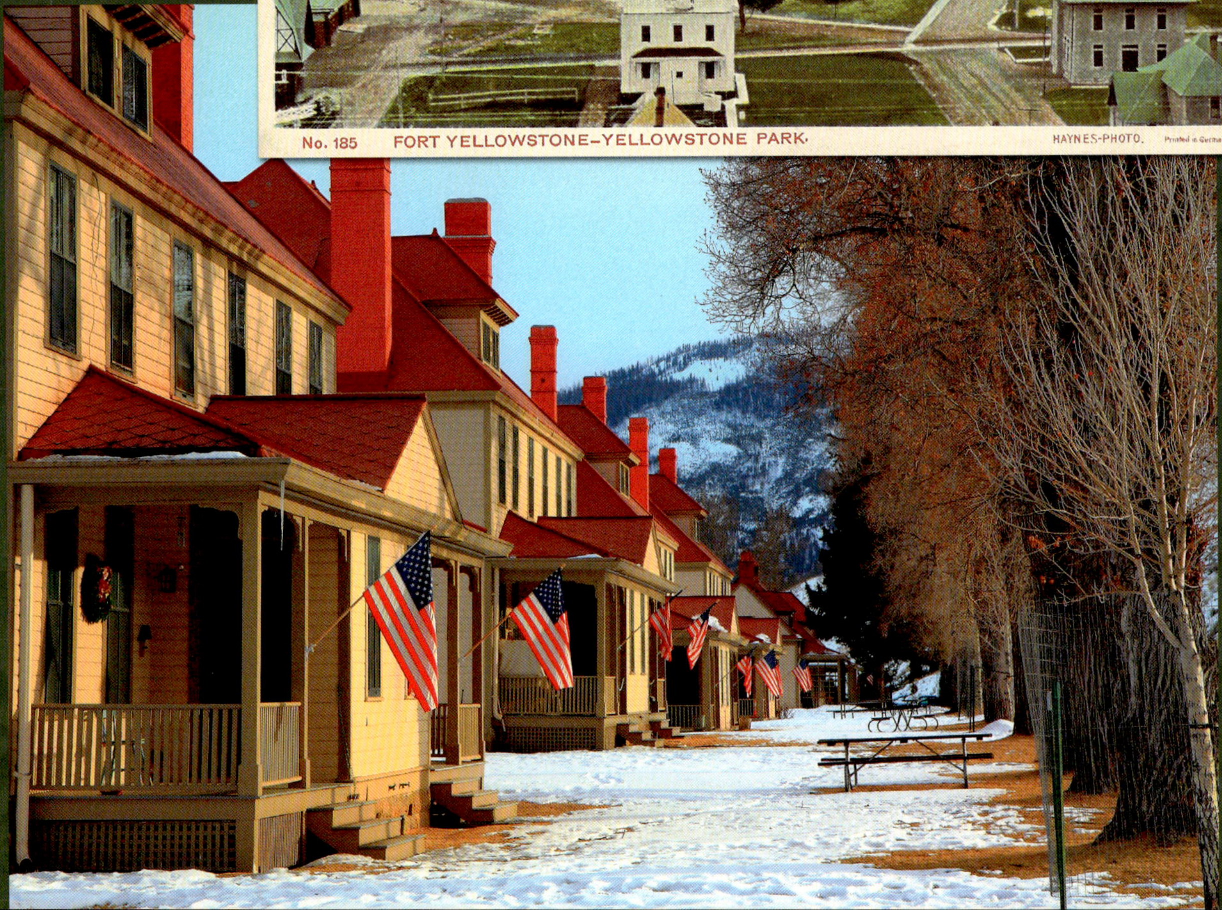

The Fort Yellowstone buildings are still standing at Mammoth Hot Springs and showcase the park's earlier occupation by the Cavalry. Many of the buildings are now used to house senior park staff. Park headquarters are also located here. Fort Yellowstone was designated a National Historic Landmark in 2003.

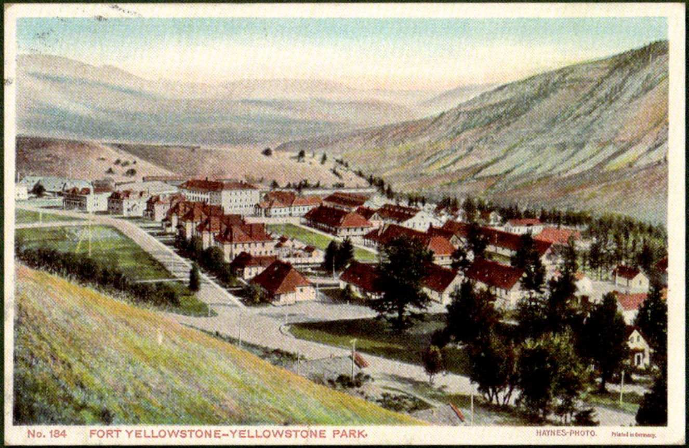

A hospital was added to Fort Yellowstone in 1893. The last structure built for the troops was the chapel added in 1913. A cemetery was also available. Entertainment included dances, bowling, movies, swimming, and baseball. This Haynes-Photo postcard of Fort Yellowstone was sent in 1912 and pictures many of the buildings built to accommodate the troops. This arrangement lasted until the National Park Service was created as a bureau in the Department of the Interior in which a civilian superintendent replaced the military administrator in the park. The transition took place from 1916 to 1918.

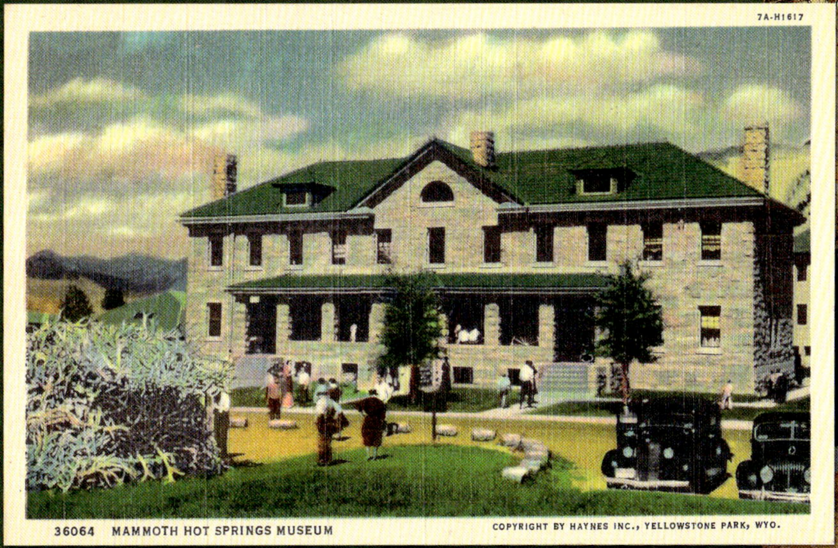

This building once housed the bachelor officers' quarters. It is now home to the Albright Visitor Center and Museum, which is open daily year-round. The museum includes works from early-day painter Thomas Moran and photographs by William Henry Jackson, members of the 1871 Hayden Survey. The linen postcard by Haynes, Inc. was postmarked in 1933.

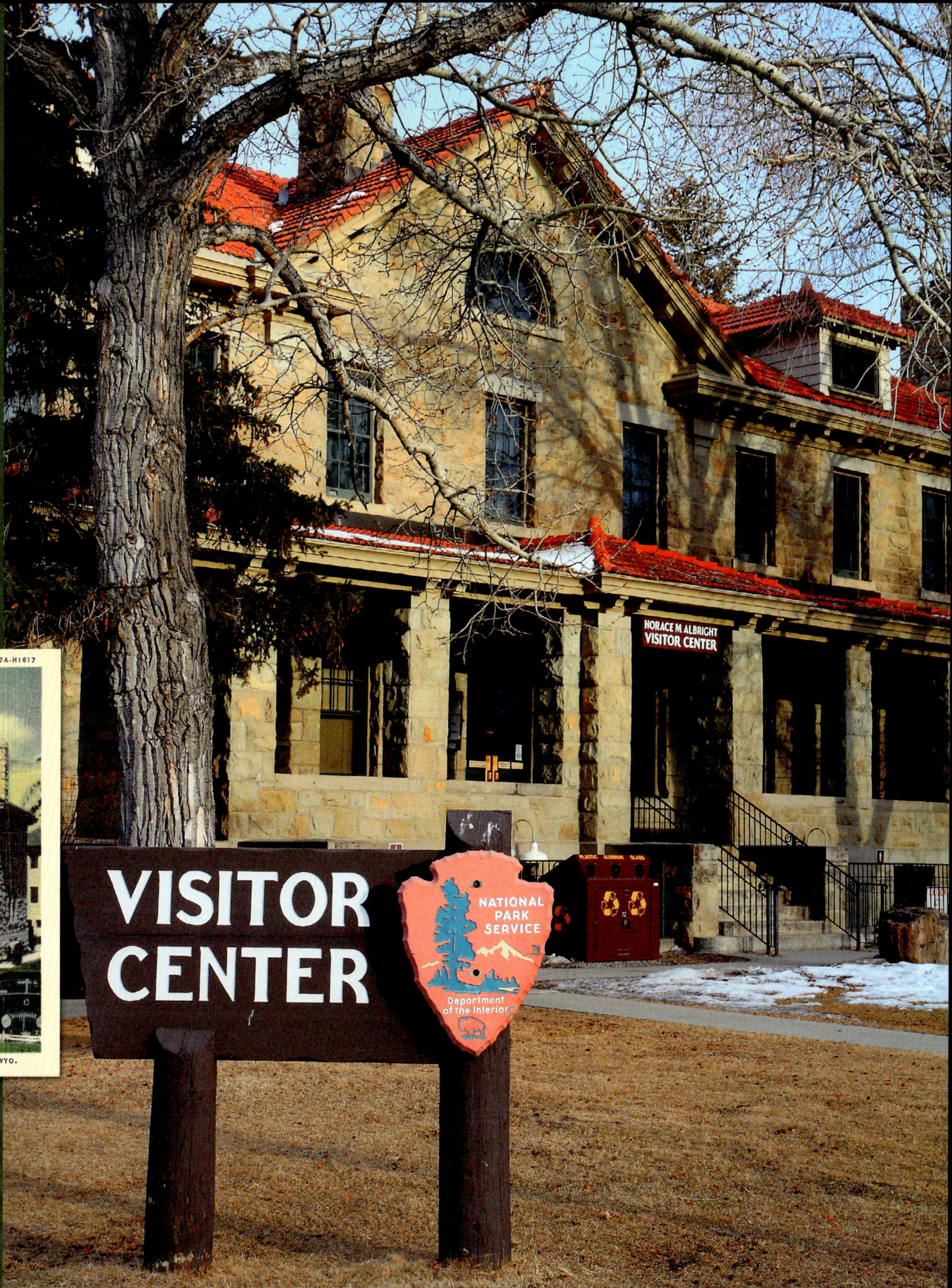

FRANK J. HAYNES

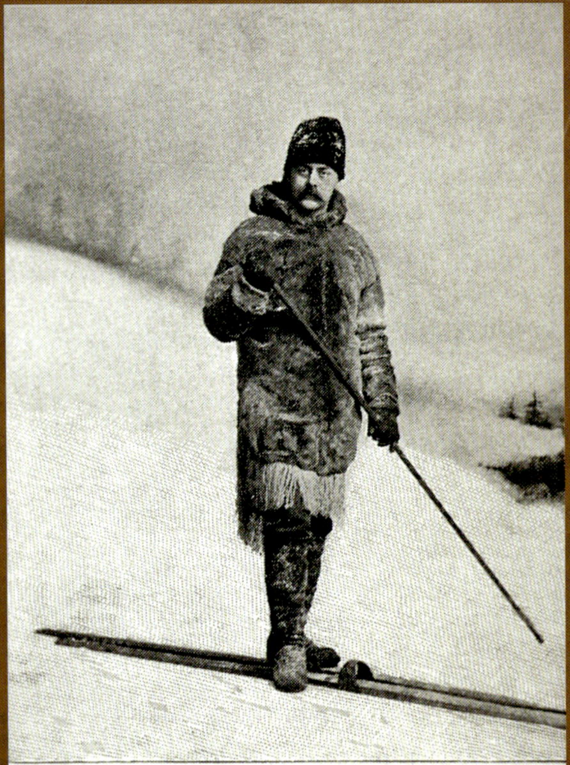

F. J. HAYNES.

Frank J. Haynes was Yellowstone's first official photographer. His photographs are included on hundreds of postcards that span numerous decades documenting the park's features. Born in Michigan in 1853, he was hired by the Northern Pacific Railway in 1876 to photograph scenery along the railroad's new route from Minnesota to the West Coast. It was during his railroad assignment that Haynes discovered Yellowstone, and he devoted the remainder of his life to the park as a photographer, publisher, and entrepreneur. This photo was taken in 1887 as Haynes accompanied a winter expedition in the park. Upon his death in 1921, Yellowstone's Mount Burley was renamed Mount Haynes in his honor.

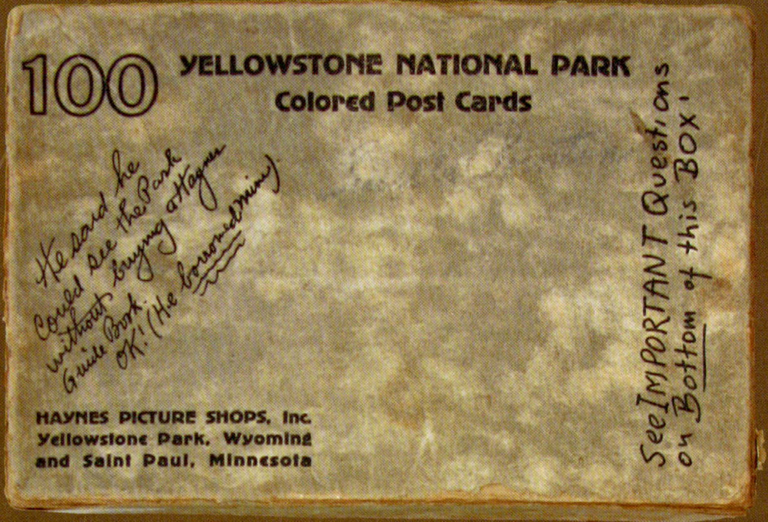

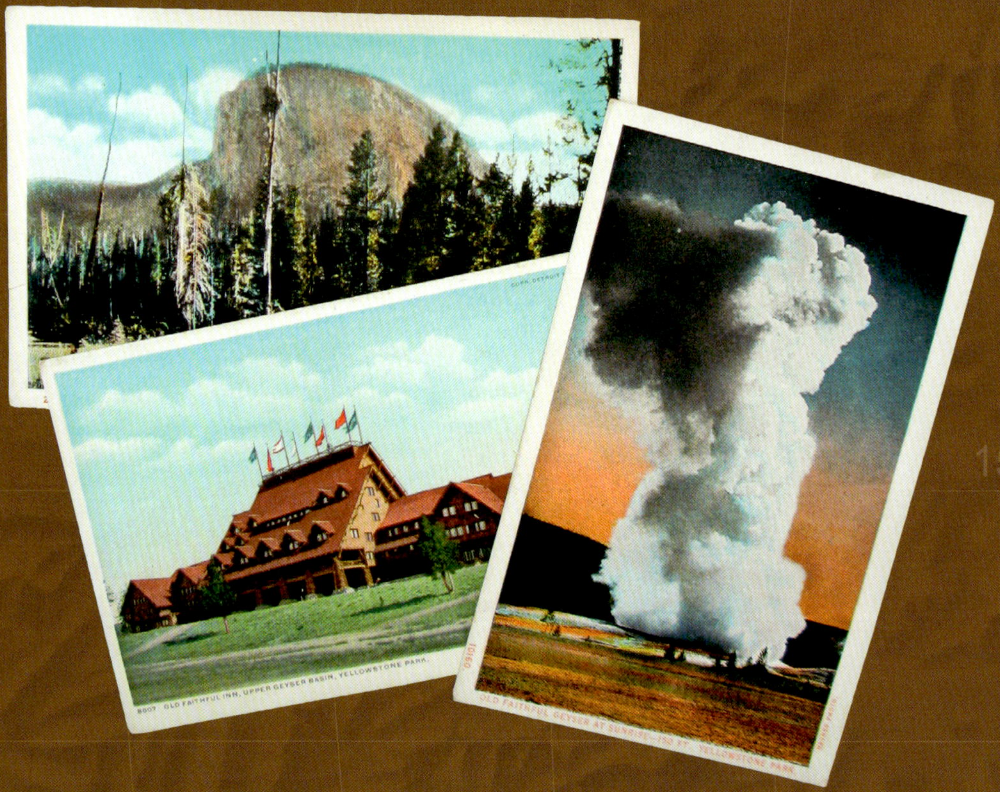

Haynes' first association with the park began in 1884 when he opened a photography studio at Mammoth Hot Springs, a business that would eventually expand to include thirteen photo shops across the park. He was also involved in several transportation companies prior to 1917 when the government created a single concessionaire. Pictured is a box of Haynes colored postcards circa late 1920s sold at the Haynes Picture Shops.

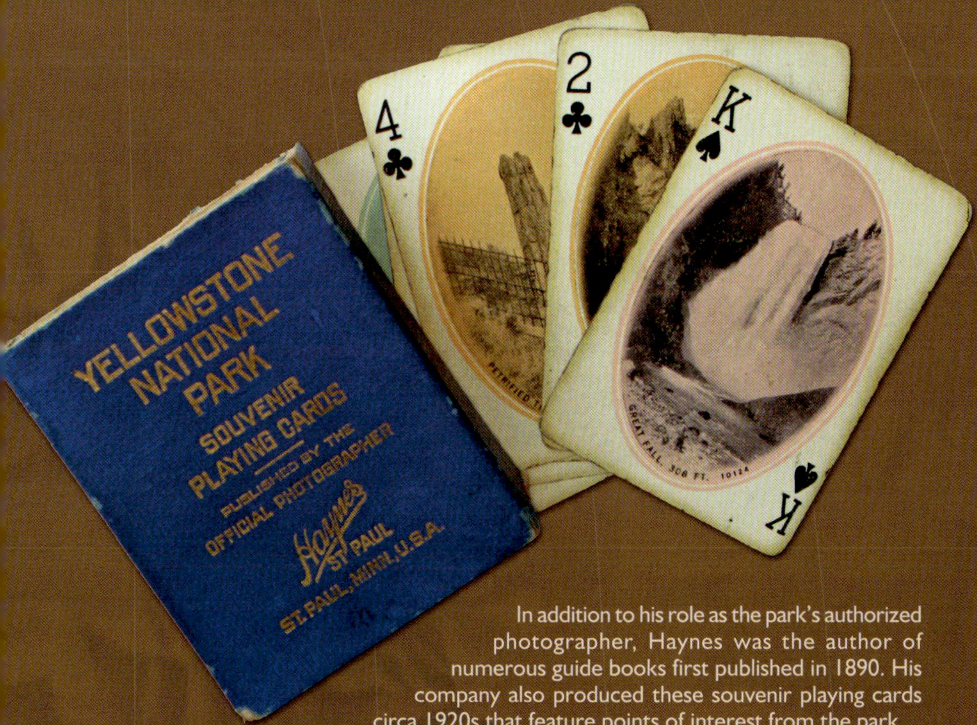

In addition to his role as the park's authorized photographer, Haynes was the author of numerous guide books first published in 1890. His company also produced these souvenir playing cards circa 1920s that feature points of interest from the park.

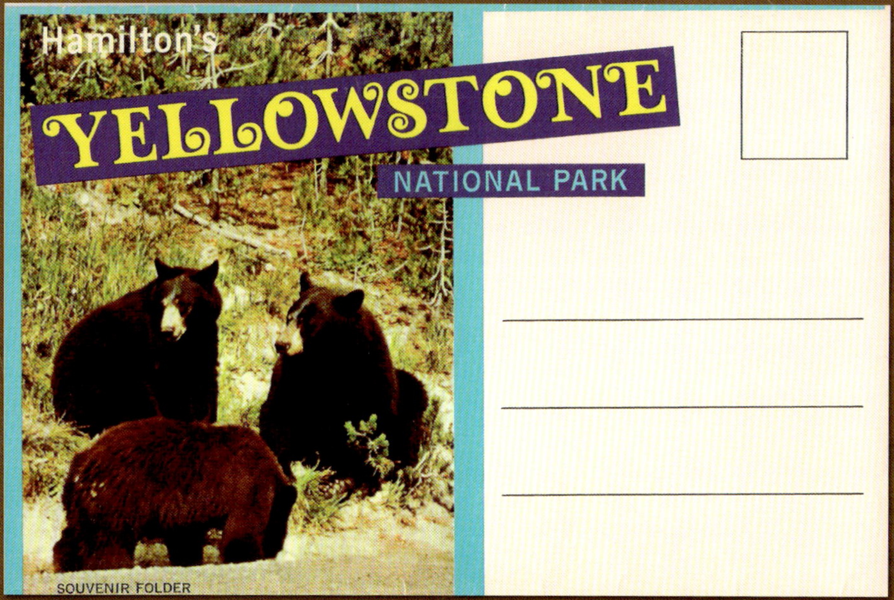

Hamilton Stores purchased the Haynes family shops in 1967. Hamilton Stores, Inc. was in business from 1915 until 2002, when it lost the concessions contract to Delaware North which now operates twelve general stores throughout the park. This Yellowstone postcard folder was published by Hamilton Stores.

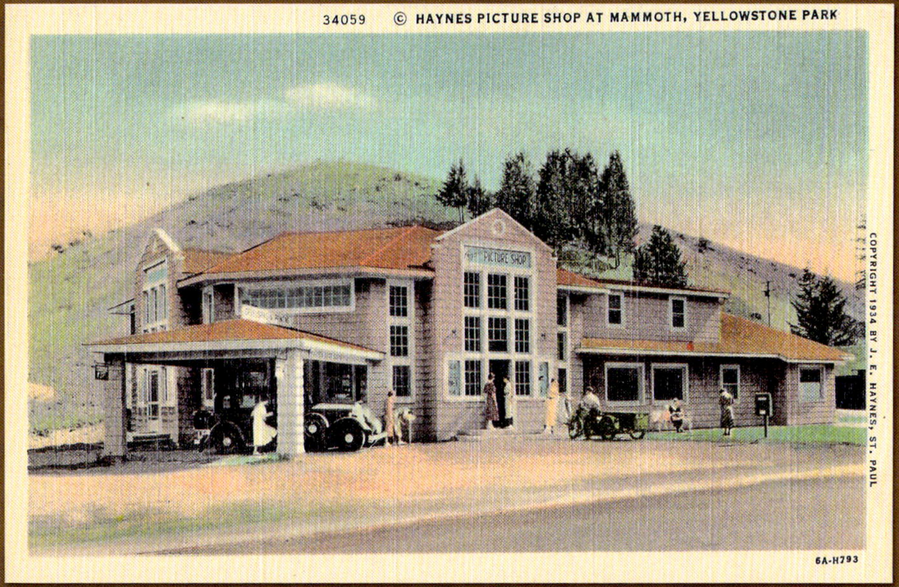

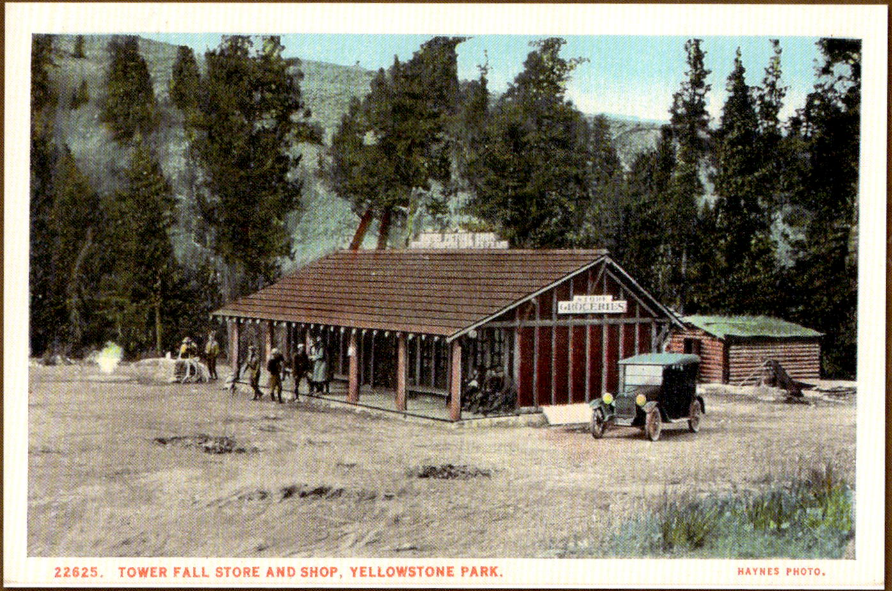

This Haynes postcard features the Picture Shop that was opened in the 1920s to replace the first Haynes shop built at Mammoth in 1884. Another Haynes Picture Shops was located near Tower Fall (right). Son Jack Haynes operated the photo shops from the 1917 season until his death in 1961. The business then continued in the Haynes family through Jack's wife Isabel's efforts until it was sold to the Hamilton Stores in 1967, ending the family's 83 - year history with the park. As a tribute, the Yellowstone Park Foundation has arranged to renovate and operate the historic Haynes Photo Shop at Old Faithful to celebrate the enjoyment of photography in the park.

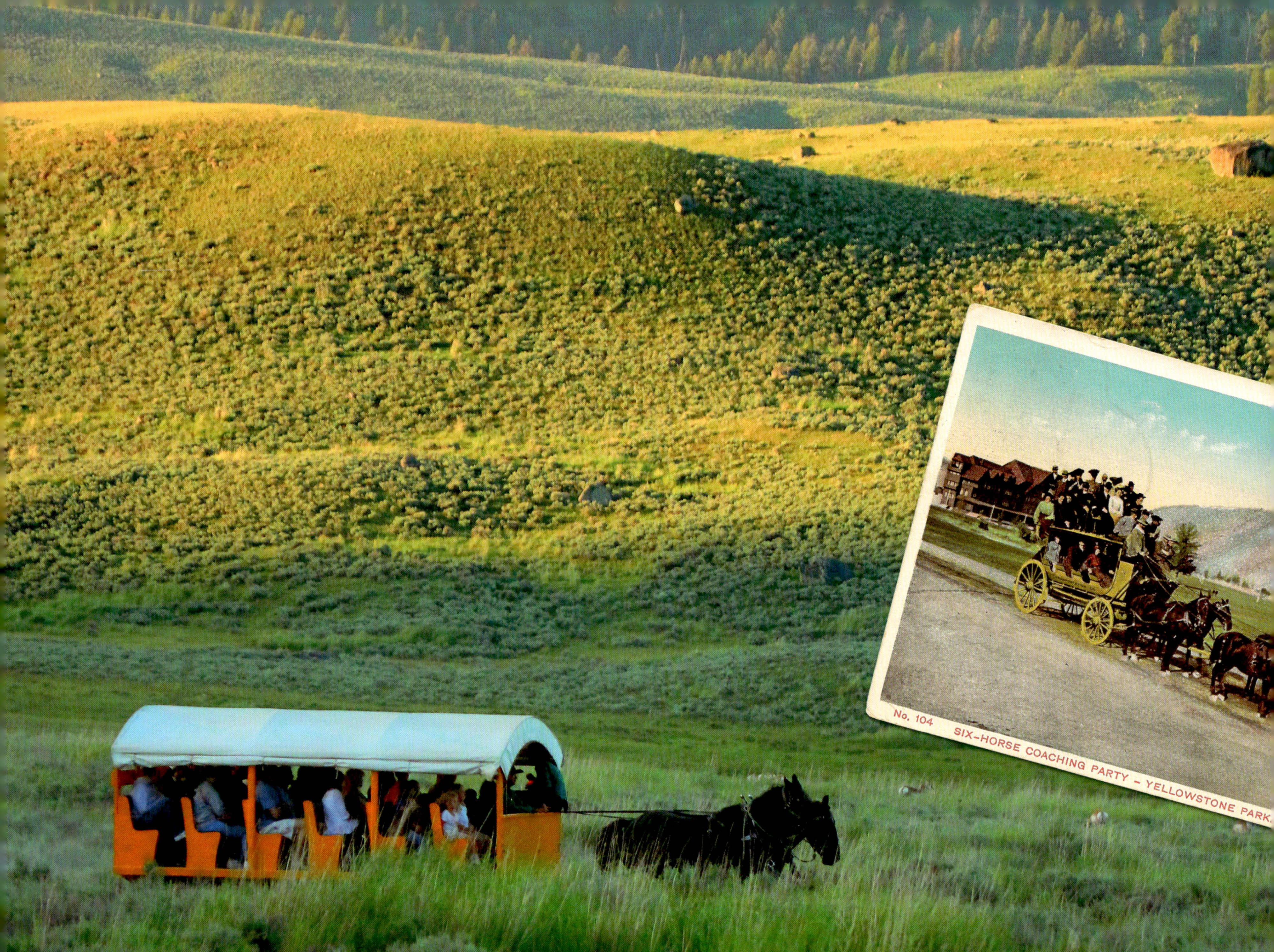

Once the primary mode of transportation in the park, horse-drawn wagon tours like this one in Tower Junction, as well as outings in replica stagecoaches, offer current sightseeing travels like those experienced during earlier times when the trails were nearly impassable.

TRANSPORTATION: RAILS AND ROADS

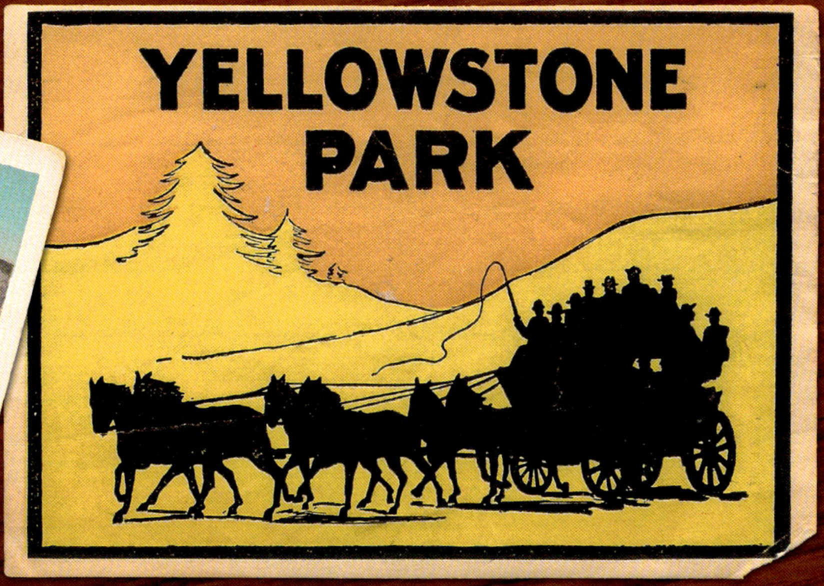

Vintage luggage label.

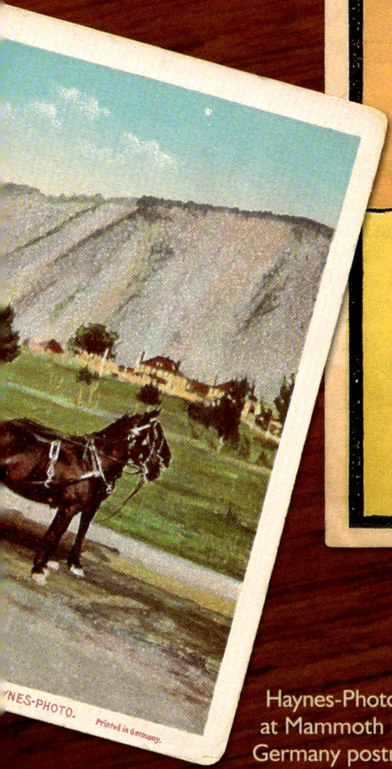

Haynes-Photo postcard of sightseers at Mammoth Hot Springs printed in Germany postmarked 1912.

Sightseers were scarce at Yellowstone National Park before the arrival of the railroads. Northern Pacific Railway was the first to provide the closest passenger service to the park with the opening of a branch line from Livingston, Montana, to Cinnabar, Montana, in 1883. The service was extended to Gardiner, Montana, at the park's North Entrance in 1902. In addition to providing transportation, Northern Pacific was also instrumental in building hotels in the park, including construction of the Old Faithful Inn which opened in 1904. Five railroads brought passengers to the park. Among these, the Chicago, Burlington, and Quincy Railroad provided service to Cody, Wyoming, beginning in 1901, and by 1908, Union Pacific was transporting passengers to what is now West Yellowstone. Once inside the park, more primitive forms of transportation were in use, including stagecoaches, mountain wagons, surreys, and saddle and pack horses. Arrival of the automobile in 1915 changed everything, making access easier and more affordable "for the benefit and enjoyment of the people" as envisioned by the park's founders.

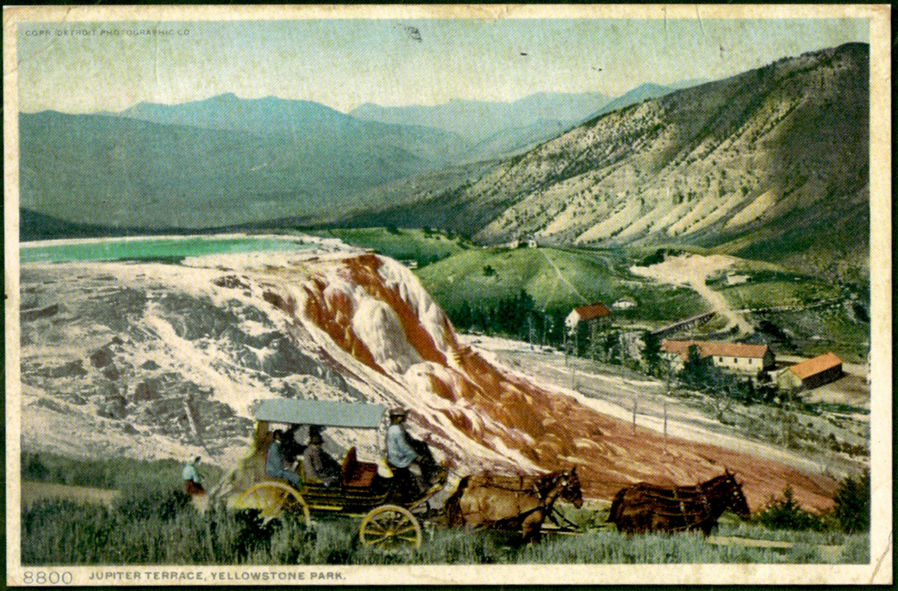

While well-appointed trains with luxury dining cars delivered passengers to Yellowstone's front door, the travelers had to adjust to a more primitive form of transportation once inside the park. Stagecoach service over rugged trails was introduced in 1881 by Marshall and Goff Stage Lines. Two years later, the U.S. Amy Corps of Engineers began building one-way roads for the coaches. The stage continued as the primary mode of transportation in the park until the automobile overtook the horse-drawn line in 1917. Phostint postcard of Yellowstone observation wagon at Mammoth made by Detroit Publishing Co., in which the sender writes, "This is one of the many great sights which we saw while passing through the park. The beauties of Yellowstone will be numbered among the most pleasant places seen."

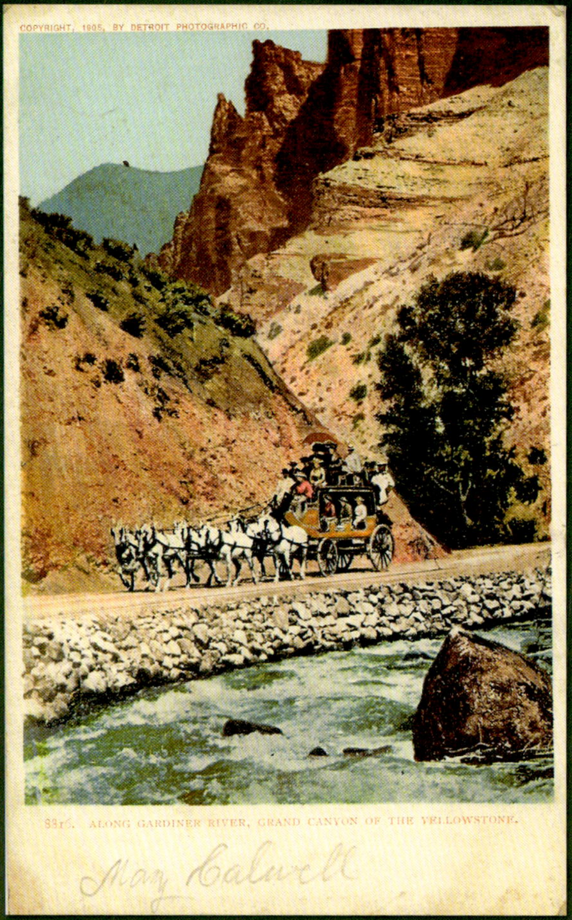

Following introduction of the Marshall and Goff Stage, future tourism prospects enticed others to sign on as early transportation concessionaires, including the Yellowstone Park Transportation Company, which operated from the North Entrance; the Monida & Yellowstone Stage Company from the West Entrance; and the Holm Transportation Company from the East Entrance. This postcard made in 1905 by Detroit Photographic Co. and postmarked 1908, shows a stagecoach with a full load of passengers along the Gardner River (also known as Gardiner River) at the Grand Canyon of the Yellowstone.

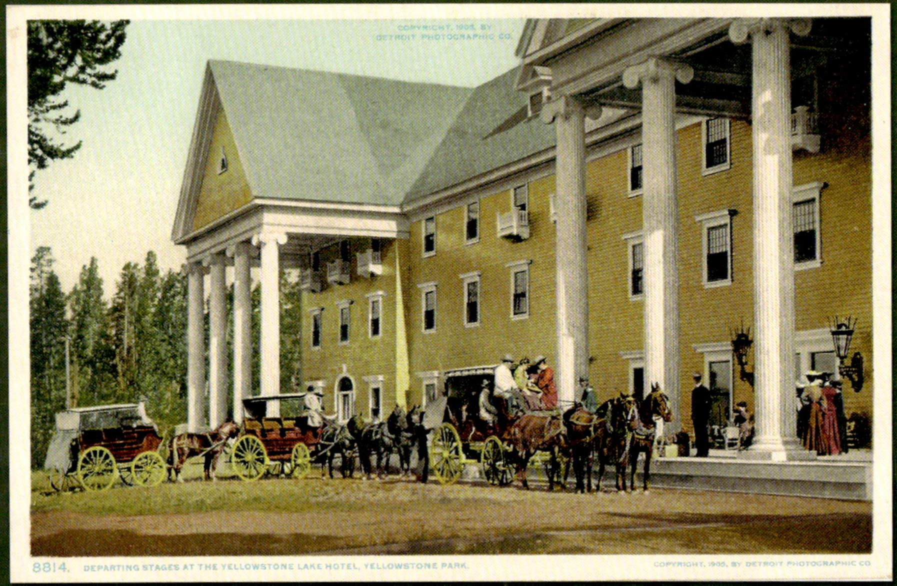

Four- and six-horse coaches were used to deliver train travelers to their hotels. Once rested, guests would climb aboard the stage for the next leg of their adventure, which included many of the sites enjoyed today. By 1909 the transportation needs of the park required more than 1,000 horses and some five hundred wagons and coaches. The stages pictured on this postcard wait outside the Yellowstone Lake Hotel for their next departure. Passengers lunched in dining tents where twenty guests could be served. This was because the horses couldn't make the trip from one fine hotel to another in time for the next meal, so other accommodations were used until the automobile was introduced. Detroit Photographic Co. postcard from 1905.

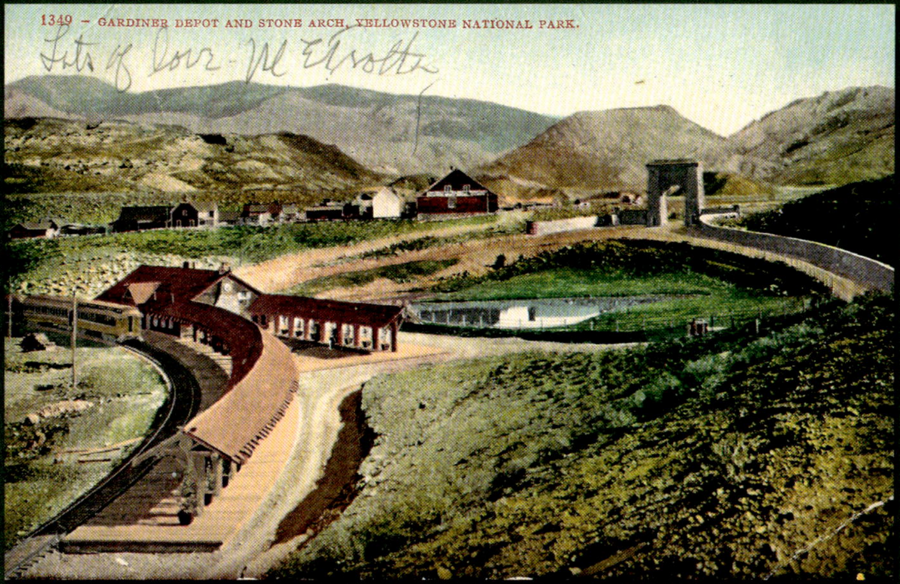

By 1929, when this time table was published for the route of the North Coast Limited, Northern Pacific was promoting its stops at Livingston and Gardiner as the Gateway to Yellowstone. Trains ran daily between June 18 and September 20 that year with morning and afternoon service between the two towns. The North Coast Limited was introduced in 1900 and became the company's flagship passenger train with service between Chicago and Seattle.

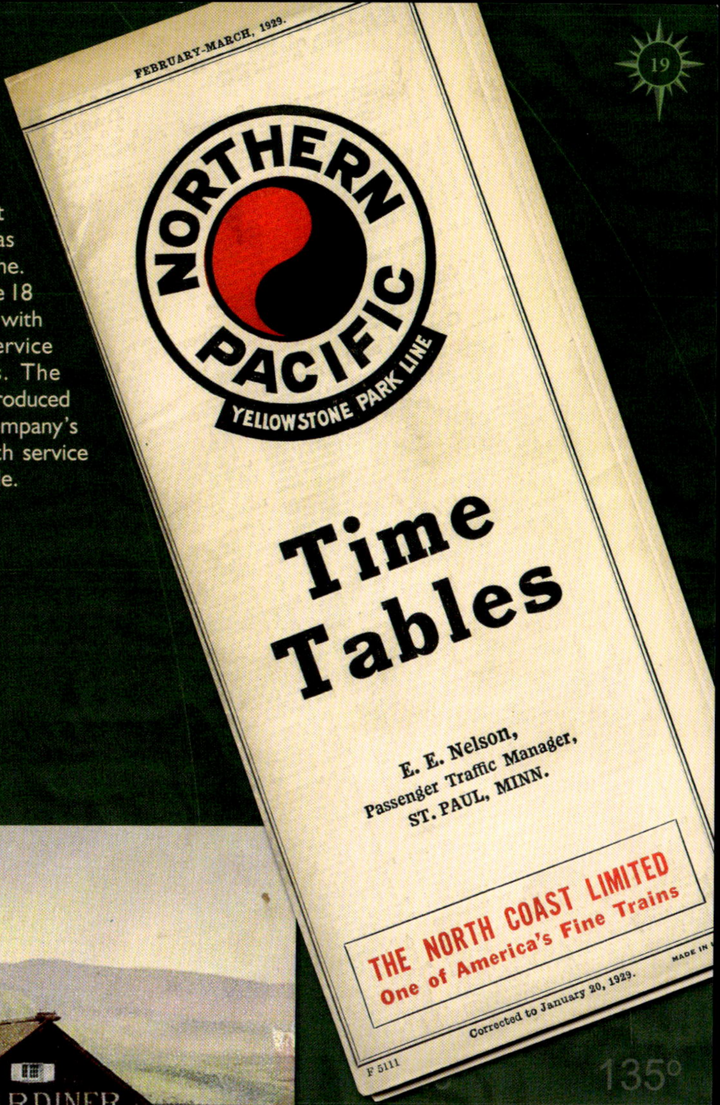

The architect for the Gardiner train station was Robert Reamer who designed and redesigned so many of the famous Yellowstone Park hotels. In 1903, at the same time he was working in Yellowstone, he was also designing the new railroad station in Gardiner on the northern border of the park. It was built by the Northern Pacific Railway to accommodate passengers as they arrived and departed Yellowstone Park. Northern Pacific was the first of the railroads to build tracks close to a Yellowstone entrance. The line from Livingston, Montana, to Cinnabar, Montana, was completed in 1883 and was extended south to Gardiner by 1902. This early postcard, postmarked in 1908 and published by Edward H. Mitchell, pictures the Gardiner Depot, a train on the railroad tracks, and the stone arch gateway that leads into the park from the Northern Entrance.

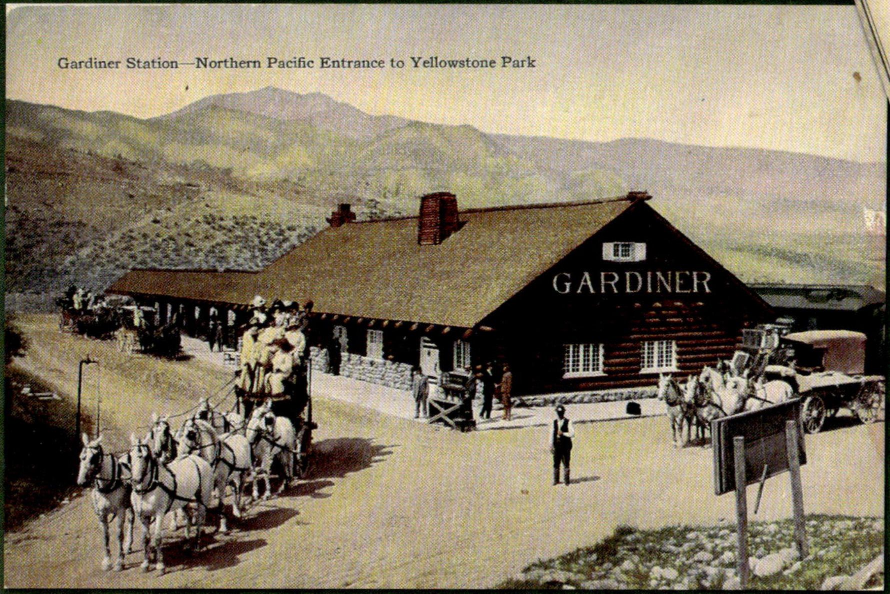

This postcard postmarked 1915 and published by Northern Pacific shows one of the stagecoaches used to bring travelers to the park. The railway station was located five miles from Mammoth Hot Springs and the beautiful painted terraces. The passenger depot was removed by the Burlington-Northern Pacific in 1956. HHT Co. postcard.

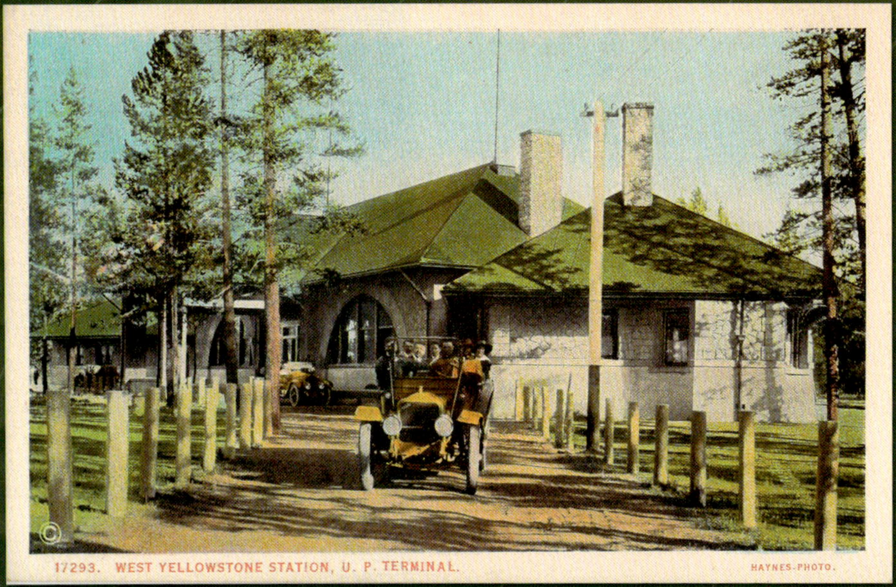

In addition to the presence of the Northern Pacific Railway to the north, the small town of West Yellowstone was established to become a stopping point for train service when the Union Pacific Railroad began operations in June 1908. Construction of a railroad station followed in 1909. This postcard pictures the station along with one of the touring cars used to transport passengers to Yellowstone Park. Published by J. E. Haynes.

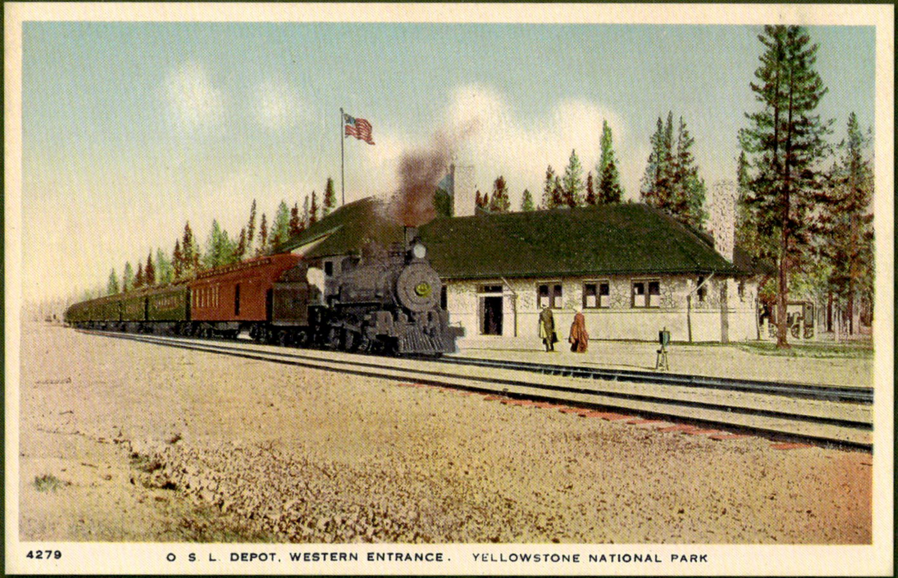

This early postcard features another view of Union Pacific Railroad Station. A train is being readied to load the passengers waiting outside. The station continued to service passengers until the railroad discontinued its operation in 1961. Postcard by HHT Co.

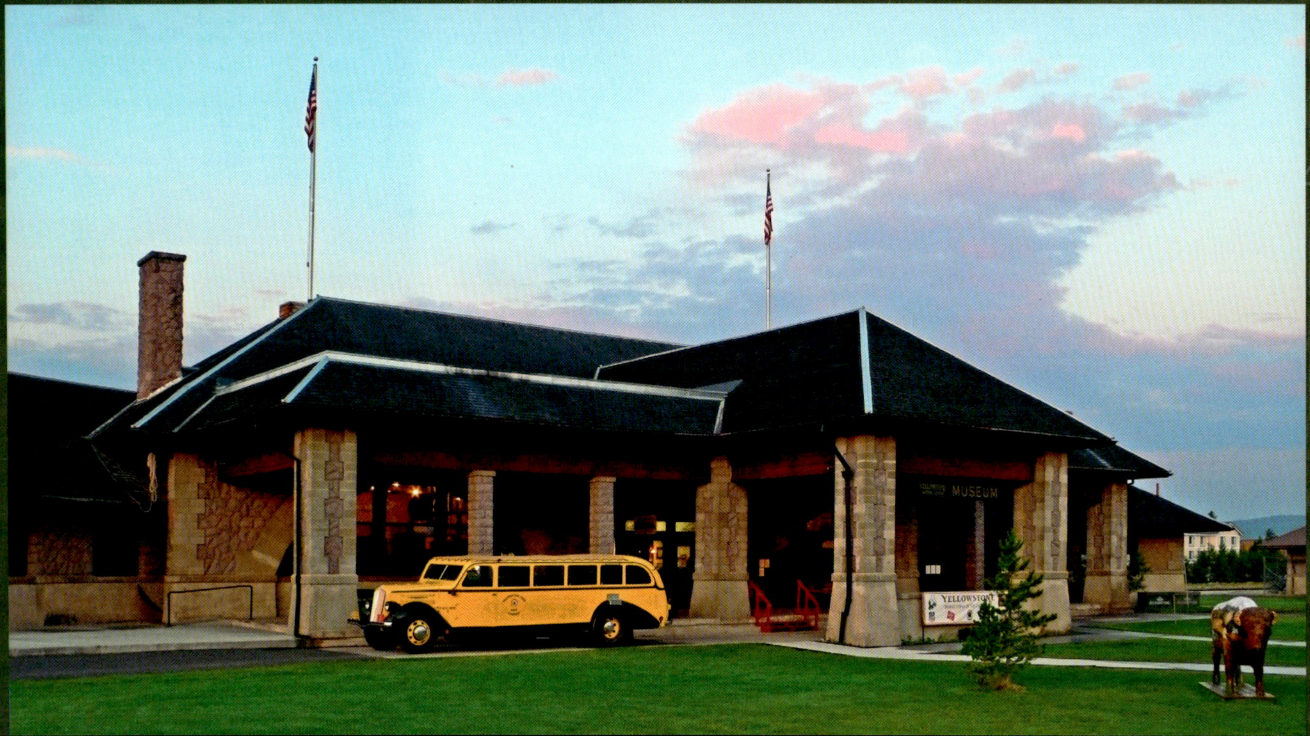

West Yellowstone's Union Pacific Depot is now home to the Yellowstone Historic Center Museum, which opened in 2001 after extensive renovation was made to the building following its use as a privately owned museum. The center contains an extensive collection of artifacts and documents that explore the heritage of travel to the park. The museum is open from mid-May to mid-October. *Photo courtesy Yellowstone Historic Center.*

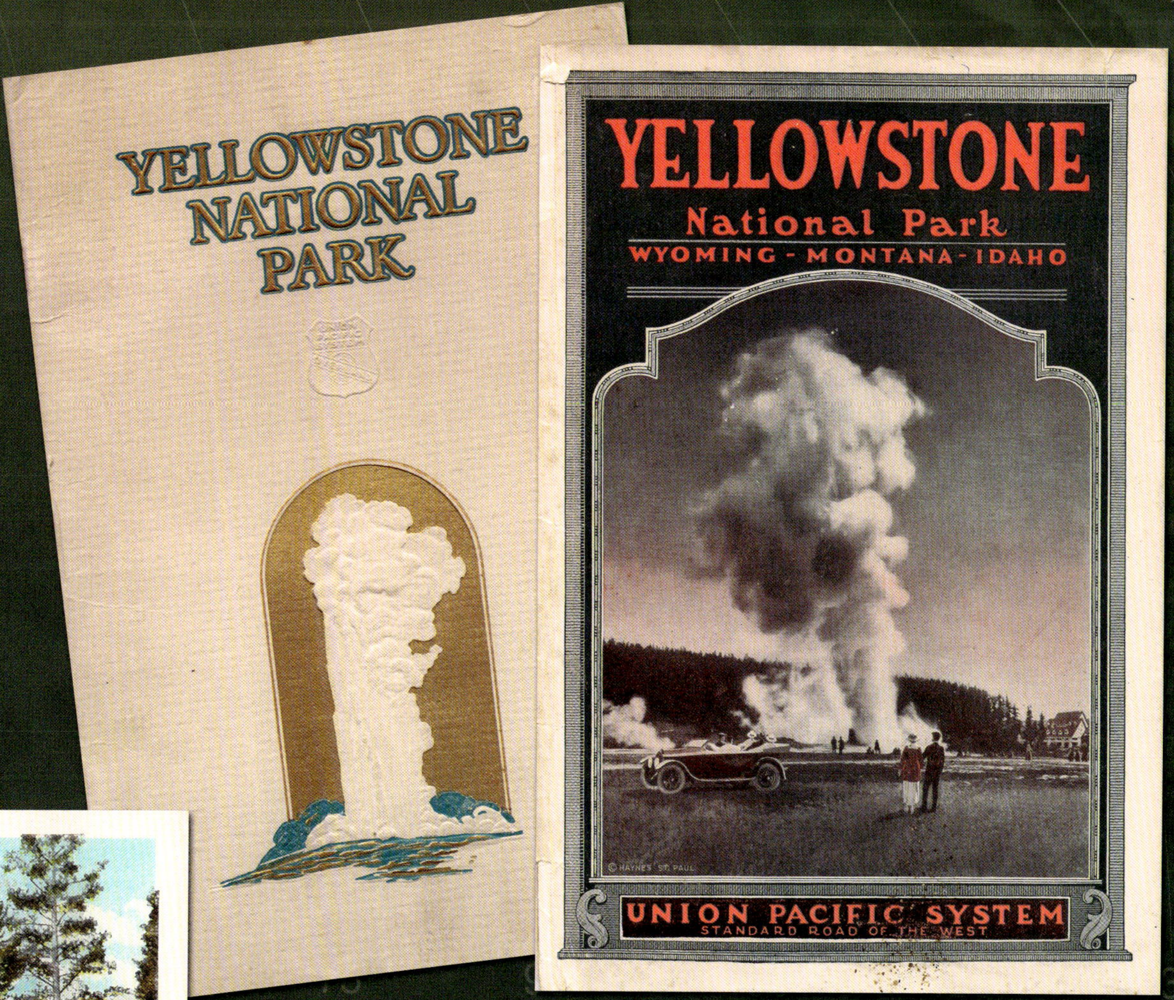

Pictured are railroad brochures from 1928 (left) and 1920 issued by the Union Pacific Railroad to promote its train tours to Yellowstone. Both booklets are illustrated with park scenes along with information on a four-and-a-half day stopover that included fourteen meals, lodging, and motor transportation. In 1920, the tour was priced at $45.00 for adults who stayed at the park's mid-priced lodges or $54.00 for guests who preferred the upscale hotels.

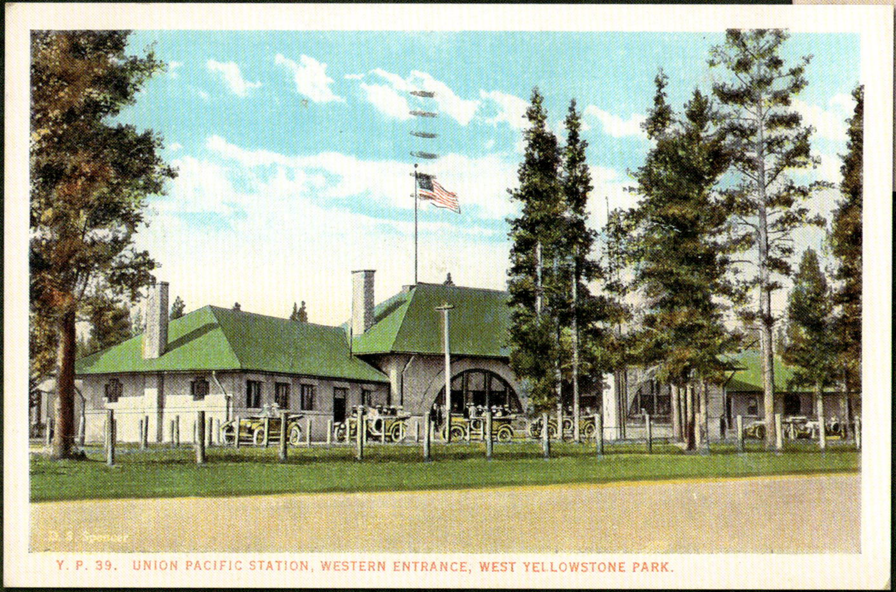

Bloom Bros. Co. postcard of the Union Pacific Station in West Yellowstone postmarked 1934.

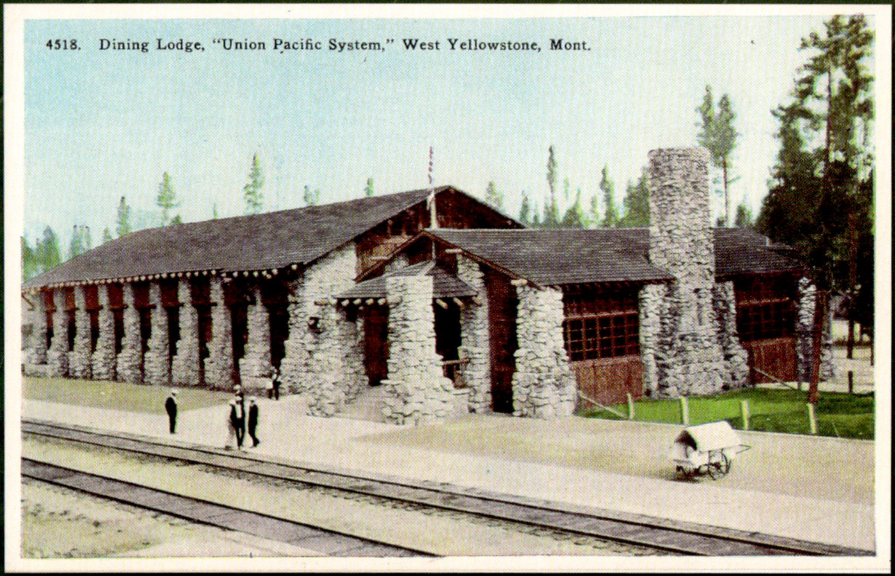

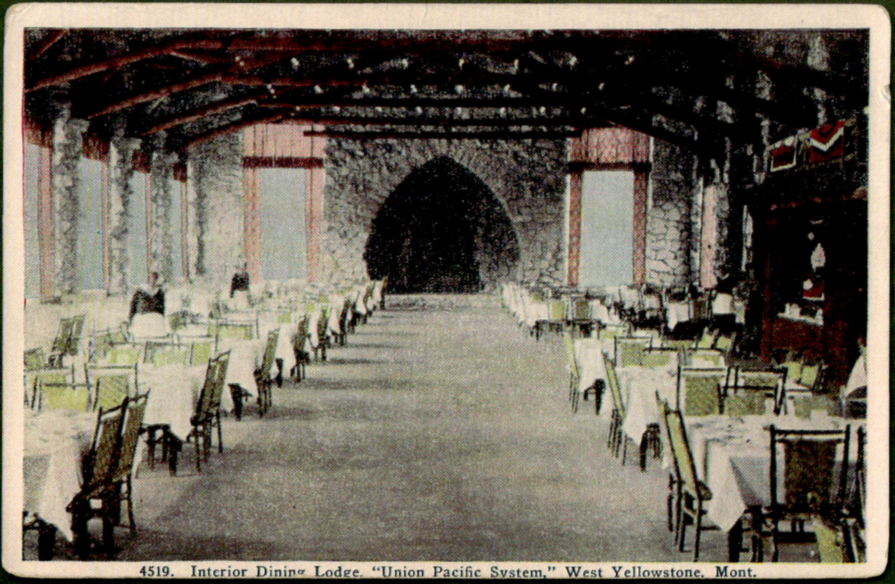

The Union Pacific Dining Lodge, located near the depot, was built in 1925. It was designed by Gilbert Stanley Underwood in the rustic architecture style. His portfolio also includes the Old Faithful Lodge in Yellowstone and The Ahwahnee Hotel in Yosemite National Park. In the days of the popular Yellowstone railroad tours, the passengers left the "Yellowstone Special" train at the railroad station and ate breakfast at this dining lodge next door. Their tour transportation consisted of ten-passenger automobiles which were designed especially for Yellowstone Park and operated by the Yellowstone Park Transportation Company. The tour left at 9:30 a.m. Haynes postcard.

The interior of the dining lodge was furnished with rustic hickory chairs and tables. A large arrowhead-shaped fireplace decorated the far wall. The kitchen was equipped to serve one-thousand meals a day. Dining service ended in 1960. Today, the building is part of the ten-acre Oregon Short Line Historic District that includes other Union Pacific Railroad facilities, including the baggage building and men's dormitory. Preservation and restoration of the structures is overseen by the Yellowstone Historic Center. A portion of the dining lodge is now used for government offices, while the remainder can be rented for special events and meetings. Postcard by HHT Co. circa 1920s.

UNION PACIFIC

The familiar red, white, and blue Union Pacific shield was introduced by the railroad in 1887 as a symbol of the company's strength. Eleven different shield designs have been used throughout the railroad's history, including this current design. Today the company operates in twenty-three states across the western two-thirds of the U.S. *Union Pacific logo is a registered trademark and is used with permission from Union Pacific Railroad.*

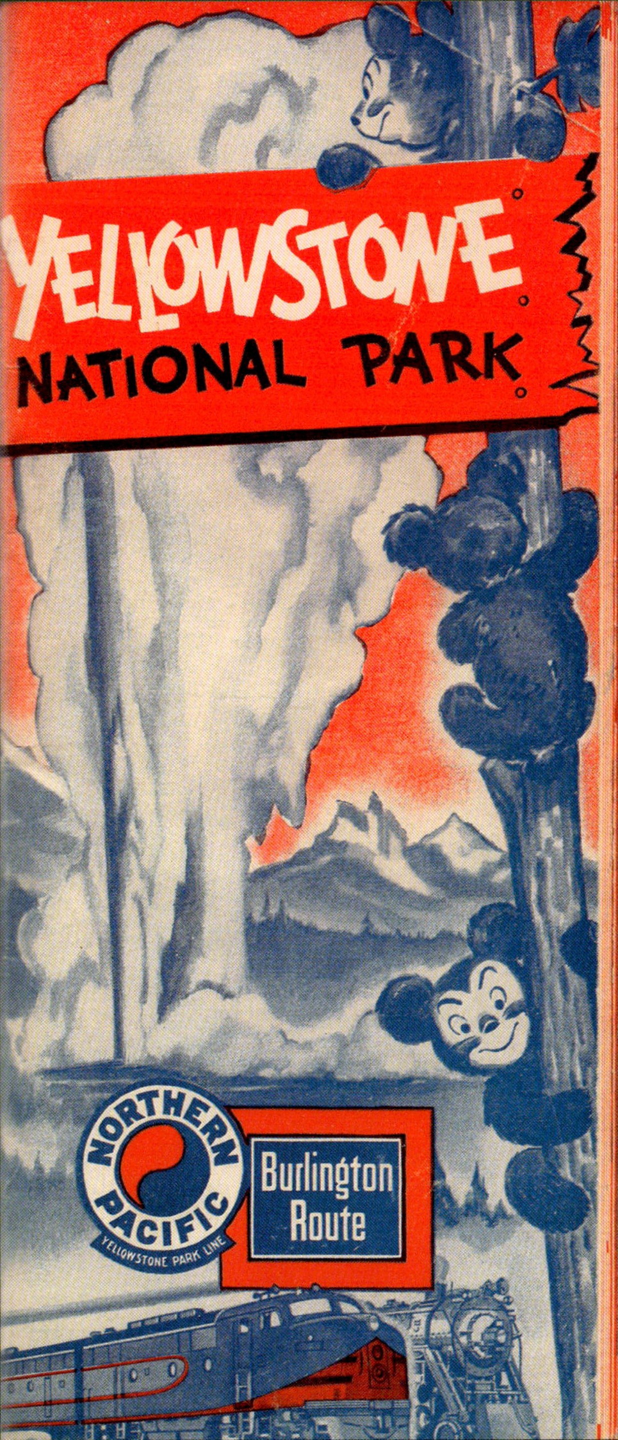

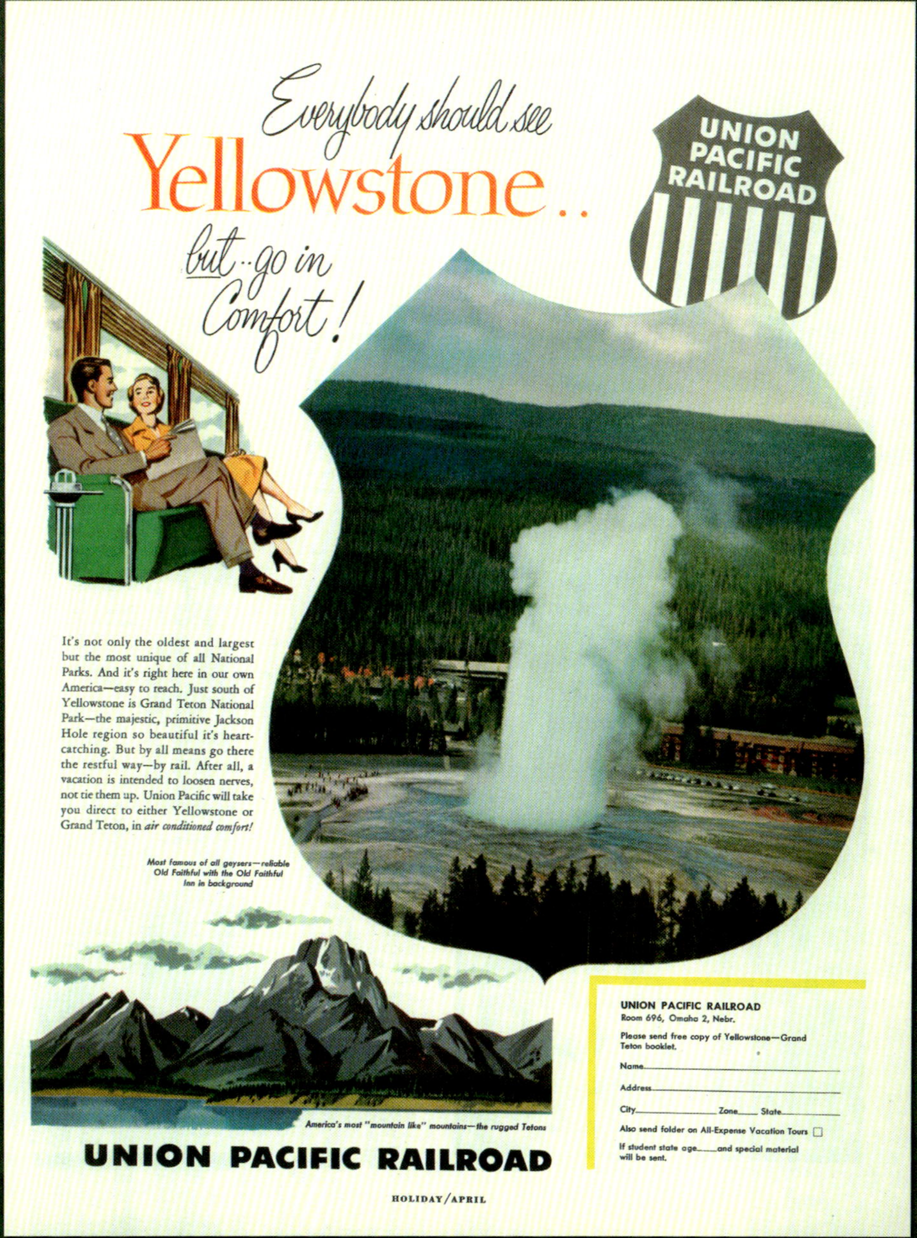

Promotion of all-inclusive tour packages to Yellowstone and other national parks caused rail travel to flourish during the 1930s and '40s. By the 1950s, threatened by the rising popularity of private automobiles, railroad marketing campaigns attempted to keep the industry alive by emphasizing the advantages of rail travel over roads. Advances in air-conditioned coaches, dining cars, and other comforts were promoted, as shown in this ad for Union Pacific in 1954. Also pictured is a Burlington-Northern Pacific pamphlet from 1951containing similar enticements. But the comforts weren't enough to keep passengers coming. Rail service to the Yellowstone area was discontinued by 1961. Today, the nearest train depots are in southeast Idaho, Salt Lake City (Utah), and northern Montana.

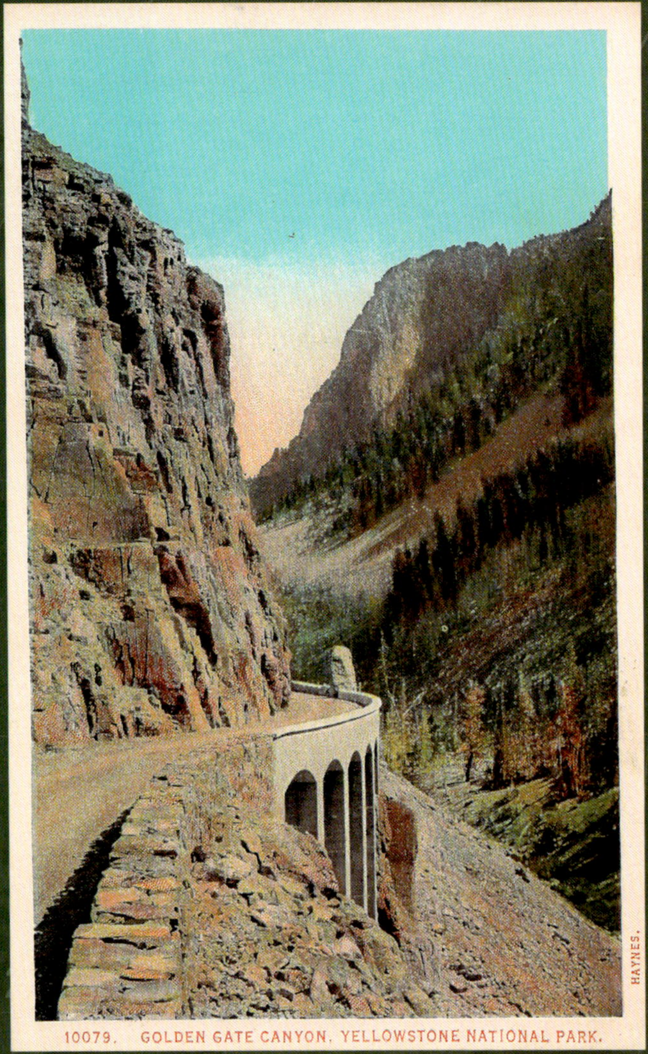

Construction of the Yellowstone Grand Loop Road was undertaken in 1883 by the U.S. Army Corps of Engineers. When completed in 1905, it dramatically improved accessibility within the park by connecting the major points of interest. Originally used for the horse-drawn stages, a project to widen the road for automobiles began in 1913 and was finished in 1915. Paving was not completed until after World War II. This early postcard pictures the road at the Golden Gate Canyon south of Mammoth Hot Springs leading to Kingman Pass. Eleven concrete arches were built into the cliff wall to support the road. Postcard by Haynes Picture Shops.

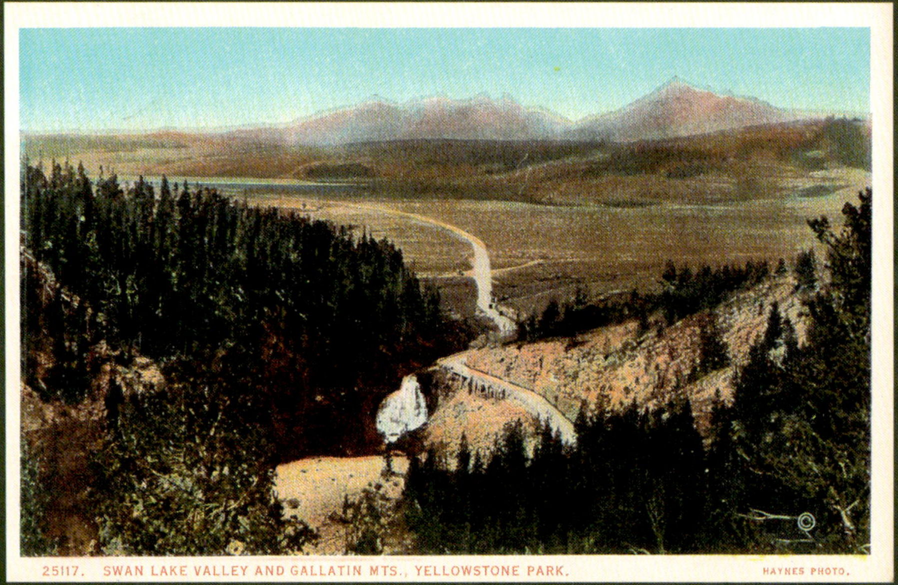

The Grand Loop Road offers panoramic views of lush valleys, streams, and mountain ranges, including this scene from the cliff above Golden Gate showing Rustic Falls in Glen Creek, Swan Lake Valley, and Gallatin Range. Postcard by J. E. Haynes.

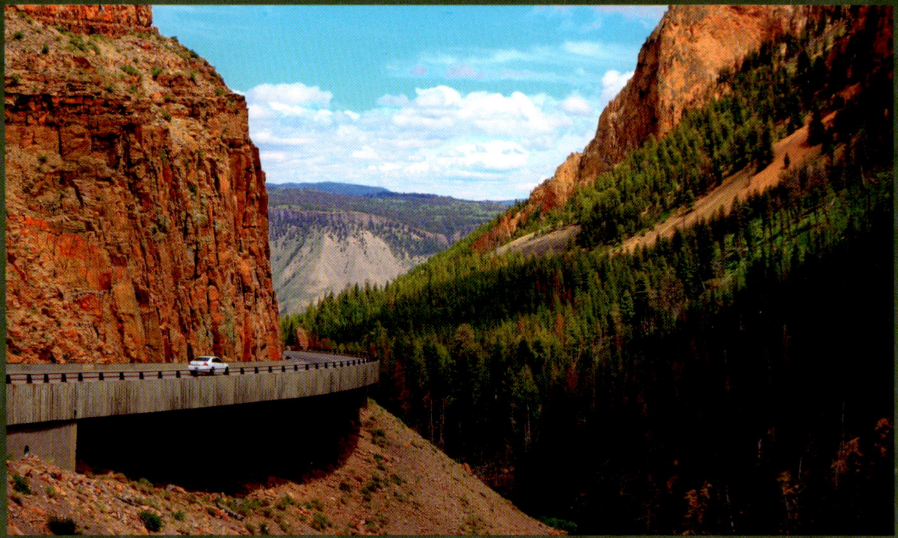

The 140-mile Grand Loop Road is in the shape of a figure-eight and provides access to the major features of the park, including the Upper, Midway and Lower geyser basins, Mammoth Hot Springs, Tower Fall, the Grand Canyon of the Yellowstone, and Yellowstone Lake. Today, the Grand Loop Road includes portions of U.S. 20, U.S. 89, U.S. 191, and U.S. 287 within the park. Due to the road's heavy use and harsh climate, rebuilding of the road has become an ongoing endeavor. This photo shows the Golden Gate Canyon as it looks now. It remains one of the most picturesque drives in the park.

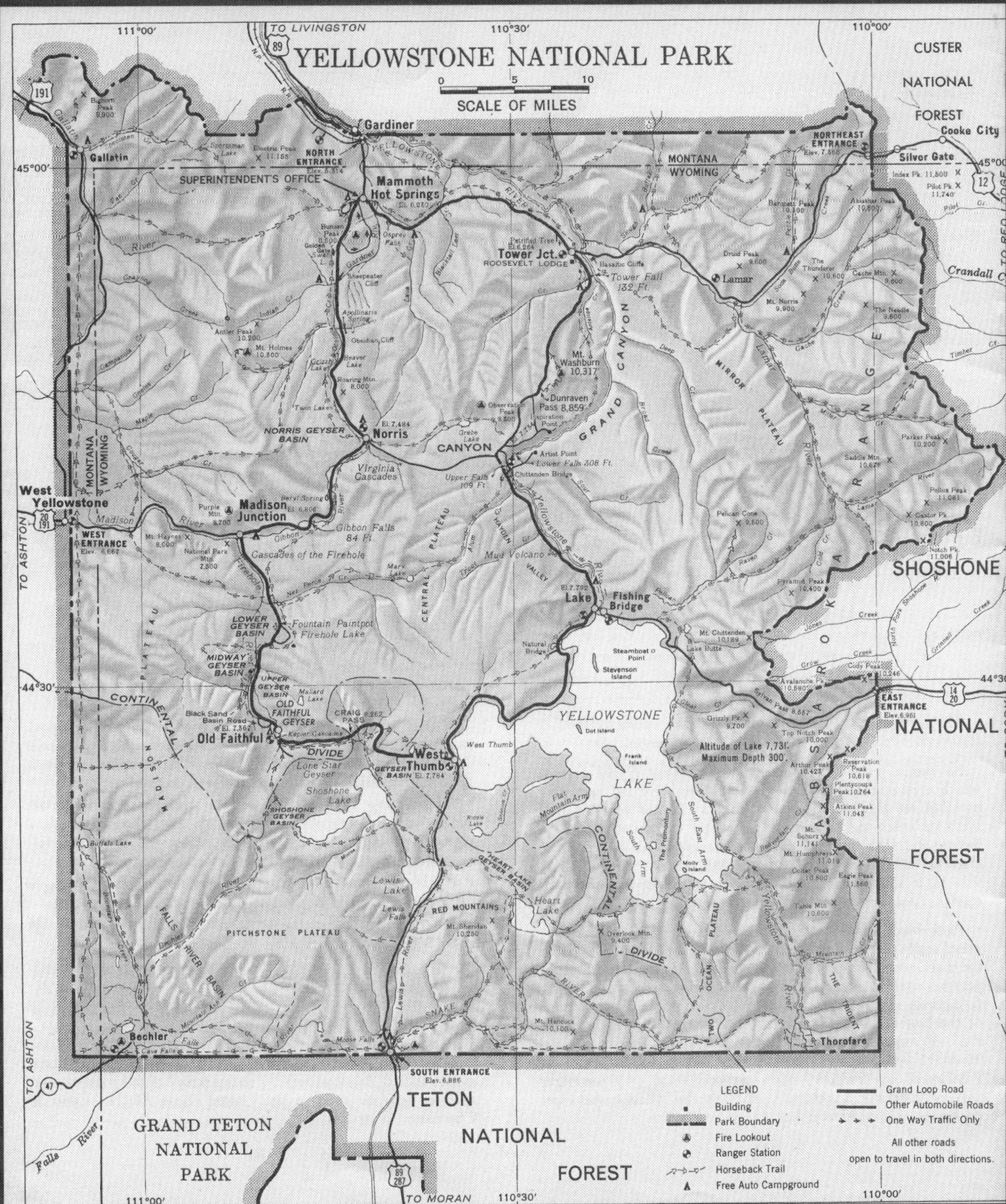

This map, issued by the National Park Service circa 1950, shows the route of the Grand Loop Road. Park Superintendent Nathaniel P. Langford had envisioned the need for a road system as early as 1872 to help spawn establishment of responsible uses that would overtake the shady practices and money-making abuses he had feared. His repeated requests for federal funding were unsuccessful, however, because of promises made during the park's establishment that money needed for road construction and maintenance would come from land leases to concessionaires rather than the government. It was not until 1878 following the appointment of Philetus W. Norris as superintendent that Congress approved its first funding appropriation to the park, where road projects were now desperately needed. This map was published before the Canyon and Grant Villages were developed during the Mission 66 project.

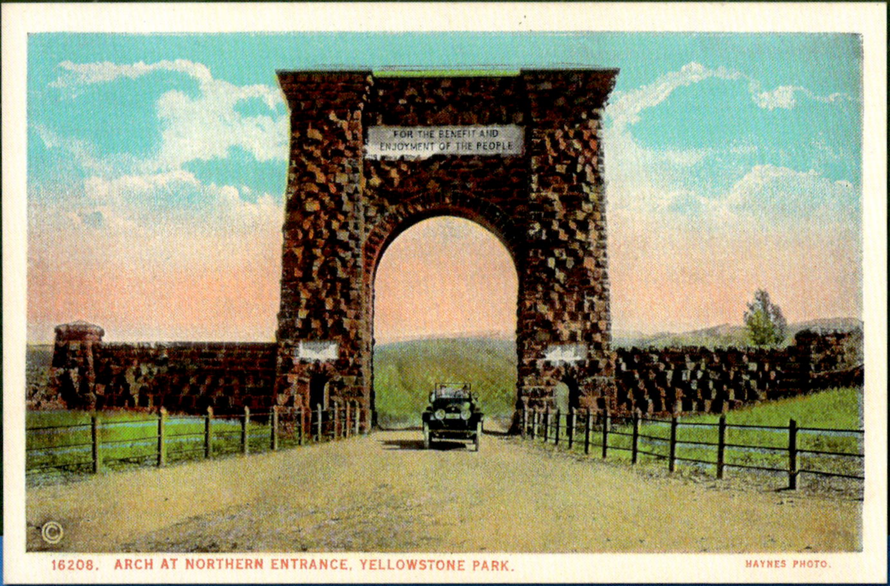

There are five entrances to Yellowstone Park, including from the west through West Yellowstone, Montana; from the south through Grand Teton National Park in Wyoming; from the north through Gardiner, Montana; northeast from Cooke City, Montana; and from the east through Cody, Wyoming. The most famous of the entrances is from the north which bears a massive arch built in 1903 by General H. M. Chittenden of the U.S. Army Corps of Engineers who became Yellowstone's greatest road builder. It was dedicated that year by President Theodore Roosevelt and bears the inscription from the Act of Dedication of the park in 1872, "For the Benefit and Enjoyment of the People." Postcard by J. E. Haynes, St. Paul, Minnesota.

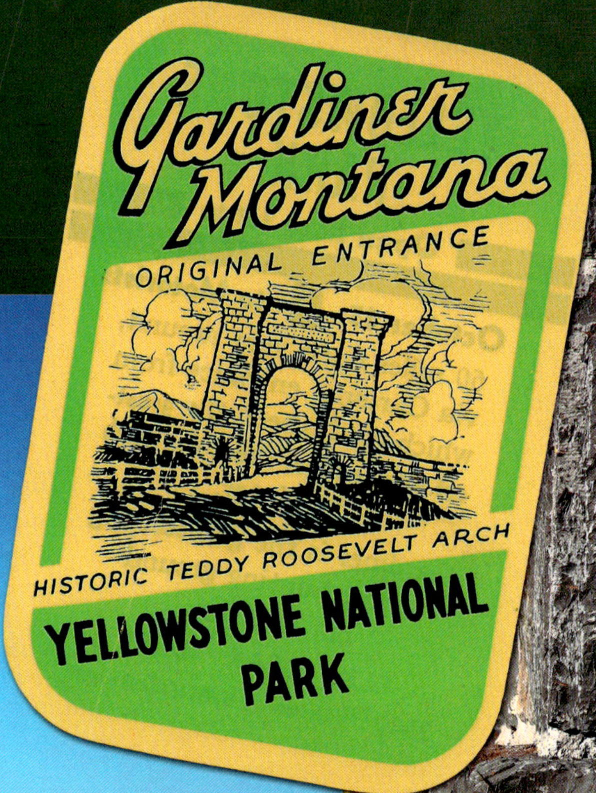

Vintage unmarked decal from Gardiner featuring the historic arch.

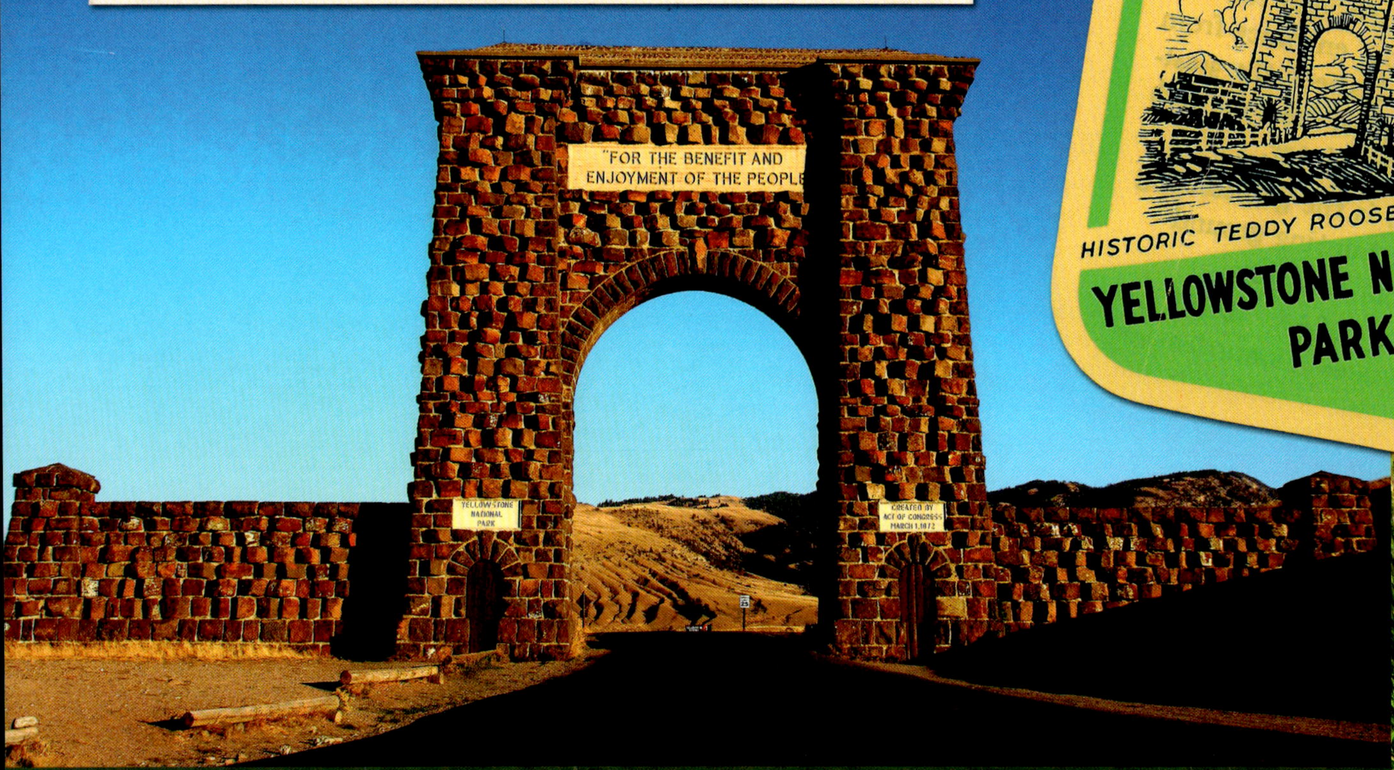

The Roosevelt Arch was built on the original road from Gardiner and is still in place today, although there is now another wider road from Gardiner to the park. Native lava rock was used in its construction. The cornerstone of the arch (shown at right) was laid by President Theodore Roosevelt on April 24, 1903.

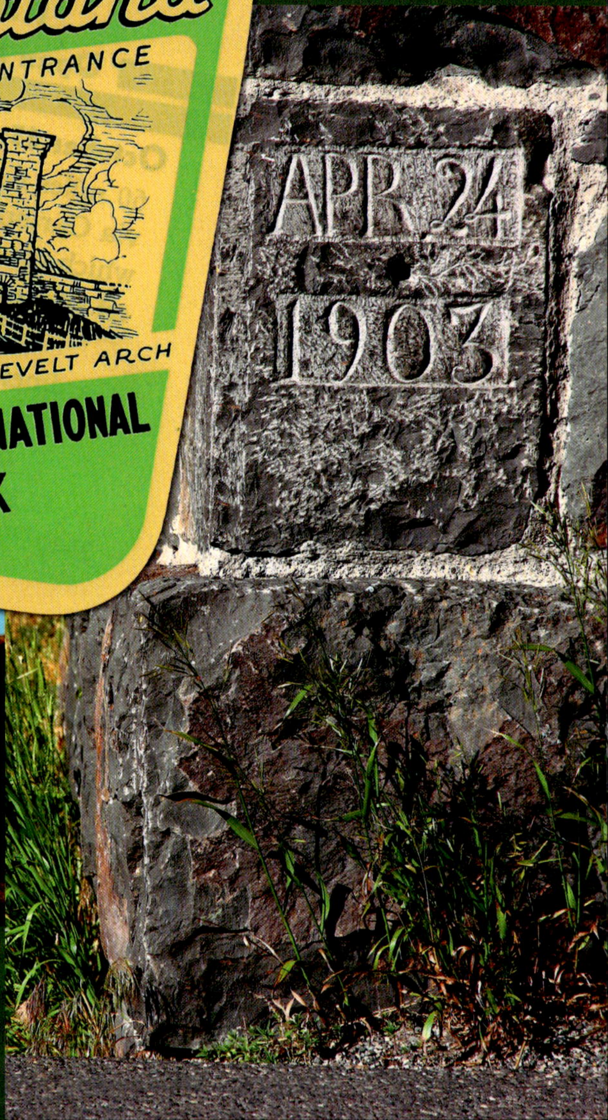

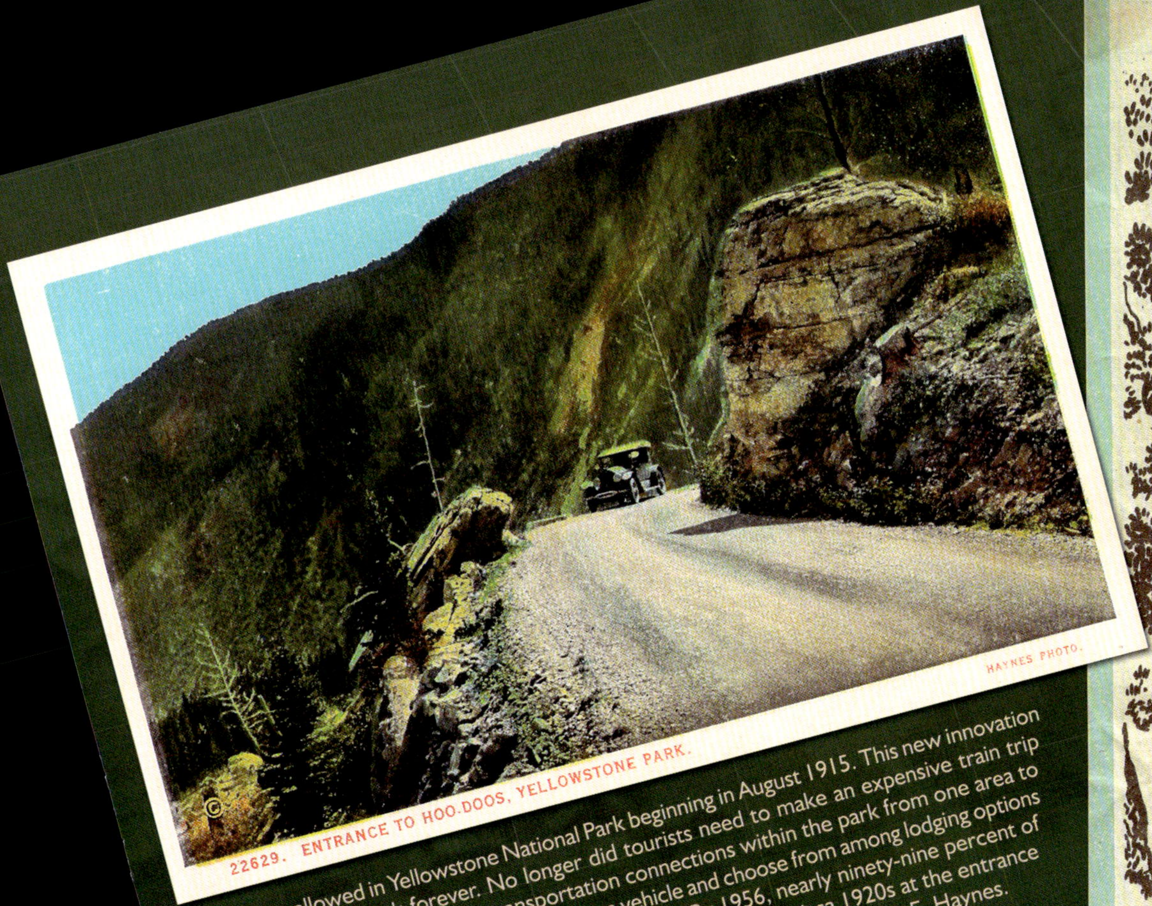

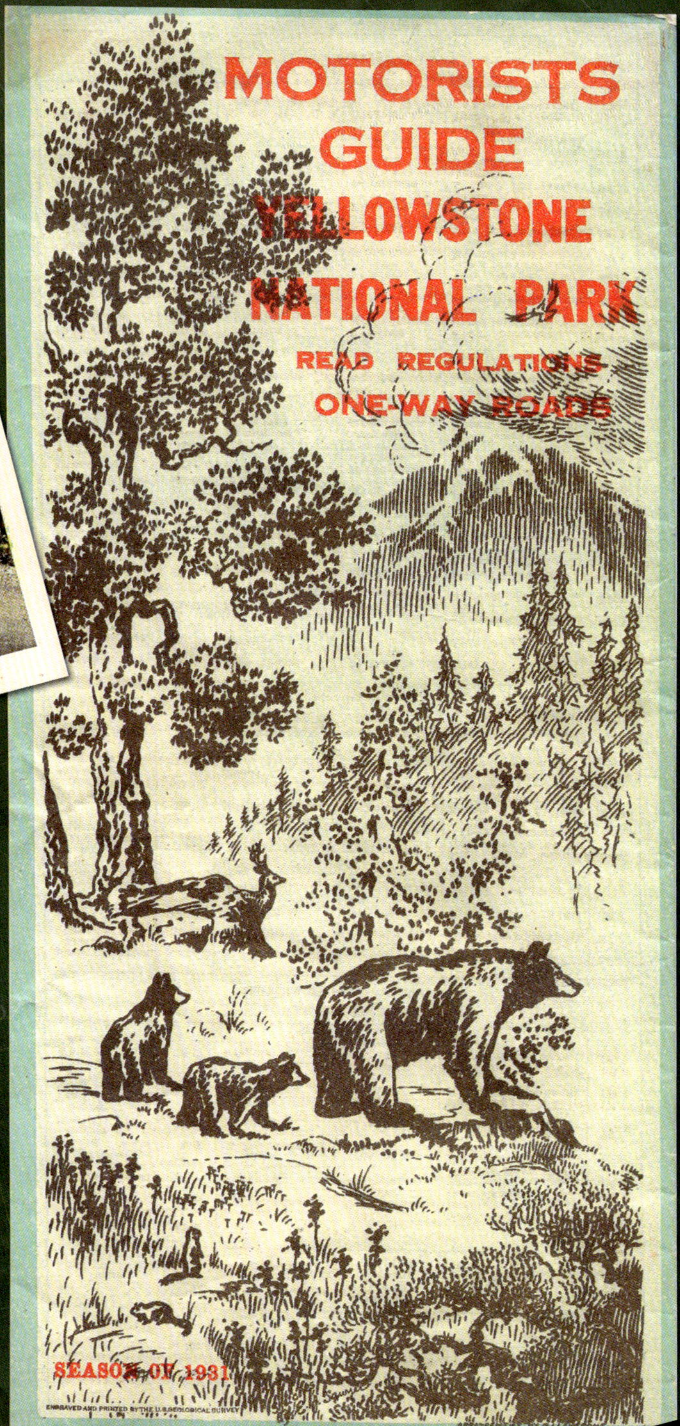

Autos were allowed in Yellowstone National Park beginning in August 1915. This new innovation would change the park forever. No longer did tourists need to make an expensive train trip across the country, followed by transportation connections within the park from one area to another. Instead, they could arrive in their own vehicle and choose from among lodging options that ranged from a campground to the grand hotels. By 1956, nearly ninety-nine percent of all park visitors came by automobile. Pictured is an automobile circa 1920s at the entrance to Hoodoos and Bunsen Peak south of Mammoth. Postcard published by J. E. Haynes.

...y the National Park Service ...included one-way ... Some

The East Entrance to the park can be reached from Cody, Wyoming. It is a 53-mile drive. In earlier days, automobiles made the trip through a more primitive road that included several tunnels drilled through volcanic rock as pictured in this circa 1920s postcard of Shoshone Canyon by Haynes Picture Shops, Inc. and the vintage decal produced by the Burlington Railroad.

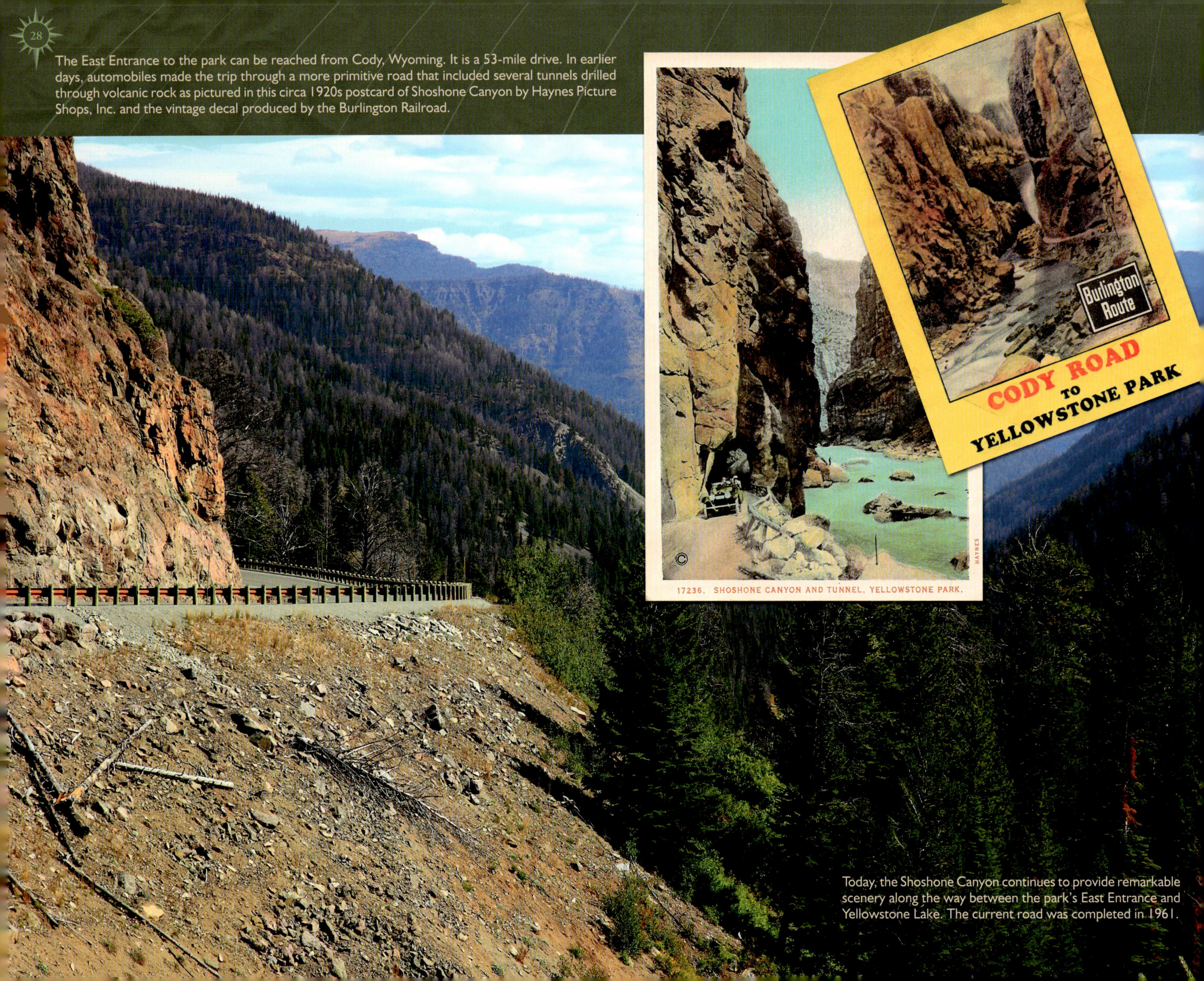

Today, the Shoshone Canyon continues to provide remarkable scenery along the way between the park's East Entrance and Yellowstone Lake. The current road was completed in 1961.

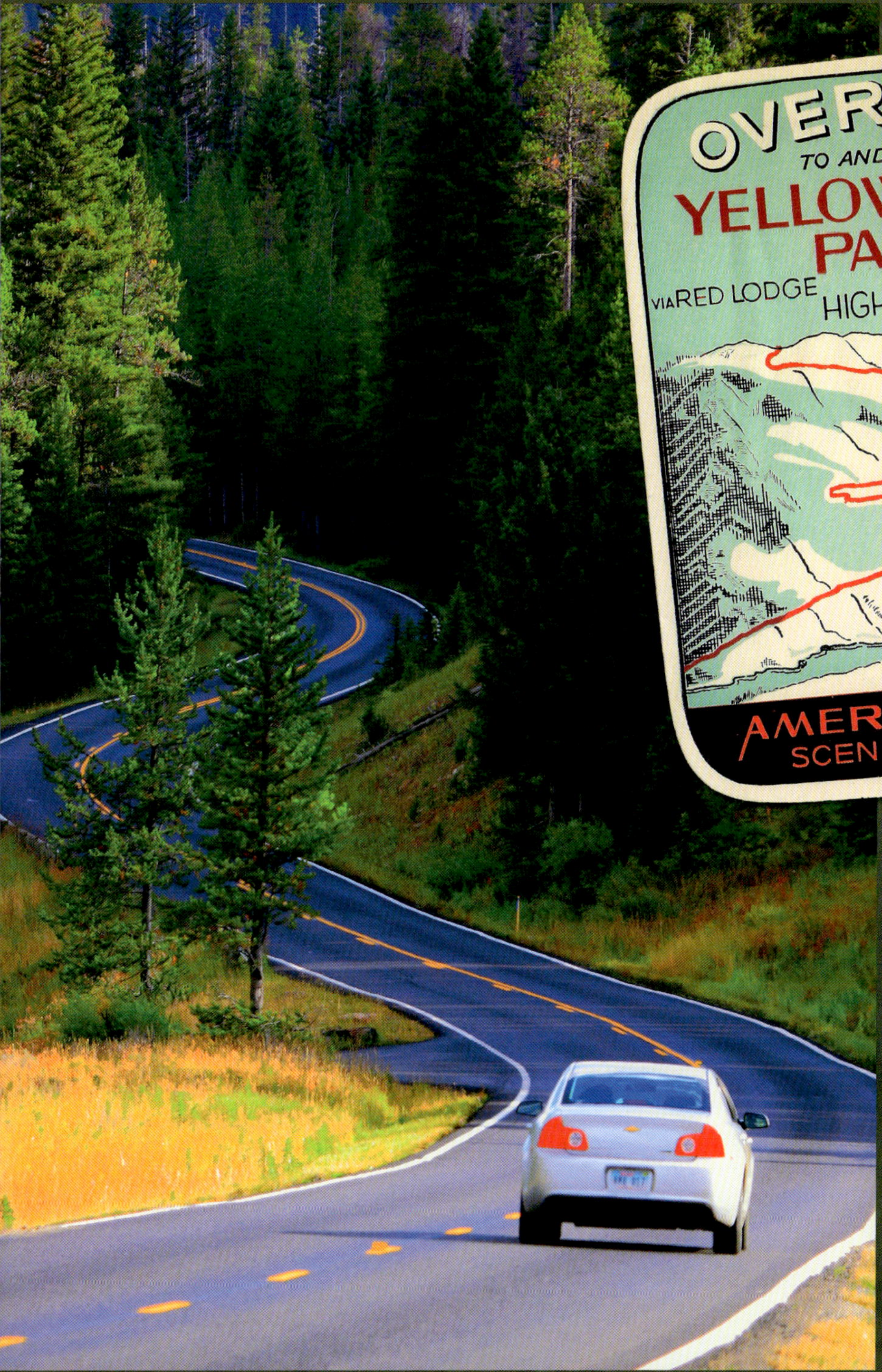

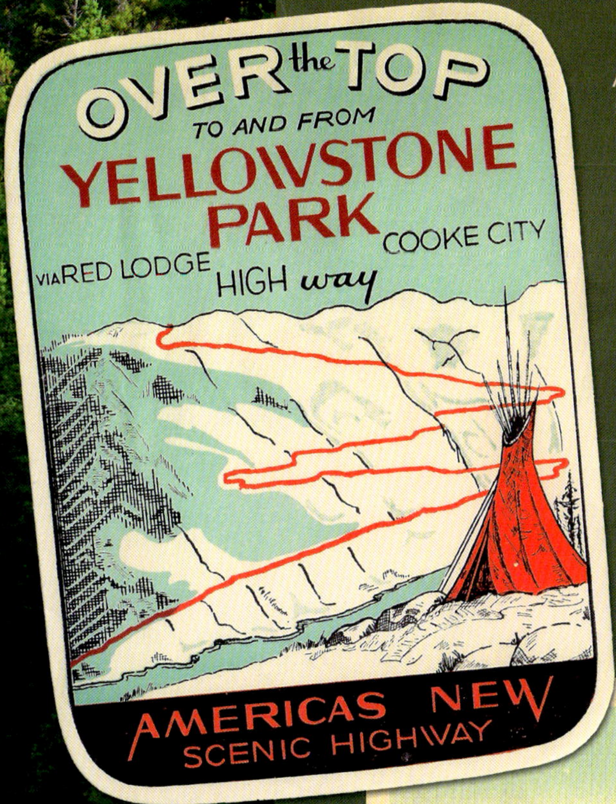

A car enters the forest near Cooke City along one of the most spectacular mountain routes in the country. U.S. Highway 212 is known as the Beartooth Highway, a sixty-nine mile route from Red Lodge, Montana. The road opened in 1936.

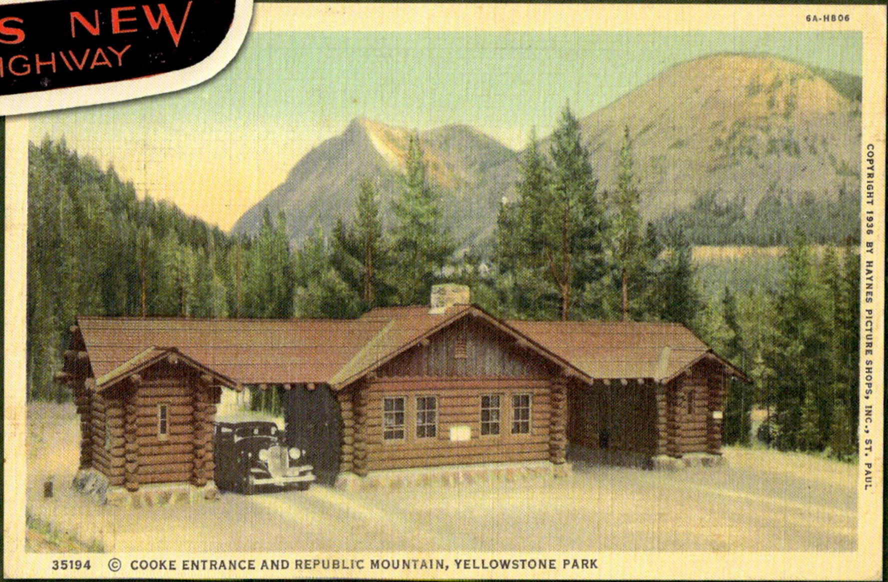

The Northeast Entrance Station is accessed from Cooke City and is one of five National Historic Landmark buildings in the park. The log structure was built in 1934-35 and reflects the "parkitecture" design that was common during the era. Postcard by Haynes Picture Shops postmarked 1937. The park's other historic landmarks are Old Faithful Inn and the museums at Fishing Bridge, Madison, and Norris Geyser Basin.

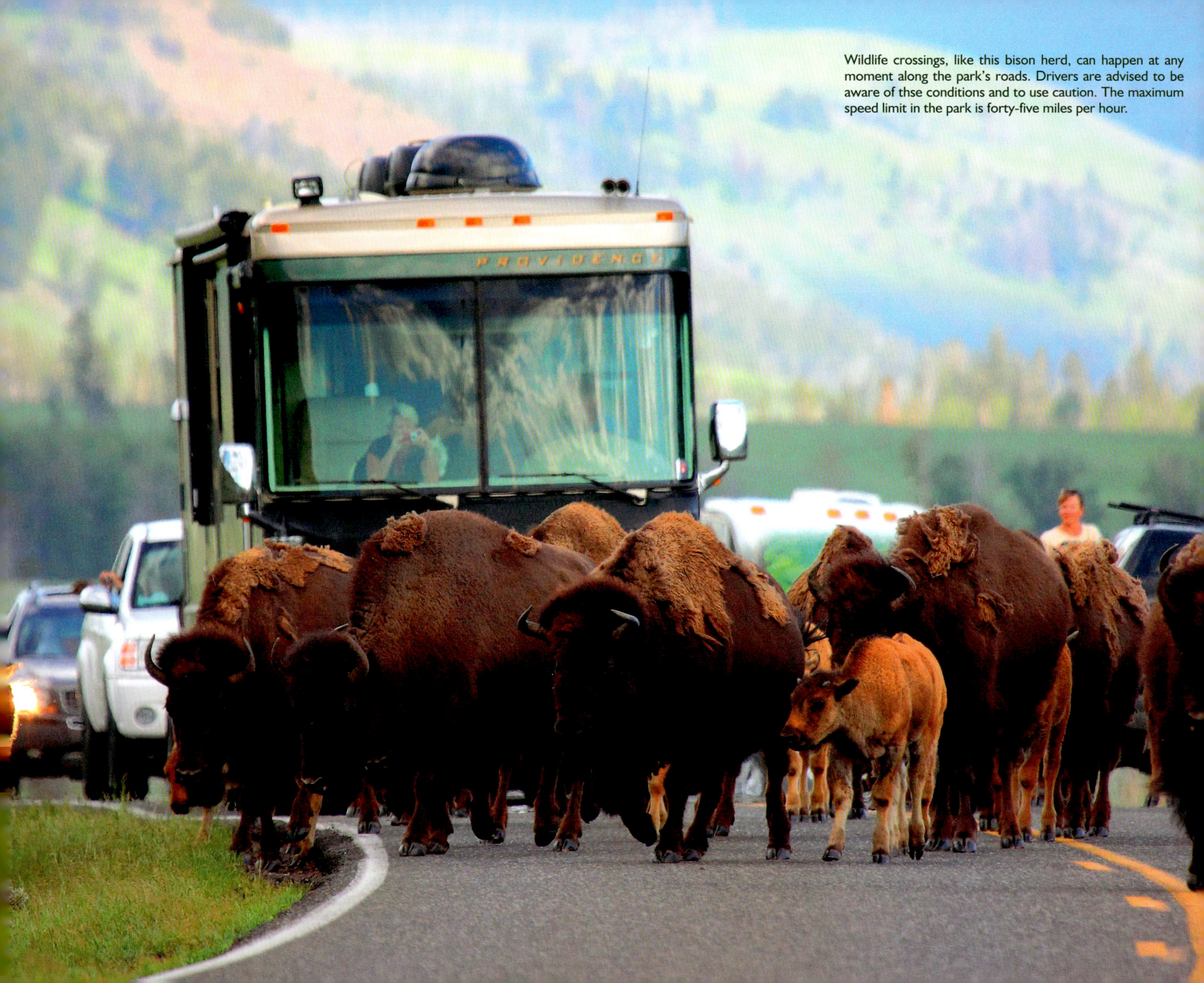

Wildlife crossings, like this bison herd, can happen at any moment along the park's roads. Drivers are advised to be aware of thse conditions and to use caution. The maximum speed limit in the park is forty-five miles per hour.

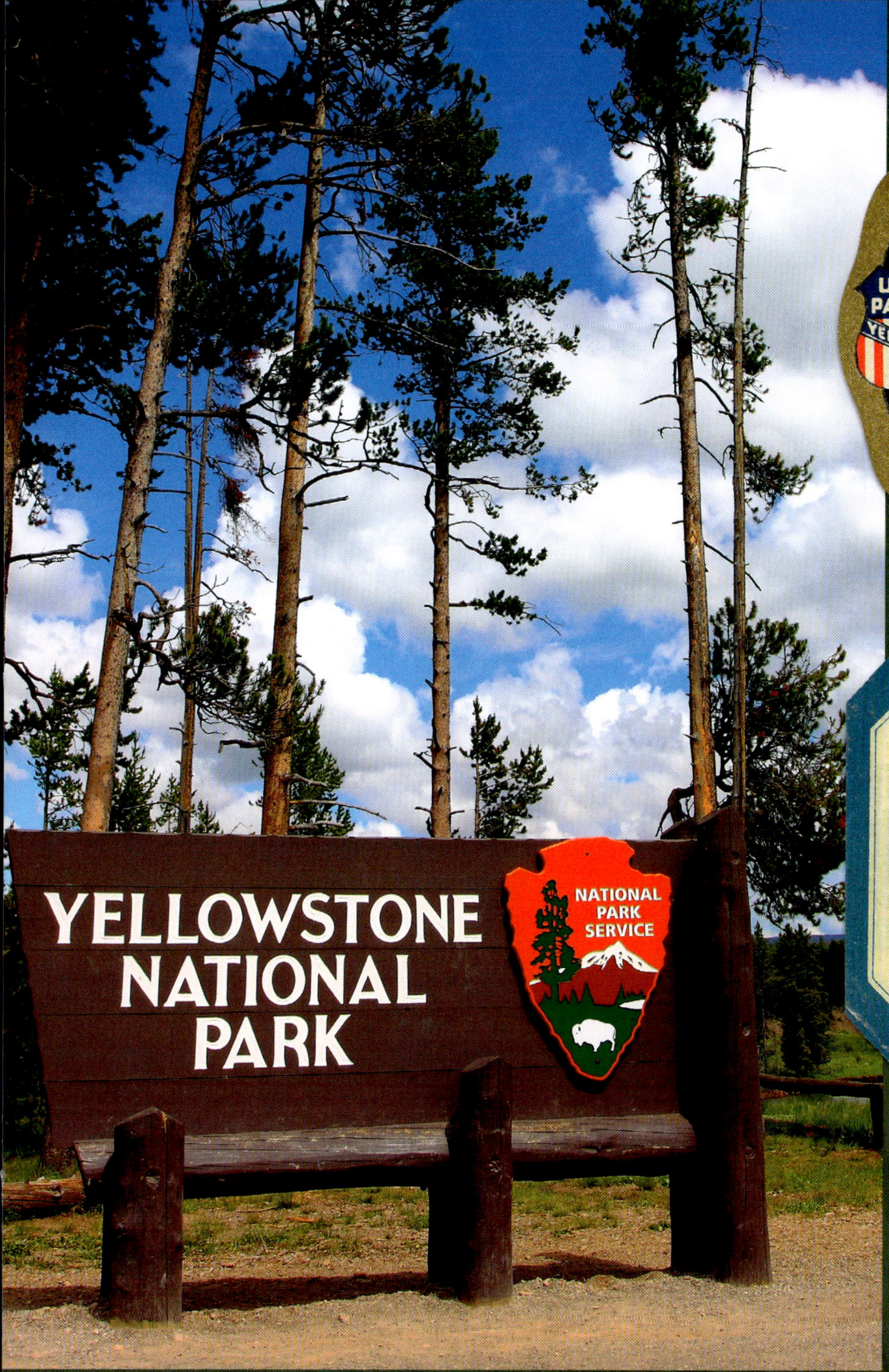

Visitation to Yellowstone has grown to more than three million annually. Entry fees are good for seven days for both Yellowstone and neighboring Grand Teton National Park. Annual passes are also sold as well as a variety of other pass types.

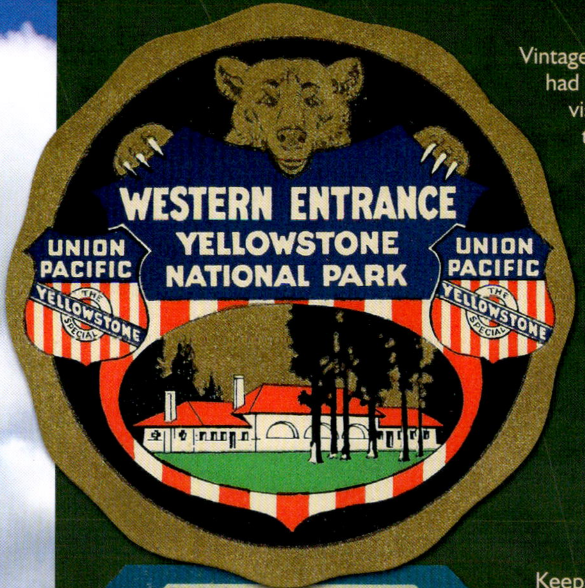

Vintage souvenir decals were given to passengers who had arrived in West Yellowstone by train for their visit to the park. The decal features a picture of the Union Pacific Railroad station.

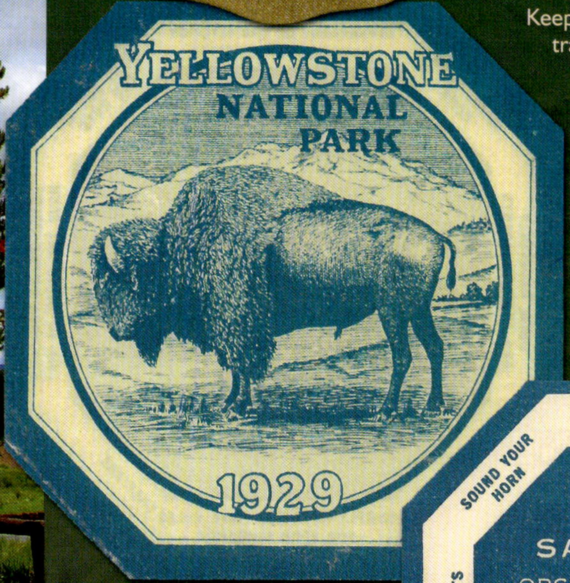

Keepsakes like this one were issued to those who traveled to the park using their own automobiles and were to be placed on the windshield. Similar decals were available from many of the other national parks. Each featured an animal or landscape scene that was most symbolic of its area. In this case, the Yellowstone decal featured a bison. This one was from 1929. The backside contains safety messages for auto travel in the park as well as a warning that "writing or carving names or initials on geysers and hot springs formations is absolutely prohibited."

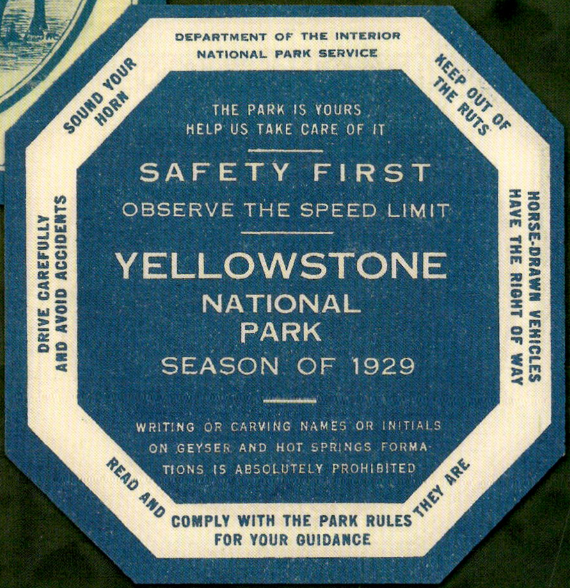

135°

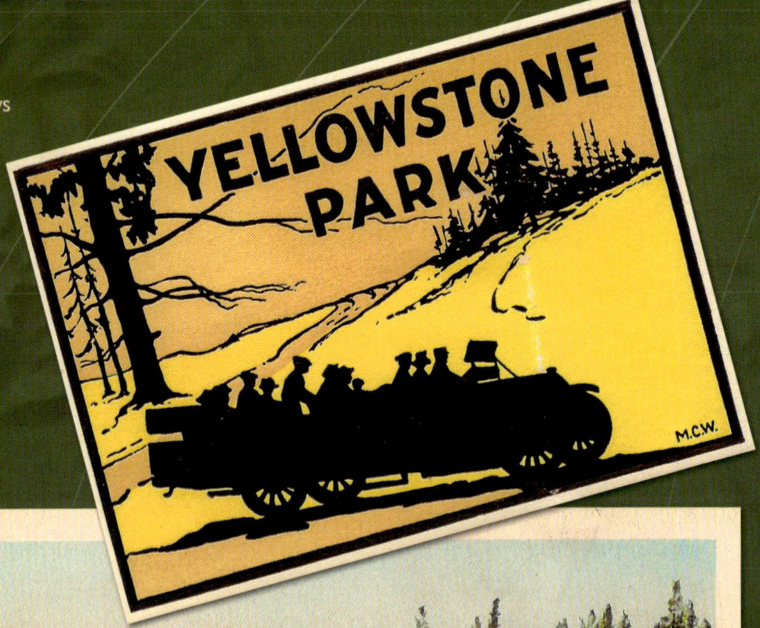

This decal from the 1920s shows a motorbus from the White Motor Company; these motorbuses were used in Yellowstone to transport visitors beginning in 1917.

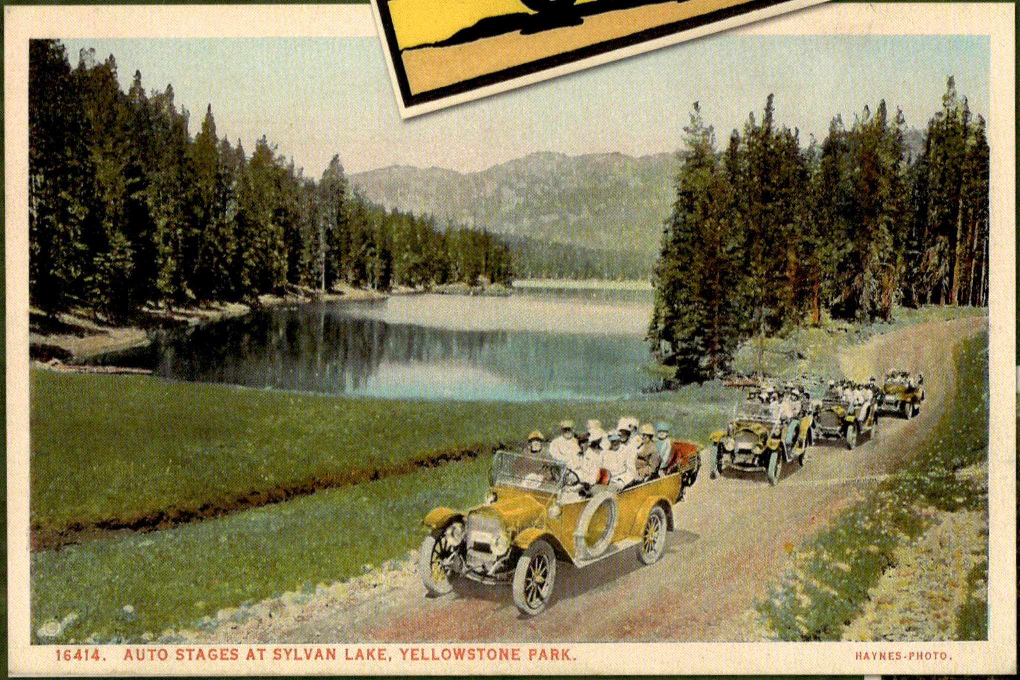

In 1916, the Yellowstone Park Transportation Company, headed by Harry W. Child, was awarded an exclusive concession contract to provide all public transportation in Yellowstone Park. The agreement required the company to fully motorize the system by the following year. In 1917, more than one hundred auto stages made by the White Motor Company of Cleveland, Ohio, were introduced, replacing stagecoach travel and ending the road sharing conflicts that had been occurring previously. Ten-passenger and seven-passenger models were produced, and like the stagecoaches previously operated by the company, these were painted yellow and trimmed in black. This postcard pictures the new touring stages at Sylvan Lake. Published by J. E. Haynes, St. Paul, Official Photographer.

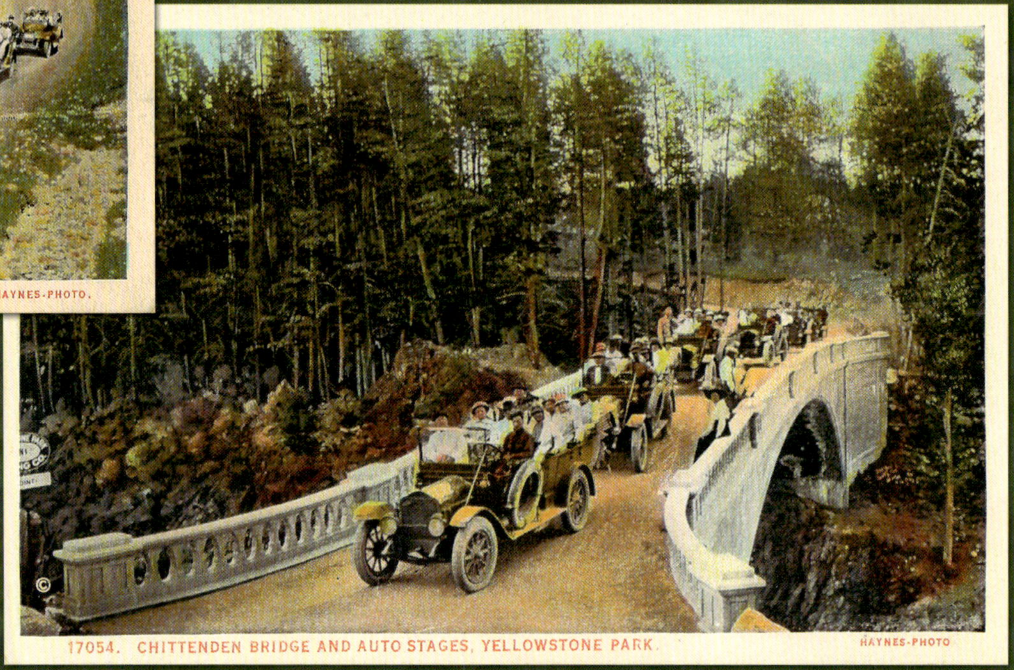

Another early postcard shows the yellow auto stages crossing the Chittenden Bridge at Grand Canyon. The auto stages had a canvas top that could be rolled back on sunny days. The bridge was built by General H.M. Chittenden. It was the longest Melan arch bridge in the world at that time. Because of wear, the bridge was replaced in 1962 and named the Chittenden Memorial Bridge. Its design is similar to the original. Postcard published by J. E. Haynes.

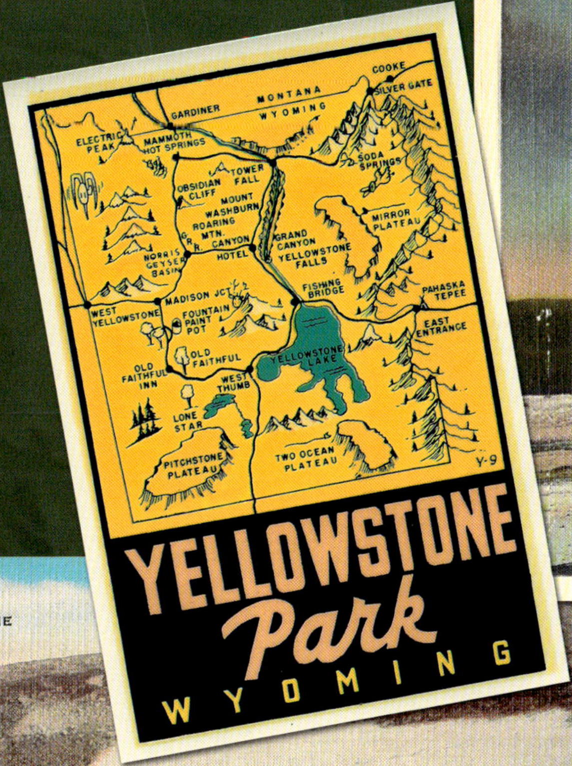

Vintage travel decal made by Lindgren-Turner showing the many points of interest in the park.

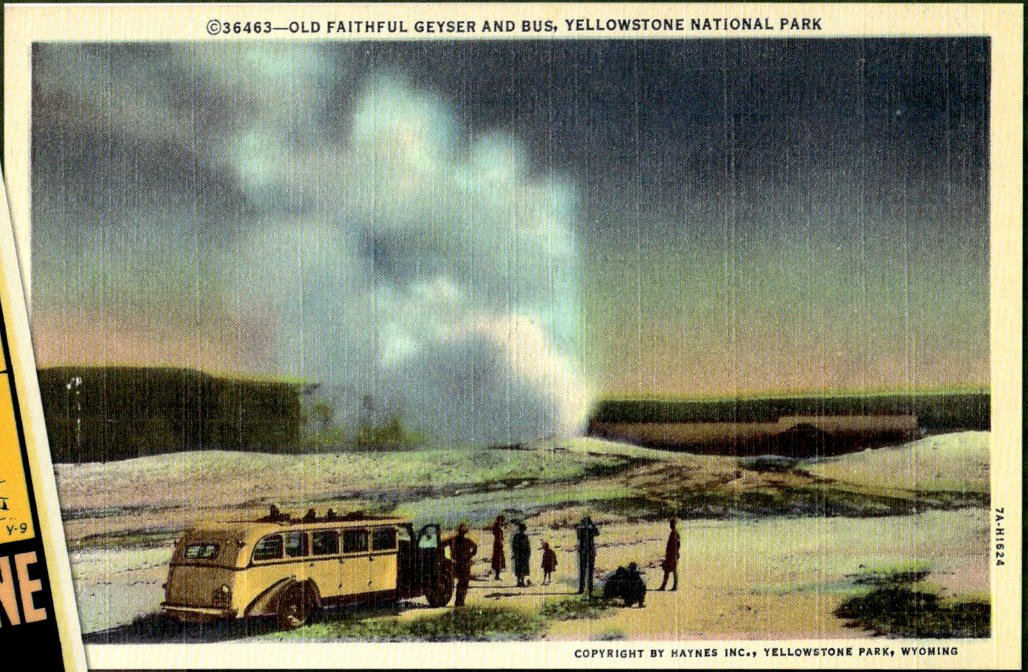

This early 1940s linen postcard pictures one of the Yellowstone Park buses as it transports tourists inside the park. The passengers watch as the Old Faithful Geyser erupts, apparently right on schedule for the bus stop. Yellowstone's bus fleet peaked at 325 vehicles by the mid-1930s, but by 1946 only 124 buses remained in service due to the decline of train travel and the increased use of private automobiles. Postcard by Haynes, Inc. Today, the park's Heritage and Research Center maintains an extensive collection of historic vehicles, including touring cars, buses, and stage coaches that were once used in the park.

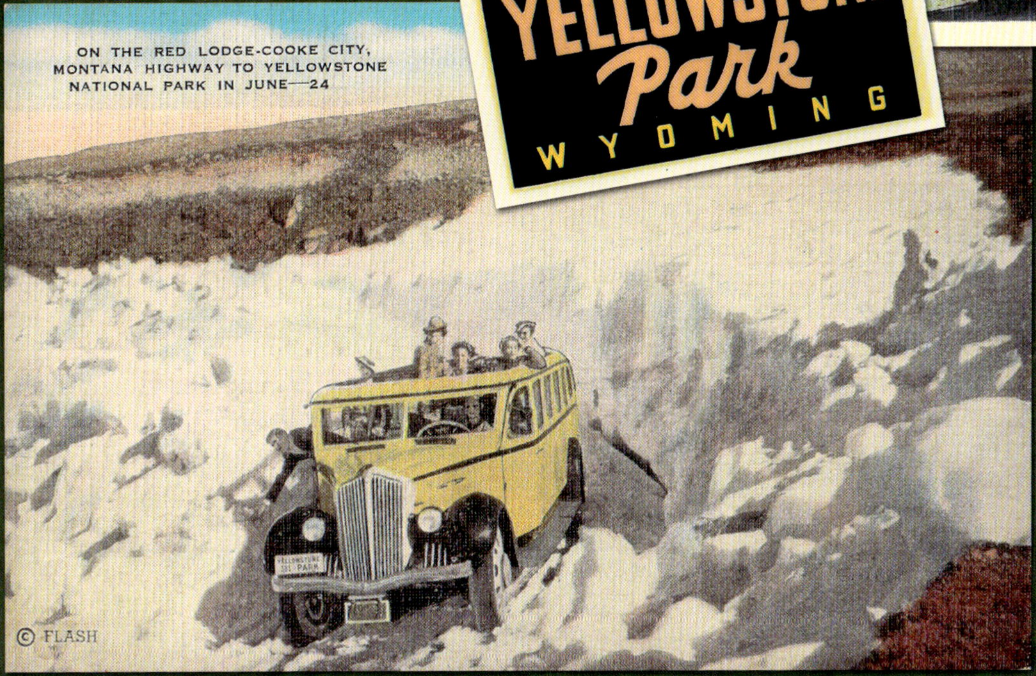

Modern buses were in use by the 1936 season when Yellowstone received delivery of the White Model 706. This linen postcard pictures one of the new buses with its top opened so passengers could see the snow still surrounding the road on June 24, 1938. The bus is on the mountain highway from Red Lodge to Cooke City. Use of the new Model 706's continued until the mid 1960s when demand for bus travel diminished and the buses were sold. Postcard by E. C. Kroff Co., Milwaukee, Wisconsin.

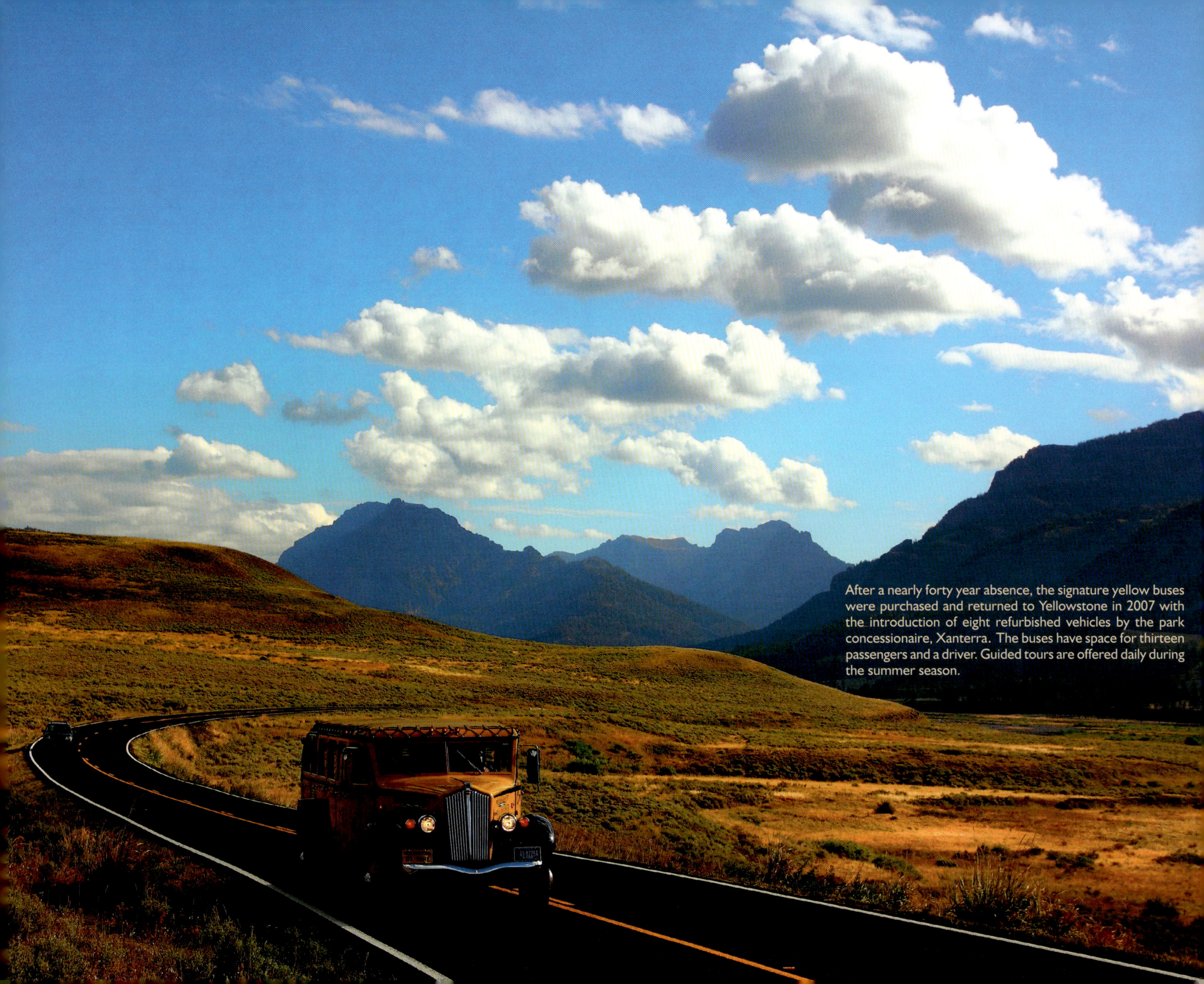

After a nearly forty year absence, the signature yellow buses were purchased and returned to Yellowstone in 2007 with the introduction of eight refurbished vehicles by the park concessionaire, Xanterra. The buses have space for thirteen passengers and a driver. Guided tours are offered daily during the summer season.

LODGING: WHERE TO STAY

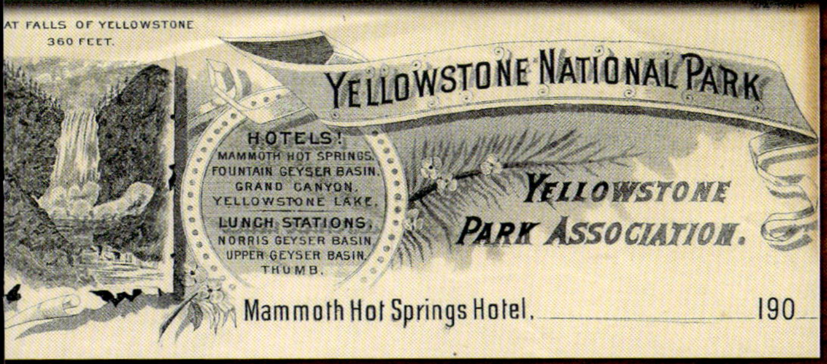

Stationery from Yellowstone Park Association circa 1900s listing the four hotels and three lunch stations in operation at the time. The Yellowstone Park Association was formed in 1886 with financial backing from Northern Pacific Railway. The company took over hotel-building operations initiated earlier by the Yellowstone Park Improvement Company.

EARLY HOTELS

Hotels began making their appearance in Yellowstone Park in the 1880s. Some of them were crude structures, including Yancey's Pleasant Valley Hotel near Tower Junction. Built by John F. Yancey in 1889, it was a two-story log hotel that featured a saloon next door. A similar structure was the Firehole Hotel, with eight rooms and little privacy for guests.

Hotels near the Norris Geyser Basin included the Norris Hotel, built by the Yellowstone Park Association in 1886; it was destroyed by fire the next year. Though another hotel was constructed around 1900, it closed when it was no longer needed as a stopover for stagecoach travel and was eventually torn down in 1927.

Other accommodations included the National Hotel which opened in 1884, the earlier Canyon Hotel built in 1890, and the Lake and Fountain hotels completed in 1891. Of those, only the Lake Hotel remains.

Today, there are nine lodging facilities located within the park that offer both rustic and modern conveniences. The properties are owned by the National Park Service and operated by Xanterra Parks & Resorts, the park's concessionaire since 1995.

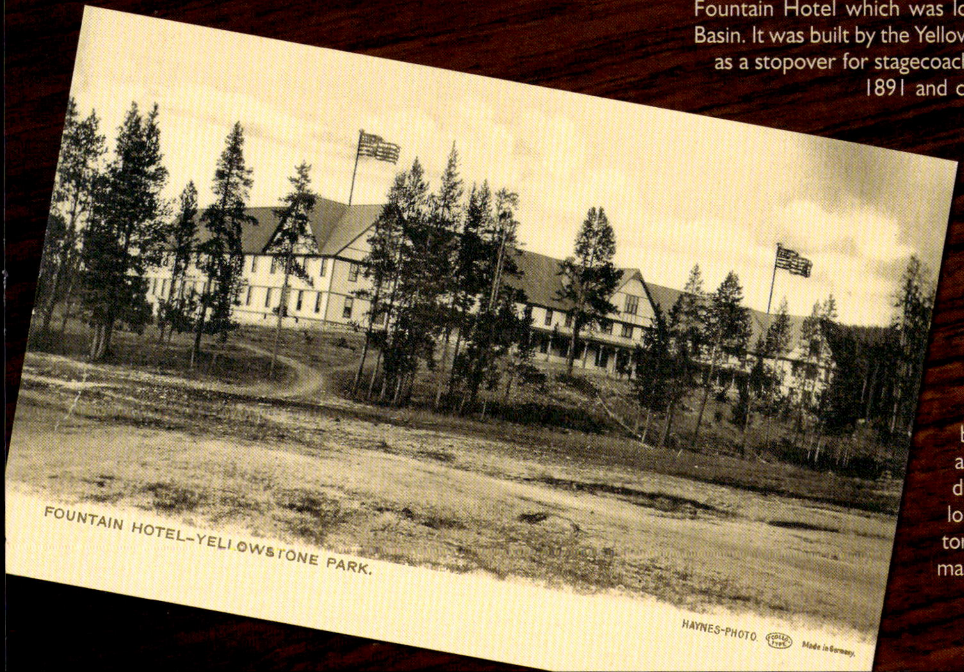

One of the most notable of the early establishments was the Fountain Hotel which was located near the Lower Geyser Basin. It was built by the Yellowstone Park Association to serve as a stopover for stagecoach travelers. The hotel opened in 1891 and could accommodate 350 guests. The facility was modern for its time and included steam heat and electric lights, while baths were drawn from the nearby hot springs. The customary practice of tossing the kitchen garbage outside to attract bears and other wildlife was first introduced at this property which served as the evening entertainment for guests. After Old Faithful Inn was built, and the introduction of the automobile made longer travel distances easier, the hotel was no longer needed and was eventually torn down. Haynes-Photo postcard made in Germany.

ARCHITECT ROBERT C. REAMER

The most famous hotels in Yellowstone National Park all have one thing in common: Architect Robert C. Reamer. It was Reamer's work that created the "parkitecture" style that has influenced rustic architecture designs throughout the national parks for more than a century. Reamer was born in 1873 in Oberlin, Ohio, where he lived during his early years. He began work at the age of thirteen as a draftsman in an architecture office. After a move to San Diego, he opened his own firm, first with a partner. Later, he continued working on his own. It was during this time that he met Harry W. Child, president of the Yellowstone Hotel Company; Child offered him the job of architect for Old Faithful Inn. Reamer began designing the famous building in 1902; the hotel opened in 1904.

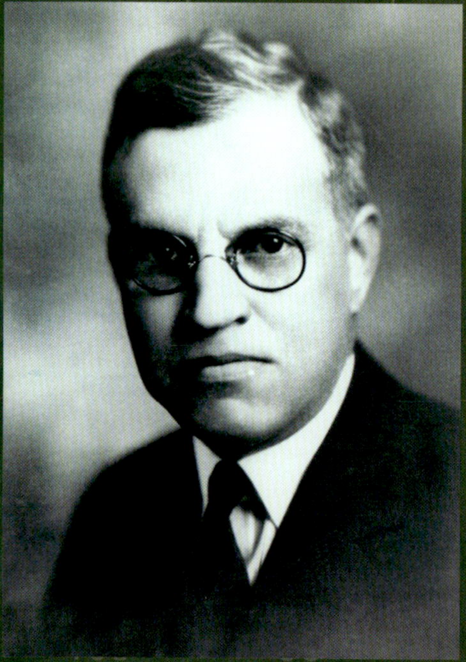

Robert C. Reamer. *Courtesy National Park Service.*

At the same time Reamer was finishing work on the inn, he was also planning the renovation of the oldest hotel still in use in the park — the Lake Hotel. This hotel was originally a clapboard barn-like structure and through Reamer's efforts, the hotel took on a different look during the remodel which took place from 1904-1905. With the

The well-known Canyon Hotel, which opened in 1911, was also designed by Reamer. The hotel was so large that it stretched nearly a full mile around its perimeter.

Reamer continued to work with the Yellowstone hotels even after the original buildings were completed. From 1926 to 1937, he completed additions to Old Faithful Inn, Canyon Hotel, Lake Hotel, and Mammoth Hotel. An additional dining room and the Bear Pit lounge were added to Old Faithful Inn while the Lake Hotel gained a new sun room that faced the lake and gave visitors a place to relax and enjoy the view.

During 1936-1937, Reamer was the architect for what is now the front section of the Mammoth Hotel. It includes the lobby, Map Room, and gift shop. The Map Room features a 17 x 10-foot map of the United States made of inlaid wood, which Reamer and his associate W. H. Fey designed and built.

In addition to designing many other park projects, Reamer was also the architect for the Gardiner train depot, as well as several theaters in Seattle, Washington. It was in Seattle where Reamer died in 1938. He was sixty-five years old.

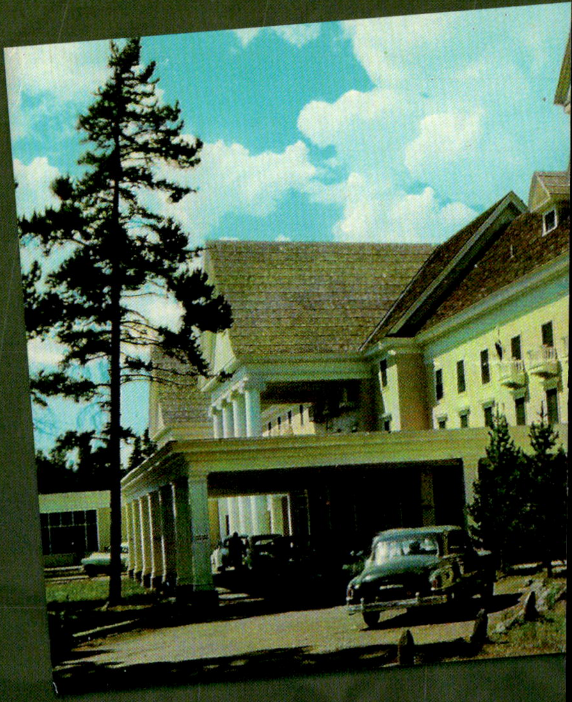

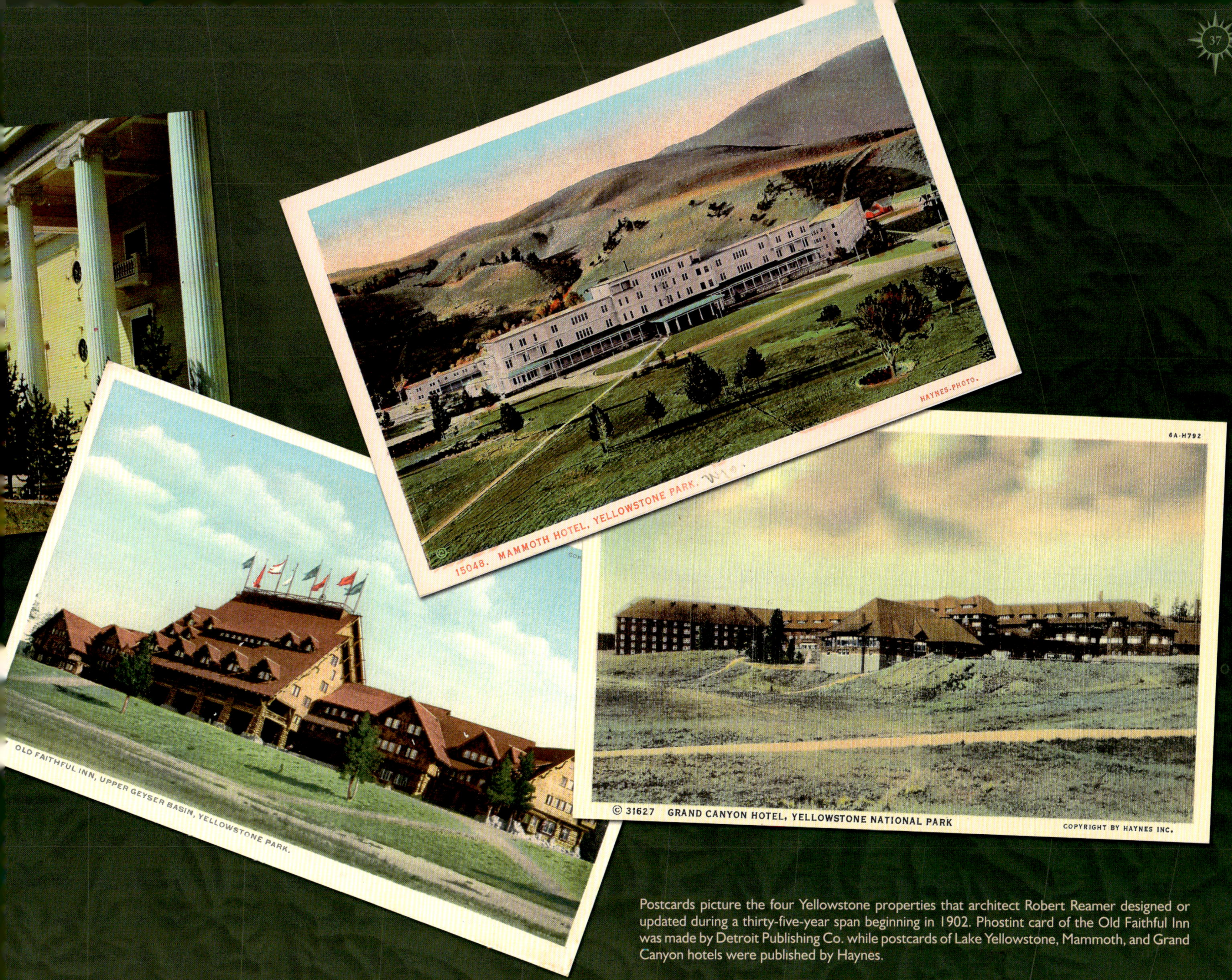

Postcards picture the four Yellowstone properties that architect Robert Reamer designed or updated during a thirty-five-year span beginning in 1902. Phostint card of the Old Faithful Inn was made by Detroit Publishing Co. while postcards of Lake Yellowstone, Mammoth, and Grand Canyon hotels were published by Haynes.

OLD FAITHFUL INN

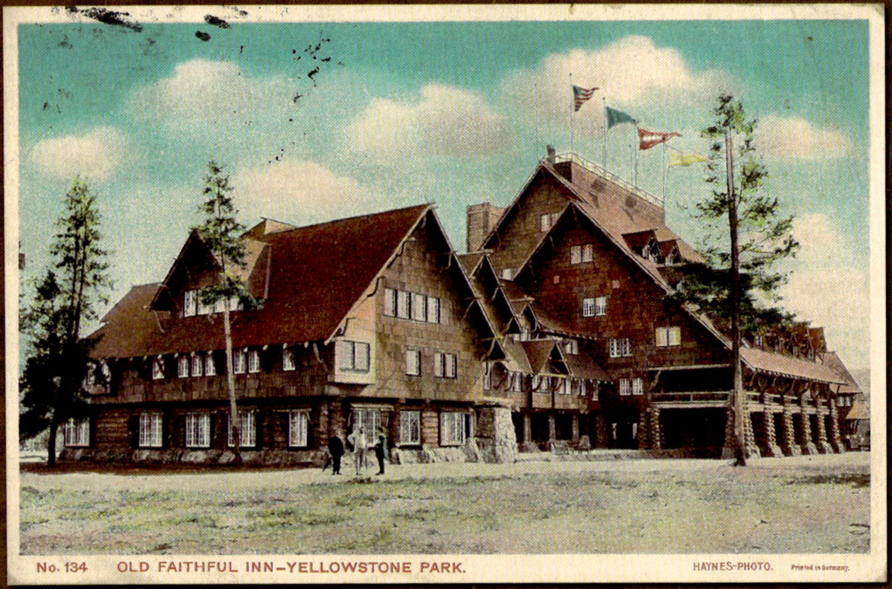

The Old Faithful Inn is located in the southwest part of Yellowstone Park, thirty miles from the station entrance at West Yellowstone and within sight of the park's most famous geyser. It was opened in 1904 after being funded by the Northern Pacific Railway at a cost of $140,000. The hotel was designed by Robert Reamer who used timber and stone from the area to blend the building with its surroundings. Because the Old House section of the hotel was so successful with its 140 rooms, the East Wing addition was built in 1913-1914. One hundred additional guest rooms were added to meet the demand. The West Wing was built in 1927. It added 150 rooms to the hotel. Both wings were updated with more private baths added in the 1990s. Haynes-Photo postcard printed in Germany.

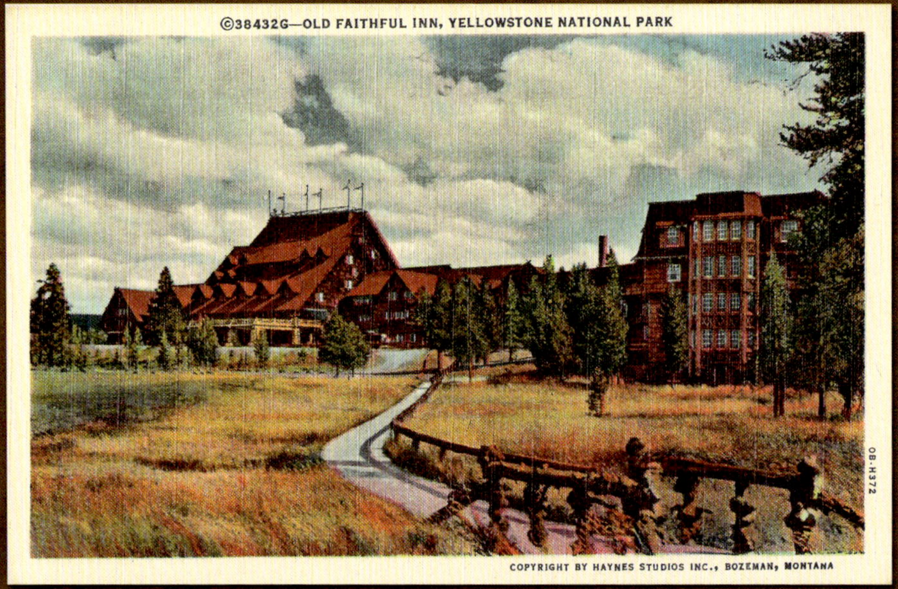

This linen postcard by Haynes Studios pictures Old Faithful Inn after the additions had been added. A spring-fed swimming pool was built in 1915 and was housed in a separate building across from Geyser Hill. Rates were $5.00 per day for two people in a room with no bath, plus $4.25 each for meals, circa late 1920s. The Old House addition is distinguished by its sloped roof while the later addition has a flat roof.

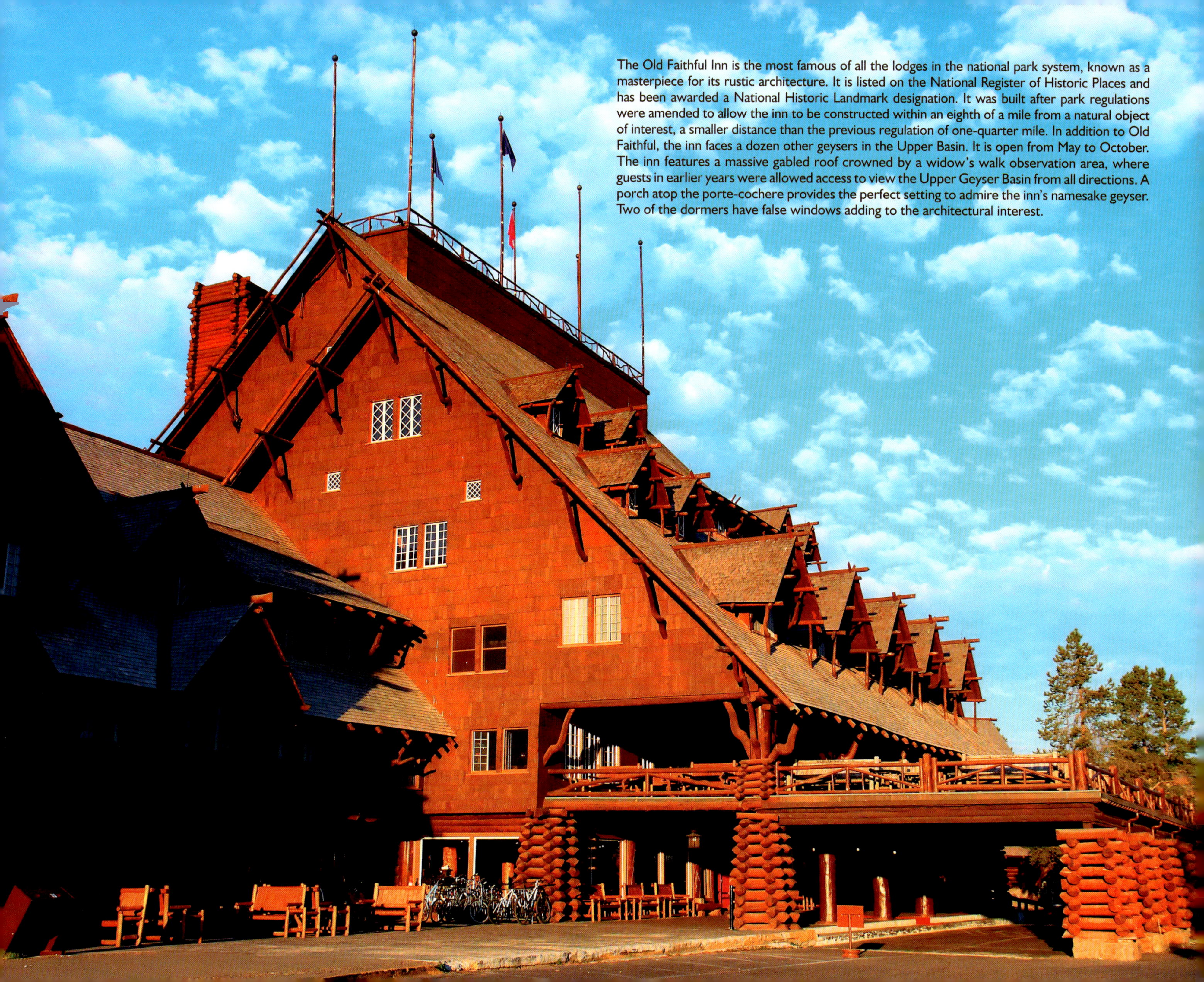

The Old Faithful Inn is the most famous of all the lodges in the national park system, known as a masterpiece for its rustic architecture. It is listed on the National Register of Historic Places and has been awarded a National Historic Landmark designation. It was built after park regulations were amended to allow the inn to be constructed within an eighth of a mile from a natural object of interest, a smaller distance than the previous regulation of one-quarter mile. In addition to Old Faithful, the inn faces a dozen other geysers in the Upper Basin. It is open from May to October. The inn features a massive gabled roof crowned by a widow's walk observation area, where guests in earlier years were allowed access to view the Upper Geyser Basin from all directions. A porch atop the porte-cochere provides the perfect setting to admire the inn's namesake geyser. Two of the dormers have false windows adding to the architectural interest.

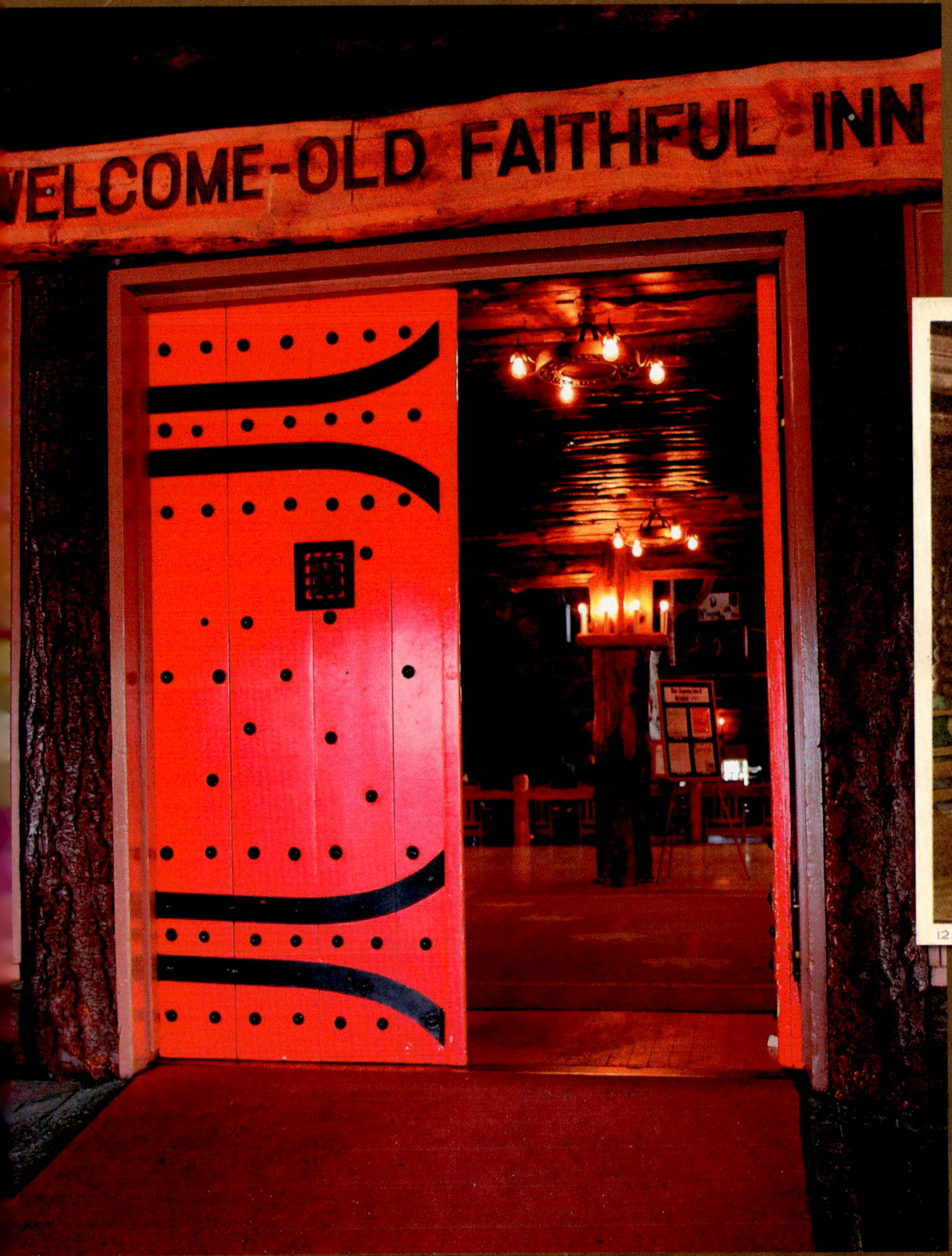

The rustic ironwork on the entrance doors offers a hint of the craftsmanship that can be found inside.

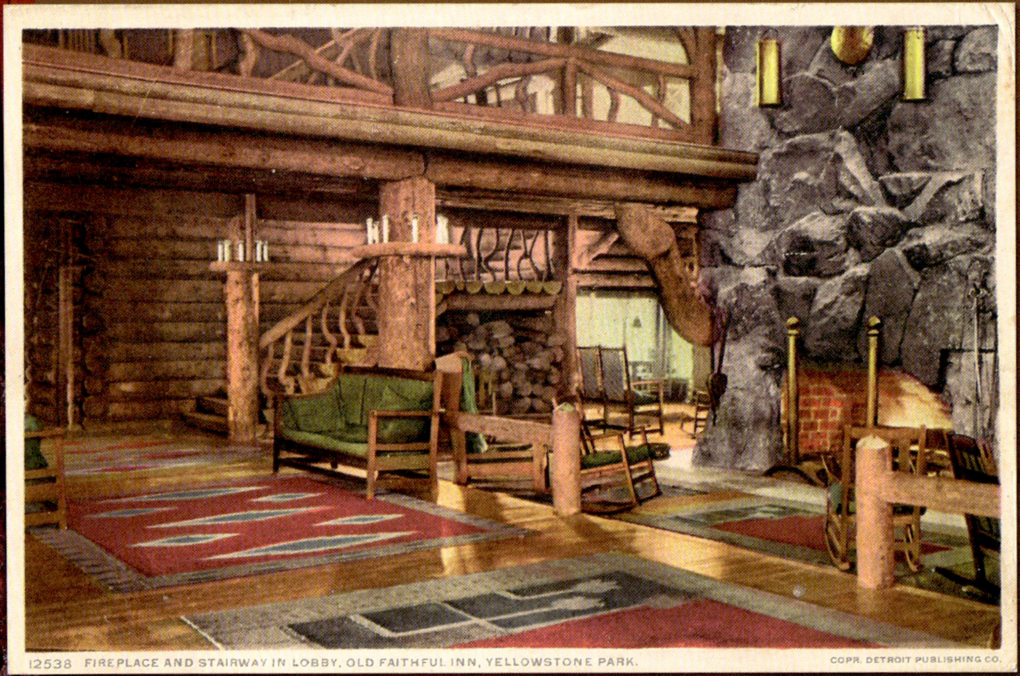

While not immediately evident upon stepping inside, the lobby is a spectacular area spanning seven stories tall. It features a four-sided stone fireplace at its base made of native rhyolite rock. The chimney continues up four stories through the roof. A giant clock was mounted on the chimney and is still in place. The mezzanine wraps around the second floor. Its lobby was furnished with Arts and Crafts style chairs and settees. This early phostint card was made by the Detroit Publishing Co.

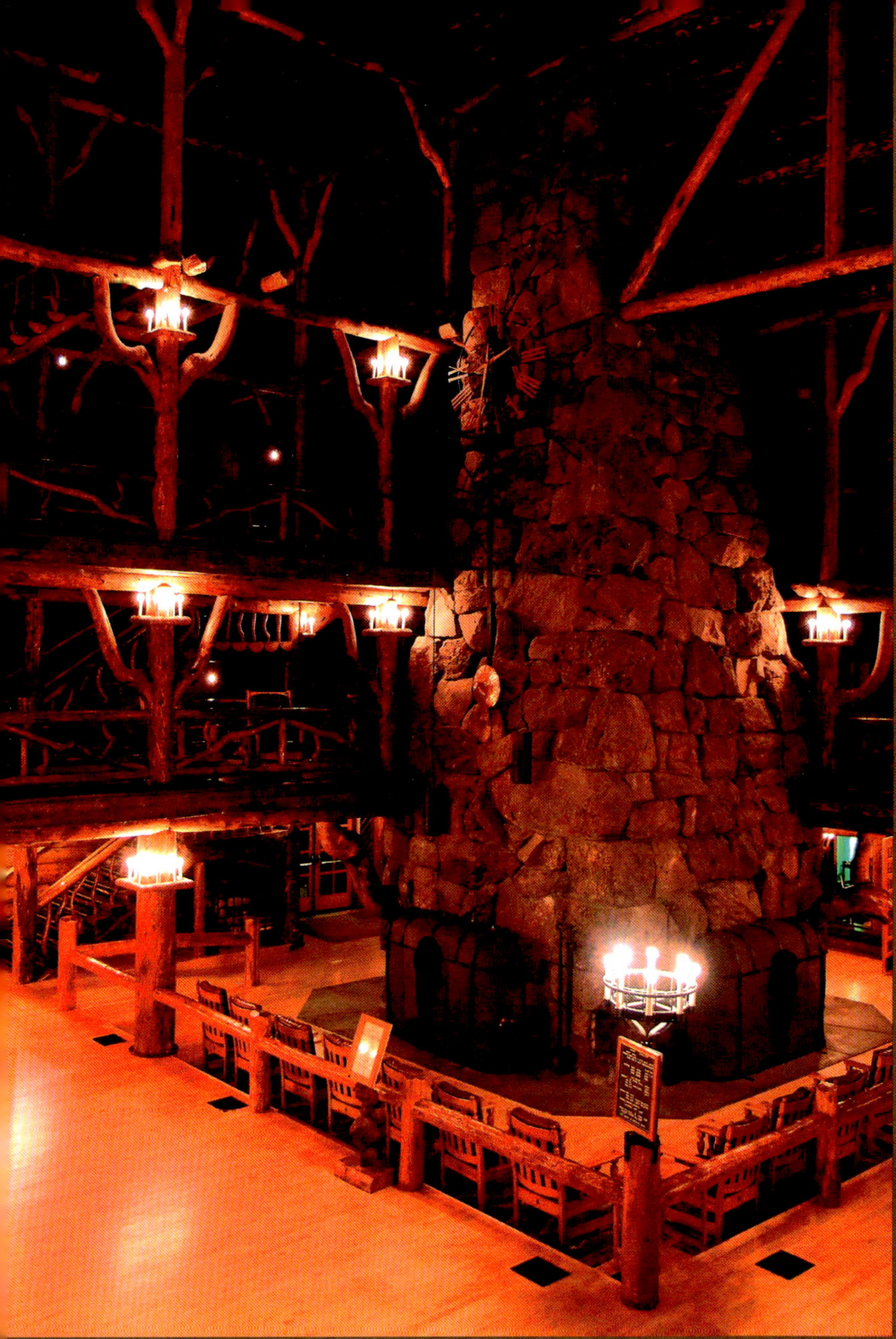

The lobby continues to offer an awe-inspiring experience for those who venture inside. With its massive fireplace and clock, it is surrounded by balconies trimmed with gnarled tree trunks. A crow's nest near the roof resembles a tree house and was used by musicians for evening entertainment during the inn's early days. The light fixtures were designed by Reamer and resemble candlelight.

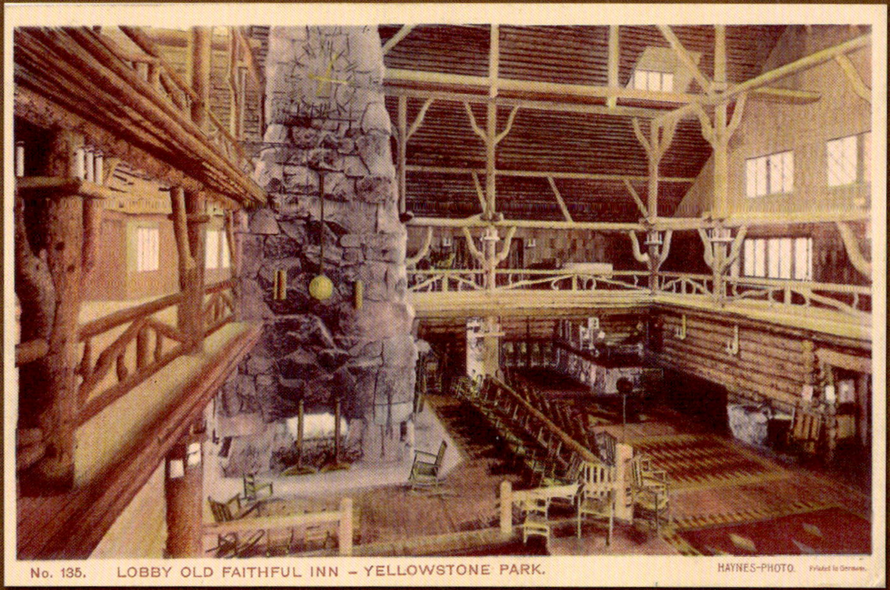

The massive lobby stands nearly eighty feet high and is pictured in this view which shows the interesting rustic railings and the enormous fireplace. The bark was stripped from the wood in the 1940s. The size of the large clock made of wrought-iron and brass and designed by Reamer can be seen in this 1909 postmarked card. The hotel was designed as a luxury hotel and only guests were allowed inside during its early days. The inn has since been opened to all visitors so they can marvel at its forest-like appearance. Haynes-Photo postcard made in Germany.

The fine craftsmanship is evident in every feature of the inn, from those who built the building and those who have worked to preserve it. Significant renovations took place in the 1980s, and again in later years, to address various structural and code issues. The most recent remodel was completed in 2012 to satisfy modern safety requirements. The inn celebrated its 100th birthday in 2004.

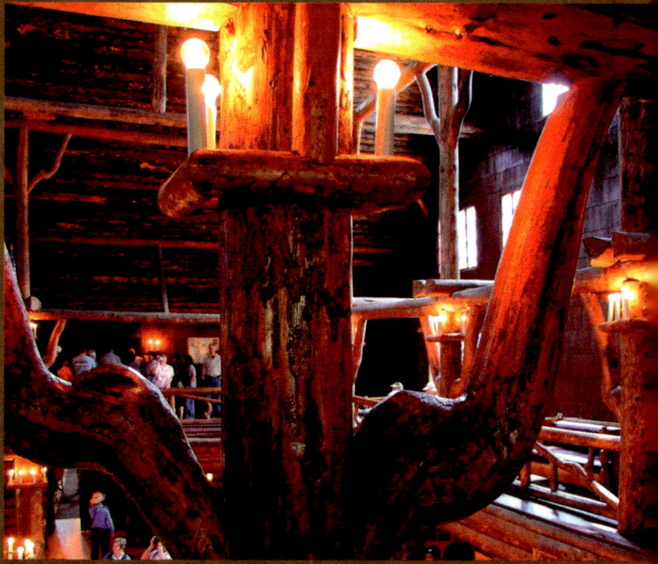

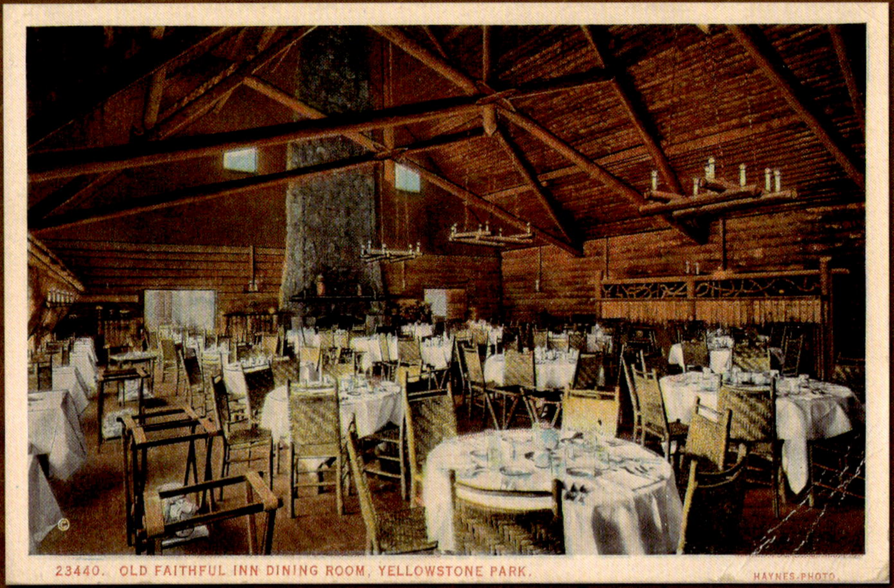

This postcard pictures the dining room furnished with rustic hickory chairs in the style still used today as well as a large fireplace. The postcard was published by Haynes, Official Photographer, Yellowstone National Park.

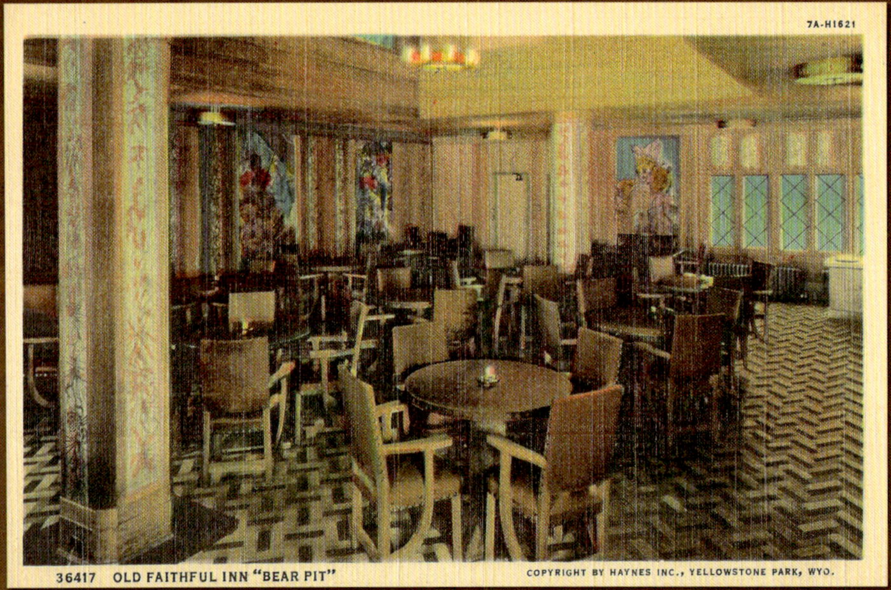

The Bear Pit cocktail lounge was added in the 1930s and was decorated with humorous wild animal scenes sand-blasted in wood. The snack bar is now housed in the original Bear Pit location. Linen Haynes, Inc. postcard marked C. T. Art-Colortone.

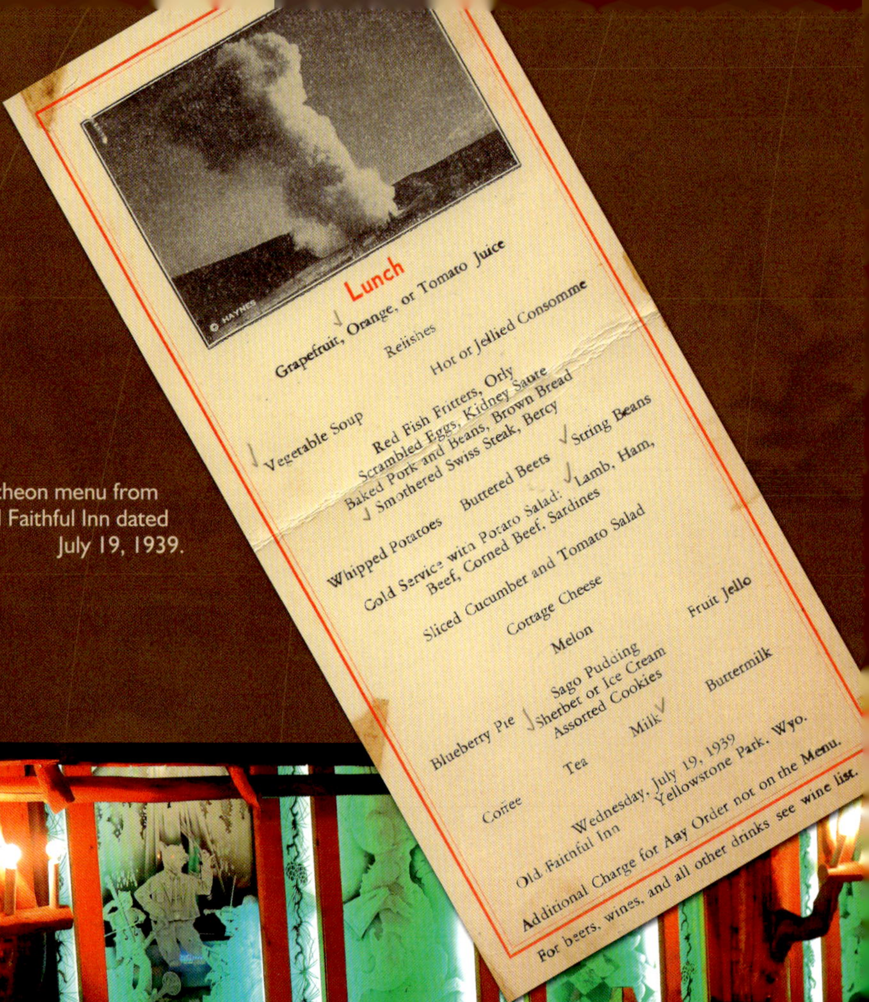

© HAYNES

Lunch

Grapefruit, Orange, or Tomato Juice

Relishes

Vegetable Soup Hot or Jellied Consomme

Red Fish Fritters, Orly
Scrambled Eggs, Kidney Saute
Baked Pork and Beans, Brown Bread
Smothered Swiss Steak, Bercy

Whipped Potatoes Buttered Beets String Beans

Cold Service with Potato Salad: Lamb, Ham,
Beef, Corned Beef, Sardines

Sliced Cucumber and Tomato Salad

Cottage Cheese

Melon

Blueberry Pie Sago Pudding
Sherbet or Ice Cream
Assorted Cookies Fruit Jello

Coffee Tea Milk Buttermilk

Old Faithful Inn Wednesday, July 19, 1939
Yellowstone Park, Wyo.

Additional Charge for Any Order not on the Menu.
For beers, wines, and all other drinks see wine list.

Luncheon menu from Old Faithful Inn dated July 19, 1939.

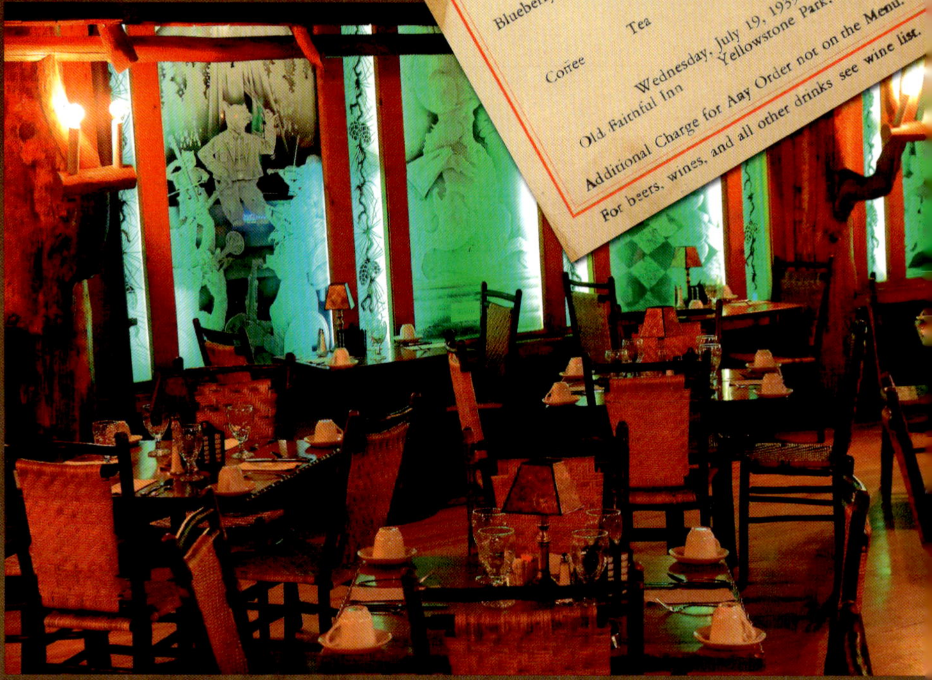

The ambiance of the dining room has been retained in today's setting. Panels of the wild animal scenes from the Bear Pit lounge were reproduced in glass etchings in 1989 and were mounted on the divider wall as pictured. The room's centerpiece, the fireplace, has been rebuilt following damage by an earthquake in 1959.

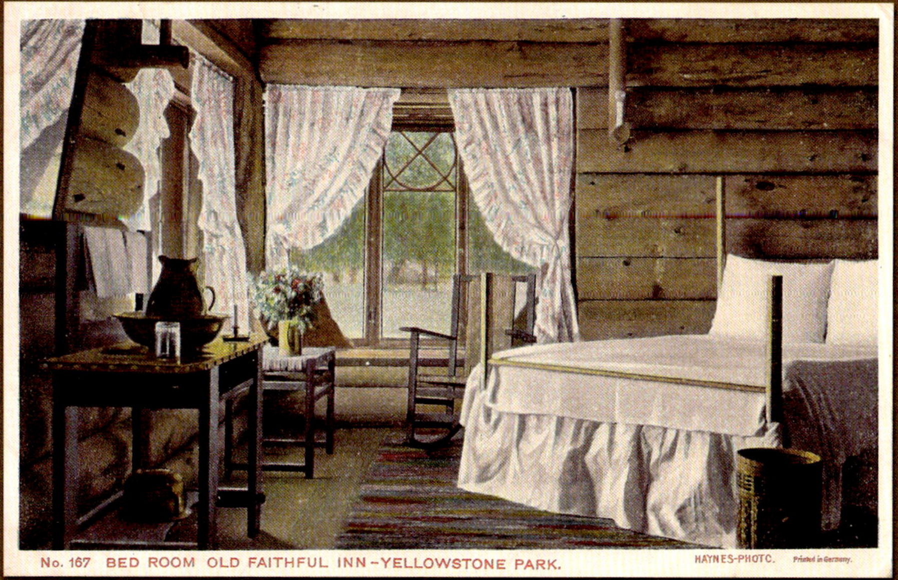

The original bedrooms of the Old Faithful Inn were modestly furnished. This one is pictured on a 1911 postmarked card. It features a rocking chair, bed, flowers on a small stool, pitcher and bowl, chamber pot, face towels on a washstand, and a mirror on the wall. In the 1920s this room with no bath would have cost $13.00 a day for two people's stay which included meals. The postcard was made in Germany using a Haynes photo.

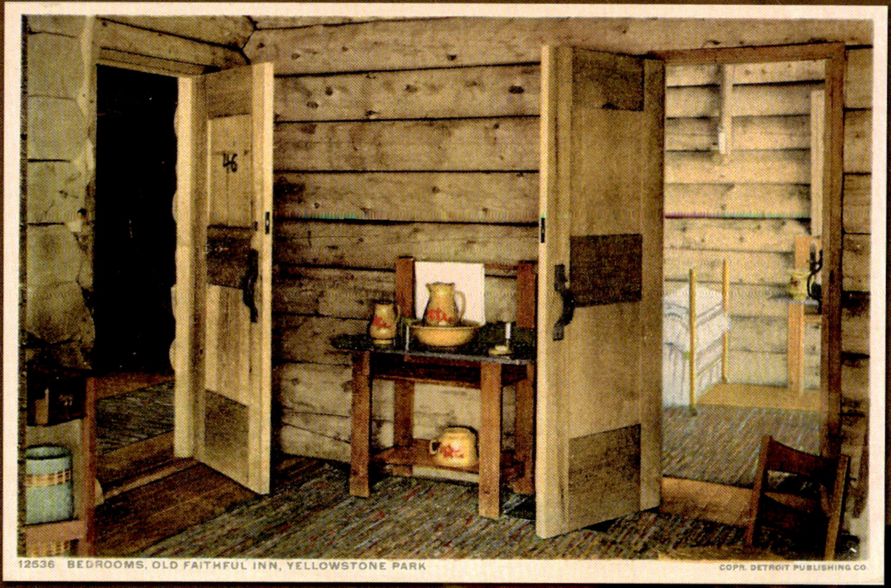

Another postcard showing the original bedrooms. Phostint card by Detroit Publishing Co.

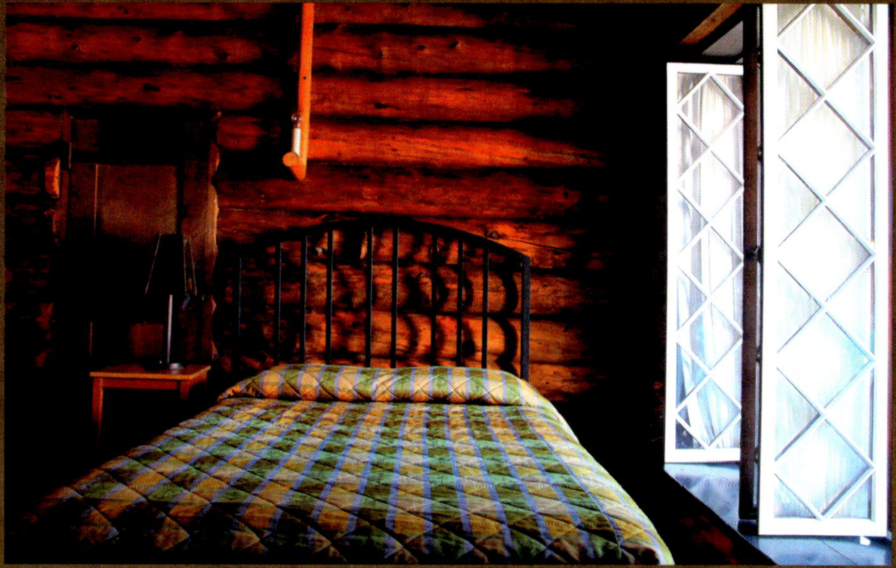

Today, guests can request to stay in one of the lodge rooms from the Old House; most of them require use of a shared bathroom down the hall. The property offers 327 lodge rooms of various comforts and configurations.

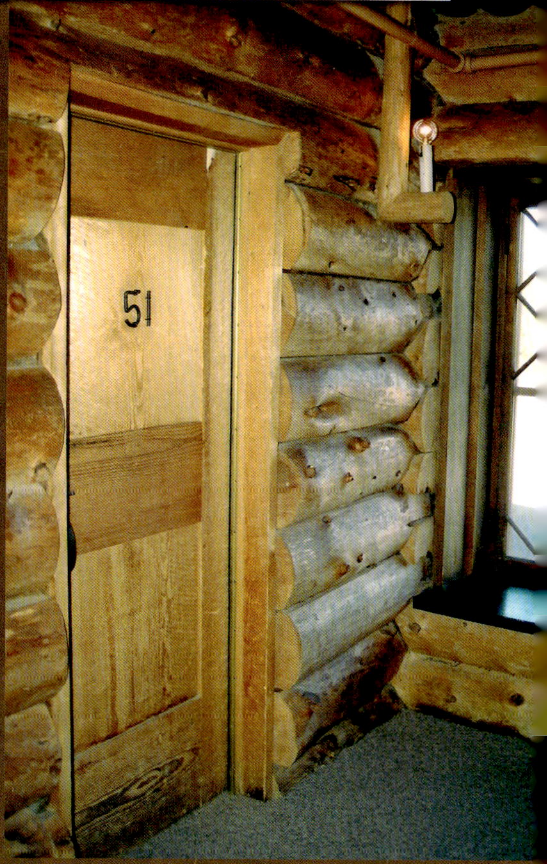

A hallway leading to one of the ninety-one guest rooms in the older section of the inn shows how the wooden door, log siding, and light fixture are unchanged from the earlier scenes. Historic tours are offered daily during the season to share the inn's rich history with today's visitors.

LAKE YELLOWSTONE HOTEL

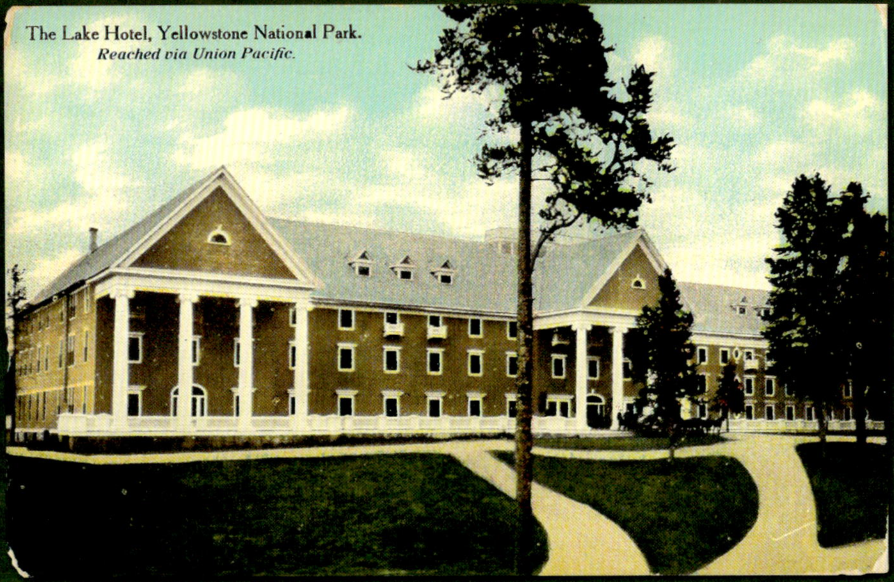

The Lake Hotel, earlier known as the Colonial or Lake Colonial Hotel, is located at the outlet of Yellowstone Lake. It is the oldest hotel still operating at Yellowstone National Park. Construction began in 1889 and the hotel opened in 1891. The hotel was remodeled in 1904-1905 when it was given a Colonial Revival look with the addition of tall pillars which formed large porticoes facing the lake. The architect for the project was Robert Reamer. By the 1920s, more additions had been made to the hotel, now called the Lake Hotel. These included the east wing with additional guest rooms, a dining room, sunroom, and porte-cochere. This vintage postcard by Barkalow Bros. pictures the hotel in its early days.

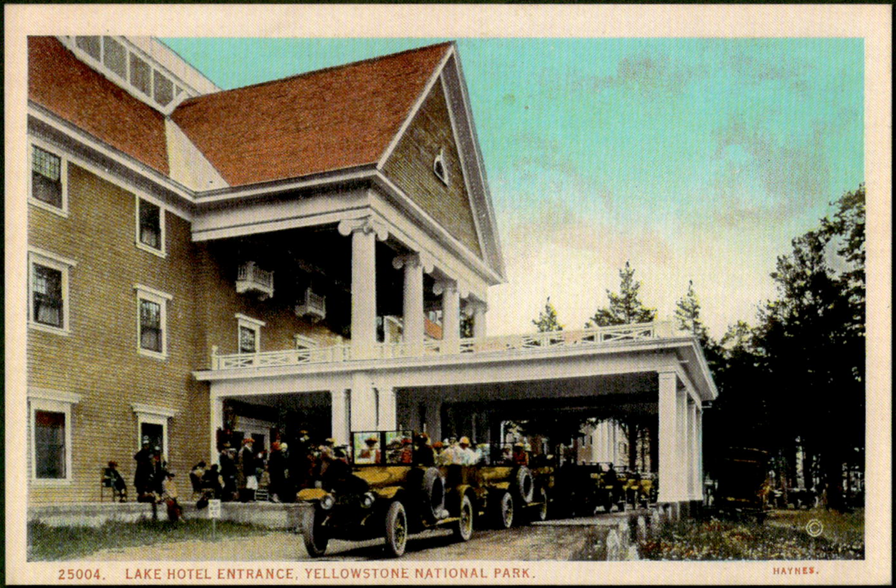

This circa 1920 postcard pictures guests in their touring automobiles at the Lake Hotel. At the time, Lake Hotel was one of four large hotels operated in the park by the Yellowstone Park Hotel Co. Postcard by Haynes Picture Shops, Inc.

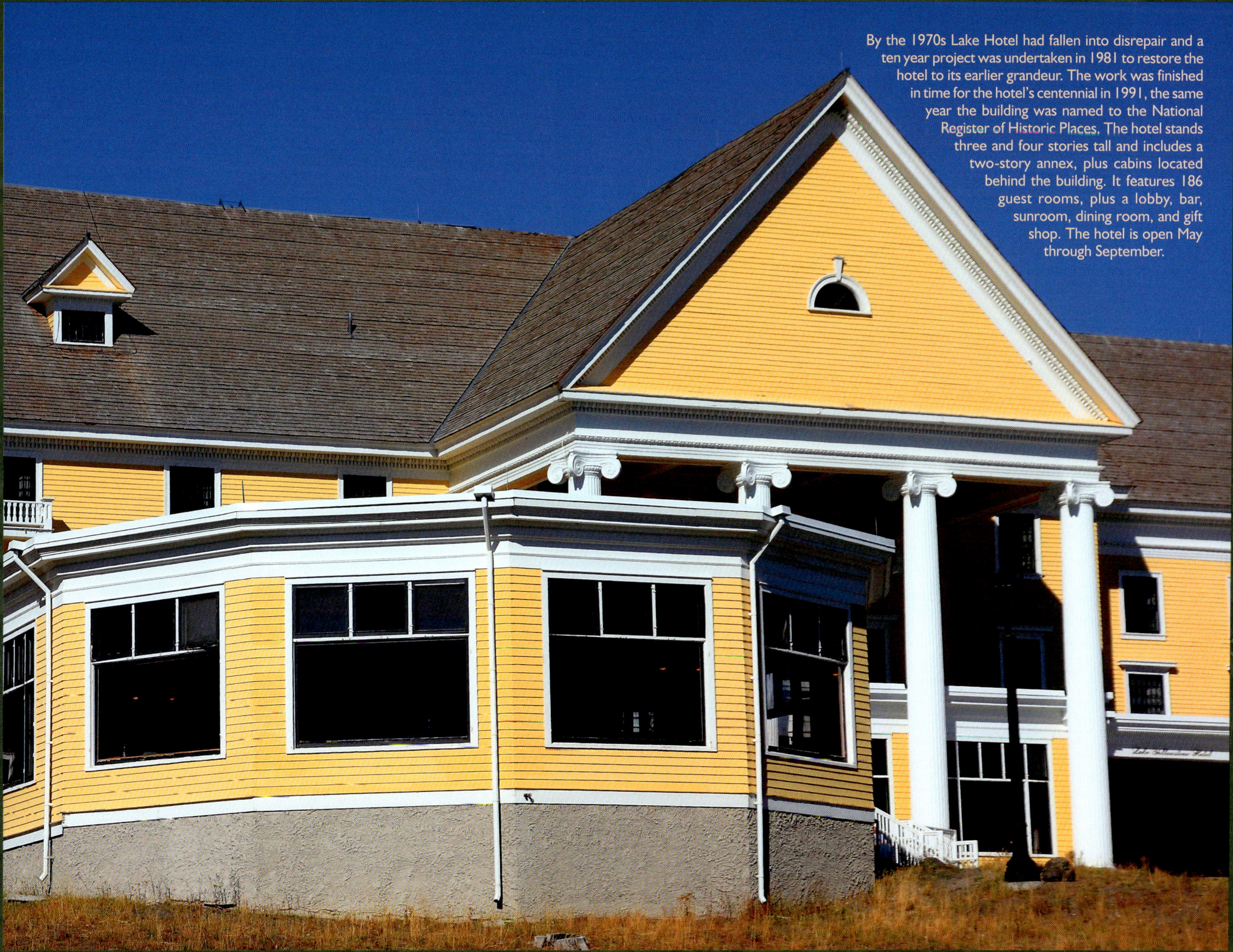

By the 1970s Lake Hotel had fallen into disrepair and a ten year project was undertaken in 1981 to restore the hotel to its earlier grandeur. The work was finished in time for the hotel's centennial in 1991, the same year the building was named to the National Register of Historic Places. The hotel stands three and four stories tall and includes a two-story annex, plus cabins located behind the building. It features 186 guest rooms, plus a lobby, bar, sunroom, dining room, and gift shop. The hotel is open May through September.

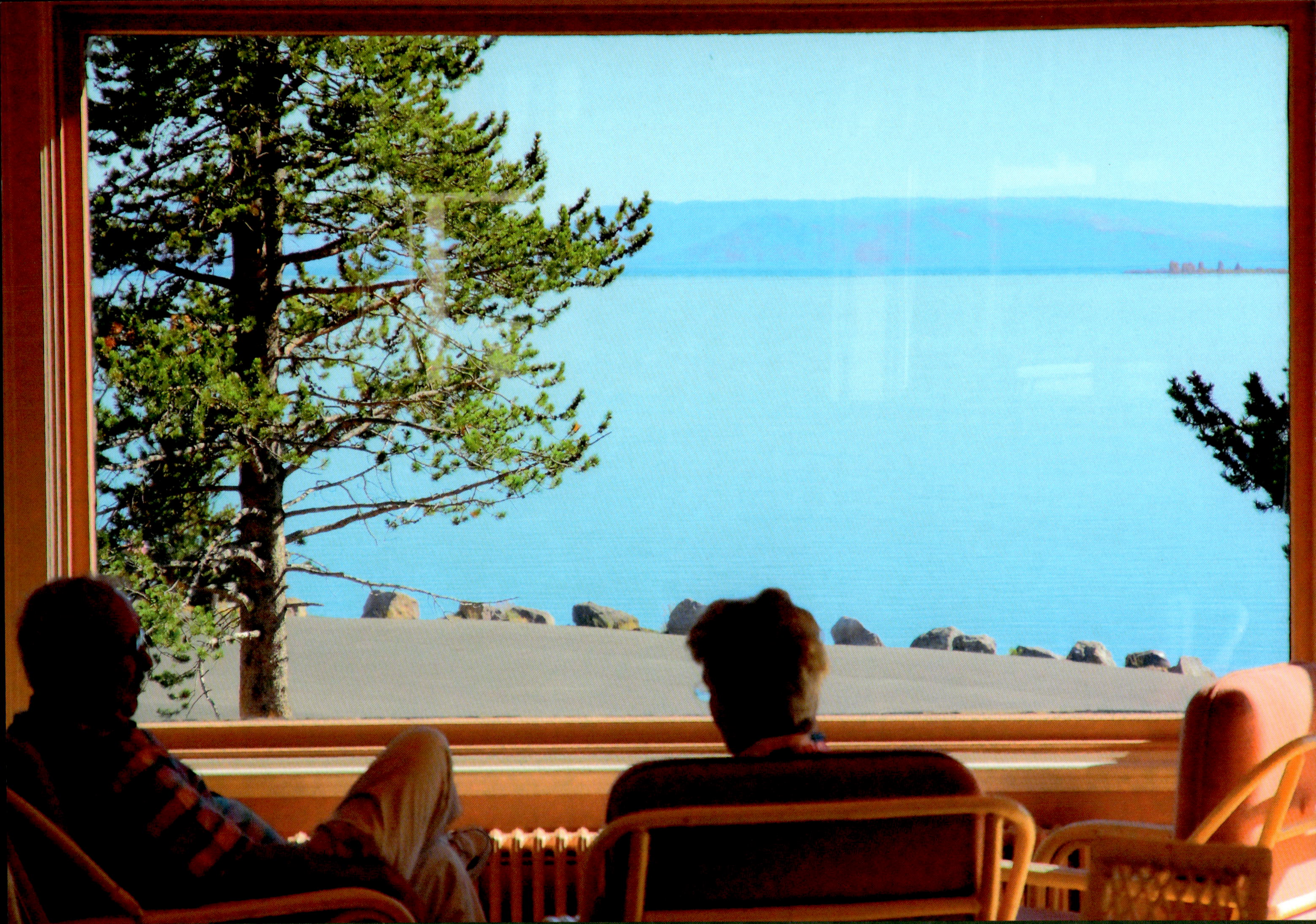

Lake Hotel offers spectacular views from the north shore of Yellowstone Lake, the largest body of water in the park. During the hotel's early years, guests could arrive by boat after boarding a steamboat at West Thumb on the lake's western edge.

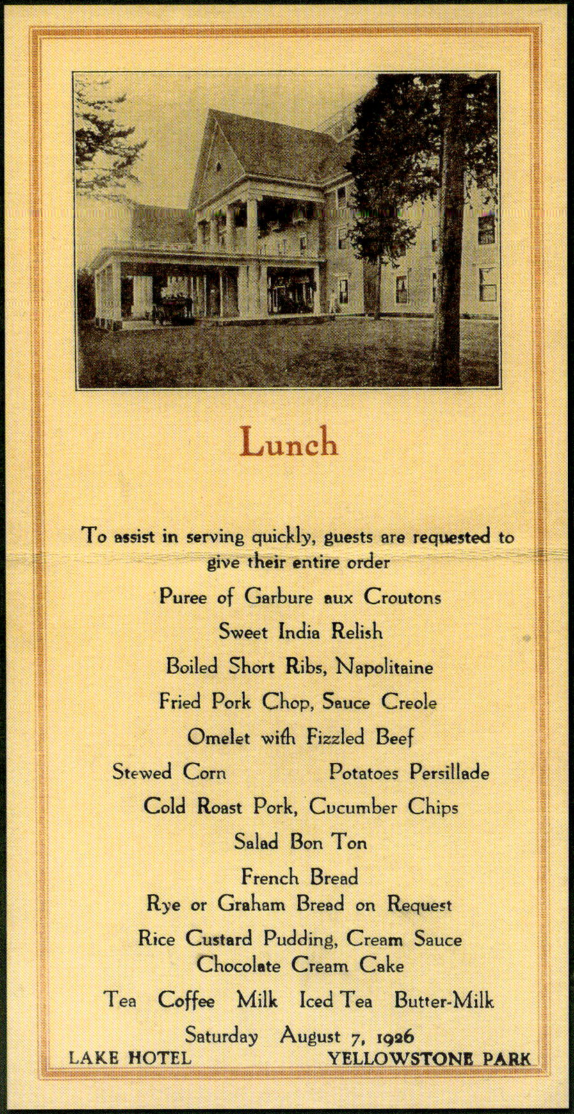

Lunch

To assist in serving quickly, guests are requested to give their entire order

Puree of Garbure aux Croutons

Sweet India Relish

Boiled Short Ribs, Napolitaine

Fried Pork Chop, Sauce Creole

Omelet with Fizzled Beef

Stewed Corn Potatoes Persillade

Cold Roast Pork, Cucumber Chips

Salad Bon Ton

French Bread

Rye or Graham Bread on Request

Rice Custard Pudding, Cream Sauce

Chocolate Cream Cake

Tea Coffee Milk Iced Tea Butter-Milk

Saturday August 7, 1926

LAKE HOTEL YELLOWSTONE PARK

Lake Hotel lunch menu from August 7, 1926. Guests were given many choices including boiled short ribs, fried pork chop, or omelet with frizzled beef.

Postcard of the Lake Hotel dining room which had been added to the hotel by the late 1920s. The postcard message reads, "Having a fine time. Here is where we wine & dine." Postcard by Haynes Picture Shop, Inc.

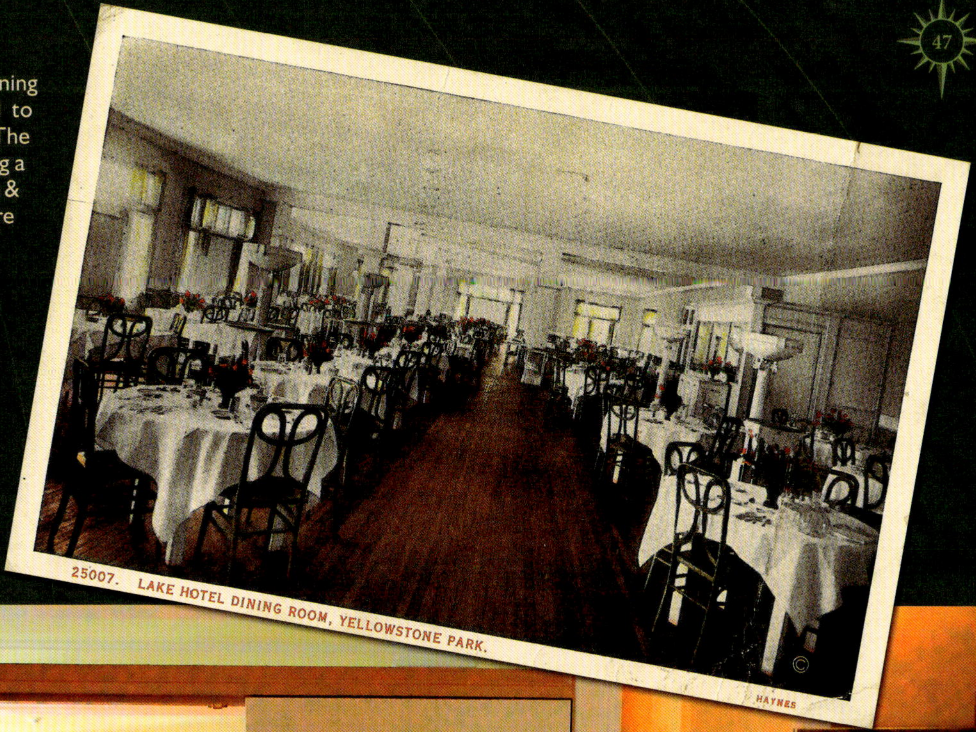

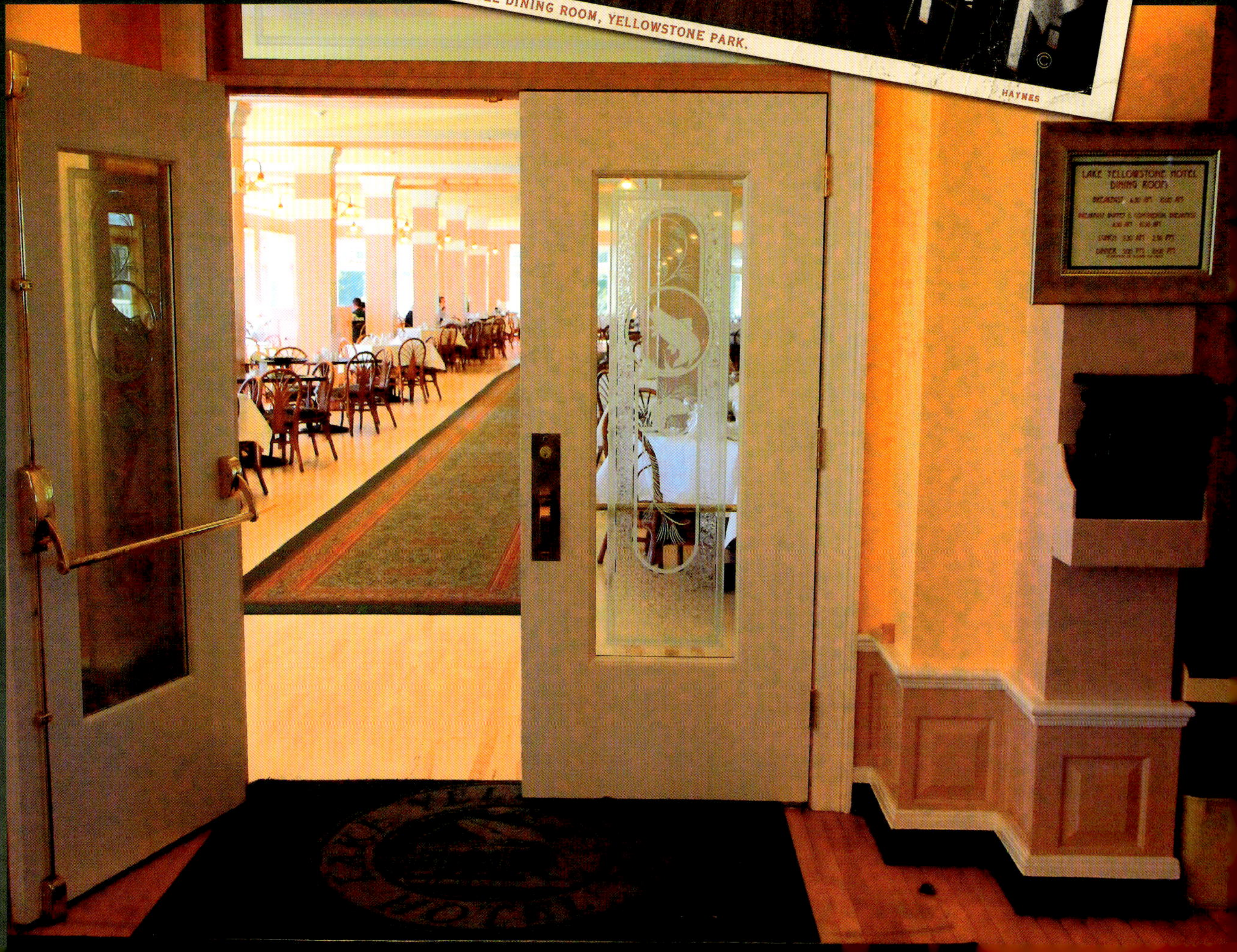

The dining room is open for breakfast, lunch, and dinner and continues to provide enjoyment for today's guests.

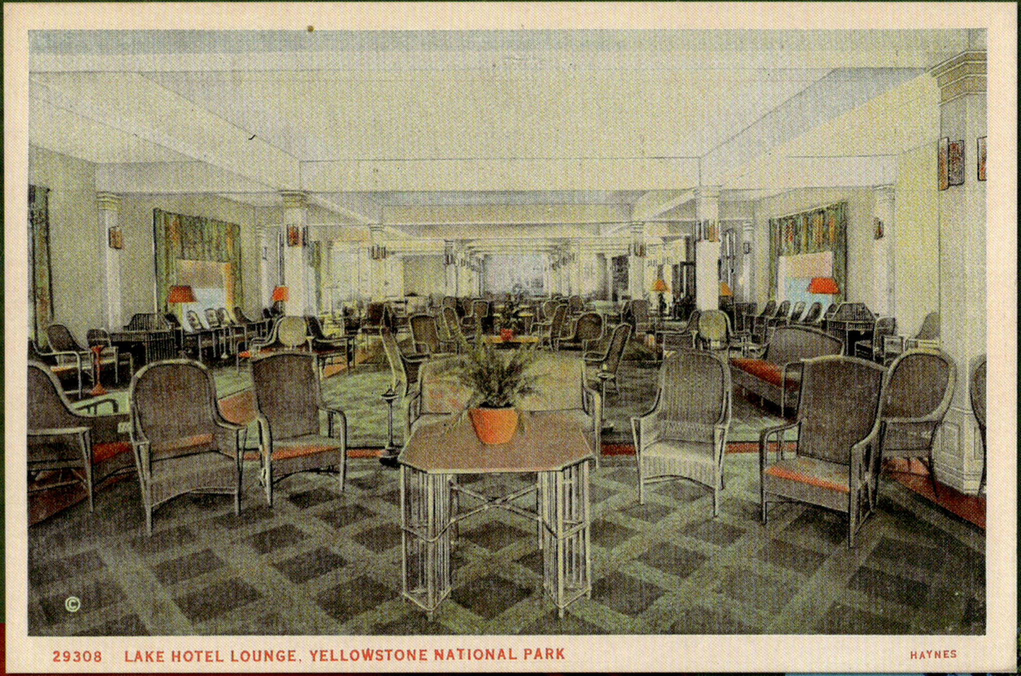

Lake Hotel lounge circa 1920s, where Lake Yellowstone can be seen from the windows. The area was furnished with wicker type furniture. Postcard by Haynes Picture Shops, Inc.

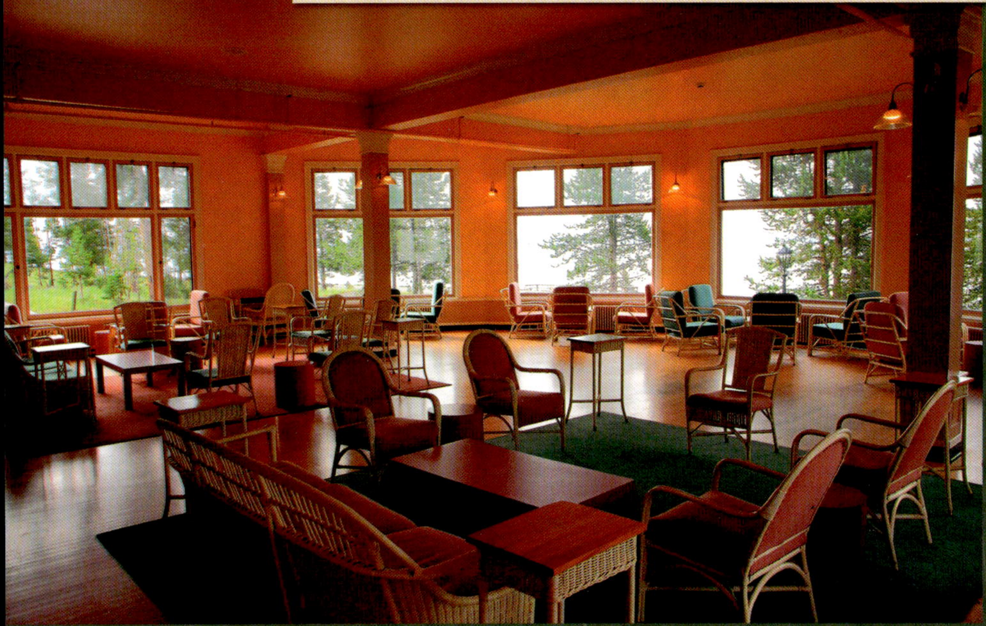

Some of the hotel's original wicker furniture is still used in the lounge, now called the sunroom. The earlier postcard describes the setting as a peaceful interlude for the busy park visitor.

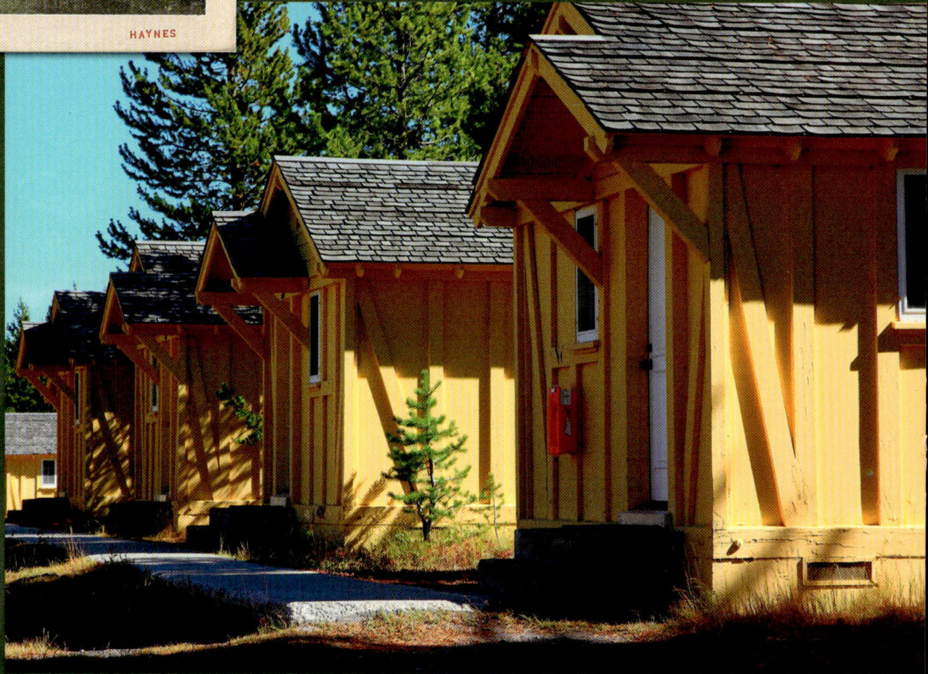

The Lake Yellowstone property also includes 110 cabins located behind the hotel. The cabins have private baths and showers.

MAMMOTH HOT SPRINGS HOTEL

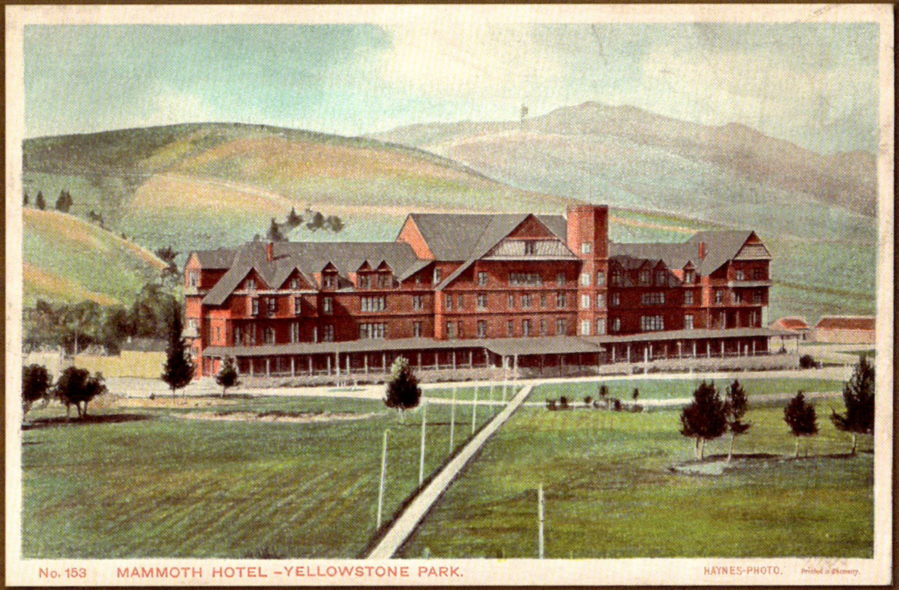

The first hotel in Yellowstone was built by James C. McCarthy at Mammoth Hot Springs in 1871. His claim was taken over by the government after the area became a national park and he was reimbursed $5,000 for his rights and improvements. Rufus Hatch secured the first franchise for a hotel in the park in 1883. He built the National Hotel at Mammoth which opened in 1884. In 1886 the Yellowstone Association was formed and with financial help from the Northern Pacific Railway, the National Hotel was purchased and it became the Mammoth Hot Springs Hotel. This postcard pictures the hotel as it looked in its early days after it became the Mammoth Hotel. The card was made in Germany from a Haynes photograph.

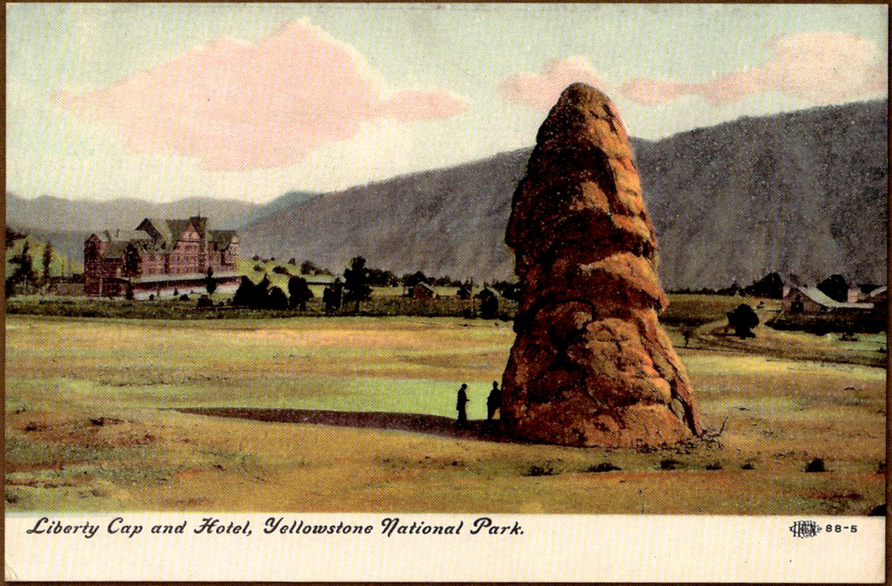

35¢

The Liberty Cap is pictured in this early postcard along with the Mammoth Hot Springs Hotel in the background. From the hotel, guests could explore the thirty-seven-foot-high geothermal feature as well as other points of interest before moving on to another area of the park. The hotel was used as the first tour stop by train travelers who arrived from the North Entrance at Gardiner. Postcard publisher unknown.

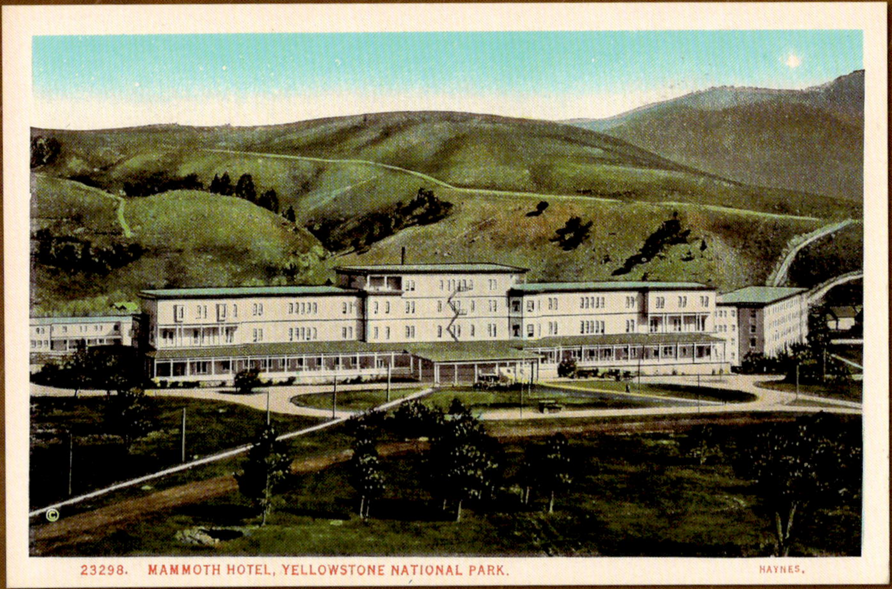

This later postcard pictures the Mammoth Springs Hotel following extensive remodeling by architect Robert Reamer circa 1913, which resulted in a change of roof-line and a dramatically different look from the original Queen Anne style. The project also added a three-story wing to the rear of the hotel. Postcard by Haynes Picture Shops, Inc.

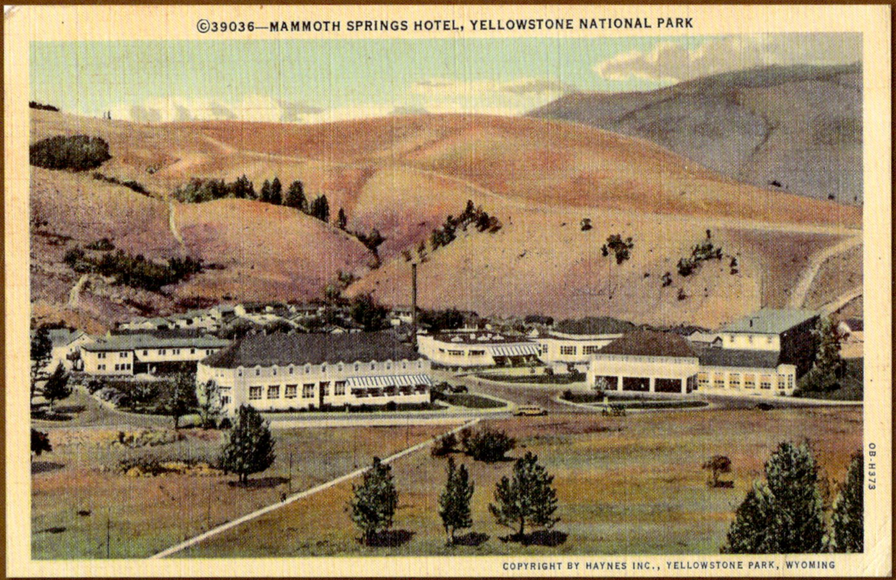

Other additions and renovations by Reamer occurred circa 1934-1938 as pictured, with demolition of the remainder of the original hotel also taking place during the decade. This linen postcard by Haynes is postmarked July 10, 1948. The message reads, "We're spending several days in Yellowstone and enjoying it. We were in this place July 8th where the boys went for a swim in the spring water." The old military parade ground is shown in front of the hotel.

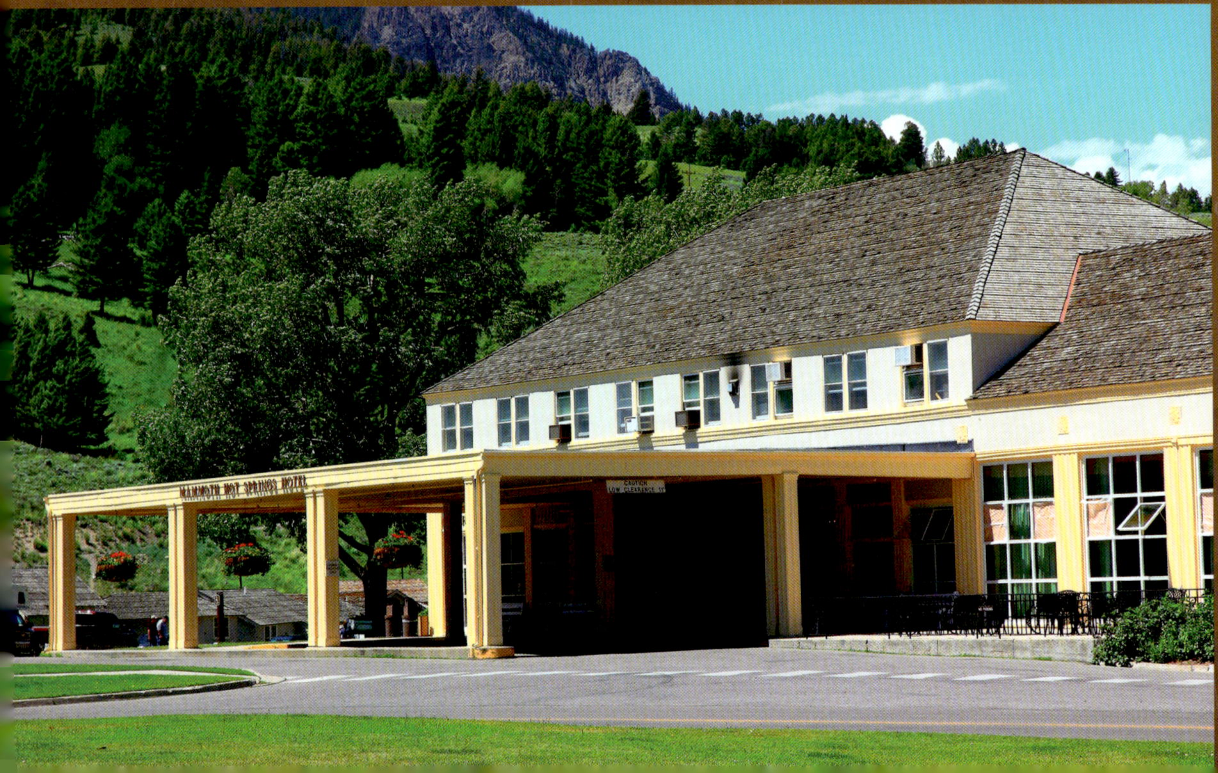

The Mammoth Hot Springs Hotel is one of only two properties in the park that remain open during the winter. There are 124 guest rooms, most of them containing a private bath.

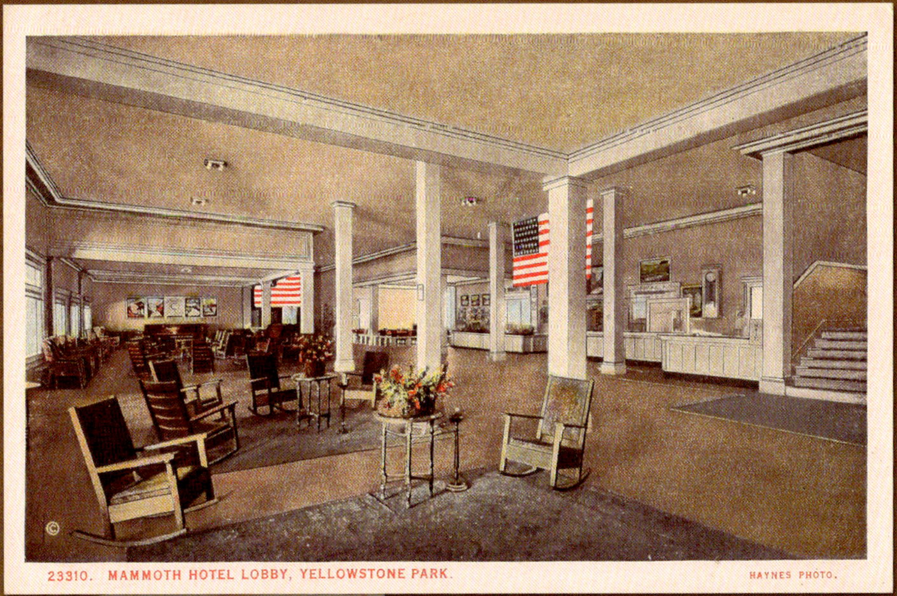

Mammoth Hotel lobby circa 1920s. During this era, daily rates for a guest at the hotel were $2.75 for a room without a private bath or $4.00 and up for a room with bath. Meals cost $1.00 each. Postcard by J. E. Haynes, St. Paul, Minnesota.

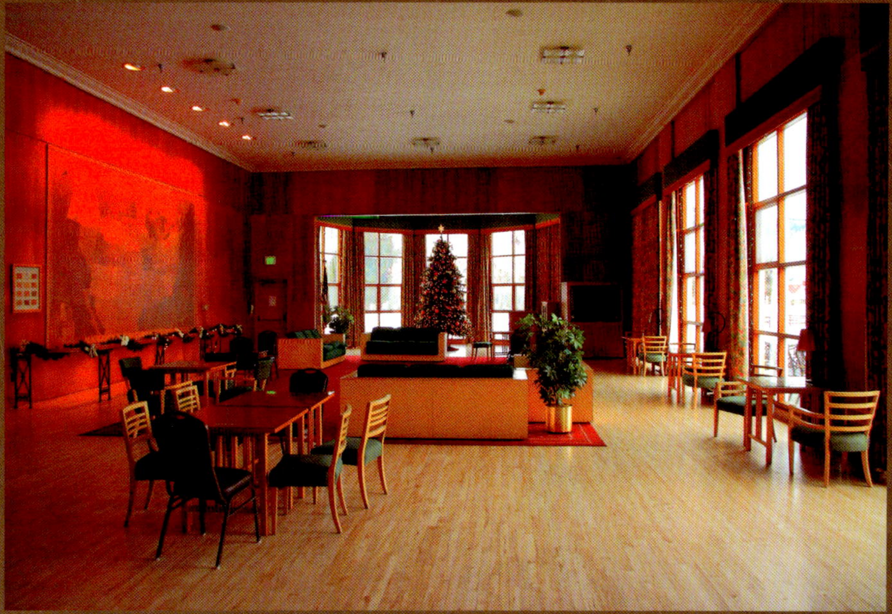

One of the most interesting features of the hotel is a 17 x 10-foot map of the United States (on left side of room) made of inlaid wood, which was designed and made by architect Robert Reamer and his associate W. H. Fey during his work on the hotel.

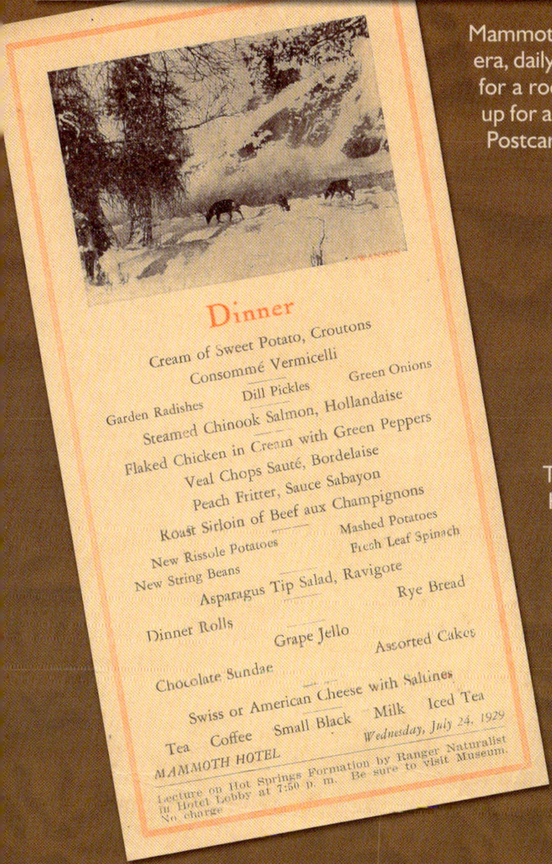

Dinner

Cream of Sweet Potato, Croutons
Consommé Vermicelli
Garden Radishes Dill Pickles Green Onions
Steamed Chinook Salmon, Hollandaise
Flaked Chicken in Cream with Green Peppers
Veal Chops Sauté, Bordelaise
Peach Fritter, Sauce Sabayon
Roast Sirloin of Beef aux Champignons
New Rissole Potatoes Mashed Potatoes
New String Beans Fresh Leaf Spinach
Asparagus Tip Salad, Ravigote
Dinner Rolls Rye Bread
Grape Jello Assorted Cakes
Chocolate Sundae
Swiss or American Cheese with Saltines
Tea Coffee Small Black Milk Iced Tea
MAMMOTH HOTEL Wednesday, July 24, 1929
Lecture on Hot Springs Formation by Ranger Naturalist in Hotel Lobby at 7:50 p. m. Be sure to visit Museum. No charge

This dinner menu from the Mammoth Hotel is dated July 24, 1929. Some of the choices included Steamed Chinook Salmon, Flaked Chicken in Cream, and Veal Chops Sauté Bordelaise.

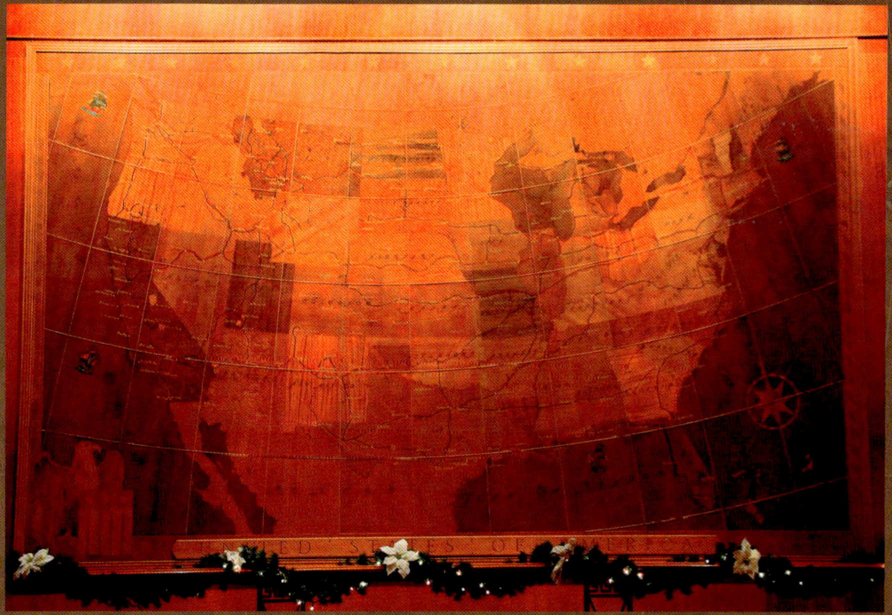

Close-up of the inlaid map.

GRAND CANYON HOTEL

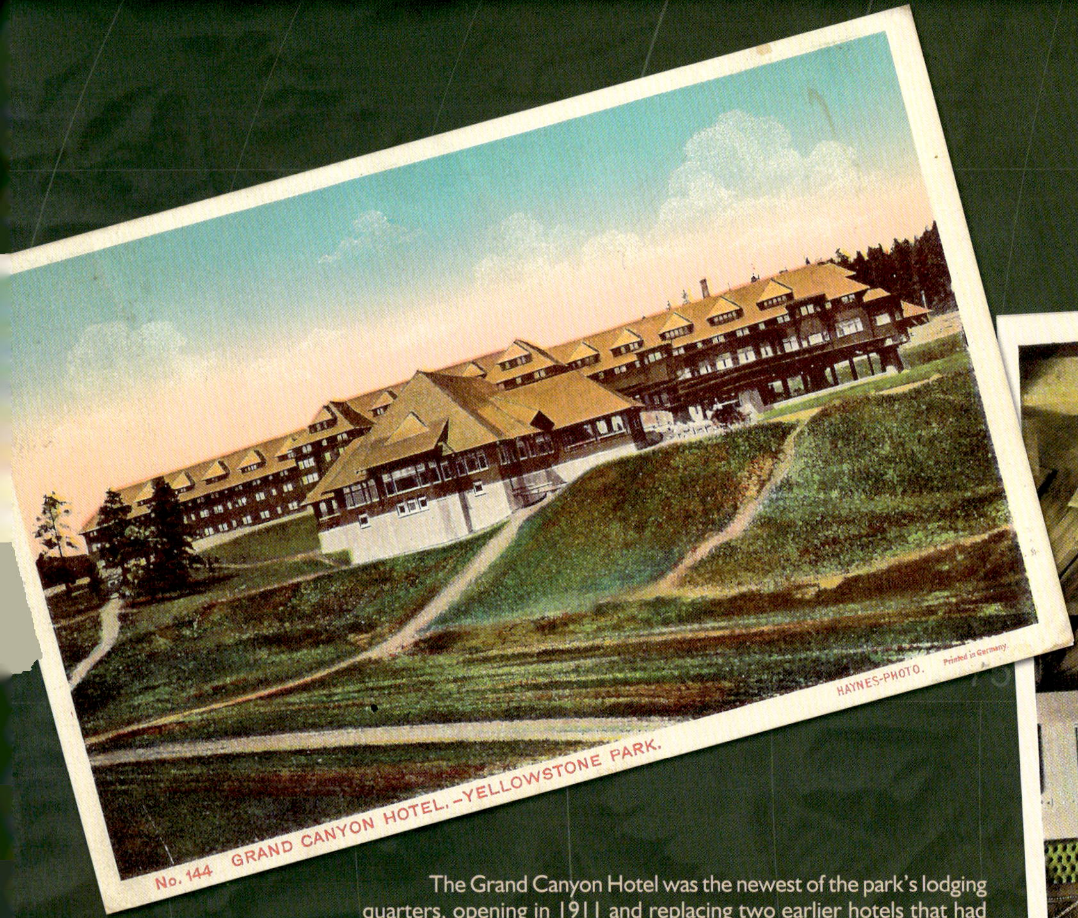

The Grand Canyon Hotel was the newest of the park's lodging quarters, opening in 1911 and replacing two earlier hotels that had been built in the area to service the scenic sights of Lower Falls and the Grand Canyon of the Yellowstone. The new hotel was the largest ever built in Yellowstone. It could accommodate over five hundred guests and cost nearly $800,000 to build. The building included a power and heating plant as well as an ice plant. The hotel was designed and built by architect Robert Reamer at the direction of the Yellowstone Park Company. The hotel was closed in 1959 following damage from an earthquake and new replacement lodging facilities. It burned the next year as the building was being demolished. This postcard was printed in Germany from a Haynes photo and was postmarked in 1913.

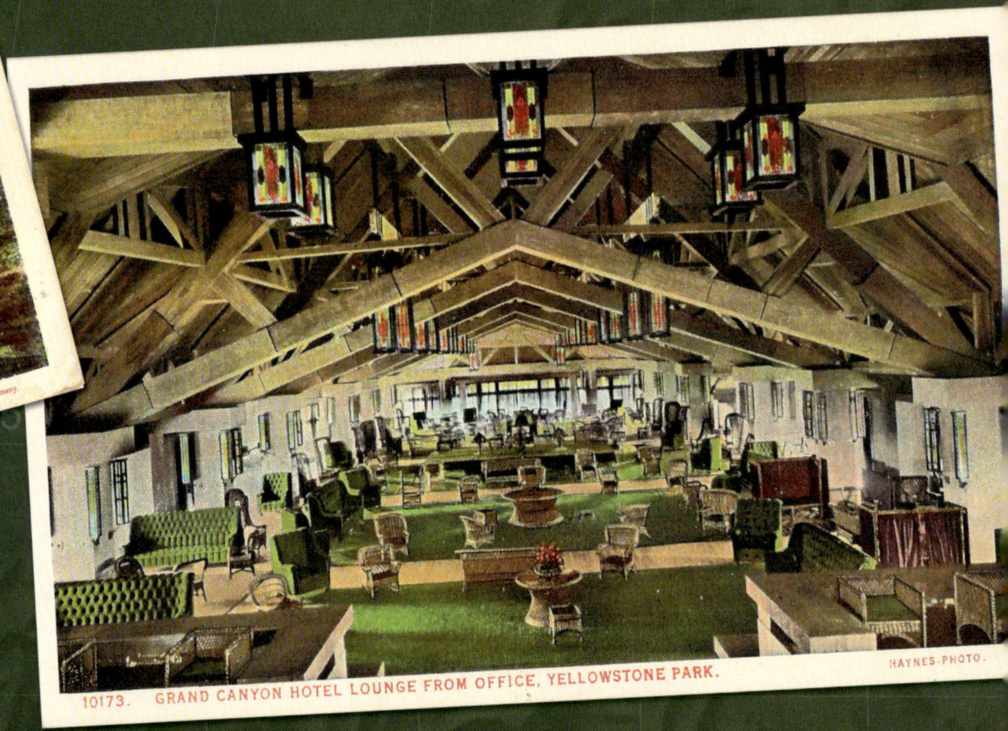

The most spectacular room in the hotel was the lounge which combined the functions of a reading room, writing room, music room, and smoking room. It was also used for dancing and concerts. The space was two hundred feet long and one hundred feet wide. The floor was made of polished oak and its walls and ceiling made of red birch. Postcard by Haynes Picture Shops, Inc.

THE YELLOWSTONE LODGES & CABINS

Park visitation increased dramatically when travelers began arriving in their own automobiles. To accommodate the new visitors, lodges with cabins were built in the 1920s by the Yellowstone Park Lodge Company to offer an overnight experience appropriate for those who were once unable to afford to travel to the park. The new lodges were designed with more comfort than the tent camps, but were not as elaborate as the luxury hotels in order to satisfy the new demand.

OLD FAITHFUL LODGE CABINS

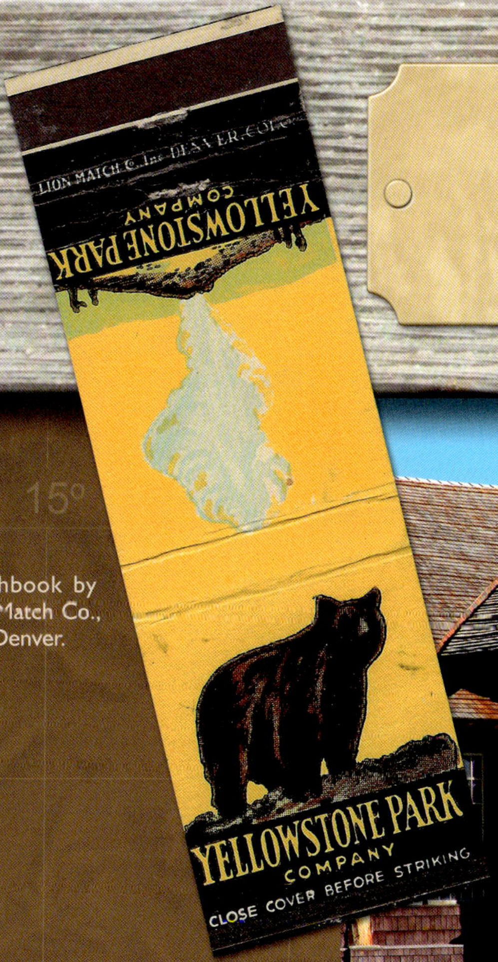

Matchbook by Lion Match Co., Inc., Denver.

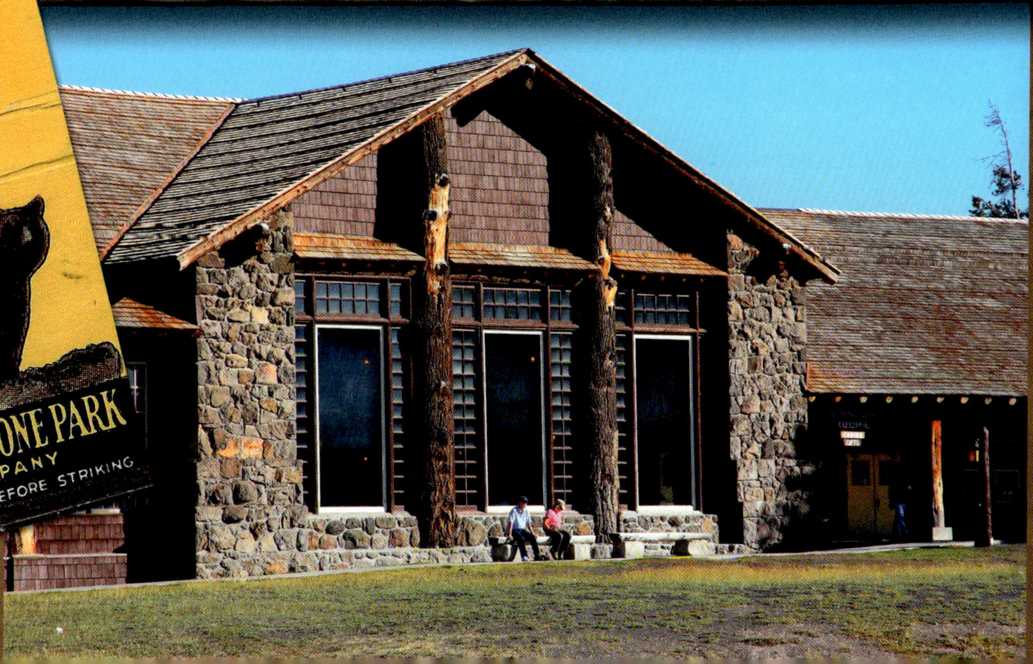

Old Faithful Lodge faces the Old Faithful Geyser and is included in the Old Faithful Historic District. Today, the lodge building houses dining facilities, an ice cream shop, bake shop, gift shop, showers, and restroom facilities, plus the Geyser Hall assembly space. The lobby's three large windows offer ample views of the Old Faithful Geyser.

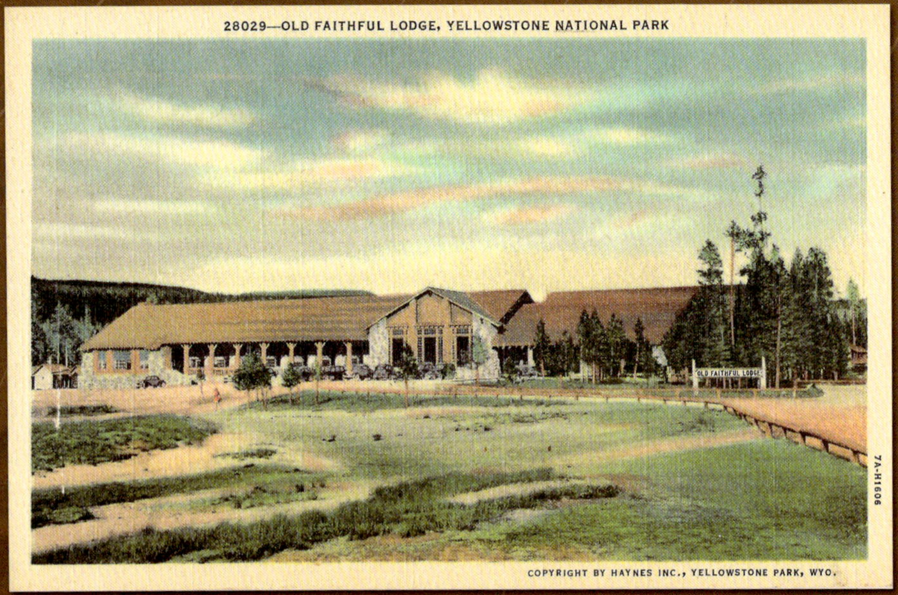

The lodge was built from 1923-1927, first as a series of detached buildings that were then reworked into one large structure. The building included a dining hall and a large social assembly hall to be used by guests who rented the many cabins nearby. Linen postcard by Haynes, Inc.

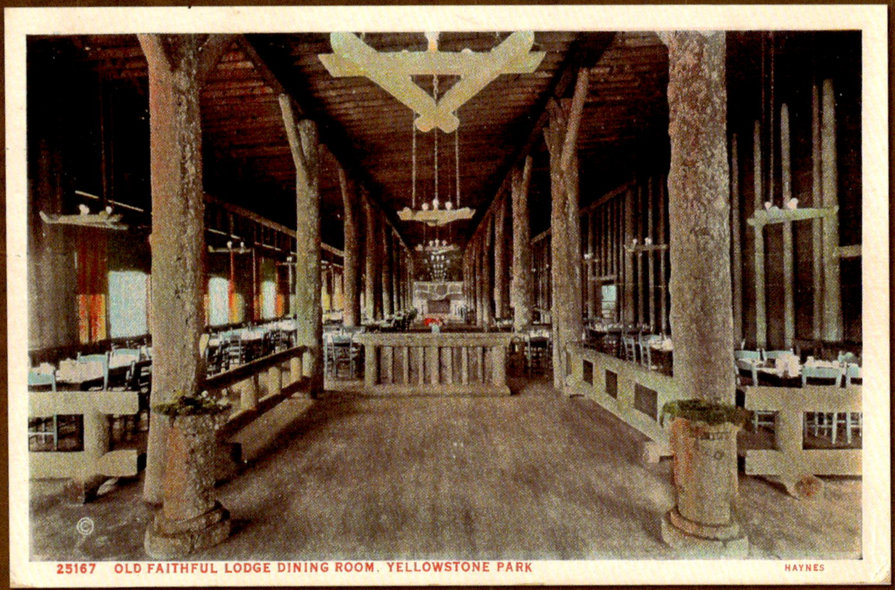

Old Faithful Lodge dining room circa 1920s. The cost of lodging and meals in the Yellowstone lodges during the 1920s was $4.50 per day per person without private bath. Haynes Picture Shops, Inc. postcard.

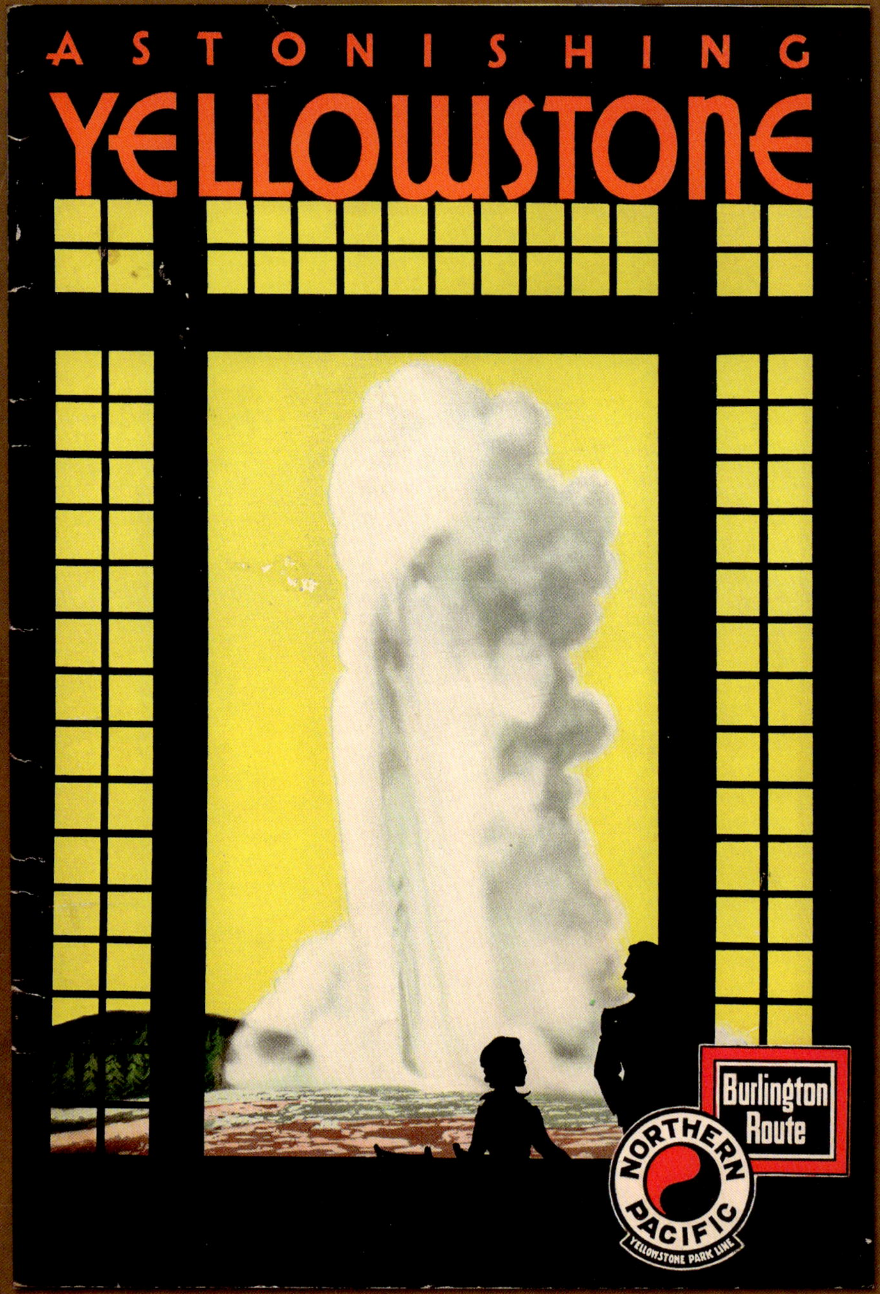

The massive windows of the Old Faithful Lodge frame a view of the famous geyser in this booklet published in 1939 by Burlington-Northern Pacific. With promotional backing from the railroads, visitation to "Wonderland" attracted nearly 500,000 visitors that year.

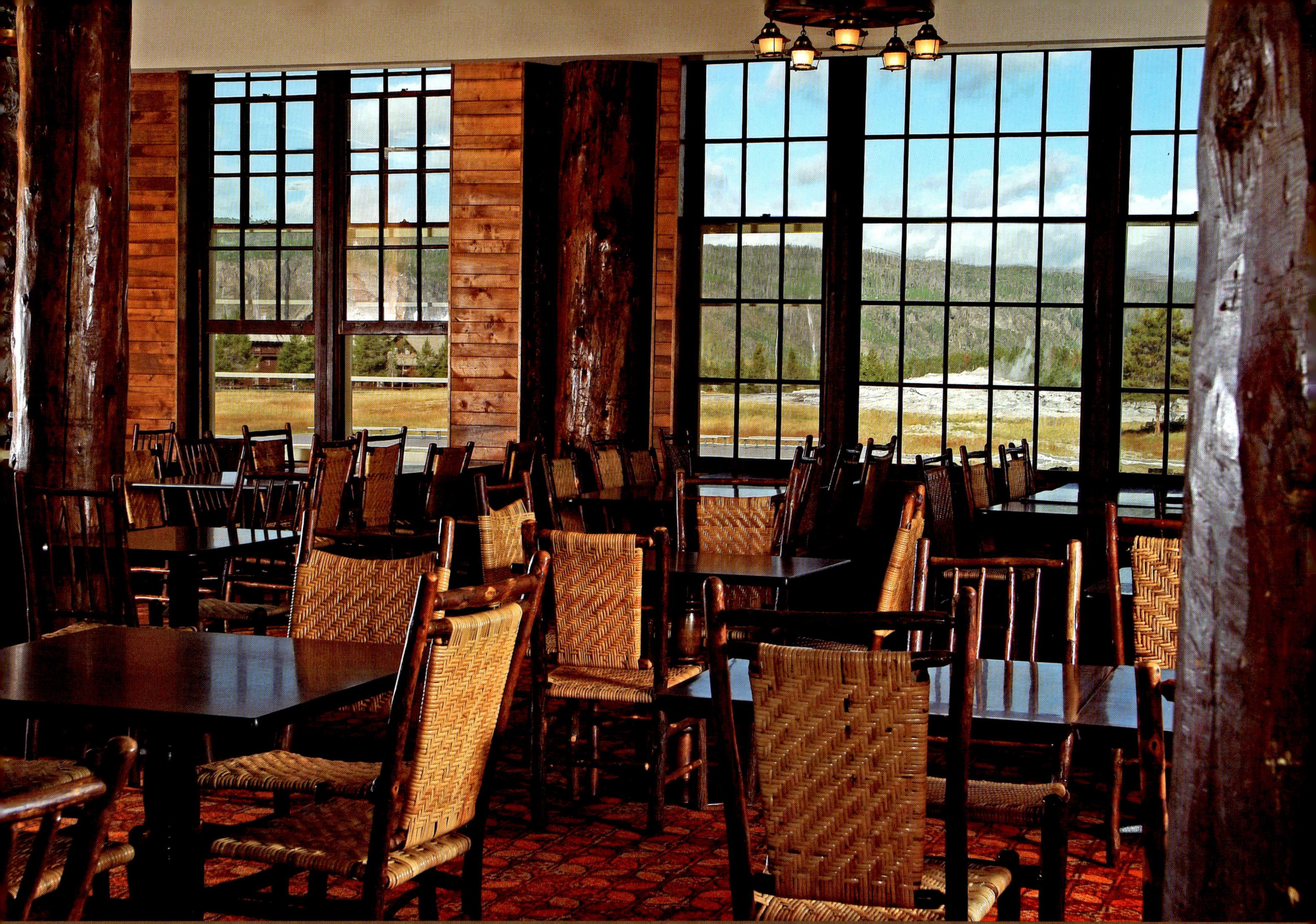

The Old Faithful Lodge is furnished with vintage hickory chairs to maintain the building's rustic ambiance. There are ninety-seven cabins within the lodge complex, most with private baths. The cabins are open from May to September. *Courtesy Xanterra Parks & Resorts.*

LAKE LODGE CABINS

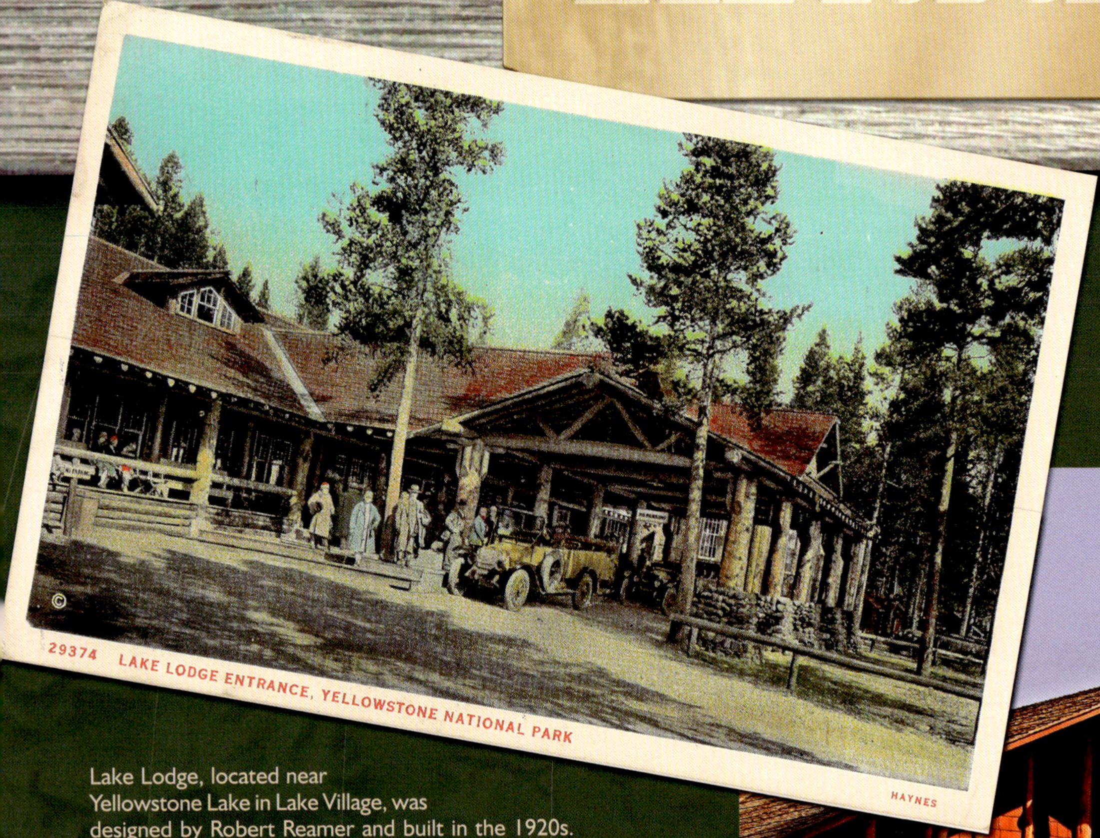

Lake Lodge, located near Yellowstone Lake in Lake Village, was designed by Robert Reamer and built in the 1920s. Later additions included the east wing for use as a dining area and the west wing for a dance hall. The front porch was also added overlooking Yellowstone Lake. Postcard by Haynes Picture Shops, Inc.

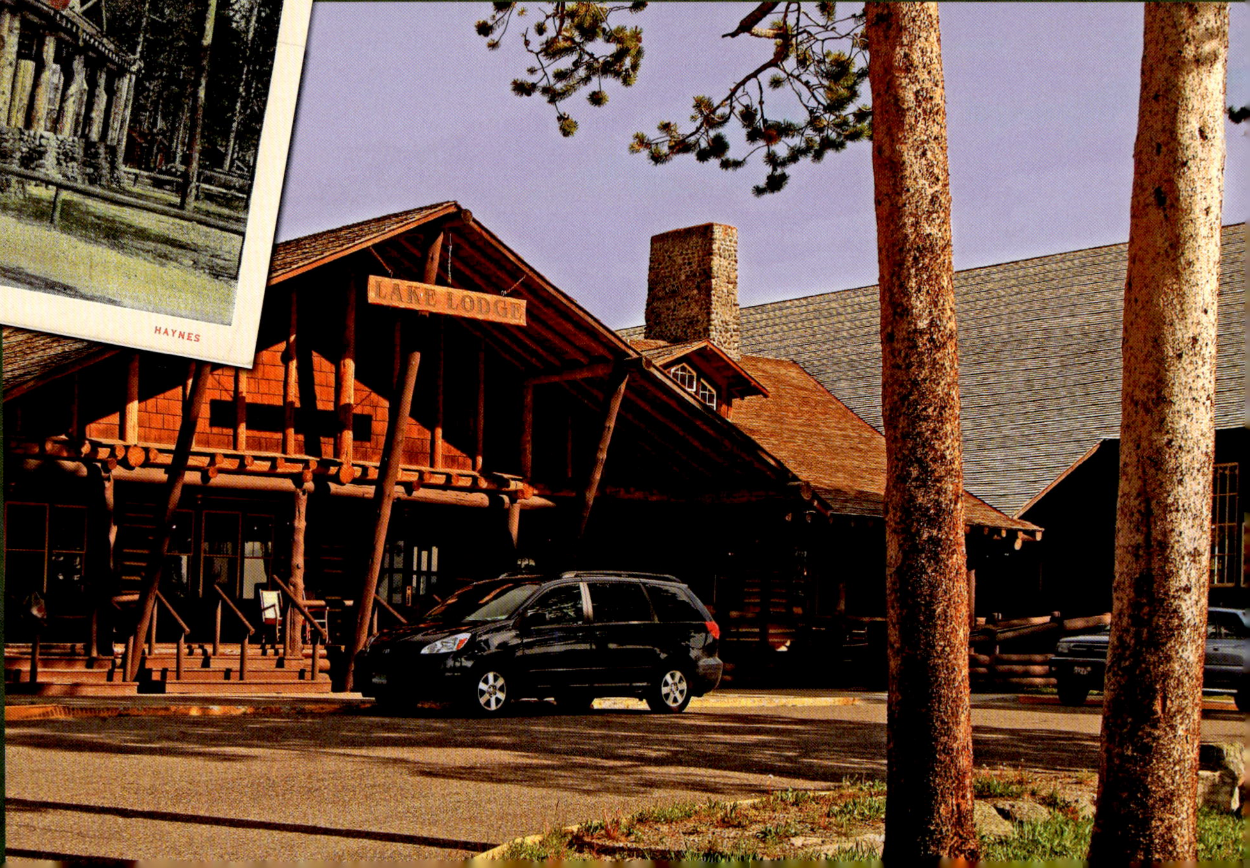

Today, the lodge building includes a gift shop, lobby, and bar. *Courtesy Xanterra Parks & Resorts.*

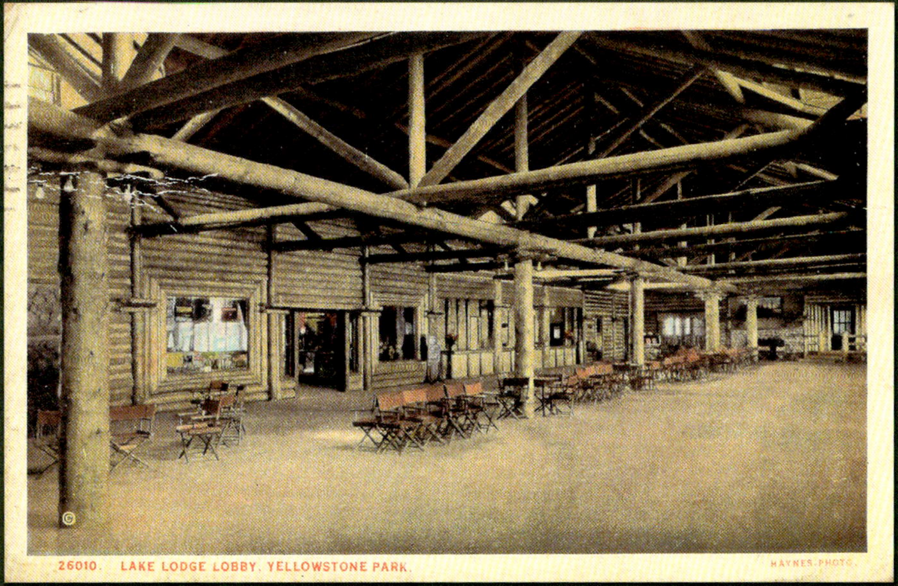

The Lake Lodge lobby is featured in this Haynes-Photo postcard postmarked July 30, 1928. The message on the back reads, "We went over here last night to an 'entertainment.' This is Hazel's first experience with anything like the outdoors so I have to do the hikes alone. Tomorrow morning I am going to climb to the bottom of the canyon on a new trail."

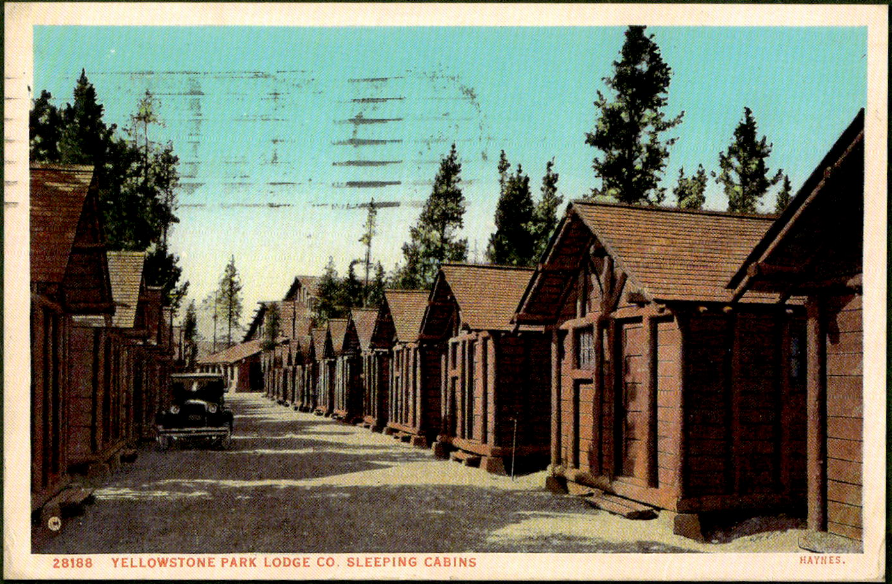

The Lake Lodge Cabins continue to look much as they did when this 1920s Haynes postcard was mailed. The description on the back offers a no-frills overview, "In the Yellowstone Park Lodge Company system, this typical street of individual cabins suggests the orderly arrangement of its facilities, including the substantial, comfortable and well furnished sleeping accommodations." Today, there are 186 cabins serviced by the lodge building, all with private baths. The cabins are open June through September.

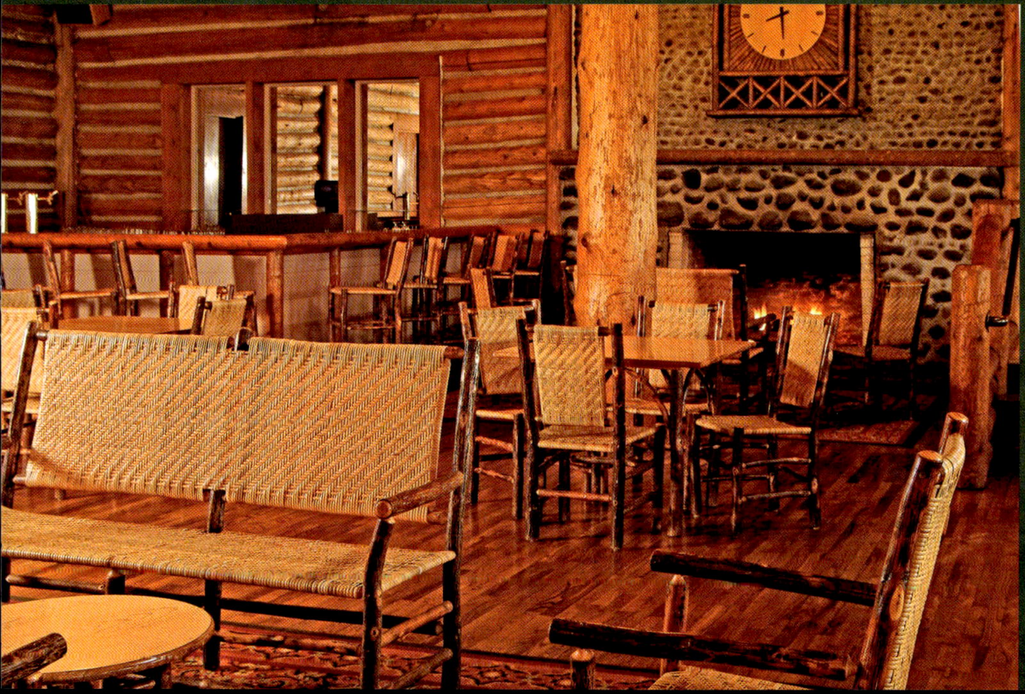

The Lake Lodge lobby as it looks today. *Courtesy Xanterra Parks & Resorts.*

MAMMOTH HOT SPRINGS LODGE CABINS

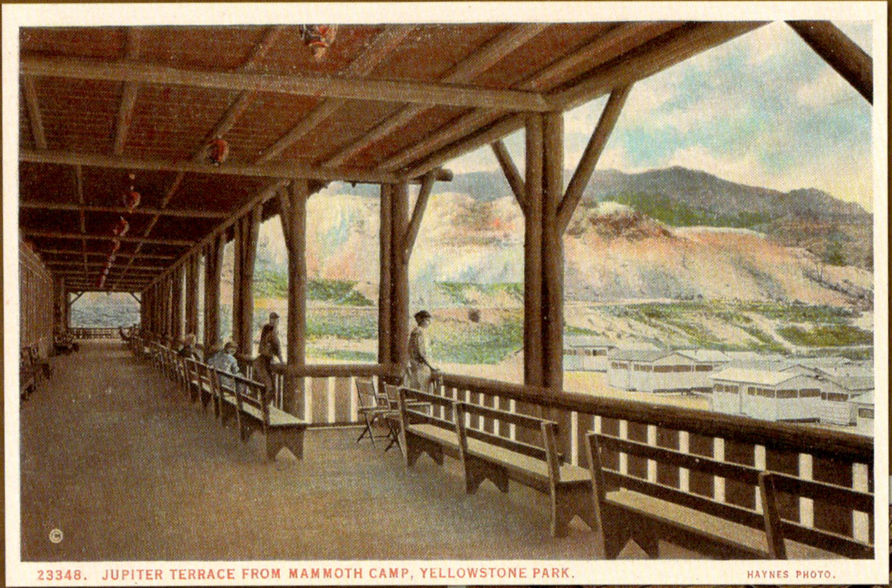

The Mammoth Hot Springs Lodge was also built in the 1920s with views of Terrace Mountain and Jupiter Terrace. Postcard published by J. E. Haynes.

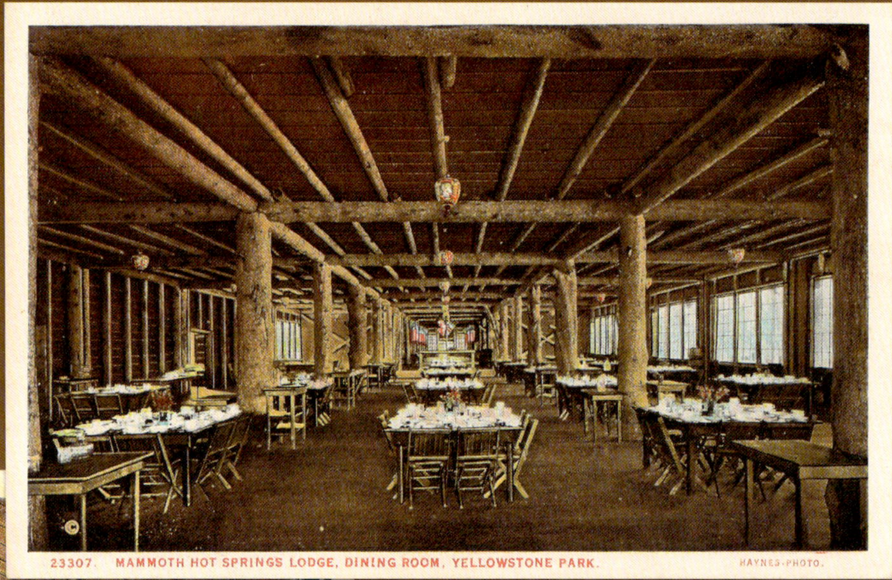

Mammoth Hot Springs Lodge dining room. Each of the early lodges in Yellowstone featured rustic architecture with exposed logs both inside and outside the structure. The information on the back of the card lists the locations of other lodges in operation at the time, including Old Faithful, Lake, Sylvan Pass, Grand Canyon, and near Tower Junction. Postcard published by J. E. Haynes.

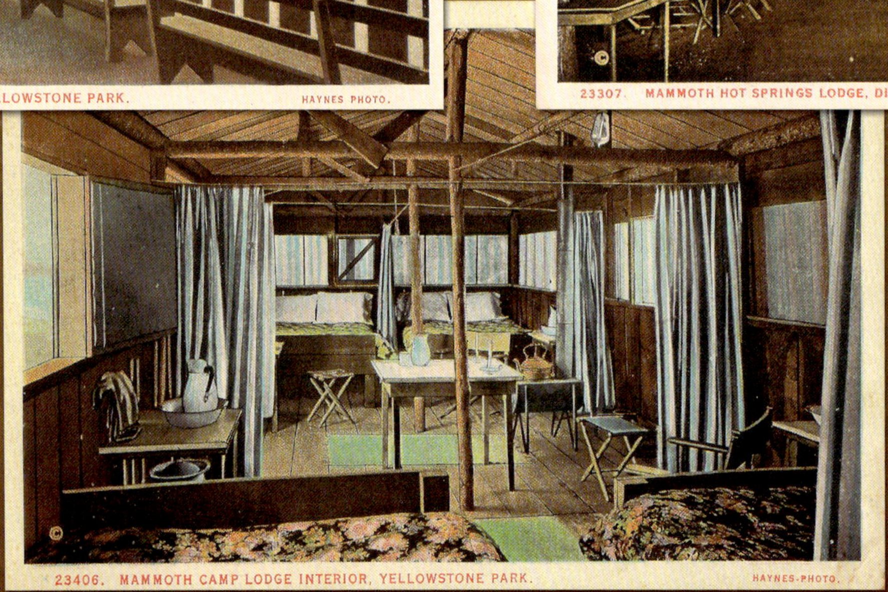

Mammoth Camp Lodge cabin interior which included four double beds with curtain dividers. Postcard published by J. E. Haynes.

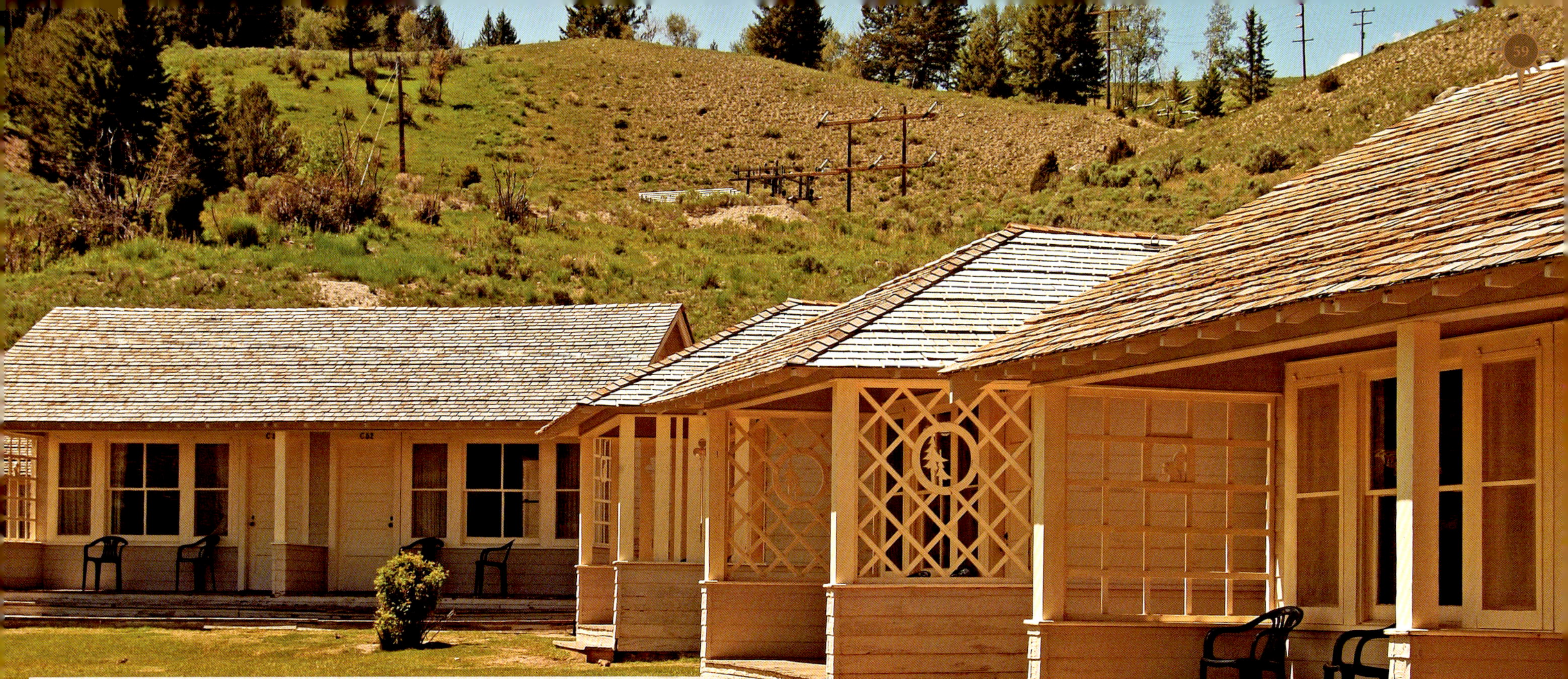

New cottages designed by Robert Reamer were built at Mammoth circa 1936 in anticipation of the eventual closure of the lodge facilities which were torn down in 1949. Today, there are 115 Mammoth cabin units, with and without private baths. The cabins are open May through October. *Courtesy Xanterra Parks & Resorts.*

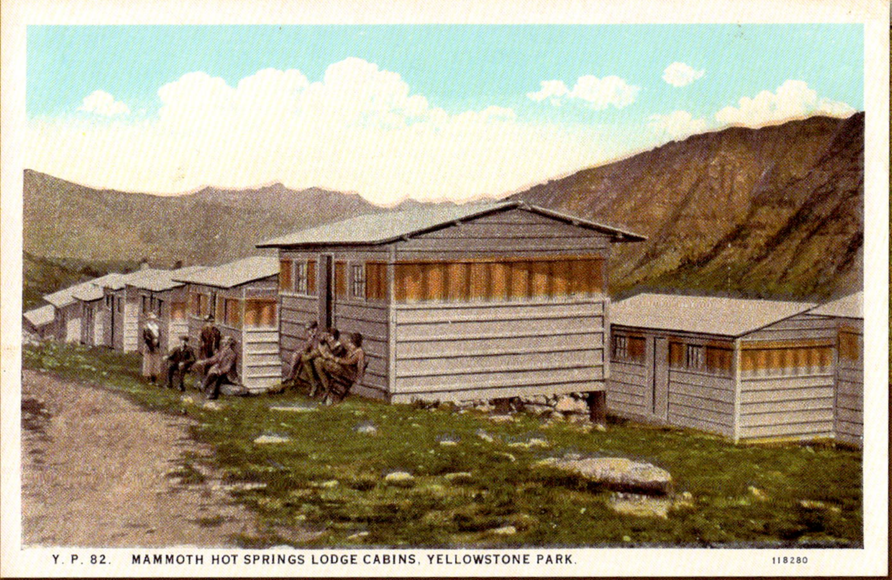

The lodge cabins at Mammoth and throughout the park included electric lights and were heated by wood burning stoves. They came in one, two, or four room units. Many of the Mammoth cabins are pictured in this Bloom Bros. Co. postcard.

CANYON LODGE & CABINS

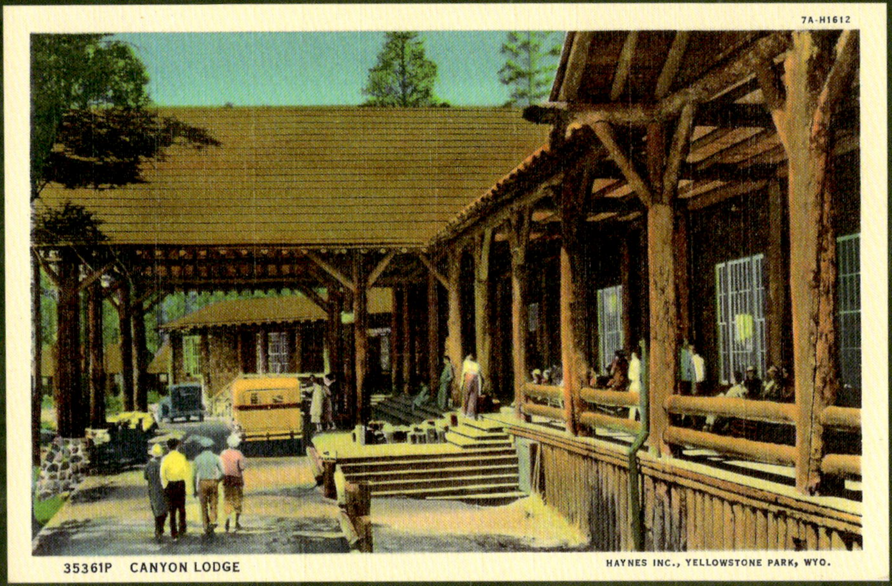

Canyon Lodge was located near the rim of the Grand Canyon of the Yellowstone and was built in the 1920s. The lodge included dining facilities and space for recreation including dances. The message on the back of this card reads, "Ten of us kids went to dance here in the evening. Had a wonderful time." This lodge building was closed at the end of the 1956 season and was replaced by a new lodge as part of the Mission 66 project. Cabins were also constructed in the 1950s and '60s. Postcard published by Haynes Inc.

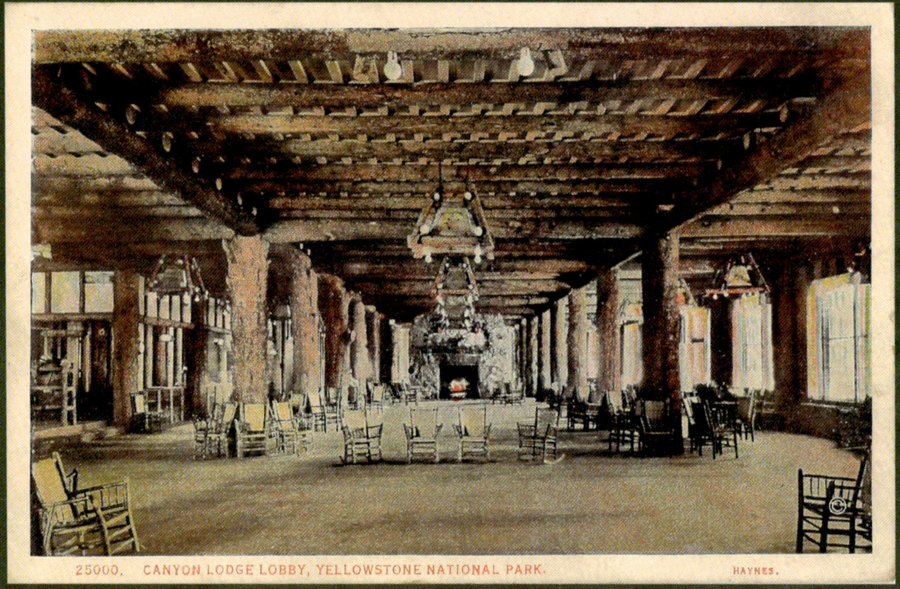

The early Canyon Lodge lobby is pictured on this Haynes Picture Shops postcard. It was a huge room furnished with hickory furniture. There was plenty of room for dancing in this unique lobby. The information on the back of the postcard reads, "Canyon Lodge, one of the largest structures in the entire camp system in the park was completed in 1925."

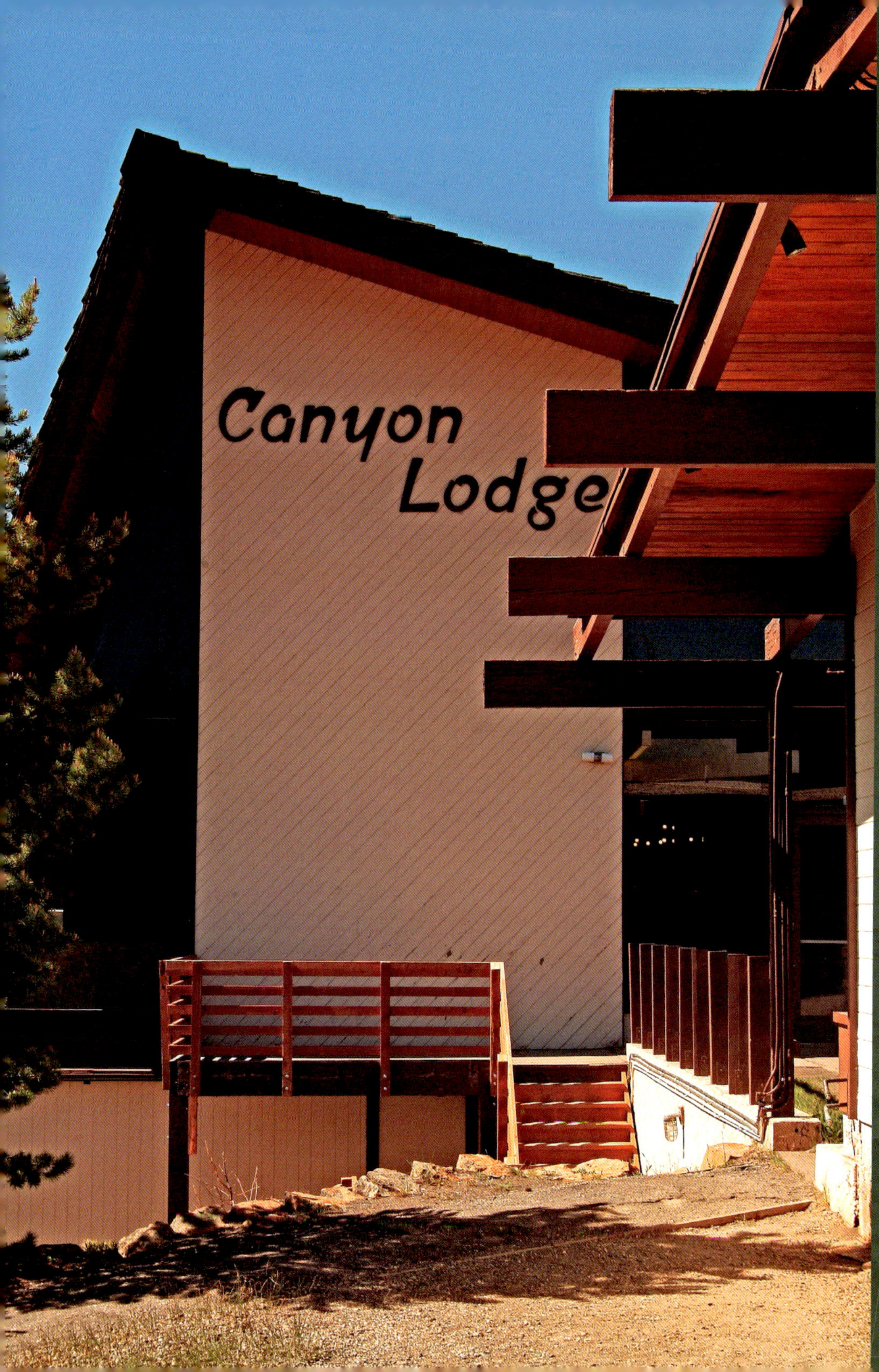

In the years after World War II, the park was directed to shift its attention away from luxury travelers and focus on lodging options that were better suited for guests who were arriving in their cars in lieu of the train. This was the inspiration for Canyon Village which included construction of a new Canyon Lodge as pictured. The Village opened in 1957 and was the park's largest undertaking. It included a visitor center, employee housing, and other amenities that could accommodate up to 5,000 people. Grant Village, on the southern shore of Yellowstone Lake, was also developed as part of the Mission 66 project to modernize the facilities in use at West Thumb. *Courtesy Xanterra Parks & Resorts.*

ROOSEVELT LODGE & CABINS

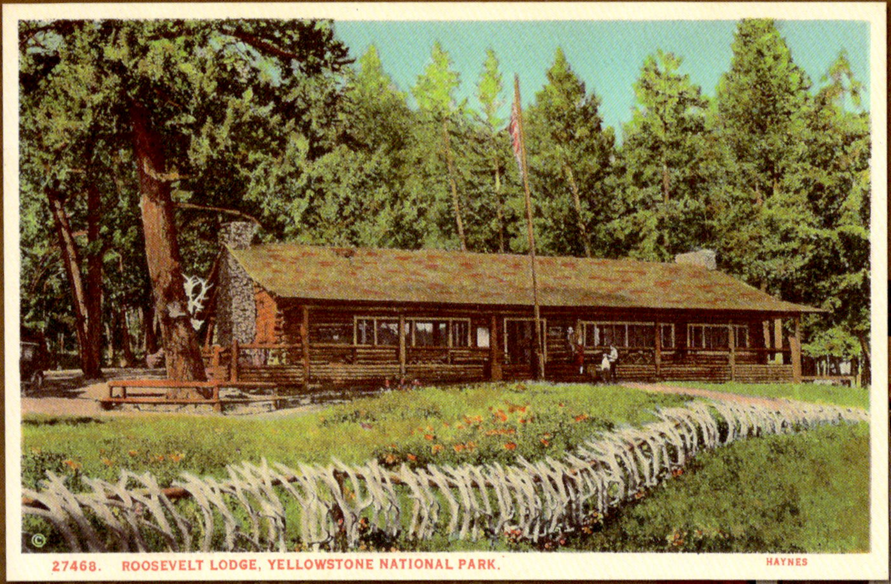

Roosevelt Lodge is located near Tower Junction where an early Wylie Camp once stood. It is named for President Theodore Roosevelt who visited the area. The lodge was built in the 1920s along with a cluster of cabins. There are eighty cabins in use today, including sixty Rough Rider cabins. These include a wood stove and no water or bathrooms. Other more modern cabins are also available. The cabins are open from June to September. Postcard by Haynes Picture Shops, Inc.

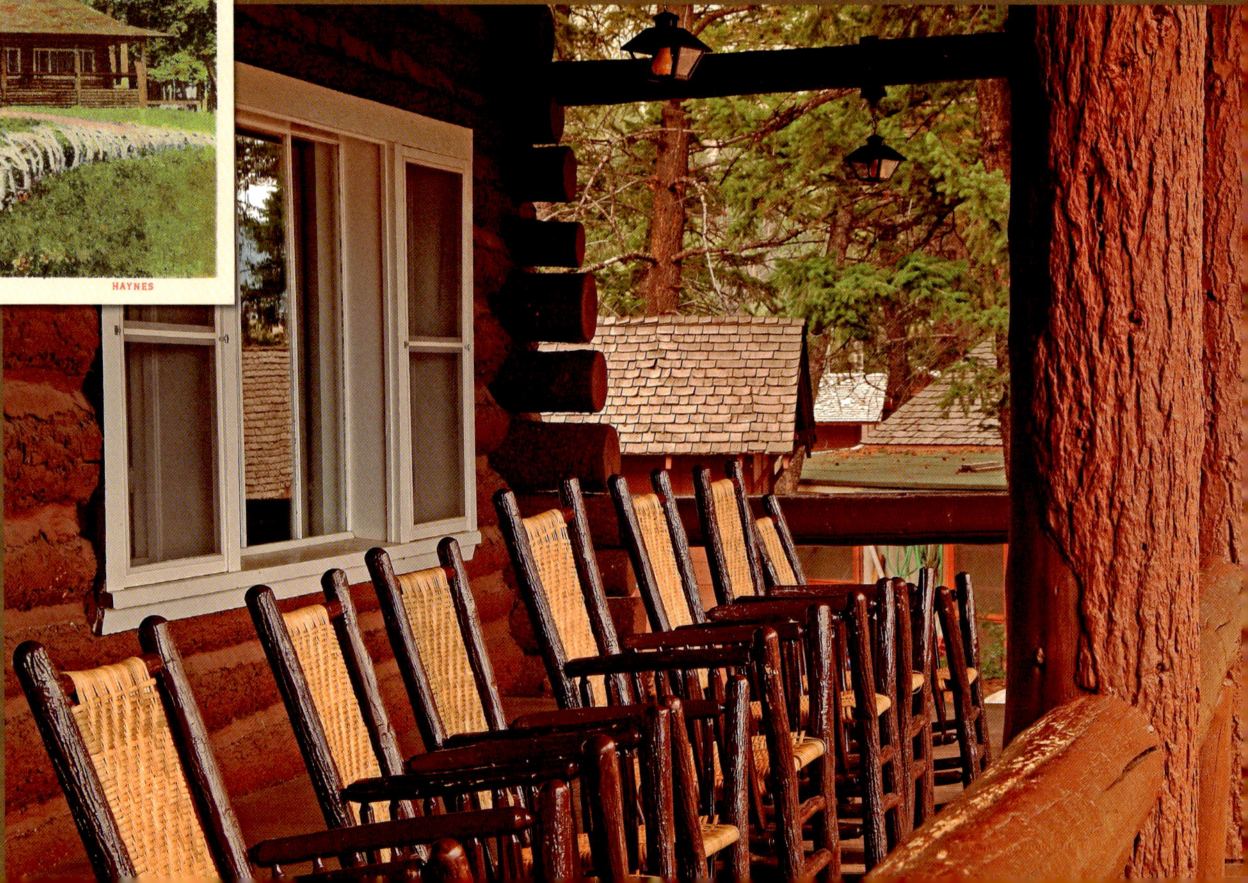

The area around Roosevelt Lodge is quieter and more secluded than other facilities in the park making it a favorite place to relax on the porch of the lodge and enjoy the outdoors. *Photo courtesy Xanterra Parks & Resorts.*

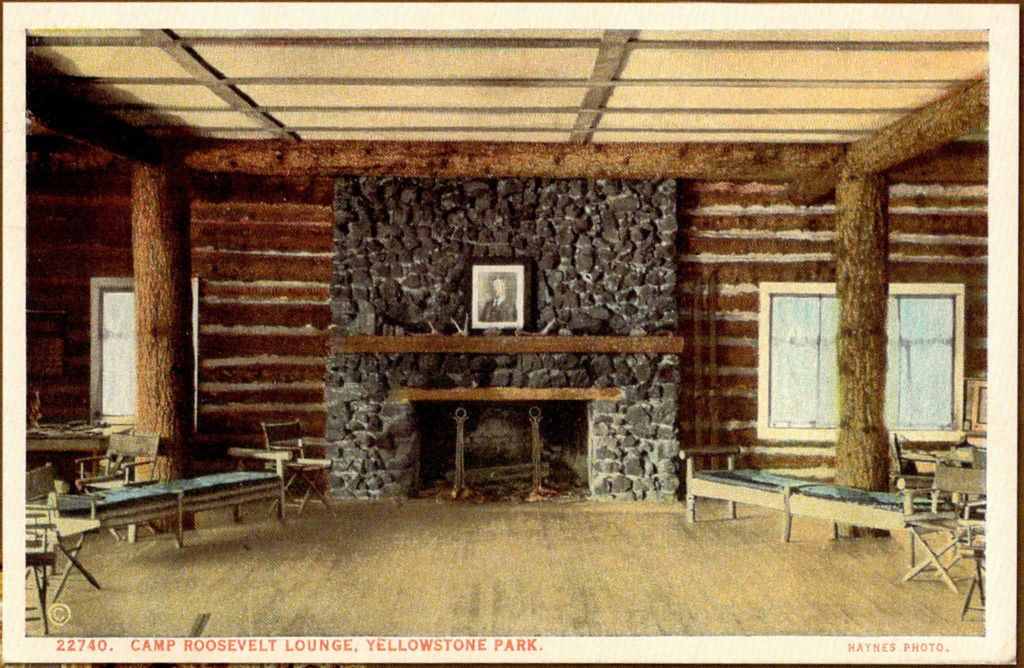

The inside of the Roosevelt Lodge features a large stone fireplace. The message on the back of this 1926 postmarked postcard reads, "Surprised? So was I when an opportunity came. Francis bought a Buick and we are taking this trip thru the park. It's wonderful. Today went up Mount Washburn 10,307 ft. Some climb." Postcard by J. E. Haynes.

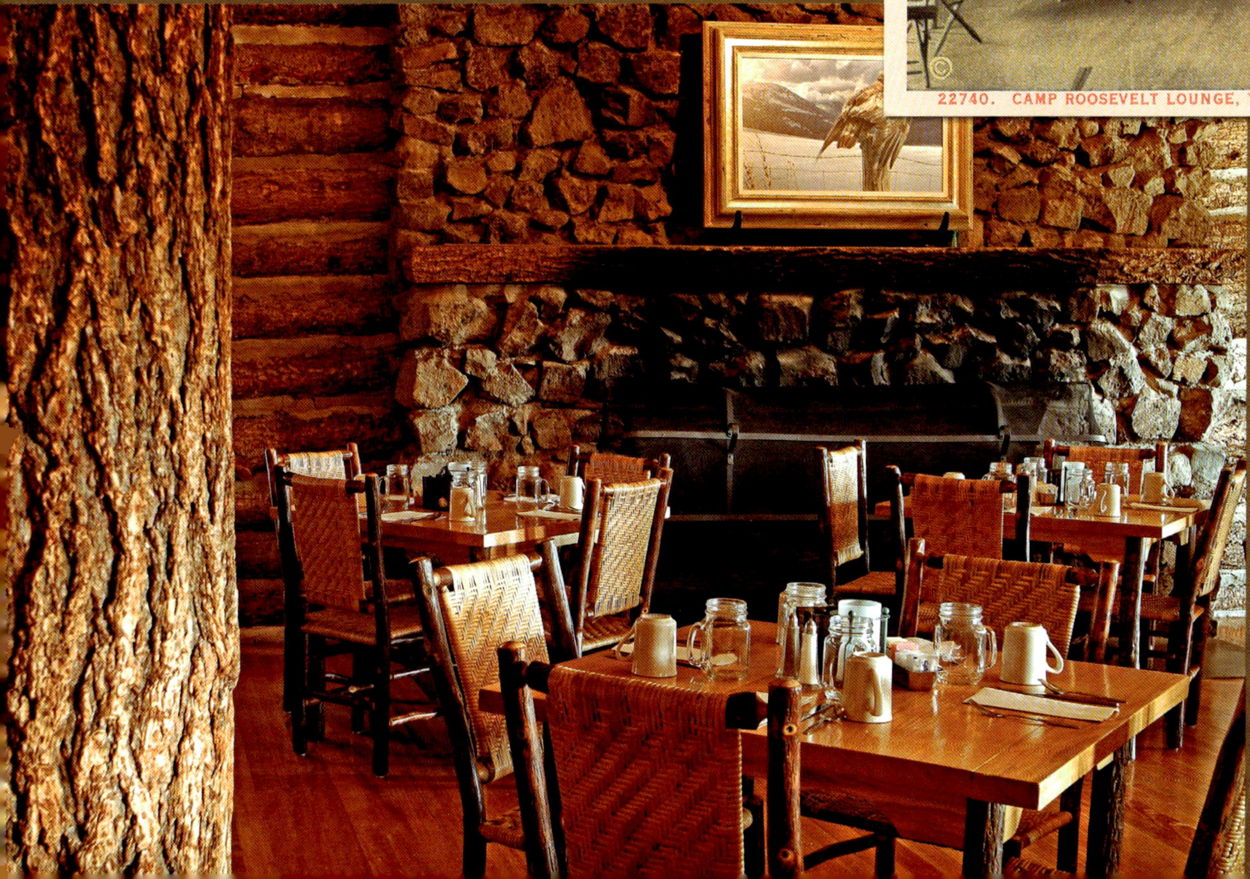

The lodge building is now used for registration and dining. *Photo courtesy Xanterra Parks & Resorts.*

THE YELLOWSTONE CAMPS

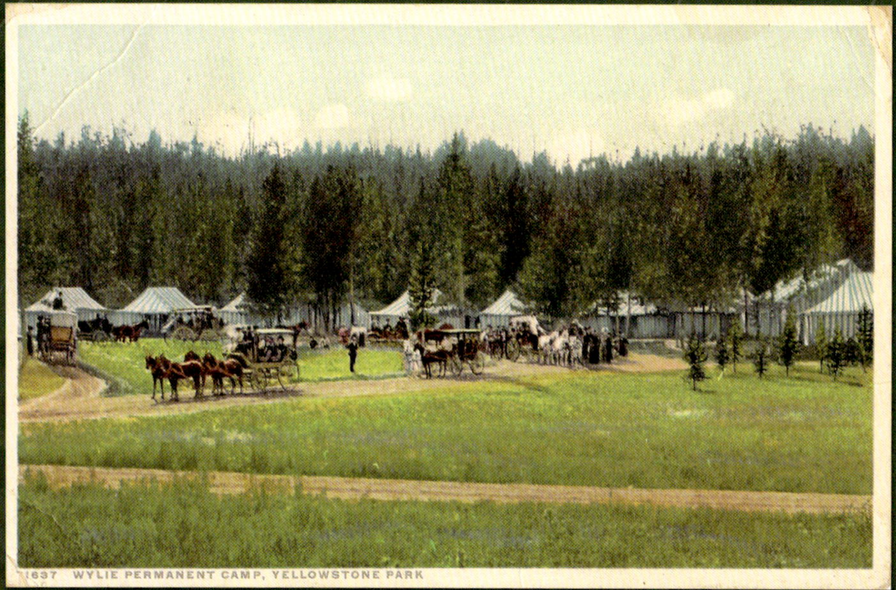

The Wylie Camping Company was established in Yellowstone in 1893 by W. W. Wylie, a public school superintendent from Bozeman, Montana. The business provided permanent camps throughout the park including Swan Lake, Gibbon, Riverside, Upper Basin, Thumb, Lake Sylvan, Canyon, and Roosevelt. The company also offered transportation using a Concord stage and six horses. This phostint postcard made by Detroit Publishing Co. shows an early scene of a Wylie Permanent Camp and the coaches and horses used for transportation. The striped tents were used by all the Wylie Camps.

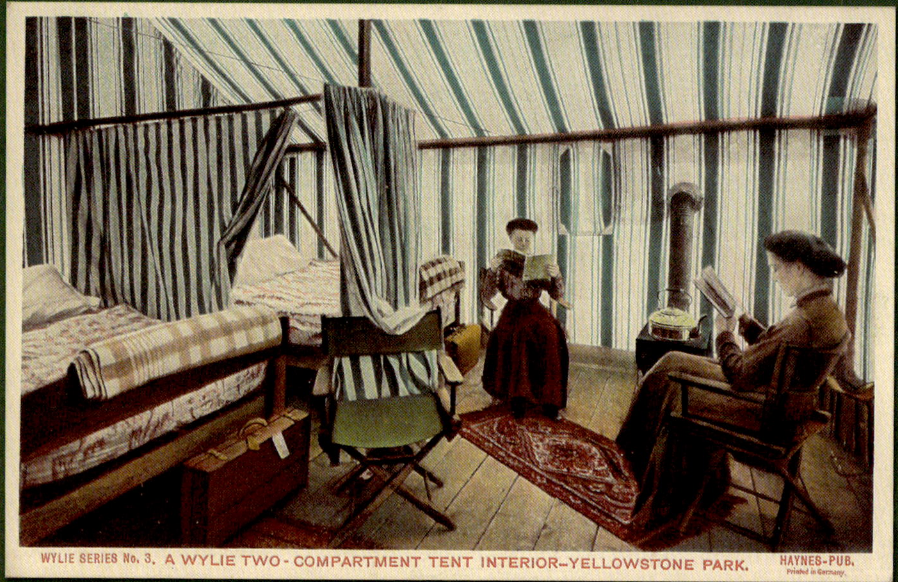

Because lodging at the Wylie Camps was less expensive than the cost of hotel rooms or cabins, these camps continued to be successful. The "Wylie Way" was also responsible for several innovations that eventually made their way into parks across the country. The management hired school teachers and college students to work for the company during their summer breaks. These educated workers made great guides for tourists because they were able to provide interesting information about the sights they were seeing. In addition, these young college students could help provide evening entertainment for the guests. This Haynes-Germany postcard pictures a Wylie two-compartment tent interior which includes a wood floor. The ladies appear to be quite comfortable in their quarters. A wood stove is visible on the far side.

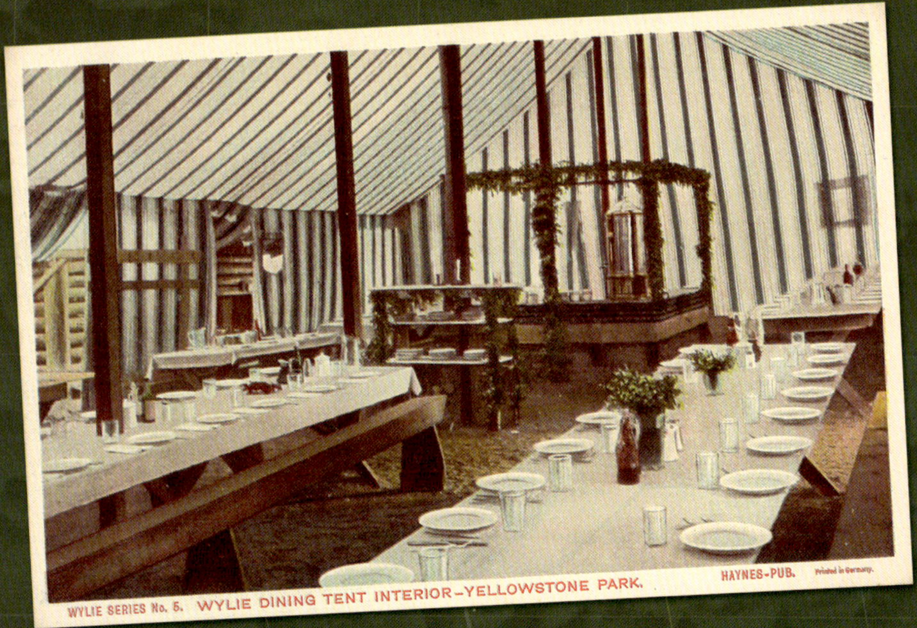

Although his camps were successful, Wylie was unable to obtain a long-term lease from the park. After the 1905 season, he sold the company to Arthur W. Miles who was successful in negotiating a ten-year lease. The Shaw & Powell Company also provided tent accommodations in the park. In 1917 the two companies merged to form Yellowstone Park Camping Company. This firm eventually became the Yellowstone Park Lodge and Camps Company in 1928 when it came under the control of H. W. Child. This Haynes-Germany postcard pictures the inside of a Wylie dining tent where the tables are elegantly set with tablecloths, dishes, and flowers, despite the rustic surroundings.

Wylie Camps were the first to introduce entertainment at night for guests sitting around a campfire and the practice spread to other national parks across the U.S. The entertainment presented by Wylie Camp employees included pantomimes, theatricals, a songfest, and campfire stories, according to information on the back of this card published by Haynes Picture Shops, Inc. circa 1920s. Also pictured is an unmarked decal.

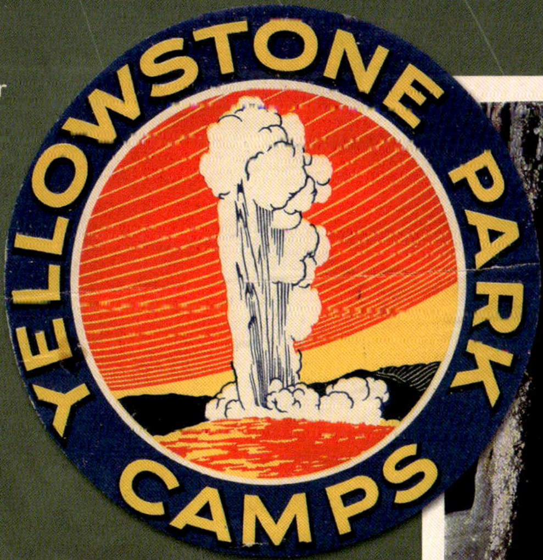

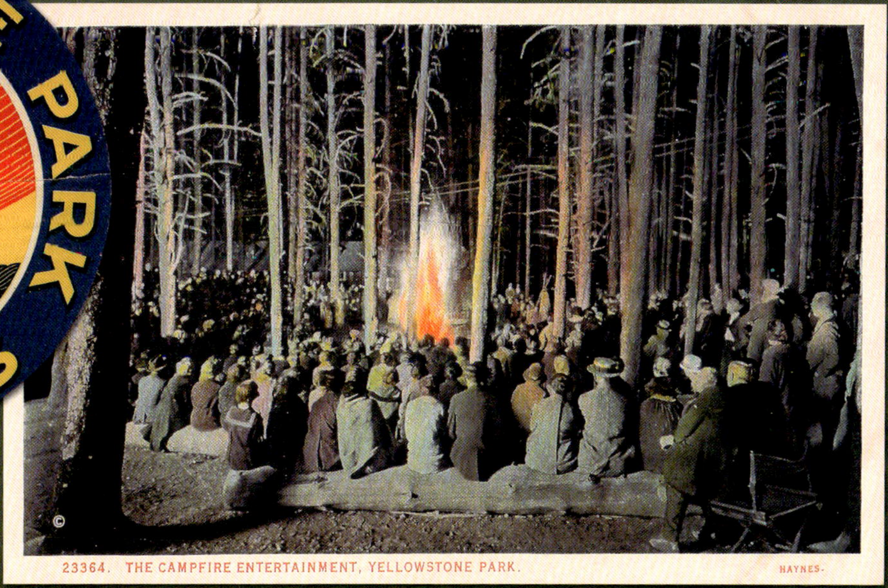

23364. THE CAMPFIRE ENTERTAINMENT, YELLOWSTONE PARK. HAYNES.

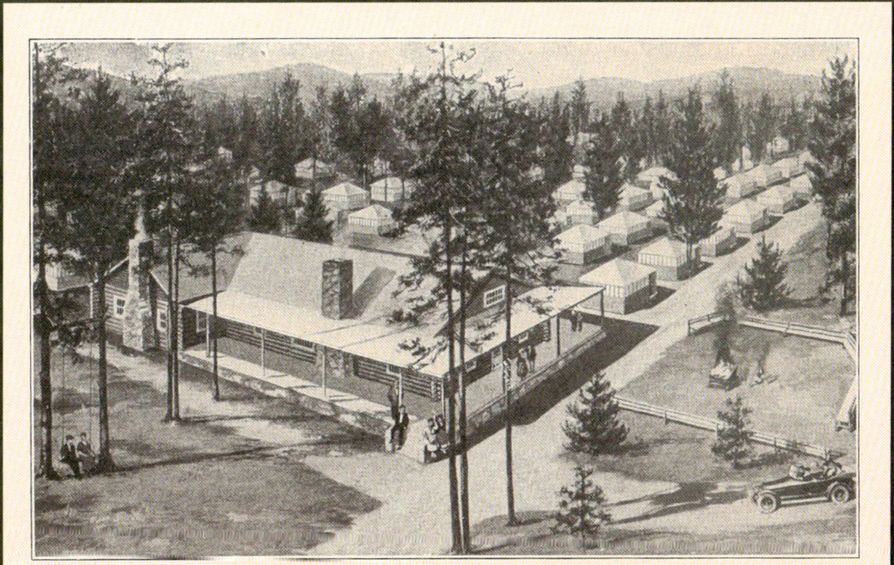

One of the several permanent camps—For years camping in comfort has been a feature of Yellowstone travel

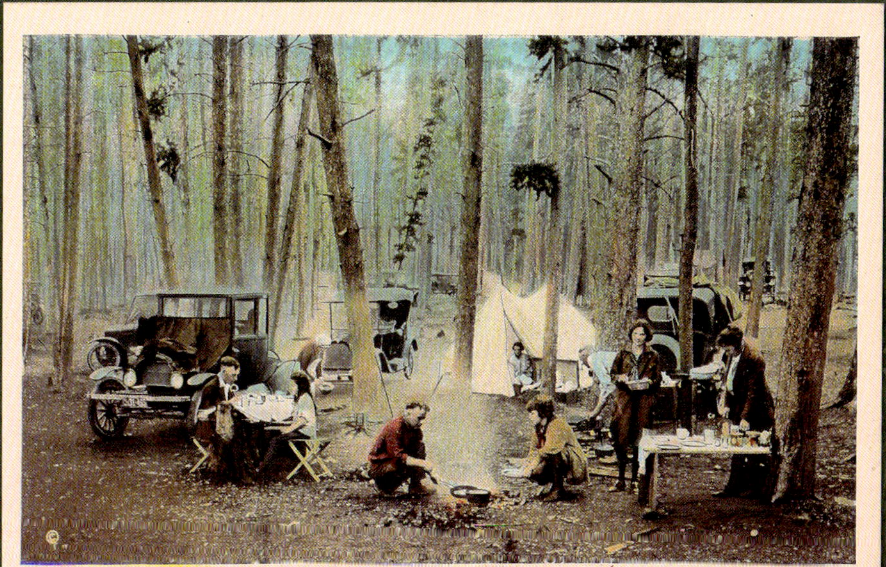

23397. A YELLOWSTONE PUBLIC AUTOMOBILE CAMP, YELLOWSTONE PARK. HAYNES PHOTO.

By 1920, the permanent camps in Yellowstone had canvas sleeping tents with four-foot-high wooden sides. They each had wood doors with locks and screened windows. Heat was provided by wood burning stoves and each tent had full-sized beds. According to the advertising provided by Yellowstone, the food was served in dining halls, and large pavilions were provided for dancing and other recreation. The camps were located at Mammoth, near Old Faithful Inn, at Grand Canyon near Artist Point, in Camp Roosevelt, near Tower Falls, and at Lake Camp near Yellowstone Lake. One of the permanent camps which appeared in a Yellowstone advertising brochure issued by the Union Pacific Railroad for the 1920 season is pictured.

Automobile Camps were established in 1916 to accommodate visitors who could now drive to the park on their own. The camps were located at Mammoth, Old Faithful, Canyon, and Lake. The early camps were quite primitive but by the 1920s each camp site included a table and fireplace. Comfort stations with flush toilets were also provided as well as water for use at the campsites. Individuals still needed to keep food above the ground by tying it to a tree limb because of the many bears nearby. For many years there was no charge for using these camps. This Haynes-Photo postcard pictures tourists using one of the campgrounds.

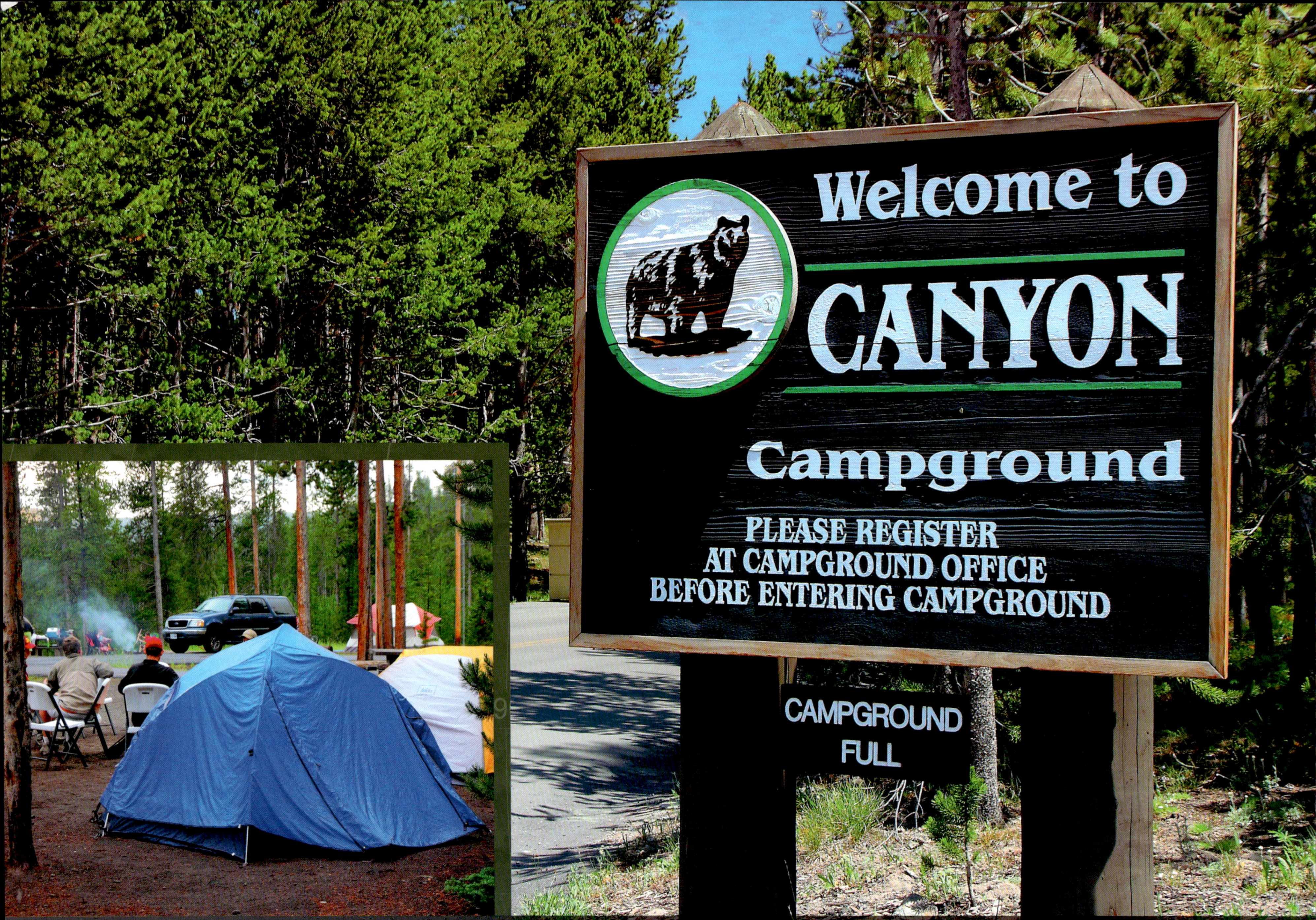

Campgrounds continue to be a visitor favorite in Yellowstone. There are twelve campgrounds with over 2,000 campsites as well as approximately three hundred backcountry sites located throughout the park. Seven of the campgrounds — Indian Creek, Lewis Lake, Mammoth, Norris, Pebble Creek, Slough Creek, and Tower Fall — are managed by the National Park Service with availability on a first-come, first-served basis. The remaining five campgrounds, Fishing Bridge RV Park, plus Bridge Bay, Canyon, Grant Village, and Madison are operated by the park concessionaire, Xanterra Parks & Resorts, and are available for same-day or advance reservations. The Mammoth Hot Springs campground is open in the winter and attracts numerous campers as shown, inset, at Madison Campground.

WILDLIFE

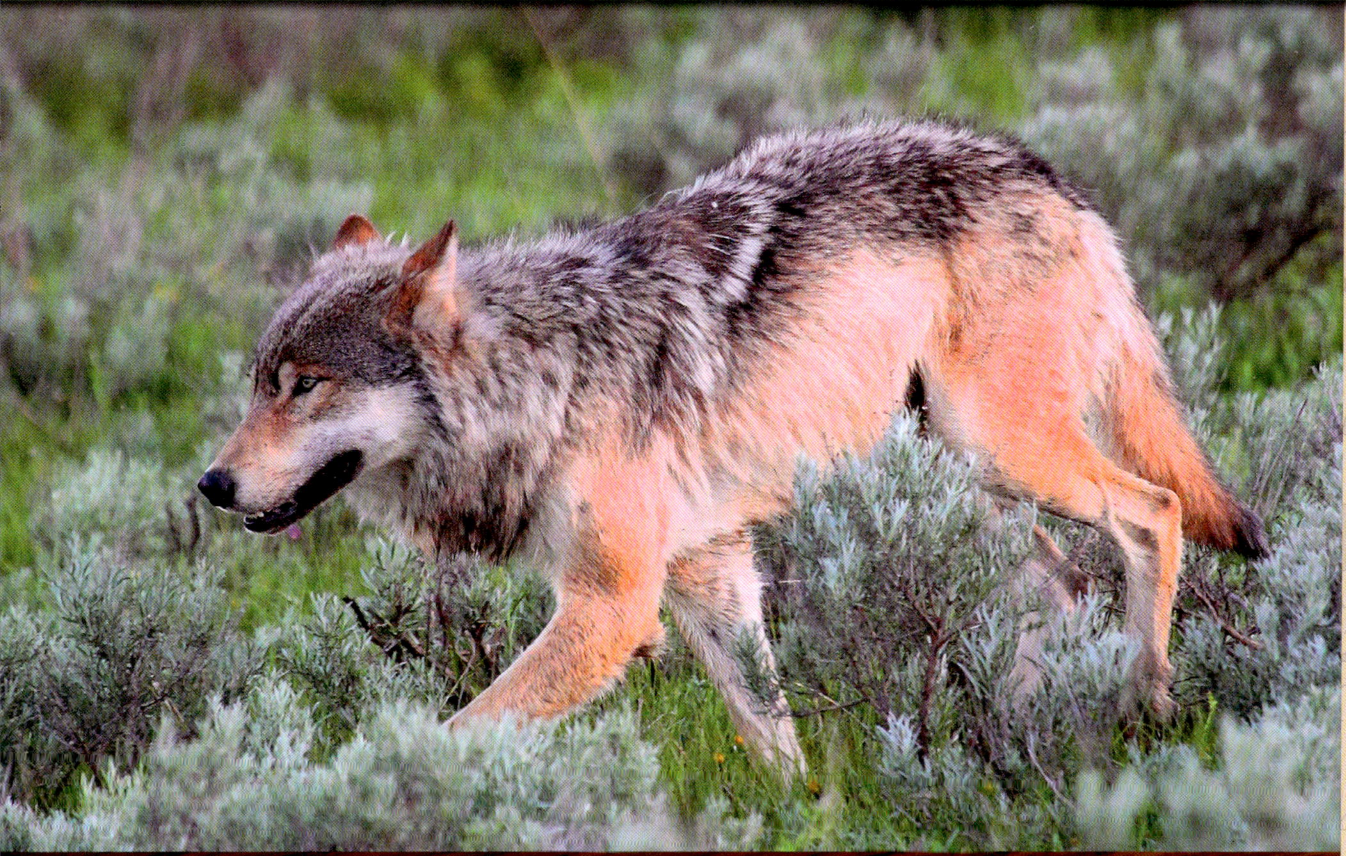

The gray wolf has been making a comeback since its controversial reintroduction in 1995 to restore balance of the park's ecosystem after a nearly seventy year absence. During the 1920s and '30s, wolves had been eliminated from Yellowstone by hunters hired by the federal government at the urging of neighboring ranchers to protect their cattle. By 1973 the wolf was listed on the Endangered Species Act. With a release of thirty-one wolves from Canada in 1995 and 1996, the wolf population increased to more than three hundred in the greater Yellowstone area, but has since declined to an estimated one hundred. Wolves prey mostly on elk, but are also known to hunt deer, moose, bison, and other animals. The best place to see them is the area between Lamar Valley and Tower Junction and in the Hayden Valley, as pictured.

In addition to scenic wonders, Yellowstone is the showplace of North American wildlife. Large mammals, such as the grizzly bear, black bear, wolf, coyote, red fox, bison, elk, moose, bighorn sheep, pronghorn, mule deer, white-tailed deer, and non-native mountain goat, are routinely seen and photographed.

As home to the largest concentration of mammals in the lower forty-eight states, the protection of these inhabitants has prompted difficult decisions throughout the park's history. From the early days of prosecuting hunters and poachers to the more recent decisions regarding the reintroduction of wolves, management policies are developed to provide long-term benefits to park habitat.

BEARS

With more than sixty species of mammals in the park, visitors are cautioned to respect the park's wildlife by keeping a safe distance and to be aware of the dangers. Instances of attacks by grizzly and black bears, while infrequent, are well documented. Park regulations require people to keep a distance of at least one hundred yards away from bears and at least twenty-five yards from other wildlife. The park's literature suggests viewing large animals from a car or from roadsides. Wildlife viewing guides are available at the park's visitor centers. The best time to see wildlife is in the early morning or evening.

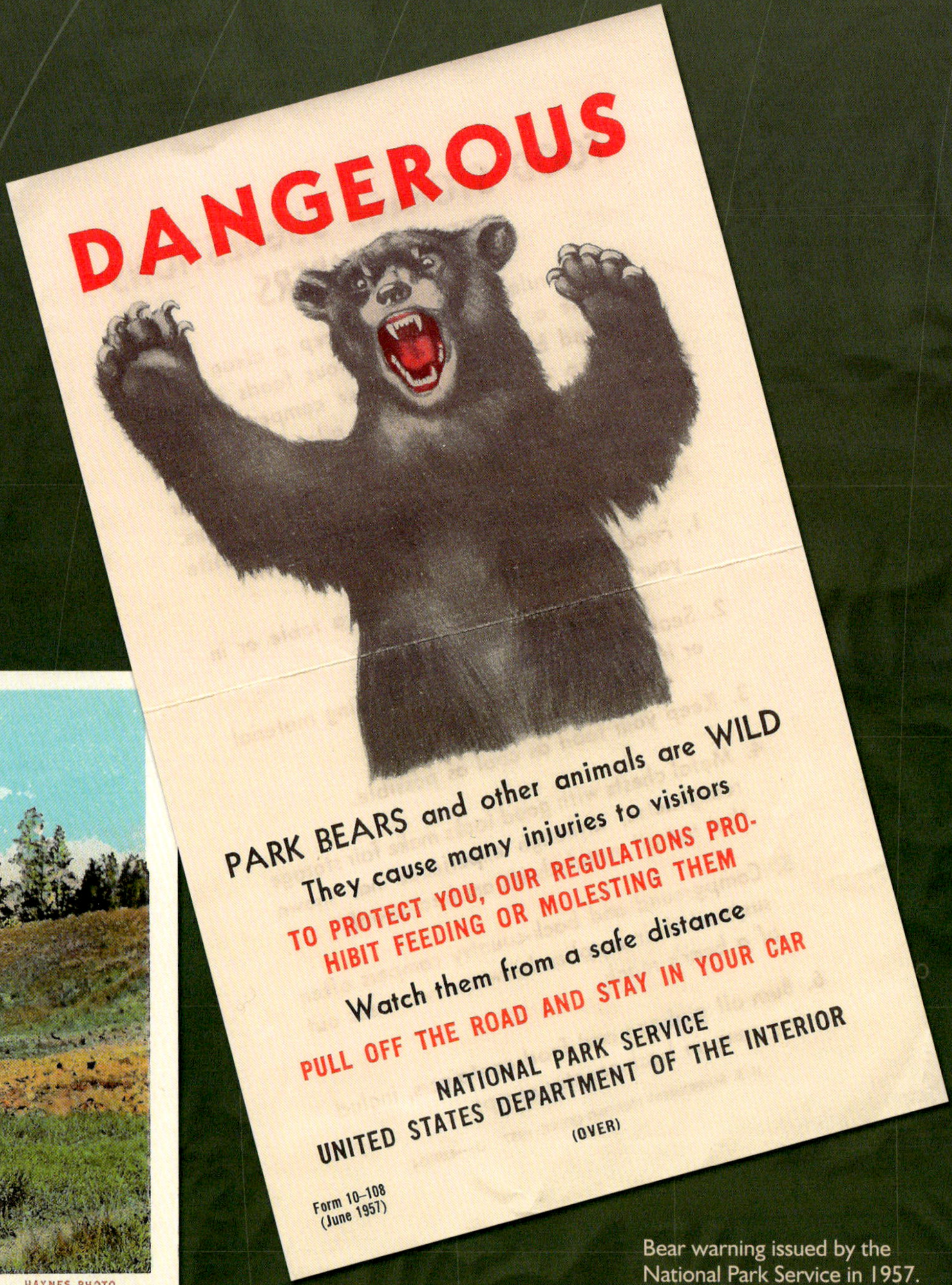

Bear warning issued by the National Park Service in 1957.

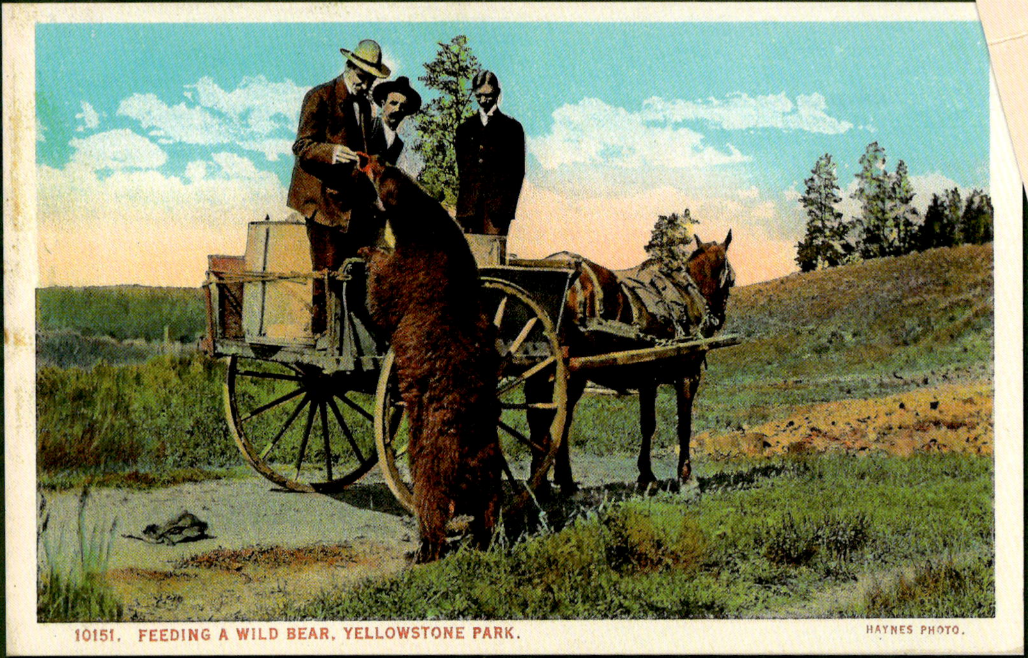

In the early days of Yellowstone Park, unlike today's policies, bears were encouraged to visit the hotels to eat the garbage left outside the kitchen doors. Guests viewed this practice as part of their evening entertainment. The back of this early postcard reads, "Guests derive great enjoyment from watching the antics of the bears." Postcard published by J. E. Haynes, St. Paul, Minnesota.

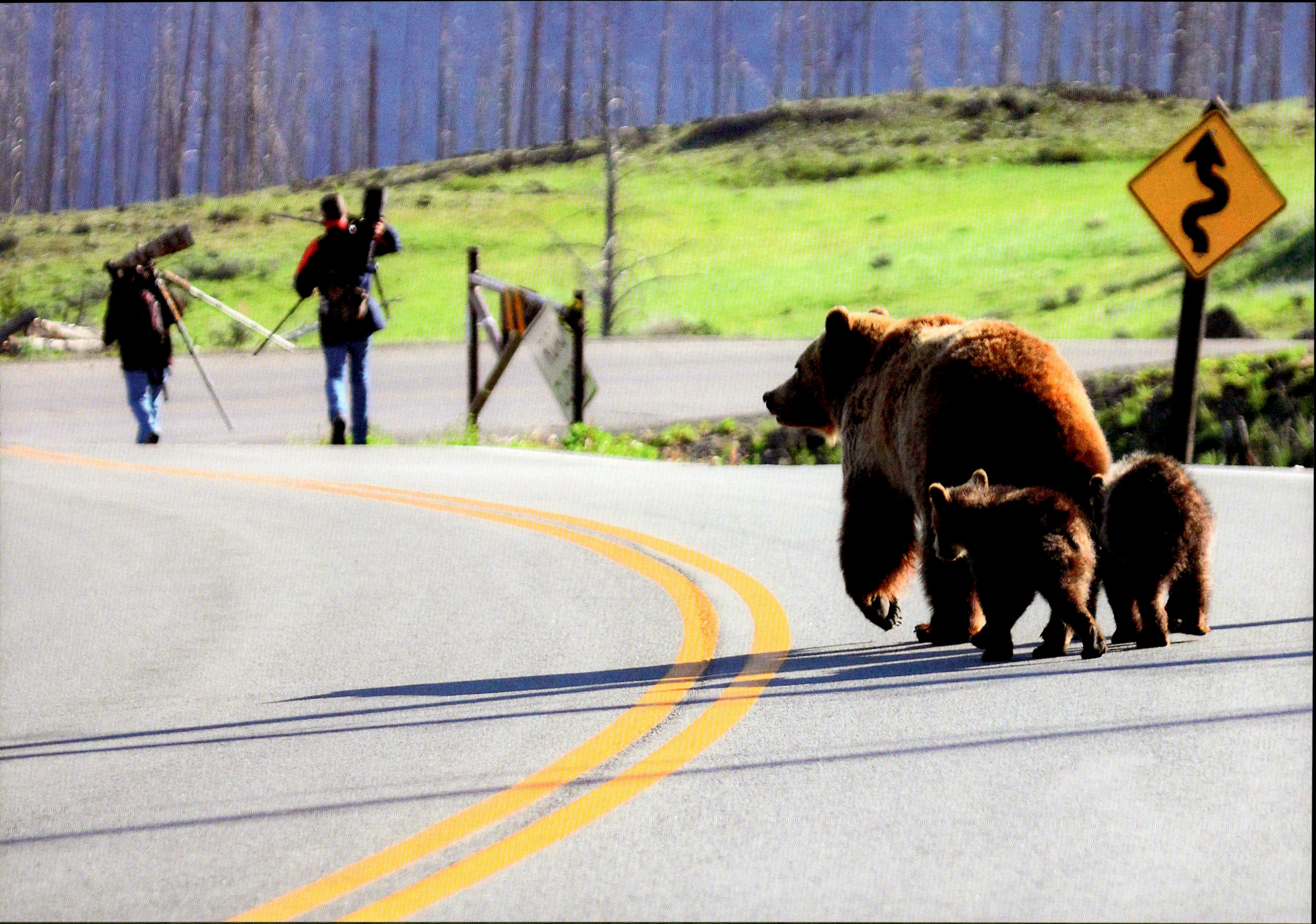

Photographers scramble to clear the area as this grizzly bear family commands the right of way while taking a stroll across the road during a recent summer outing. Park policies have changed dramatically since the days when bears were portrayed as cartoon-like characters looking for a handout.

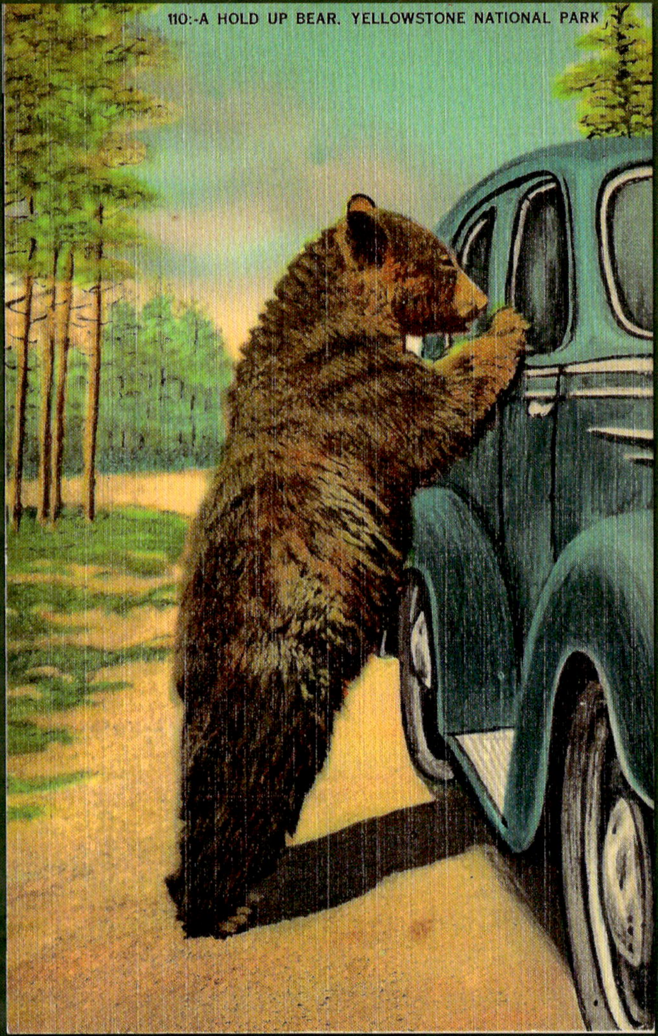

Even after the hotels stopped the practice of leaving garbage outside for the bears in 1941, visitors continued to feed them from their cars as pictured on this linen postcard. The park has since adopted strict regulations prohibiting the feeding of wildlife and promotes the use of bear-proof containers for the storage of food. Postcard published by Johnston & Bordewyk, Inc. Rapid City, S.D., which offers an explanation for the "Hold Up" heading. "These bears are called 'Hold Up' bears because they will stand on a car in anticipation of getting some food."

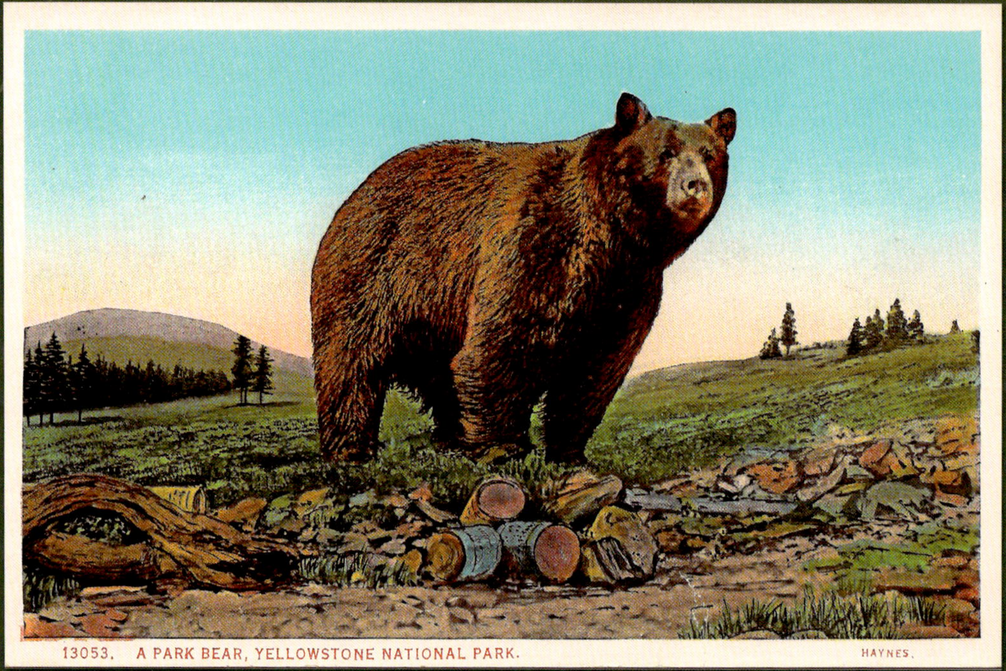

This early postcard of a park bear, published by Haynes Picture Shops, Inc., identifies the animal as a "brown bear which differs from the black bear in color only. Color is not a reliable way to distinguish between a grizzly bear and a black bear." Grizzly bears are best identified by the pronounced hump on their shoulders and a longer snout than black bears.

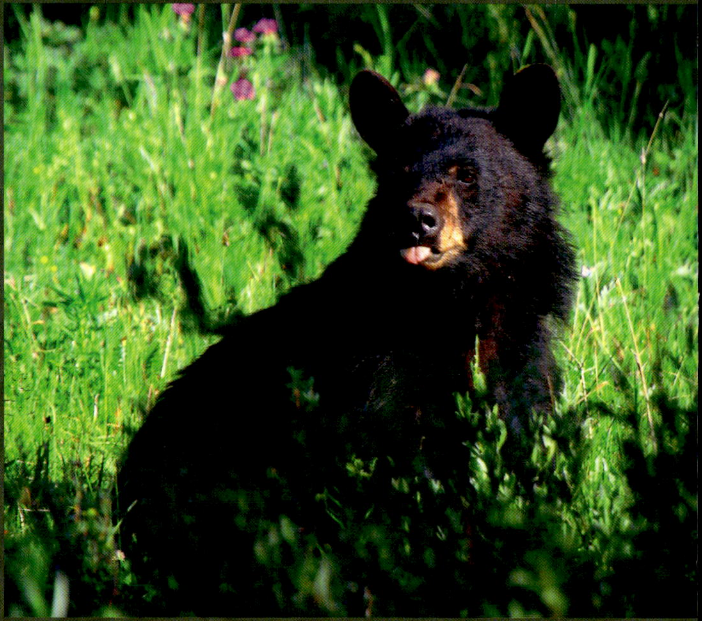

Black bears are a favorite among the park's photographers.

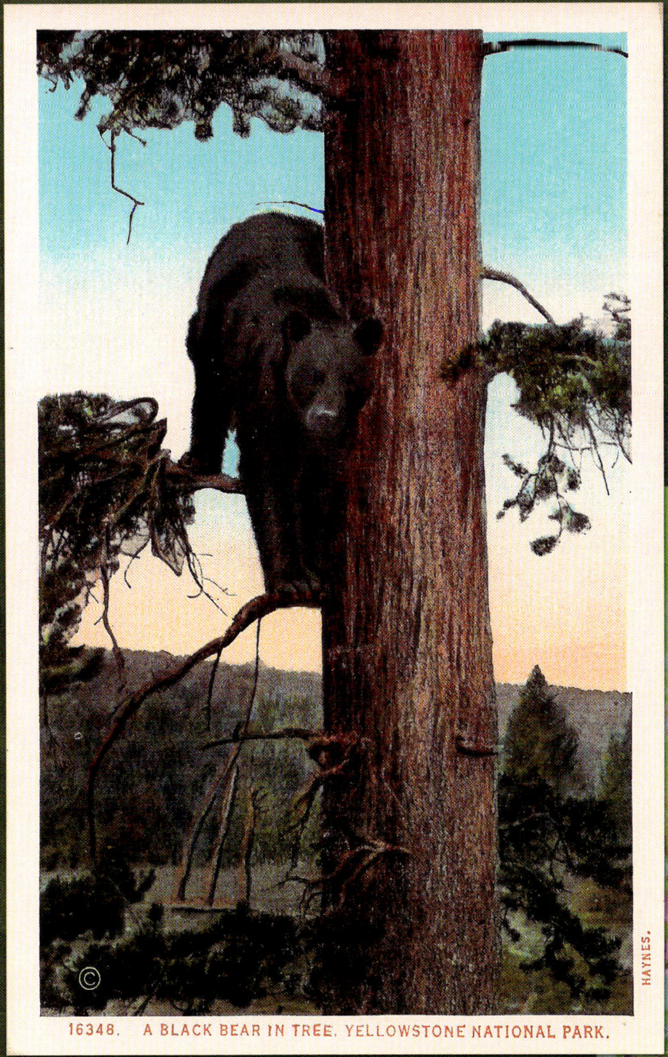

This postcard describes how black bears, unlike grizzlies, climb trees with great agility, often sleeping on slender limbs that barely support them. Postcard by Haynes Picture Shops, Inc.

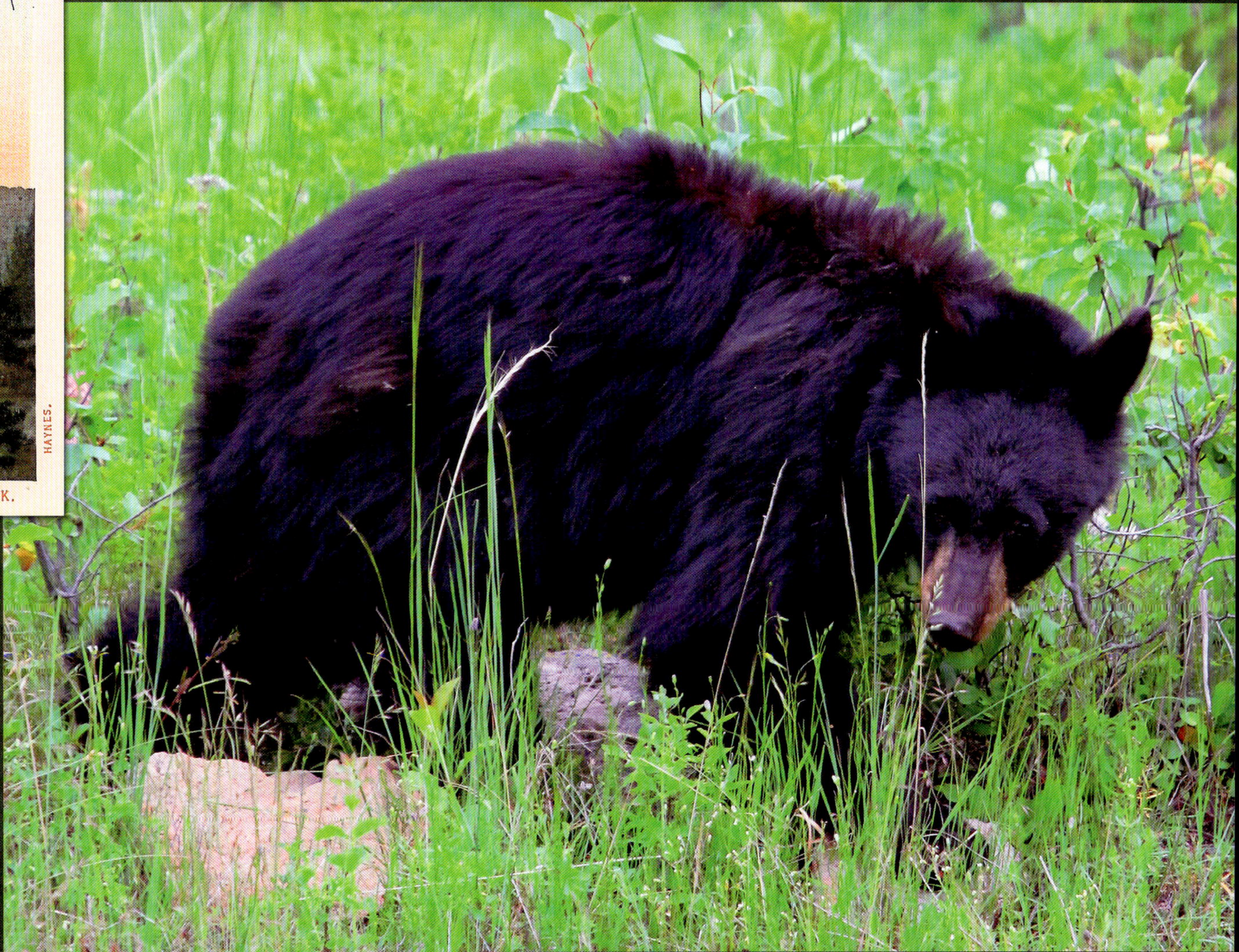

Black bears can be found along the edges of trees near Tower Junction. This black bear is among the estimated 500 to 650 bears living in the park. It was photographed from the roadside near Tower Junction.

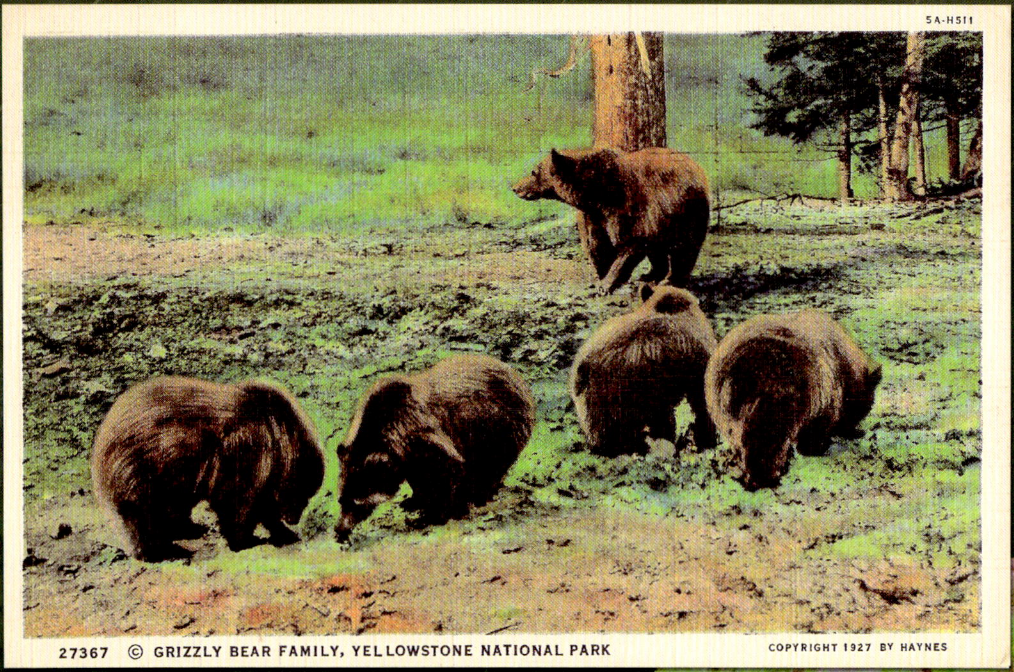

This postcard of a grizzly bear family was mailed in 1938 where the sender writes, "We saw 15-20 bears in one group tonight. One mamma bear had four cubs — a rare occurrence." Haynes Picture Shops postcard.

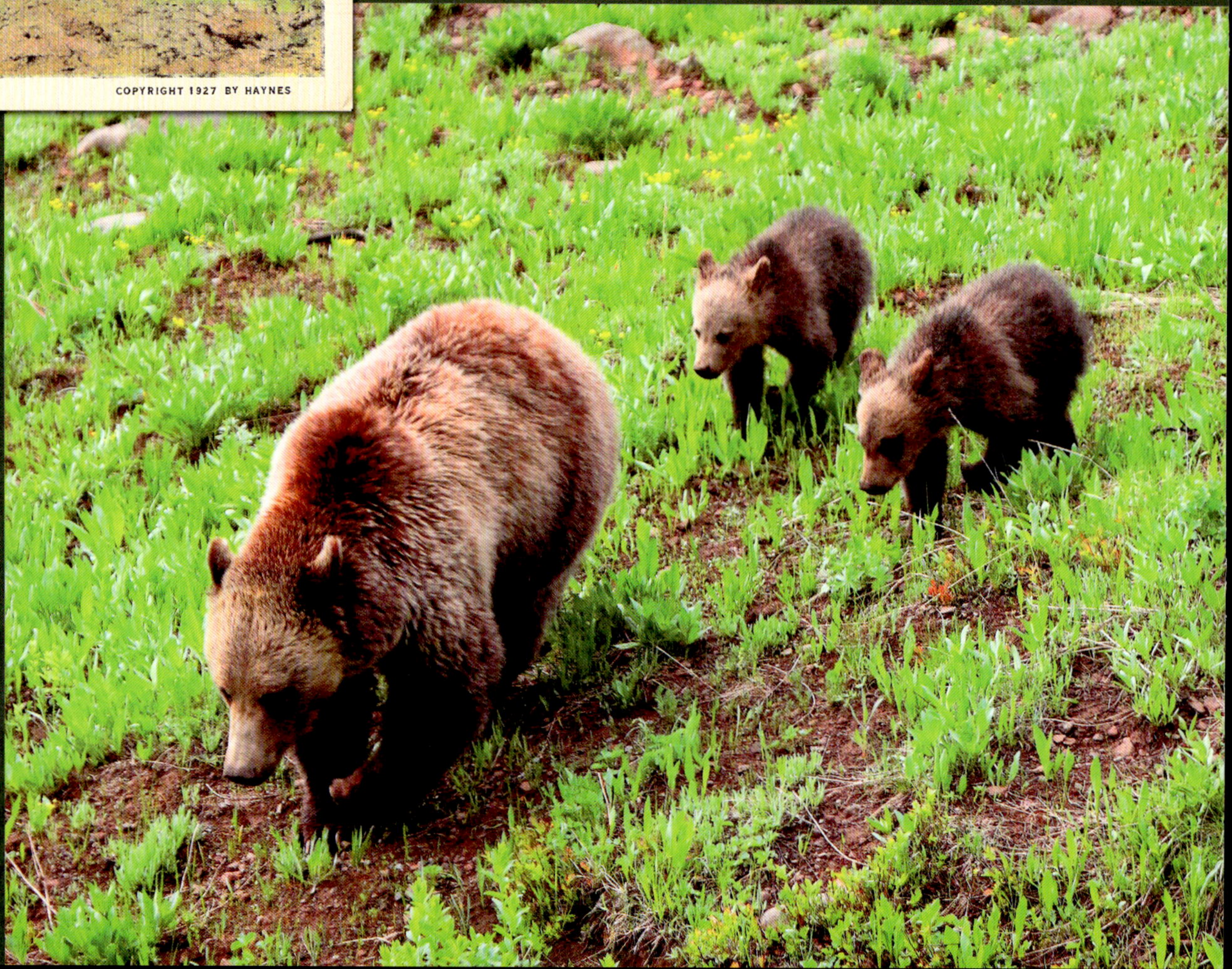

Around six hundred grizzly bears are thought to inhabit the park and surrounding area, according to recent estimates, although some biologists believe this may be a conservative count. They are regularly spotted from March through November in the area around Lamar Valley, Dunraven Pass, and Hayden Valley. This sow and her cubs were photographed near Dunraven Pass.

BISON

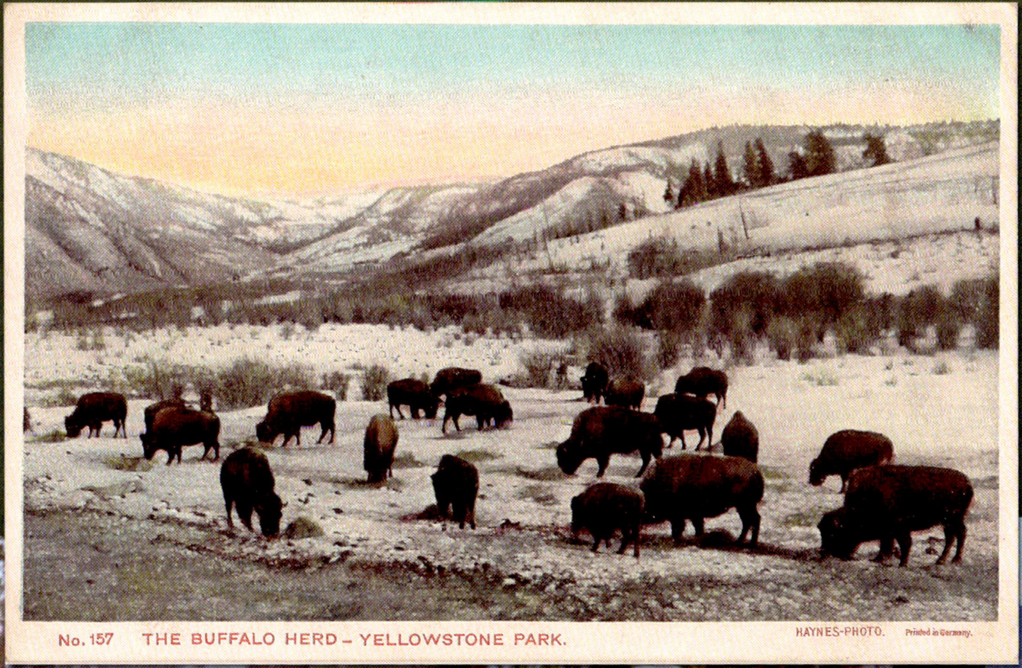

The majestic bison has been used as an iconic symbol to promote the park and its rugged landscape since Yellowstone's founding. Once on the verge of extinction because of hunting and poaching, great care has been taken by park managers to preserve what was once a small herd of fewer than fifty bison in the early 1900s to what is now the largest free-roaming herd in the country. This feat was achieved by importing nearly two dozen bison from ranches in Montana and Texas. They were placed in pens at Mammoth Hot Springs and raised like livestock. Eventually the transplanted bison were moved to Lamar Valley and in 1936 they were turned loose in the park. Today, efforts to manage bison present numerous challenges, including practices to keep cattle and bison separated across political and social boundaries. Haynes-Photo postcard printed in Germany.

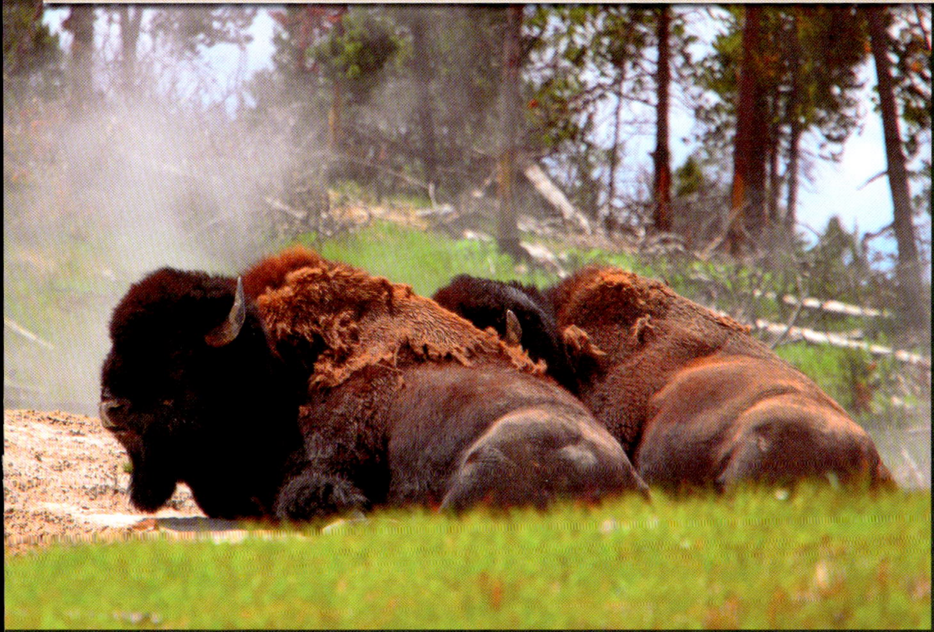

The bison is the largest land mammal in North America. Today, more than 3,000 bison roam the grasslands of the park. They can be seen almost everywhere, including thermal areas, roads, hotels, and meadows in the park. Despite their size, bison are agile and quick, and can reach speeds in excess of thirty miles per hour. Bulls are larger in size than cows and are more bearded. This photo was taken in Mud Volcano.

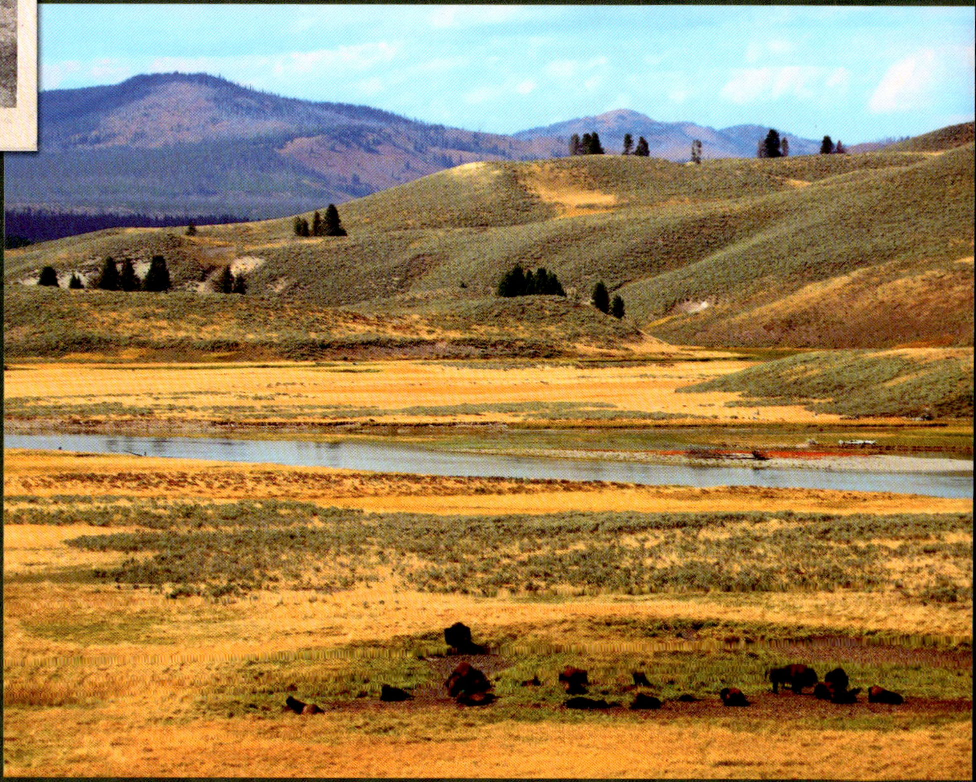

Large herds of bison are usually found in Hayden Valley, as pictured, and Lamar Valley.

ELK

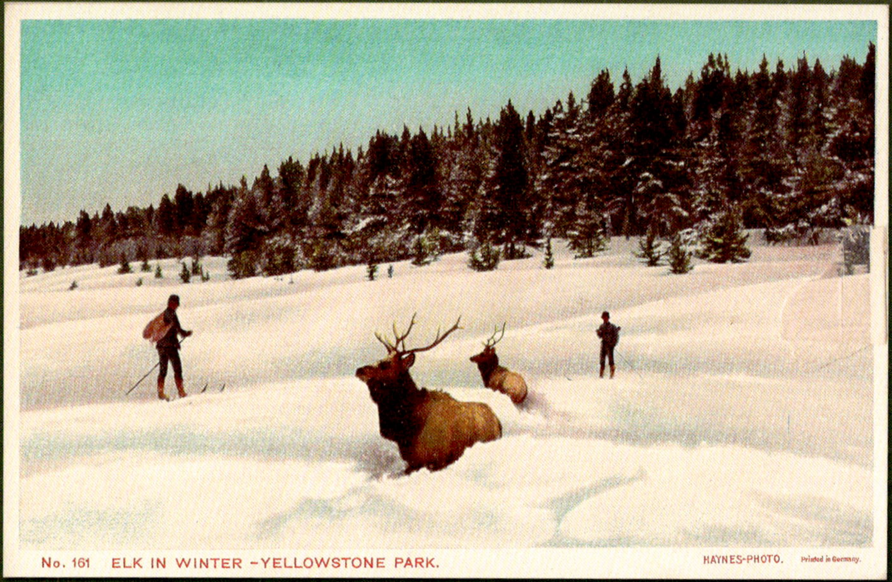

Elk are the most abundant of the large mammals in the park, with estimates up to 30,000 before the reintroduction of wolves in 1995. Prior to reintroduction, park management of elk herds extended from direct reintroduction through capture and slaughter to the hands-off approach of natural regulation. The elk use most of the park for their summer range and, in winter, remaining herds move to lower elevations, where there is less snowfall and temperatures are more moderate. Haynes-Photo postcard printed in Germany, postmarked 1922.

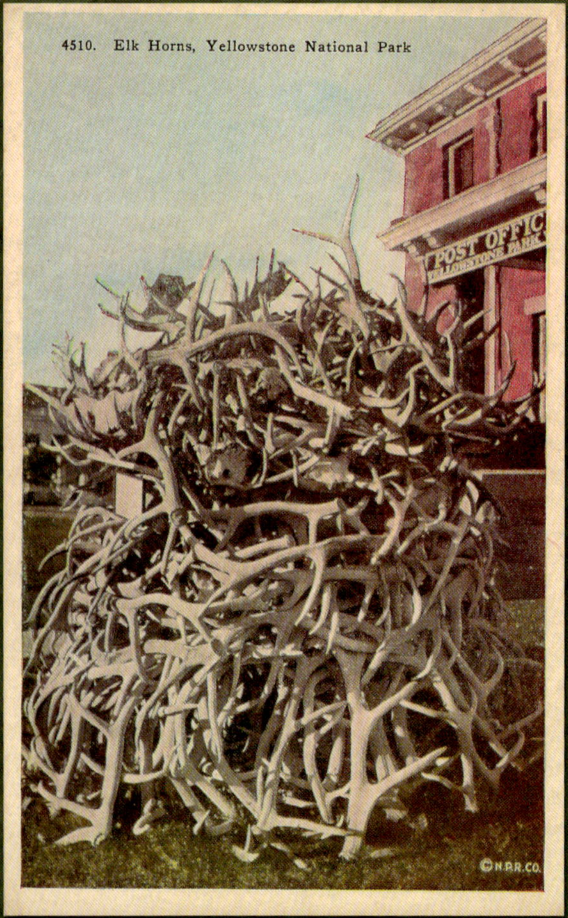

This early HHT Co. postcard showing elk, deer, and moose antlers at Mammoth Hot Springs was published for the Northern Pacific Railway Company.

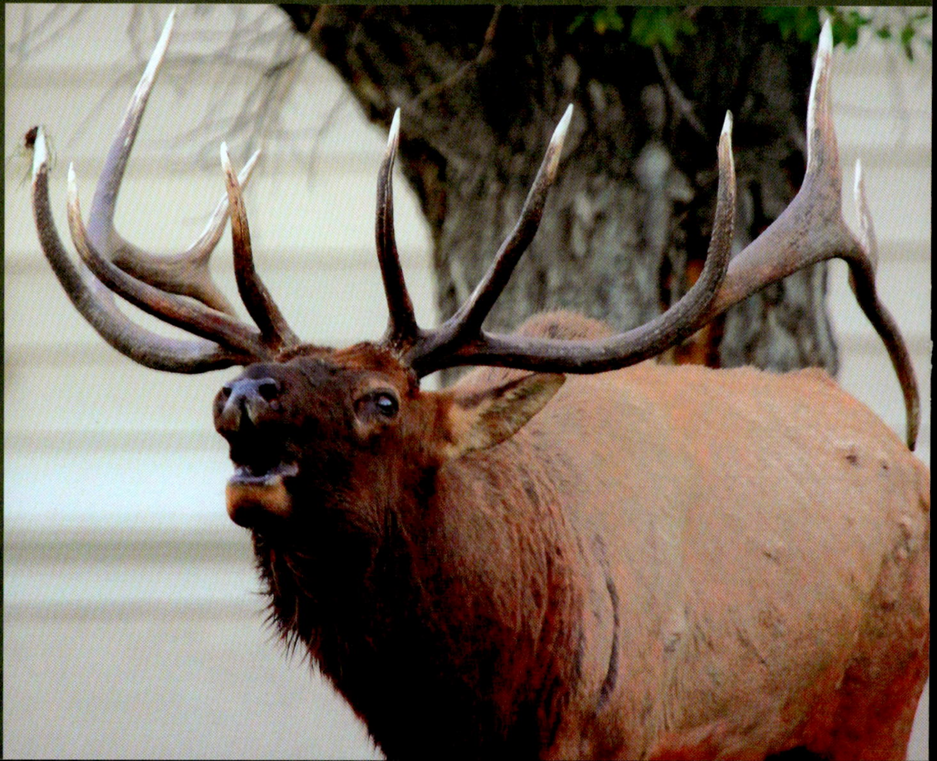

An impressive array of sights and sounds, known as bugling, take place in the fall during mating season when the bull elk clash with one another for domination of the cows. Calves are born in late May and early June. This photo was taken in Mammoth Hot Springs.

DEER

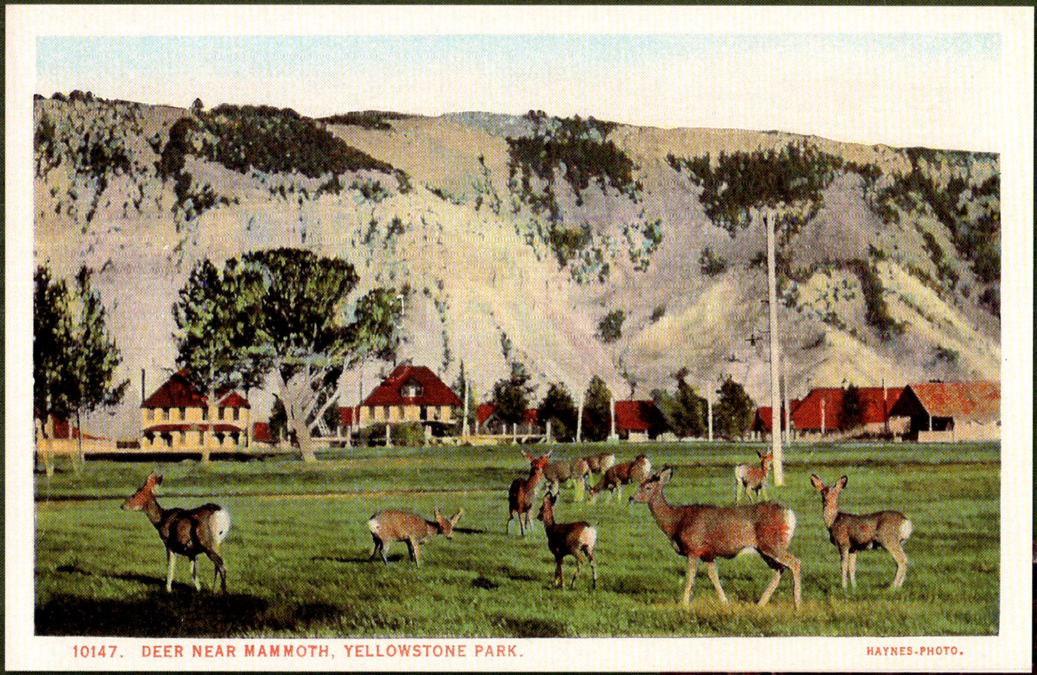

Like the elk and bison, the park provides a sanctuary for deer which were overhunted in the mid-nineteenth century before protections were added in the park. The deer population is estimated at about 2,500 today. This early postcard shows mule deer feeding near Mammoth and Fort Yellowstone. Mule deer are so-named for their large mule-like ears. They can be found throughout the park, especially along the Madison River and in the Mammoth Hot Springs area, as well as the Blacktail area between Mammoth and Tower Junction. Postcard published by J. E. Haynes.

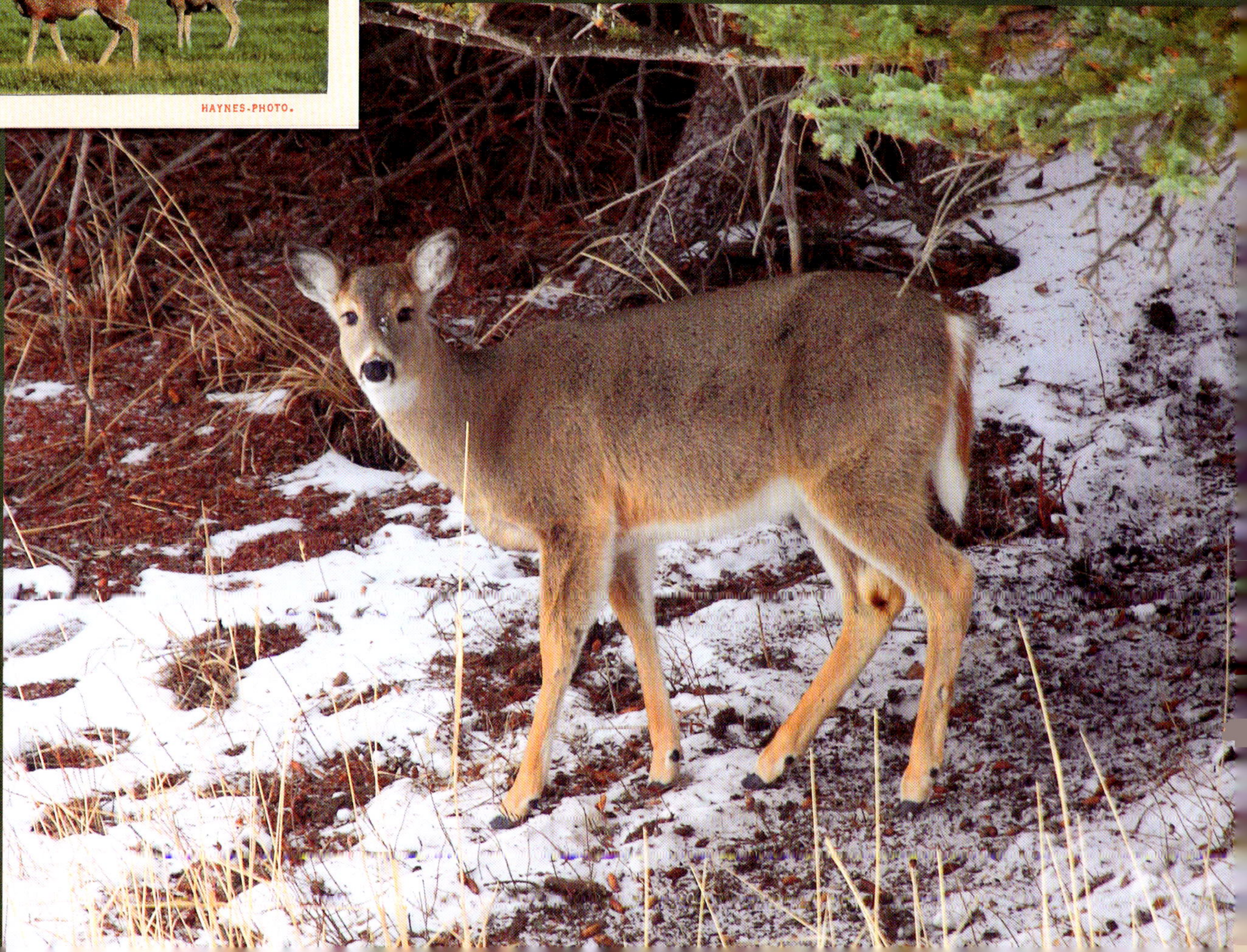

The park is also inhabited by white-tailed deer, although they are not as abundant as the mule deer. This photo was taken on a wildlife tour during the winter.

PRONGHORN

Postcard showing pronghorn, or antelope, near the Roosevelt Arch at the North Entrance. The pronghorn can be distinguished by the white patches on their rump and underside. Haynes-Photo postcard printed in Germany.

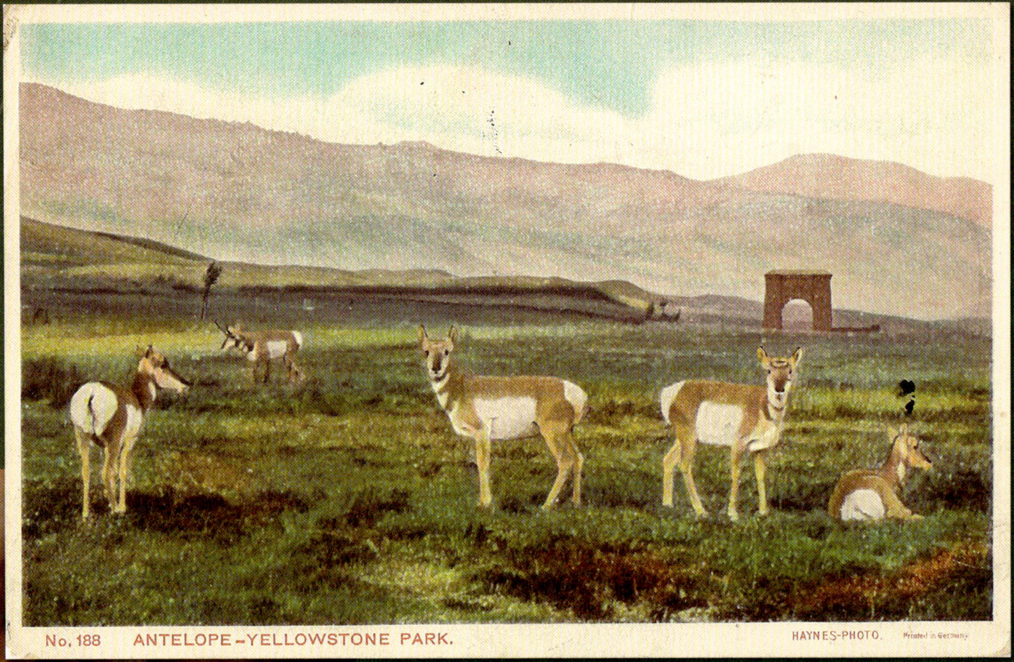

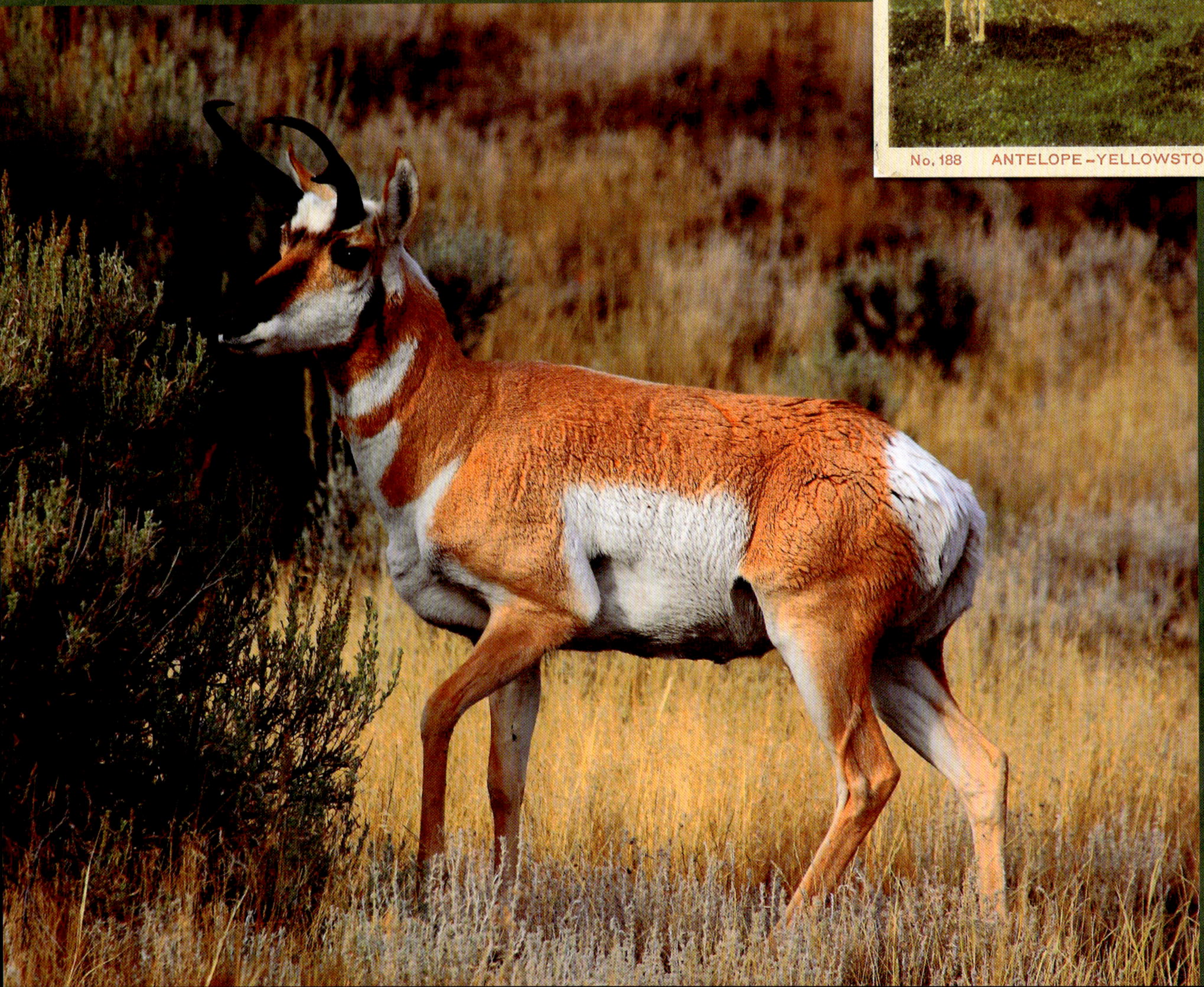

The pronghorn is the fastest land mammal in North America and is capable of reaching speeds of over fifty-five miles per hour. Equipped with keen eyesight, these two capabilities serve as its main defense against predators. They can still be found in the northern part of the park near Gardiner as well as the Lamar Valley area.

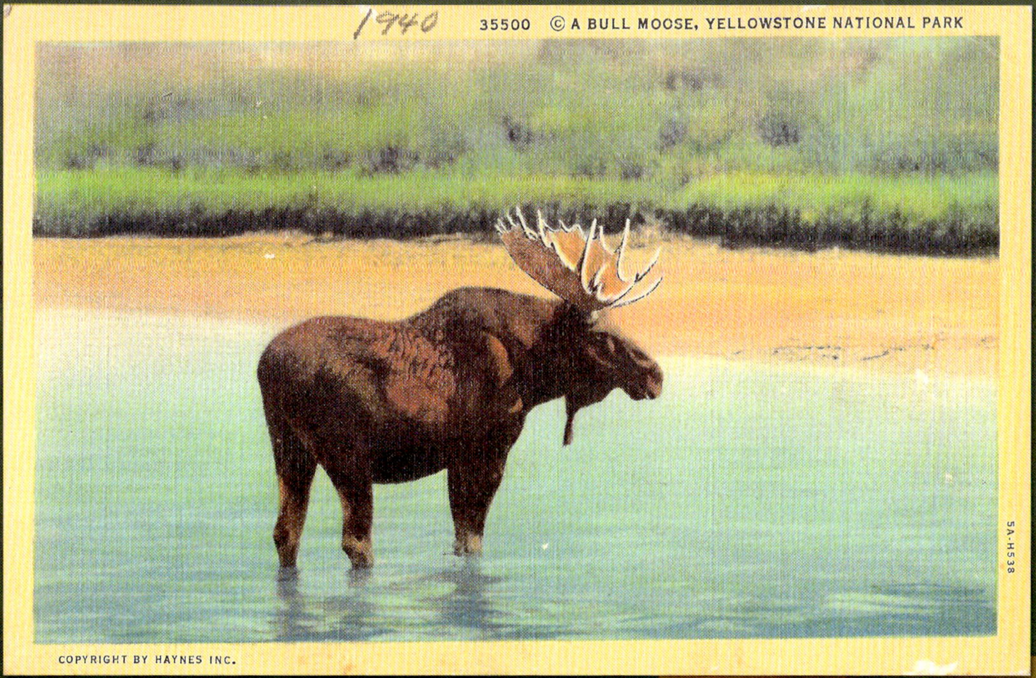

Moose can be found in several of the marshy areas of the park, including Yellowstone Lake. This linen postcard with a postmark from 1940 states that there were seven hundred moose in the park at that time. The message says, "We saw lots of these last night eating grass. We were too late to see any bears." Card by Haynes, Inc.

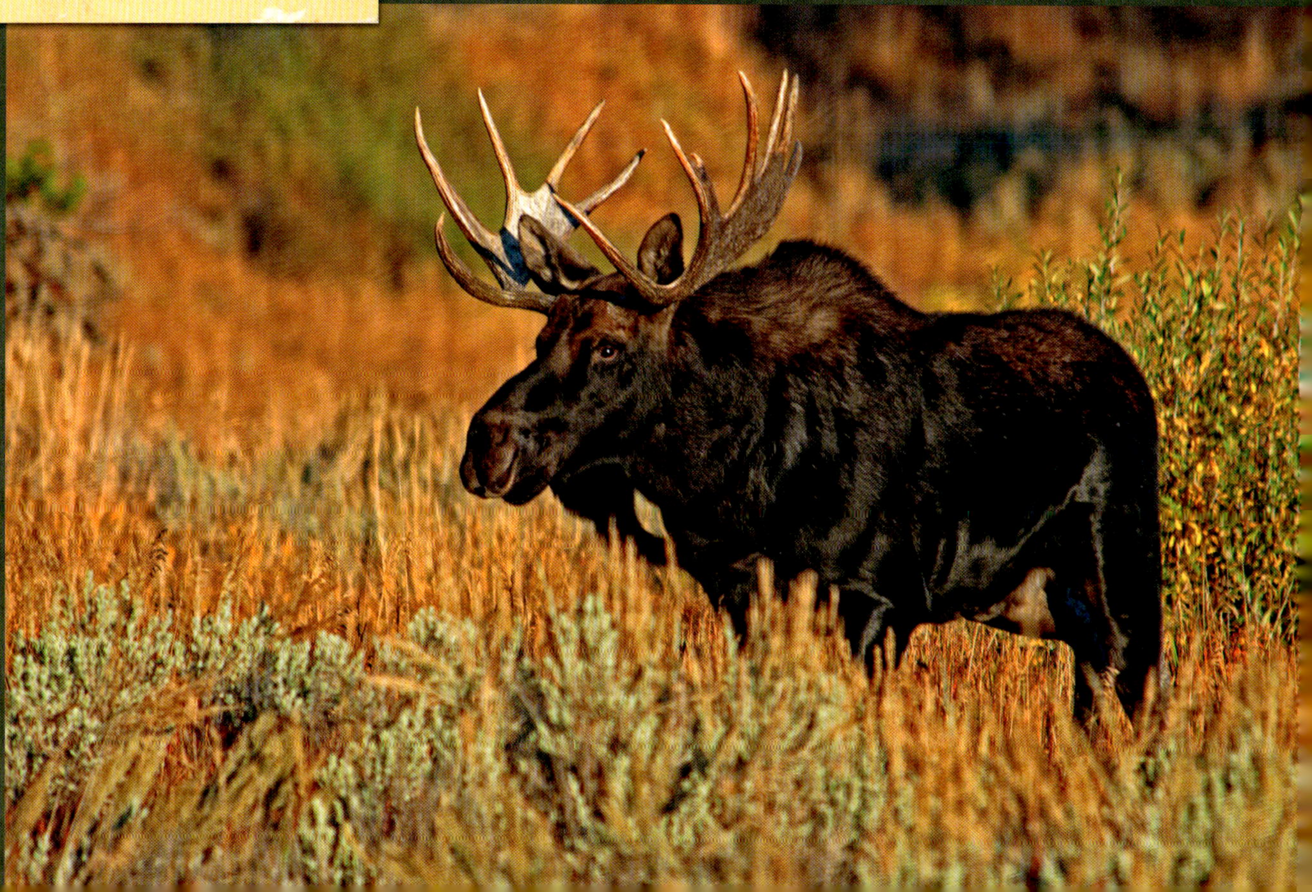

The moose population today is estimated at fewer than three hundred in the park. While fires in 1988 destroyed some of their prime habitat, moose can be found in the park's southwestern corner along the Bechler and Falls rivers, in the riparian zones around Yellowstone Lake, from the Soda Butte Creek to Cooke City, Pelican Creek, Lewis River, and Gallatin River drainages, and from Mammoth Hot Springs to Tower Junction. This bull moose was seen near Tower Junction. *Courtesy Darlene Bushue.*

BIGHORN SHEEP

Bighorn sheep also make their home in Yellowstone. The name comes from the large, curved horns found on the males, or rams, as pictured on this linen postcard by Haynes Studios, Inc.

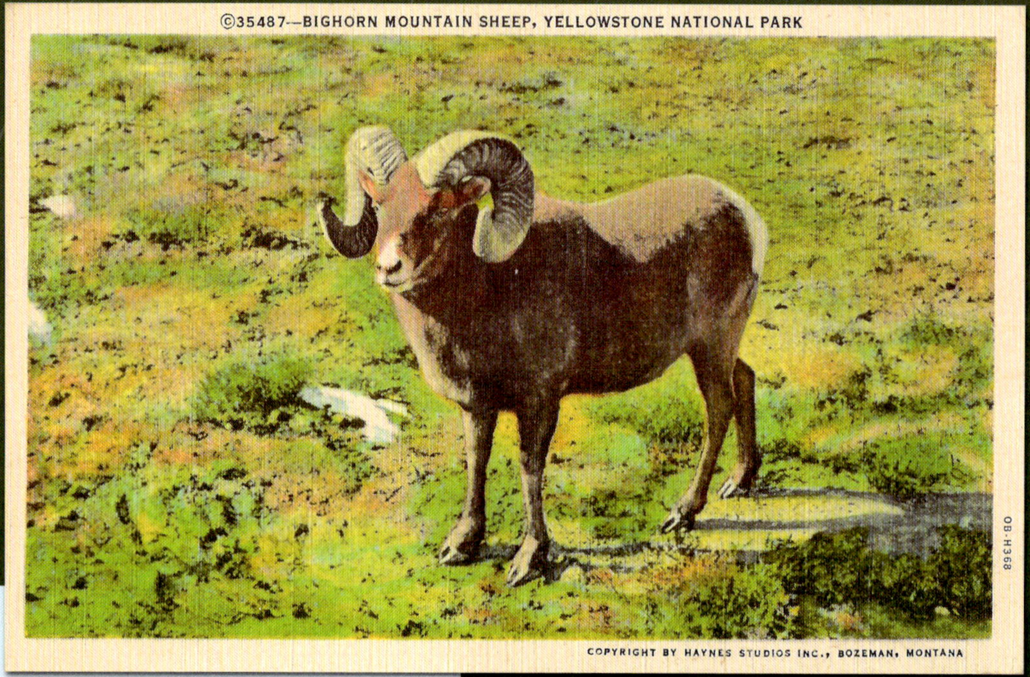

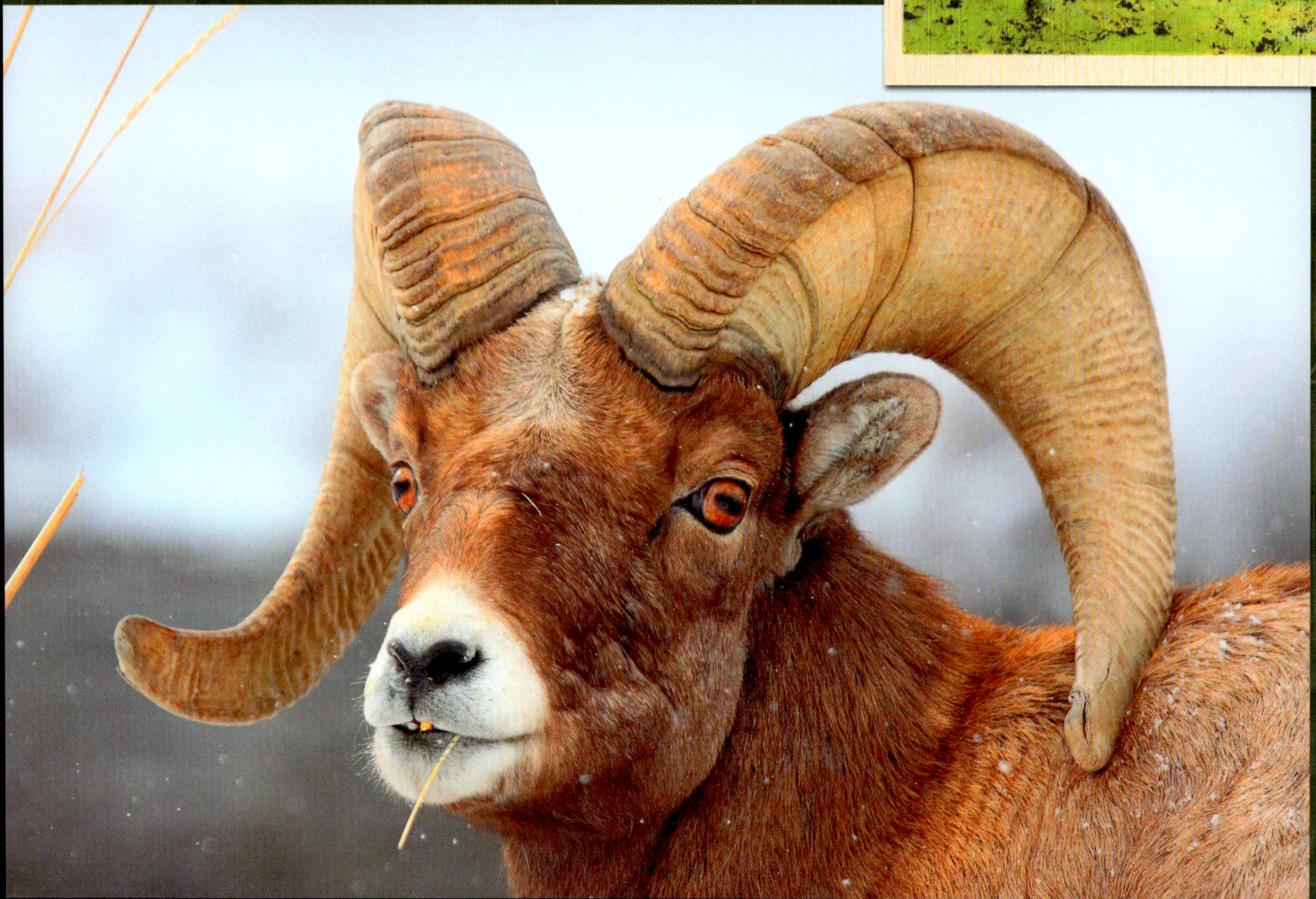

A close-up of a ram photographed along the road between the North Entrance and Mammoth Hot Springs. A ram's horns can weigh more than forty pounds. There are more than three hundred bighorn sheep in the park. Favorite winter viewing areas for bighorn sheep are the cliffs between Gardiner and Mammoth, where the sheep can climb steep terrain to escape their predators. They are often sighted in Tower Junction and Lamar Valley as well.

OTHER MAMMALS

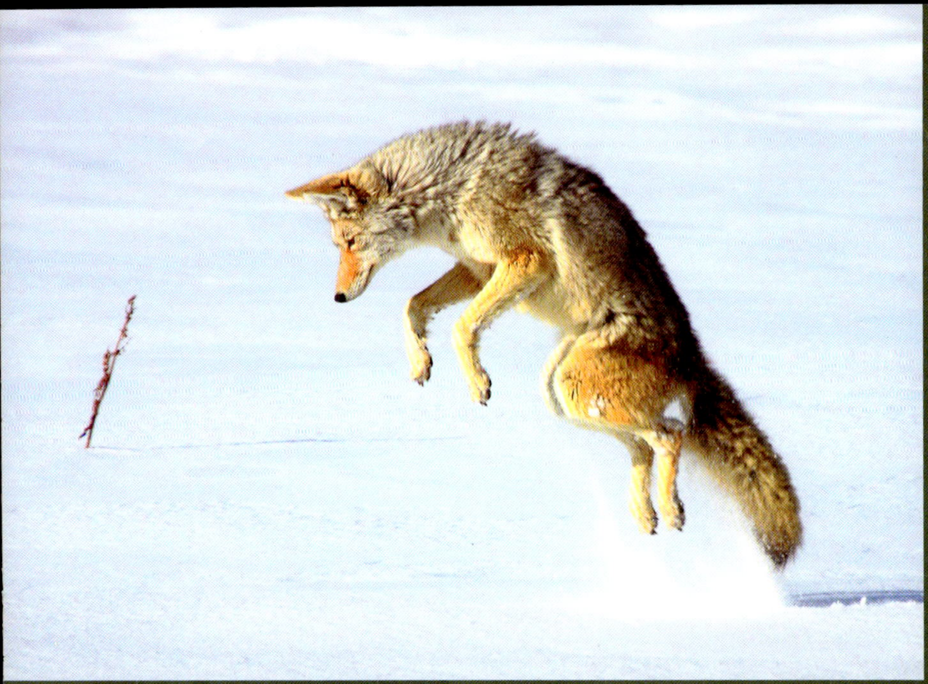

Coyotes can often be mistaken for wolves. While smaller in stature, their predatory behaviors are similar and are capable of killing large prey when they hunt in packs. One of the most studied packs is the Bison Peak Pack. When hunting alone, coyotes prefer voles, rodents, and squirrels. They are also scavengers of carcasses killed by wolves. This photo was taken around Gibbon Meadows on a snowcoach tour.

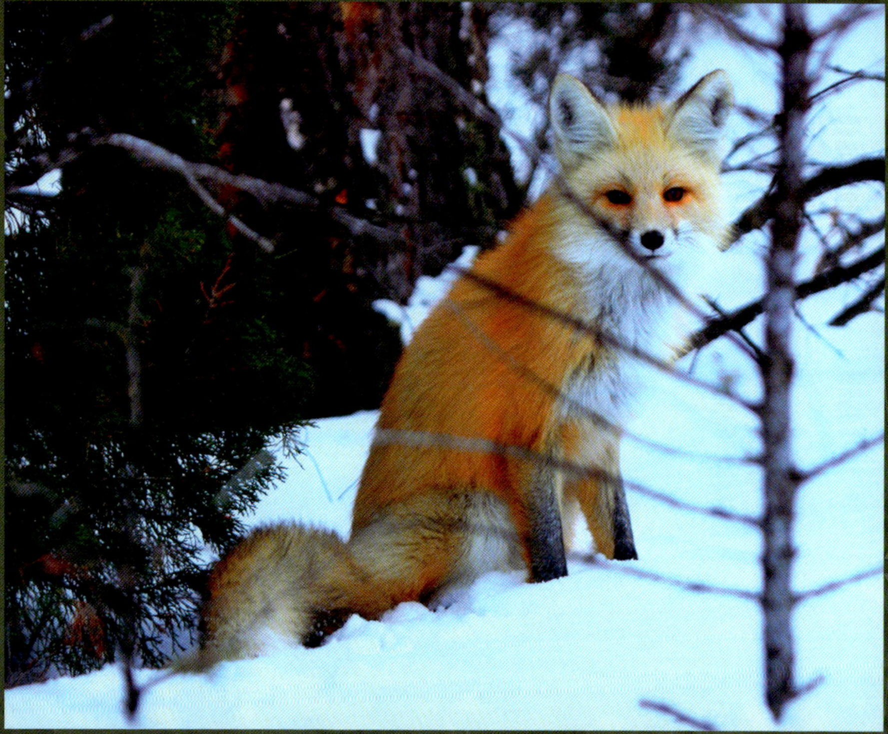

Smaller mammals inhabiting the park include the red fox, as pictured near Tower Junction in the winter, plus bobcats, badgers, martens, and weasels. The red fox is usually shy. The best time to spot a fox is early morning or evening.

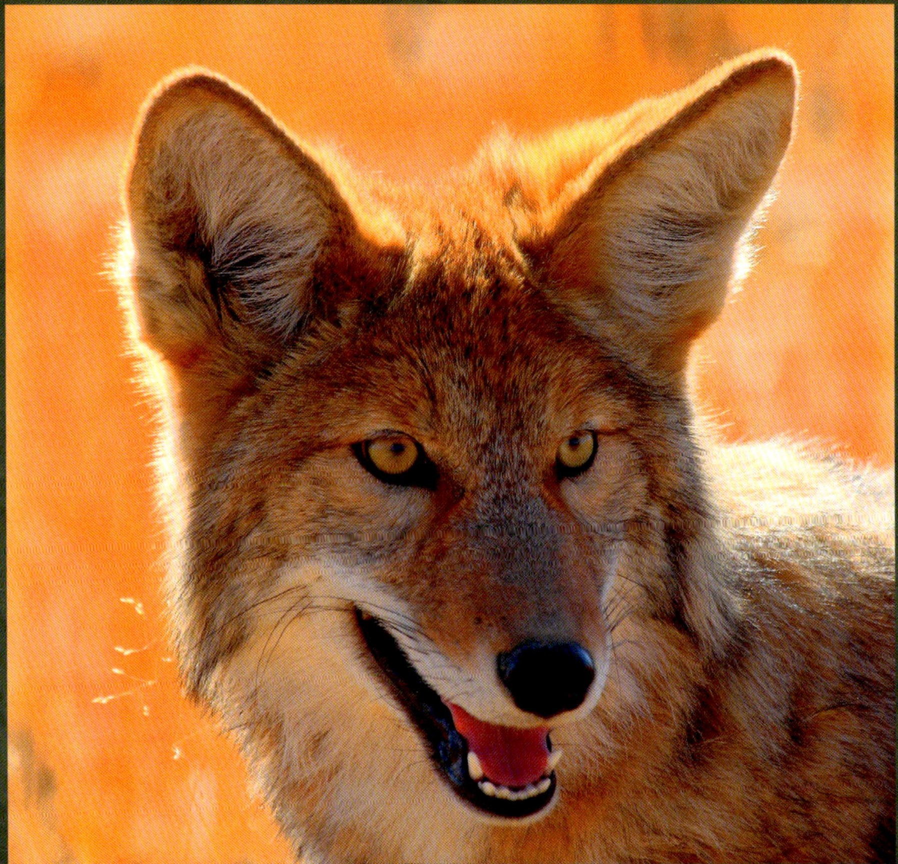

Different from a wolf, a coyote has larger ears and a more pointed nose. Since the return of wolves, coyotes are seen more frequently alongside the park's roads. This photo was taken in the Lower Geyser Basin.

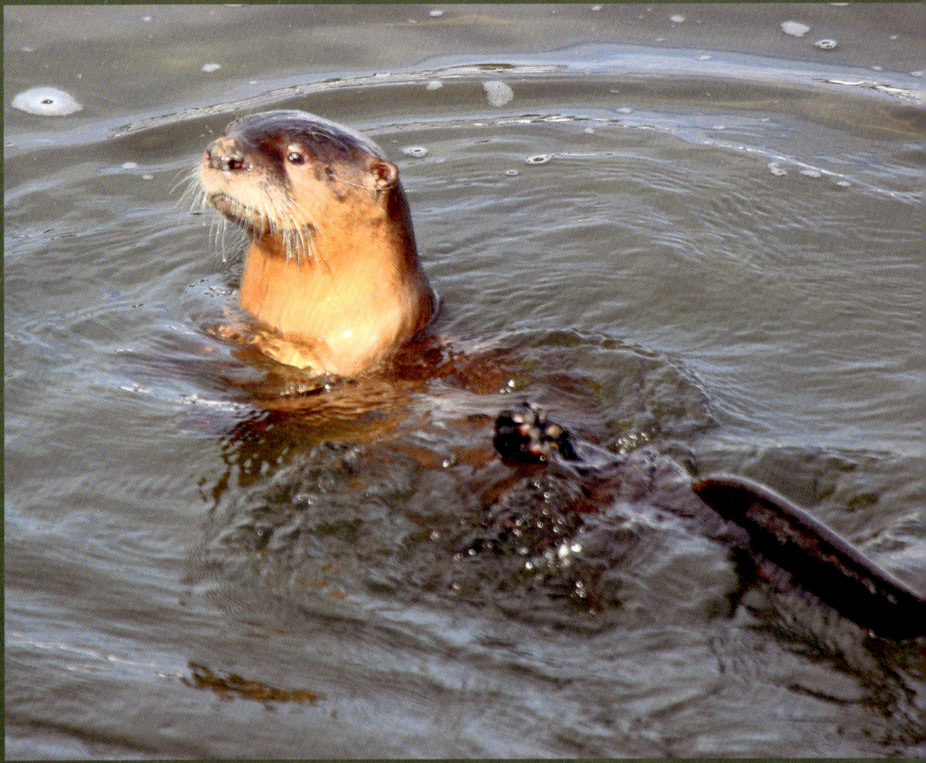

River otters can be found in Yellowstone River. They are skilled fish hunters. Eleven native fish species can be found in Yellowstone, including the cutthroat trout. Many streams are subject to a catch and release policy so as not to interfere with the food supply for other wildlife, including otters, bears, and pelicans. This photo was taken in the Yellowstone River in Hayden Valley.

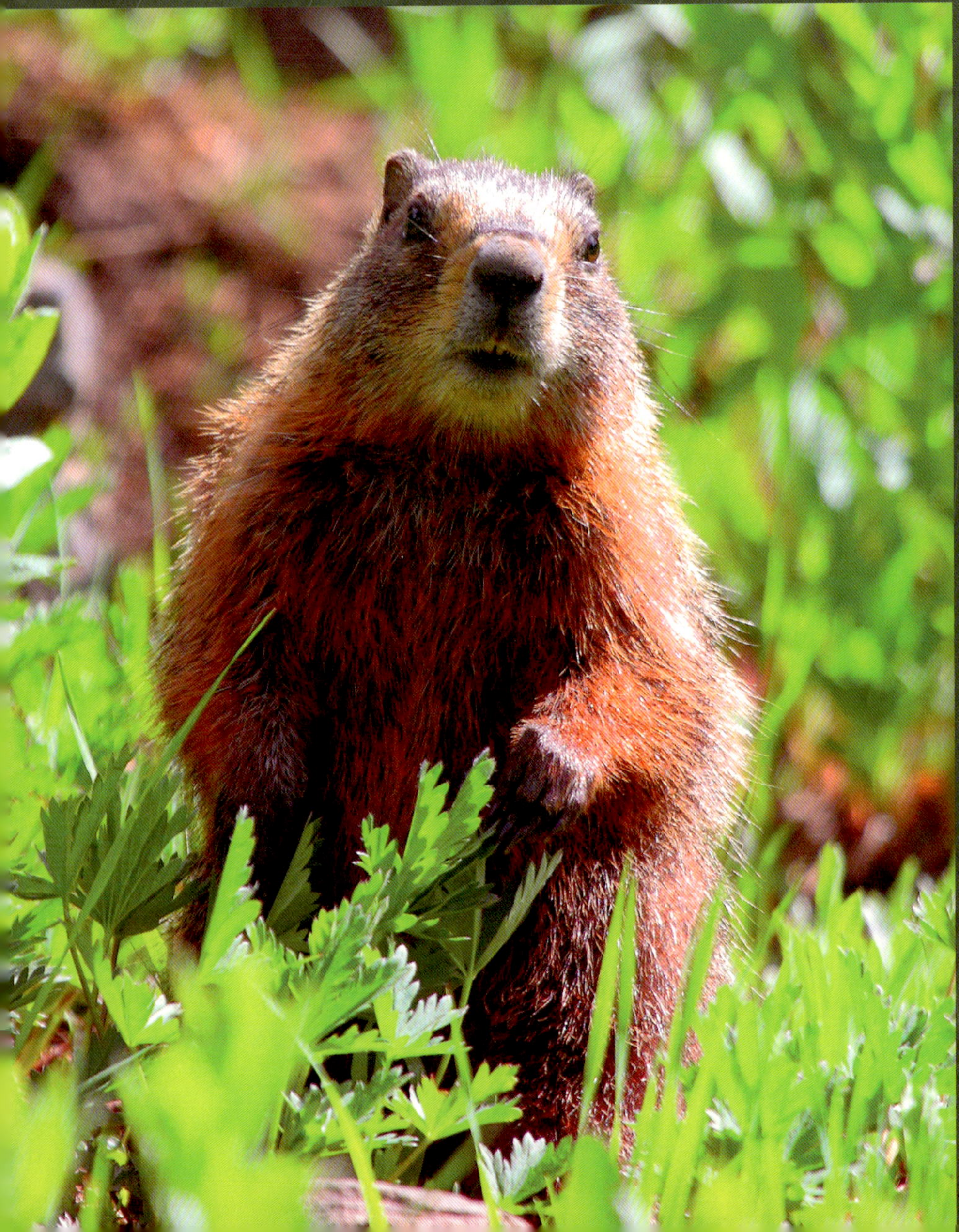

Other park inhabitants include yellow-bellied marmots, as pictured, plus squirrels, gophers, mice, and porcupines. A marmot is usually found in alpine or sub-alpine regions. They store as much fat as they can for winter hibernation. This photo was taken on the Mount Washburn Trail.

BIRDS

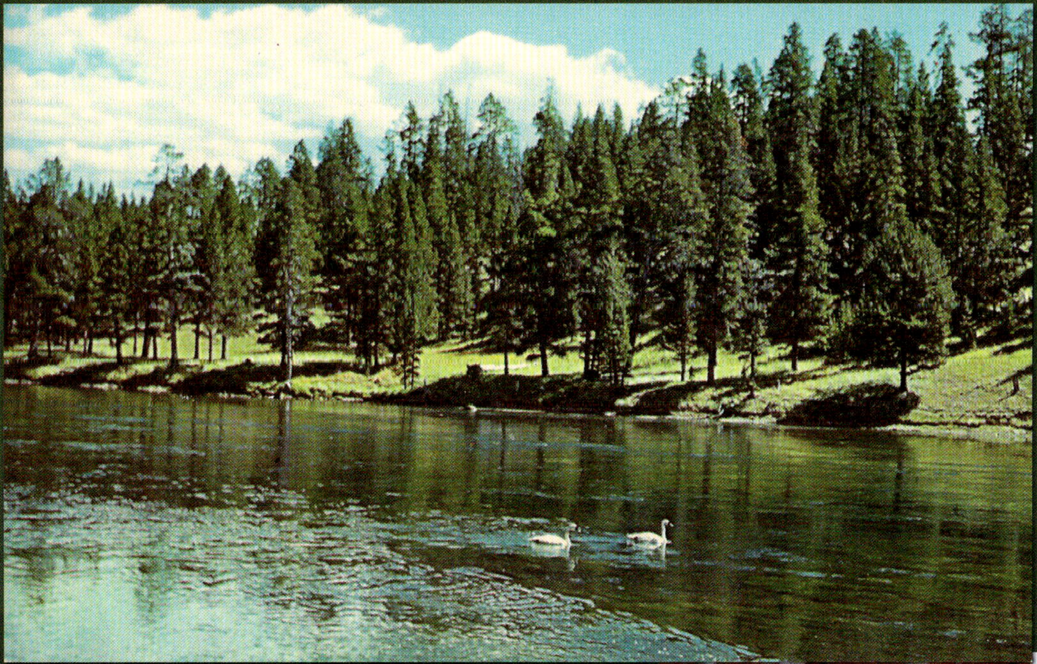

Yellowstone is a haven for bird watchers. Trumpeter swans on the Yellowstone River are featured on this vintage postcard. The description on the back tells how swans, pelicans, sea gulls, and other birds can be seen on the drive from Yellowstone Lake to the Grand Canyon, where the road parallels the river. The trumpeter swan is the largest waterfowl in North America and has become a favorite among visitors. Plastichrome postcard by Colourpicture, Boston, Mass.

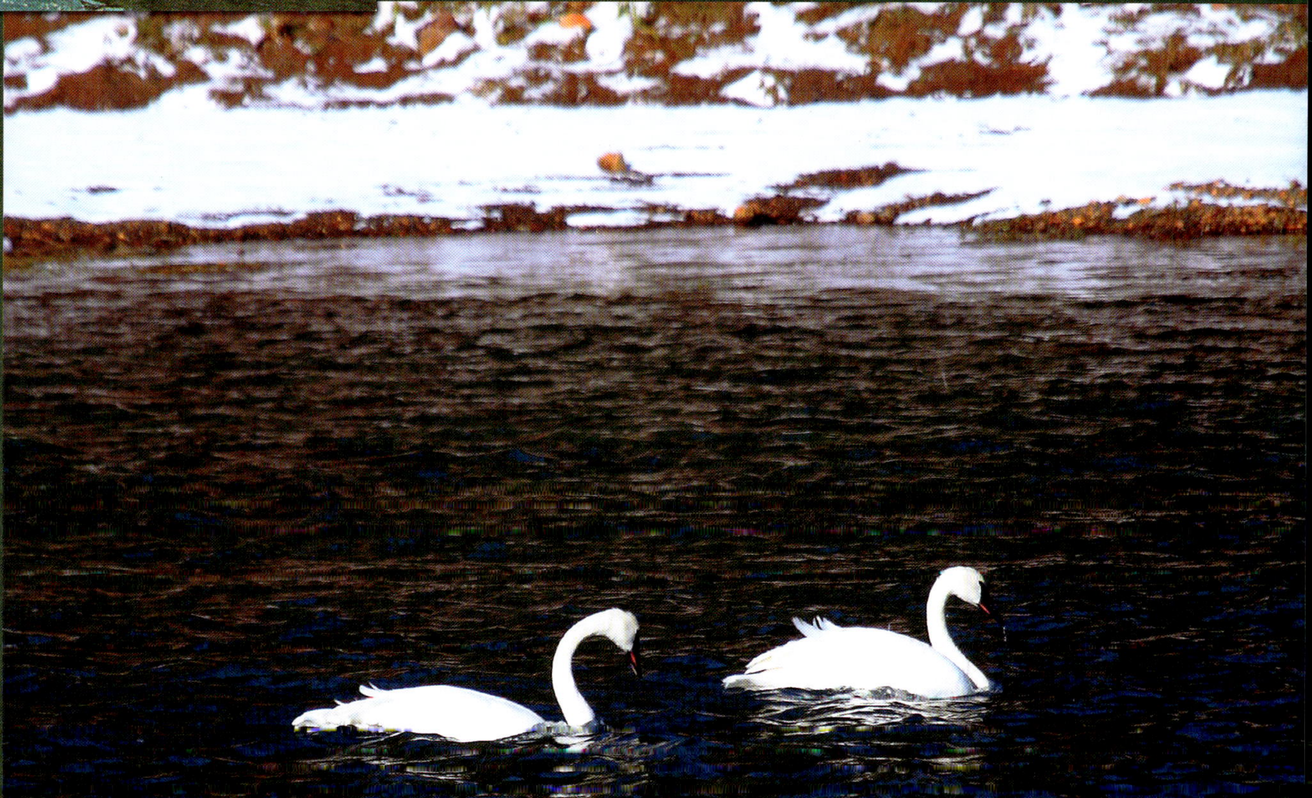

A flock of trumpeter swans has made its home in the park year-round while a migratory flock makes its home in Yellowstone during the winter. Trumpeter swans get their name from their trumpet-like call. They were near extinction in the early twentieth century due to game and plume hunting. The greater Yellowstone area was their last stronghold in the lower forty-eight states at that time and the population has improved due to tremendous conservation efforts. This photo shows swans on the Yellowstone River.

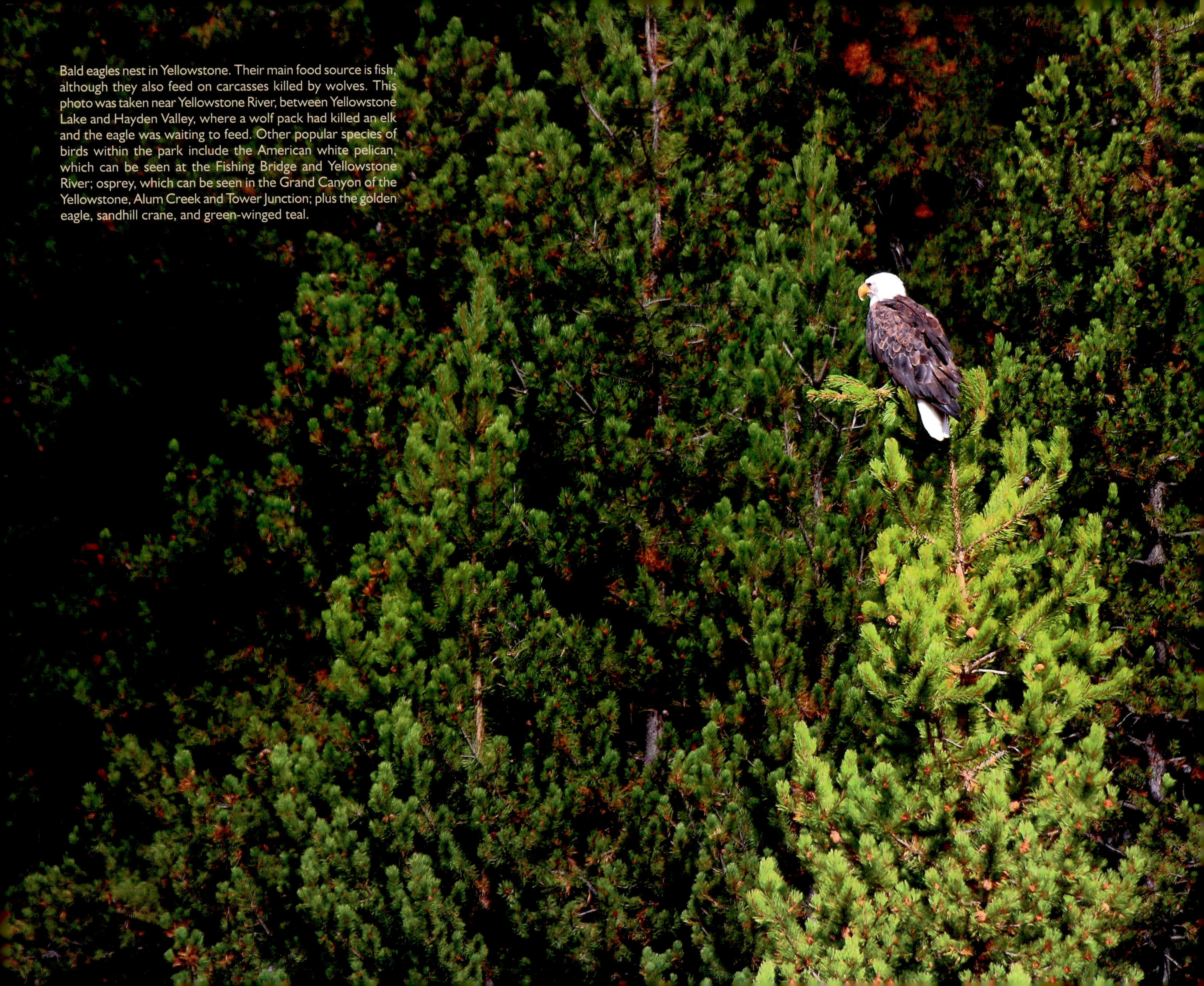

Bald eagles nest in Yellowstone. Their main food source is fish, although they also feed on carcasses killed by wolves. This photo was taken near Yellowstone River, between Yellowstone Lake and Hayden Valley, where a wolf pack had killed an elk and the eagle was waiting to feed. Other popular species of birds within the park include the American white pelican, which can be seen at the Fishing Bridge and Yellowstone River; osprey, which can be seen in the Grand Canyon of the Yellowstone, Alum Creek and Tower Junction; plus the golden eagle, sandhill crane, and green-winged teal.

OUT AND ABOUT

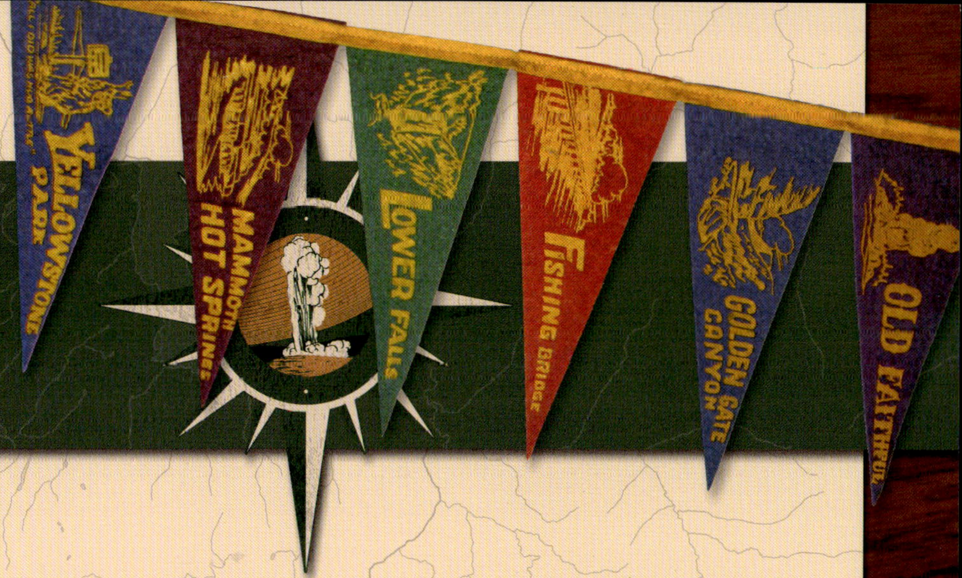

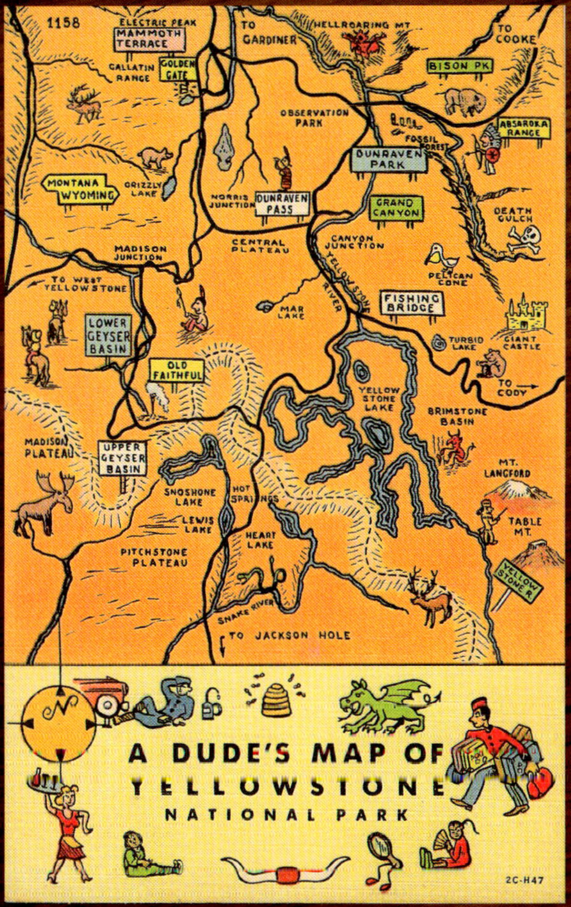

Whimsical postcard from the 1940s by C. T. Art-Colortone shows the many sights within the park. At that time, tourists were known as "dudes," part of a light-hearted Yellowstone vernacular promoted by park concessionaires.

Yellowstone National Park is a wonderland of distinct scenery and formations left behind following the eruption and implosion of a volcano thousands of years ago. The varying effects of the volcano can be found within the park's six regions. Attracting the most visitors is the Old Faithful region. It includes not only Old Faithful Geyser and Inn, but many other geysers in Upper, Midway, and Lower Basins. It also has mud pots, fumaroles, and hot pools, such as Grand Prismatic Spring and Firehole River.

The Norris area on the west side of the park is home to the Norris Geyser Museum and the National Park Ranger Museum. Several geysers are also located in this area, including Steamboat.

The Mammoth area offers the Mammoth Hot Springs Terraces not seen in any other parts of the park. Another attraction is Fort Yellowstone, which was home to soldiers who patrolled the park in the early days, the precursor of today's park ranger.

A less traveled destination is the Tower-Roosevelt area. Here, the old Roosevelt Lodge is still in use and horses are available for trail rides. Tower Fall and the Petrified Tree are also nearby attractions.

The Canyon district includes the Grand Canyon of the Yellowstone and its waterfalls with views from Artist Point, Inspiration Point, Lookout Point, and Red Rock Point. Guest facilities are abundant in this section of the park.

An entirely different area is near Yellowstone Lake. There, fishing and boating are available as well as facilities at Grant Village. For those who like historical buildings, Lake Hotel is also located in the area. Other sights to include in a trip to this region are the Fishing Bridge, Fishing Cone, and Mud Volcano.

Loop roads provide access to all parts of Yellowstone. The most popular sights are marked by maps available at the visitor centers where recommendations on day trips and other outings are offered. For a longer visit, there are trails leading to fishing lakes and other sights not seen by most visitors. Some of these include Roaring Mountain, Specimen Ridge, Bunsen Peak Trail, Shoshone Lake-Shoshone Geyser Basin Trail, and Osprey Falls Trail, as well as many more of varying degrees of difficulty.

OLD FAITHFUL AREA

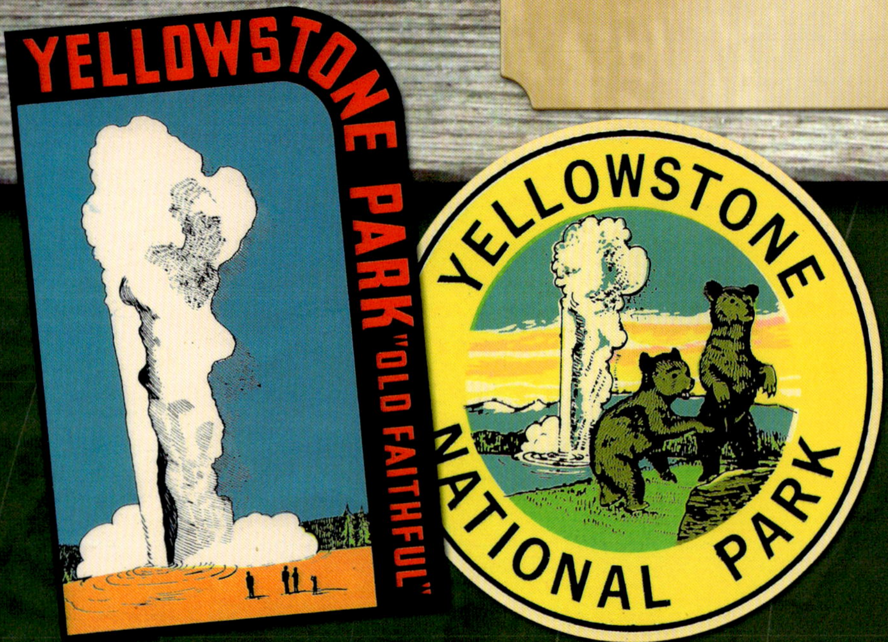

Vintage decals by Lindgren-Turner Co.

The most popular attraction in the park is Old Faithful Geyser, located within the one-mile square area of the Upper Geyser Basin. It was named by the Washburn Expedition of 1870. This card was postmarked March 1911 where the writer quips, "Does your well ever run dry? Move out if it stops." The postcard is unmarked.

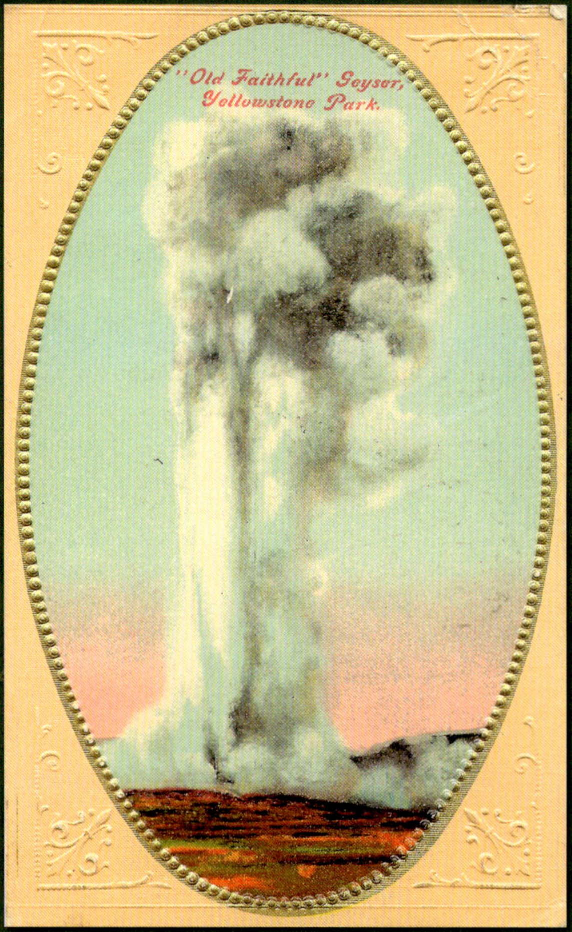

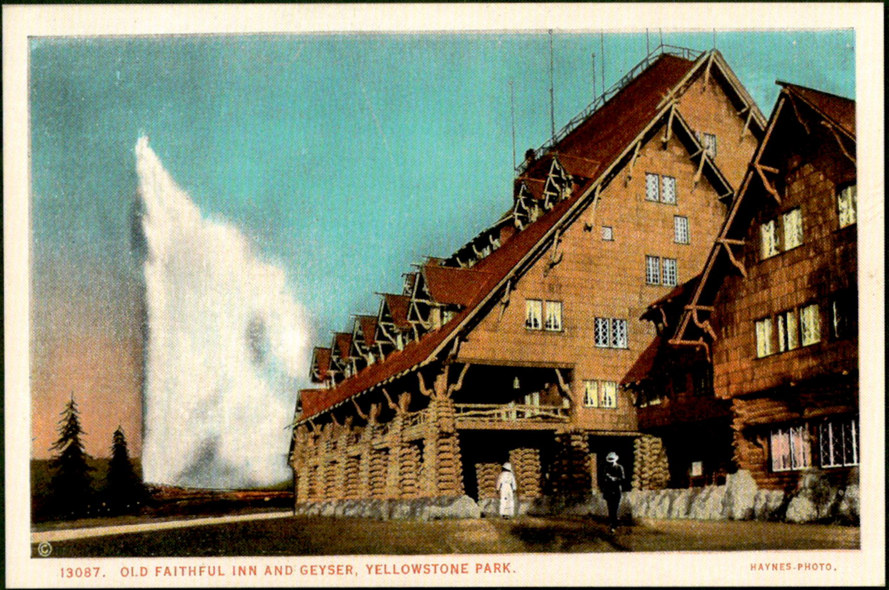

So named for its reliability, Old Faithful erupted about every sixty-five minutes during the Washburn Expedition. Today, the interval has lengthened to about every ninety minutes lasting two to five minutes. The Old Faithful Inn was allowed to be constructed in close proximity to the geyser so its eruptions could be enjoyed by the hotel's guests. For years the geyser was often lit with a search light so the eruption could be enjoyed after dark. Postcard published by J. E. Haynes, St. Paul Minnesota.

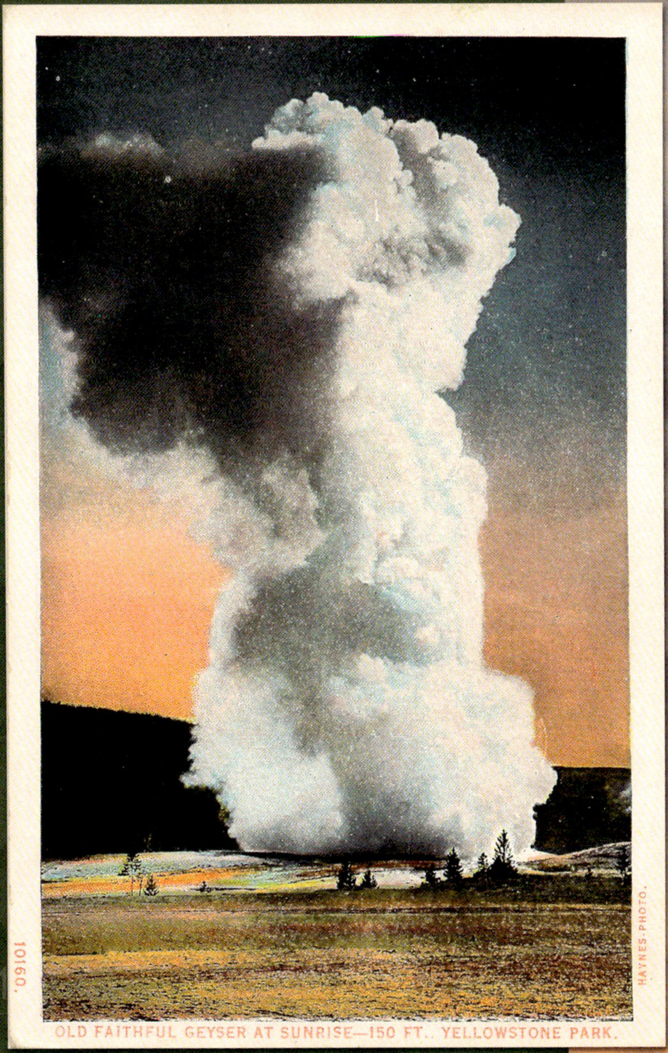

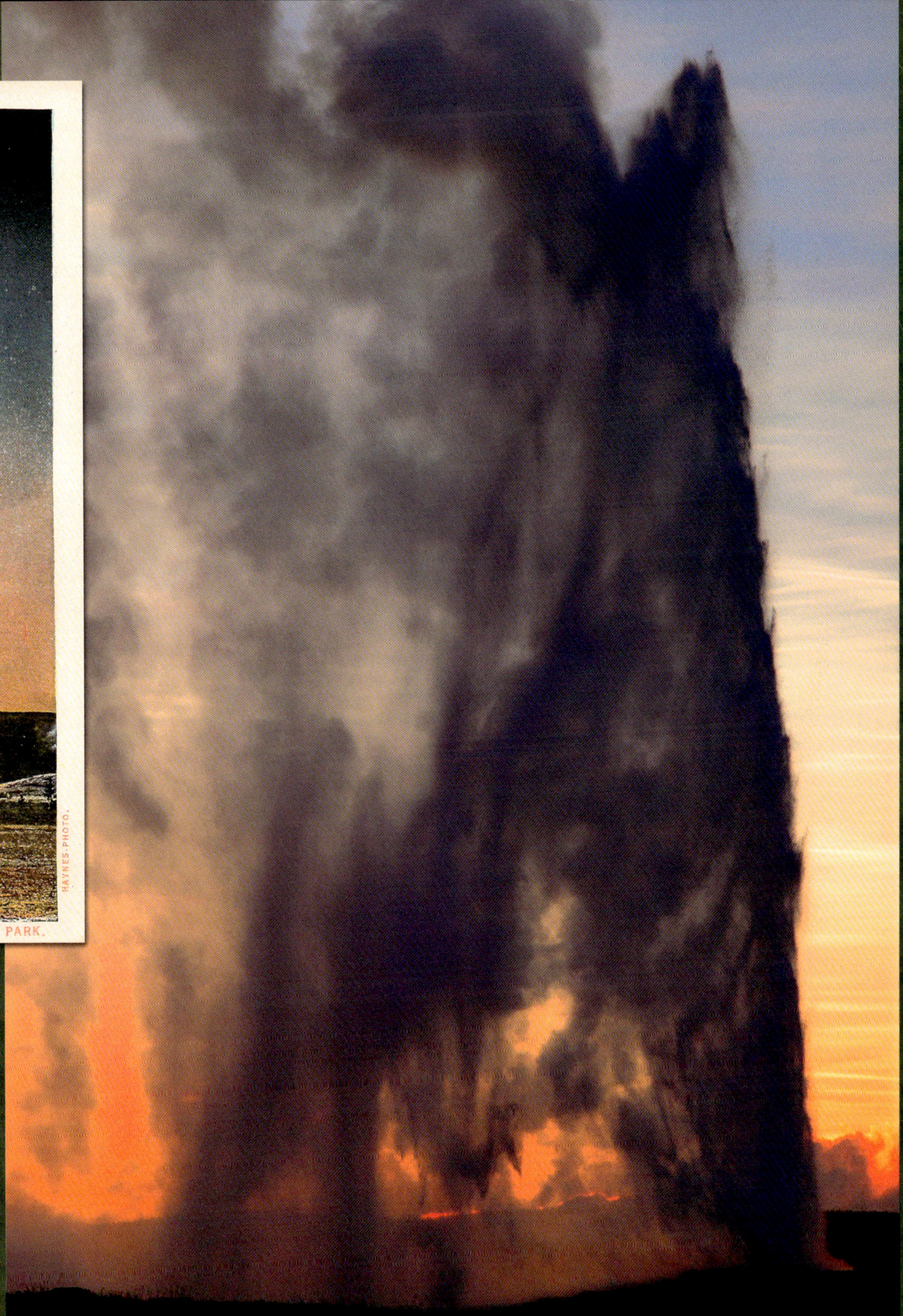

This early postcard by J. E. Haynes shows Old Faithful Geyser at sunrise, while the brilliant colors of the sky reappear at sunset on a recent summer evening.

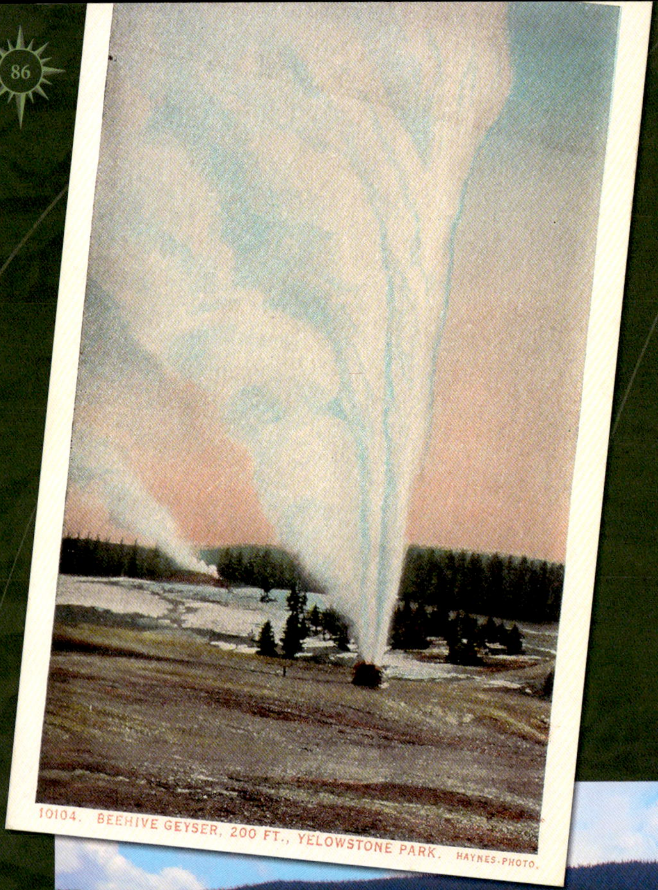

The Upper Geyser Basin is a well-traveled area and around three hundred of the hot springs have been known to erupt as geysers. Beehive Geyser is one of the famous geysers in this area. It has a narrow, beehive-shaped cone that shoots a water column high into the air. This early postcard view of the geyser was published by J. E. Haynes, Official Photographer.

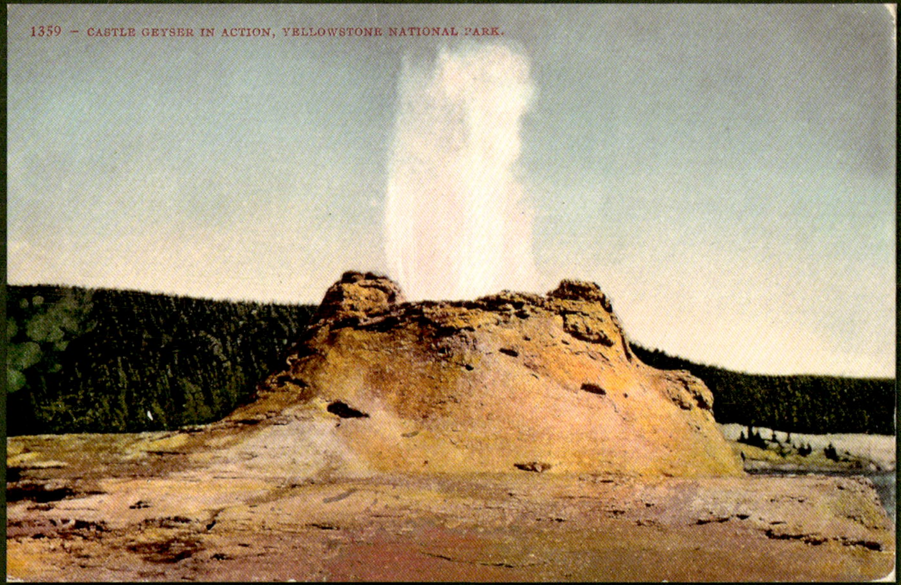

Castle Geyser is also located in Upper Geyser Basin. It has the largest cone of any of the geysers in the park, which stands nearly two feet high with a diameter of twenty feet at the top. It erupts about every twelve hours and is thought to be among the oldest geysers in the park with spectacular displays lasting half an hour. Postcard by Edward H. Mitchell published in San Francisco.

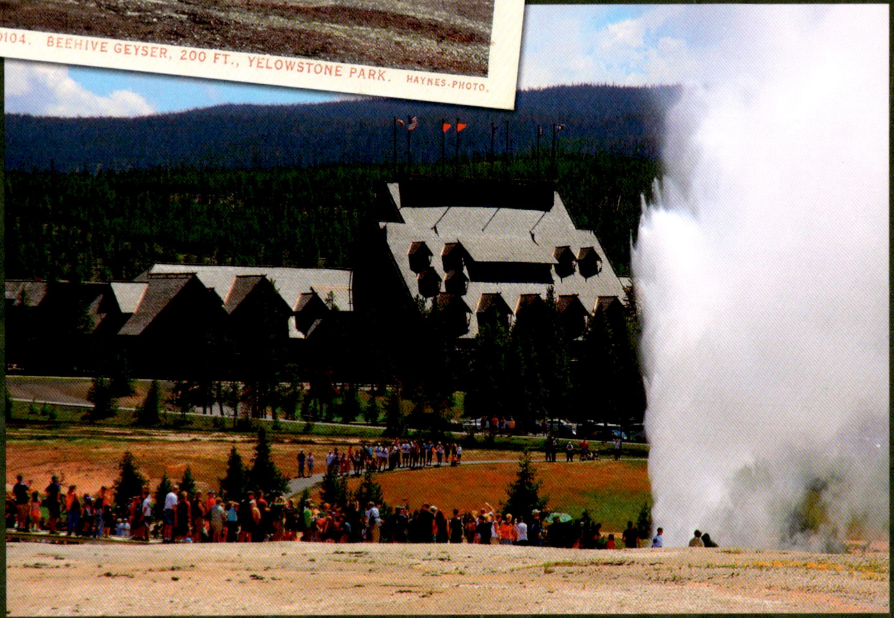

Beehive Geyser, reached by Geyser Hill Loop Trail, and Old Faithful Inn are pictured in this recent setting during one of its eruptions as visitors line up along a boardwalk to view the wonderful sight. Boardwalks are in place throughout the basin areas so as not to cause damage to the thermal features. The geyser was named by the Washburn Expedition in 1870 and has become more active in recent years. It erupts once or twice a day.

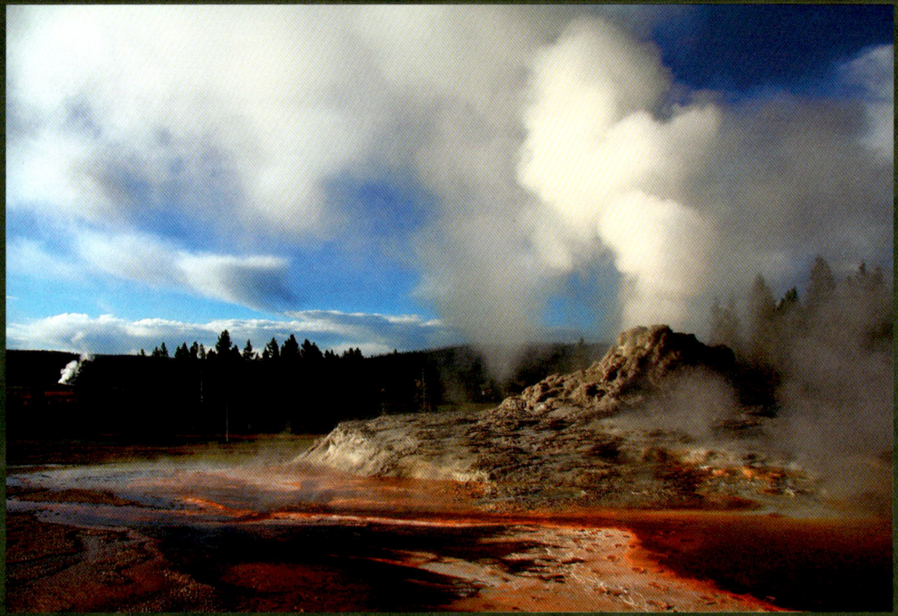

Castle Geyser was named in 1870 by members of the Washburn Expedition for its resemblance to the ruins of an old castle. It is among seven geysers in the Upper Geyser Basin named by the expedition party and reaches heights of up to ninety feet.

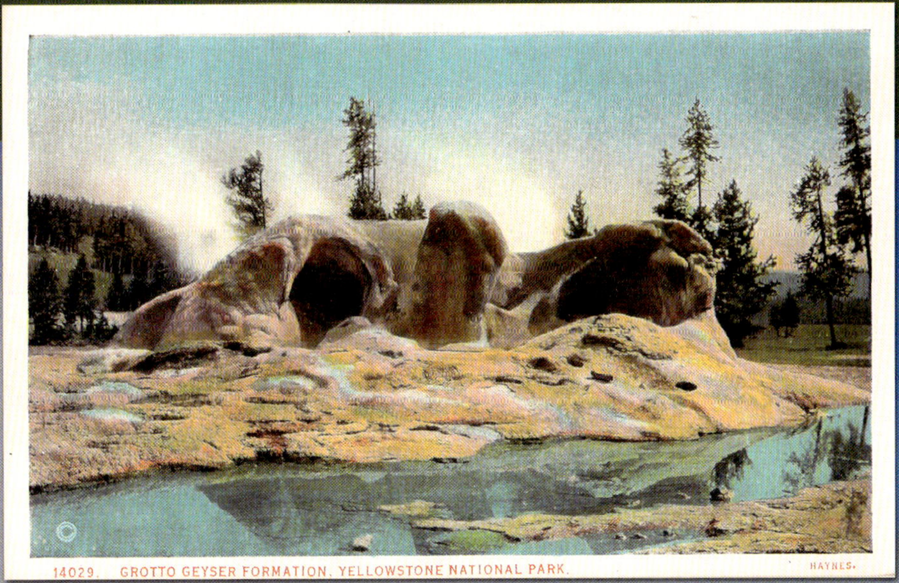

Grotto Geyser in the Upper Geyser Basin is more active than its neighbor, Giant Geyser. When this Haynes Picture Shops postcard was produced, the Grotto Geyser Formation was erupting thirty feet high at intervals varying from two to eight hours.

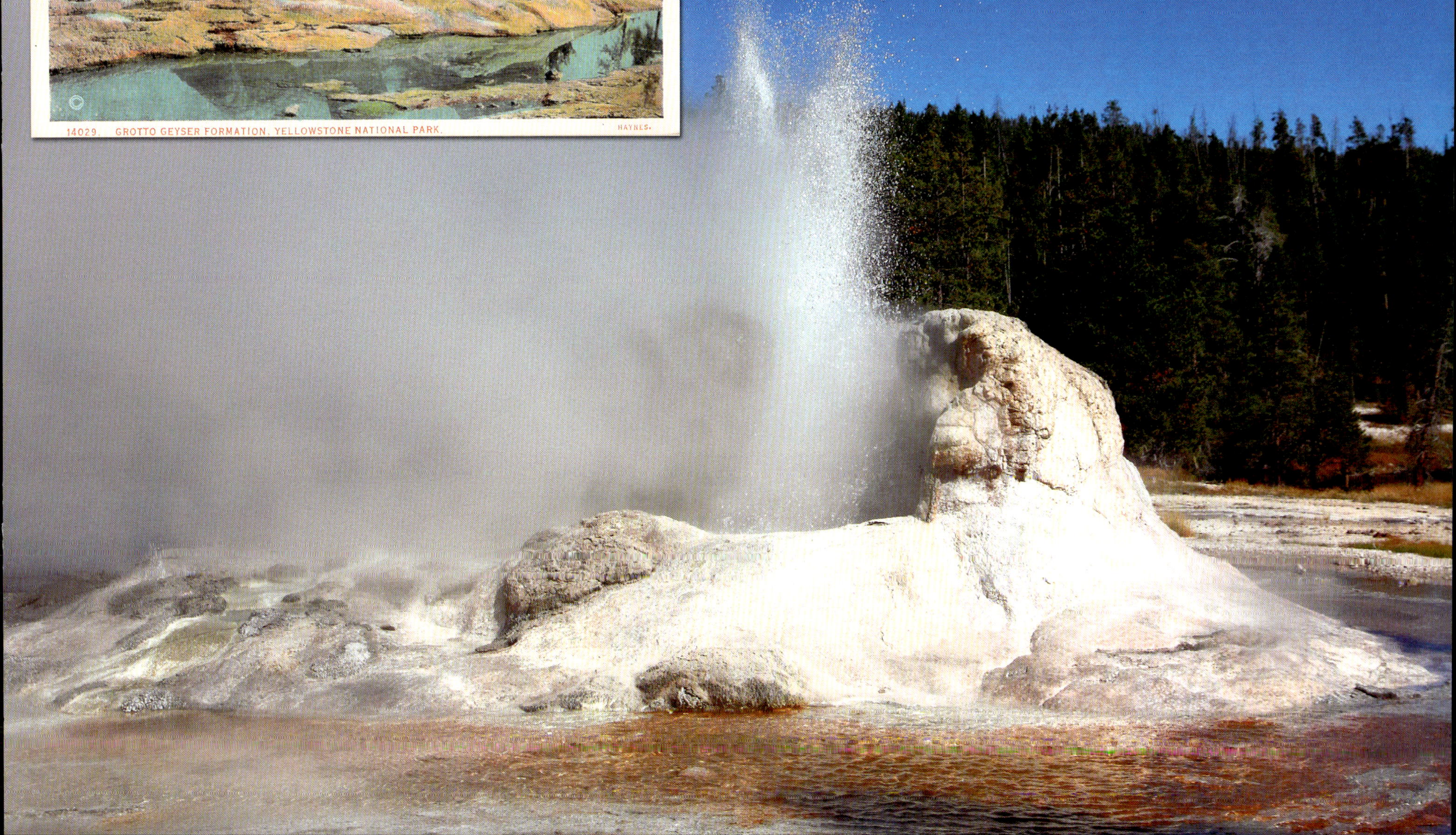

Today the Grotto Geyser is as active as before. This is one of the geysers visitors are most likely to see erupt during their trip.

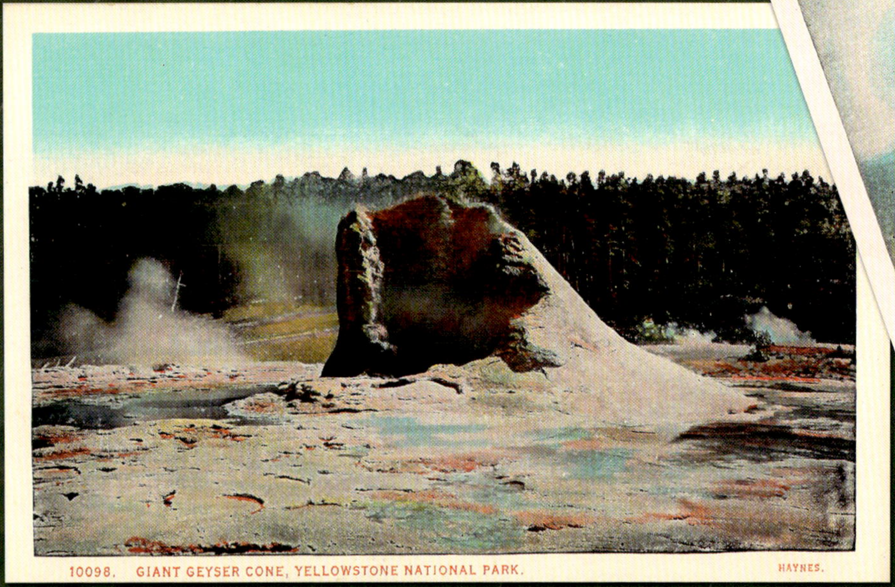

Giant Geyser was named for its huge eruptions that could reach heights of up to 250 feet. Upon its discovery, one side of its cone was gone as pictured on this early postcard by Haynes Picture Shops, Inc.

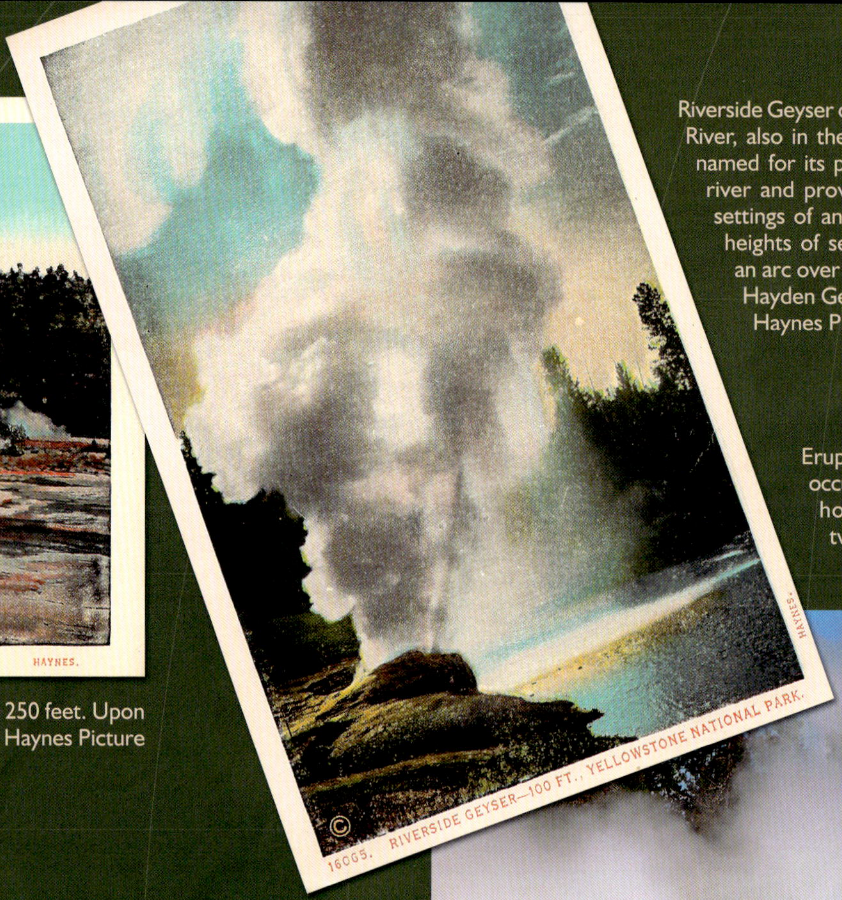

Riverside Geyser can be found along the Firehole River, also in the Upper Geyser Basin. It was named for its picturesque location along the river and provides one of the most scenic settings of any geyser. The geyser reaches heights of seventy-five feet while making an arc over the river. It was named by the Hayden Geological Survey of 1871. Early Haynes Picture Shops postcard.

Eruptions of the Riverside Geyser occur every five-and-a-half to seven hours and last approximately twenty minutes.

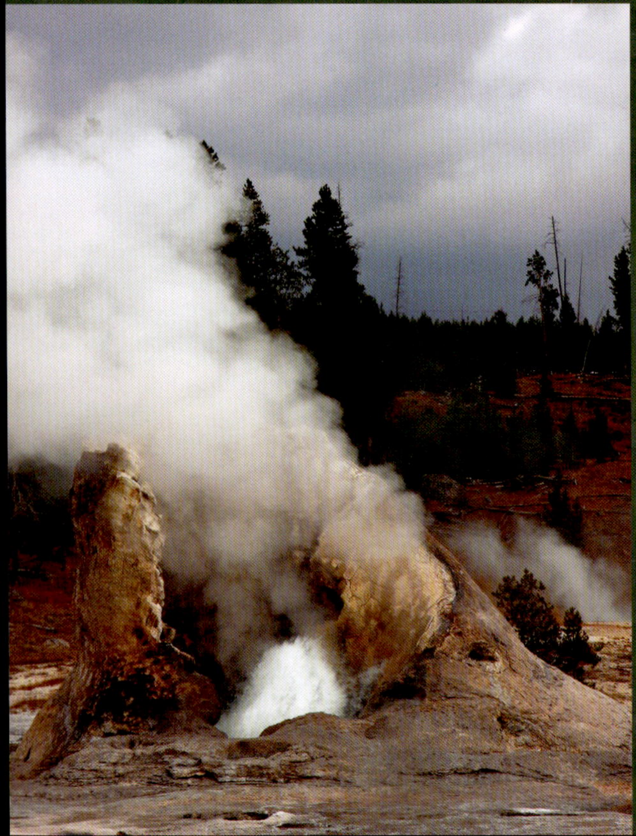

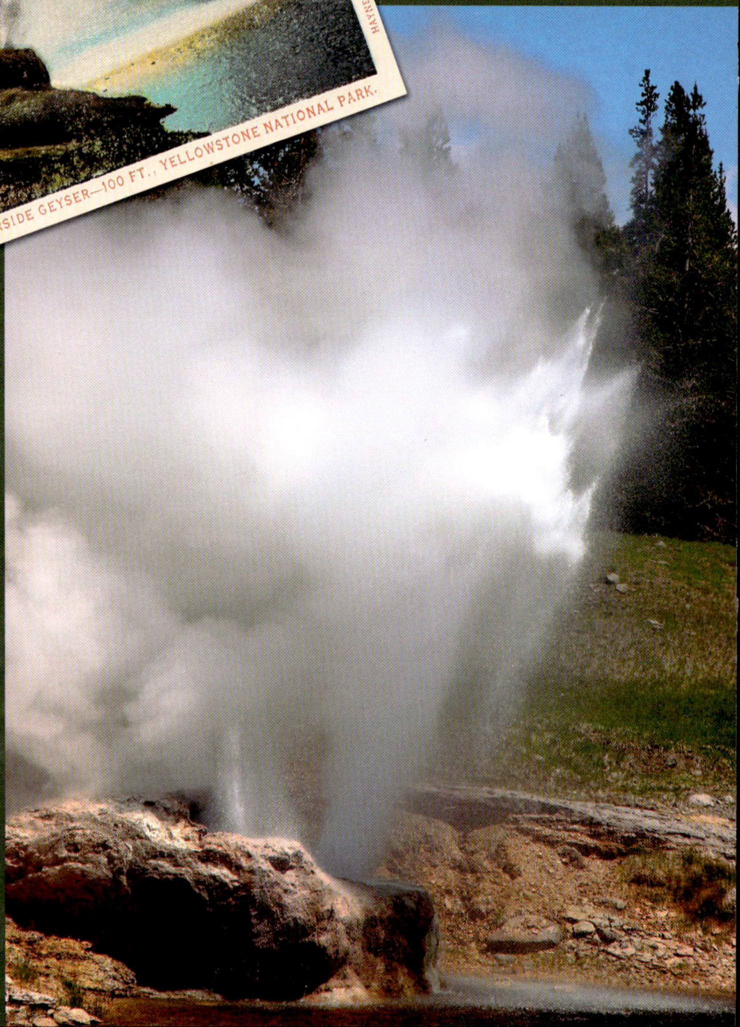

Thermal features change over time, especially when they are close to one another. Their underground plumbing system is connected and one behavior affects the others. Today the Giant Geyser is more dormant than active. Its energy is easily lost due to exchanges in functions with other nearby hot pools and geysers, and thus, visitors rarely see it erupt today.

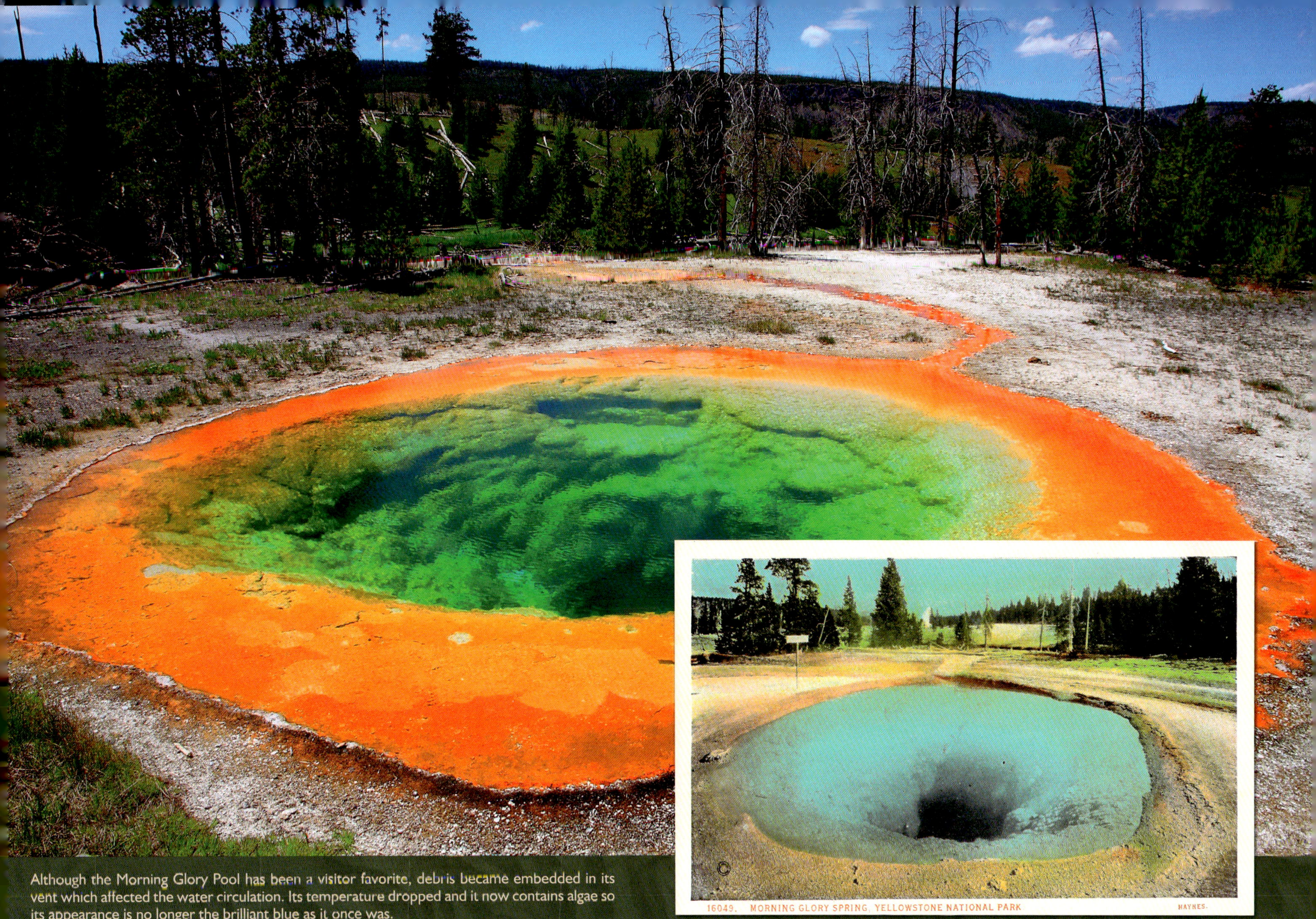

Although the Morning Glory Pool has been a visitor favorite, debris became embedded in its vent which affected the water circulation. Its temperature dropped and it now contains algae so its appearance is no longer the brilliant blue as it once was.

In addition to geysers, the Upper Geyser Basin also includes geothermal pools. One of the most popular was the Morning Glory Pool at the north end of the basin. It was given its name in the 1880s because it was the shape and color of the flower. This early postcard describes it as it was in the 1920s, "Morning Glory Spring filled with pure water over 200 degrees in temperature never erupts nor boils. It is twenty-three feet across and twenty-nine feet deep." Postcard by Haynes Picture Shops, Inc.

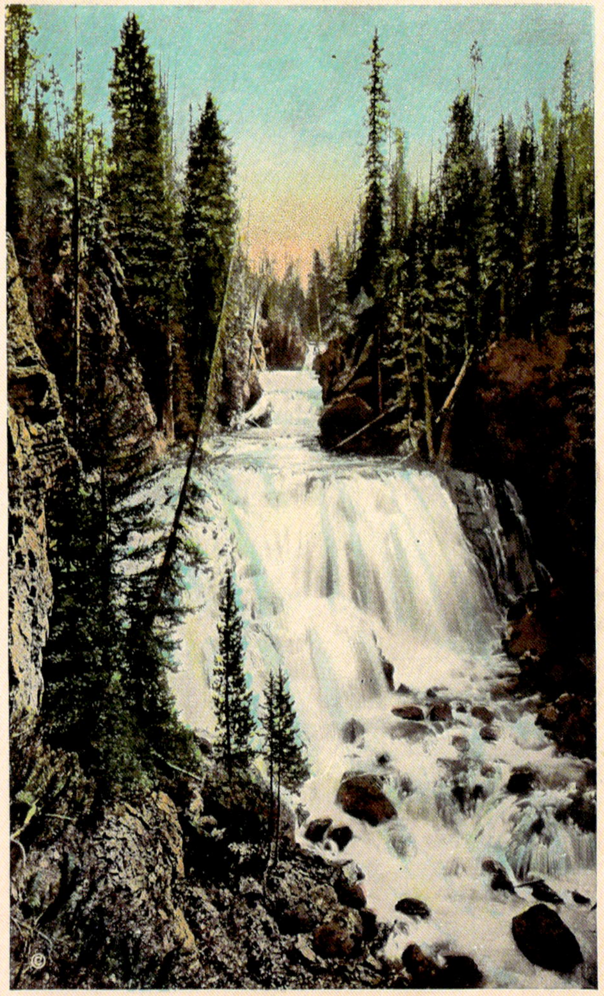

23443. KEPLER CASCADE, FIREHOLE RIVER, YELLOWSTONE PARK.

The Firehole River offers a variety of sights as it flows north from Madison Lake on the Continental Divide to join the Gibbon River at Madison Junction. Among them is Kepler Cascades. The tiered cascades drop approximately 150 feet and can be viewed from a roadside pullout. This early postcard by Haynes Picture Shops shows a summer view.

These cascades, known as Firehole Falls are formed where the river enters a narrow canyon wall. In this area, the river is fed from the surrounding geothermal features, where water temperatures are higher than upstream.

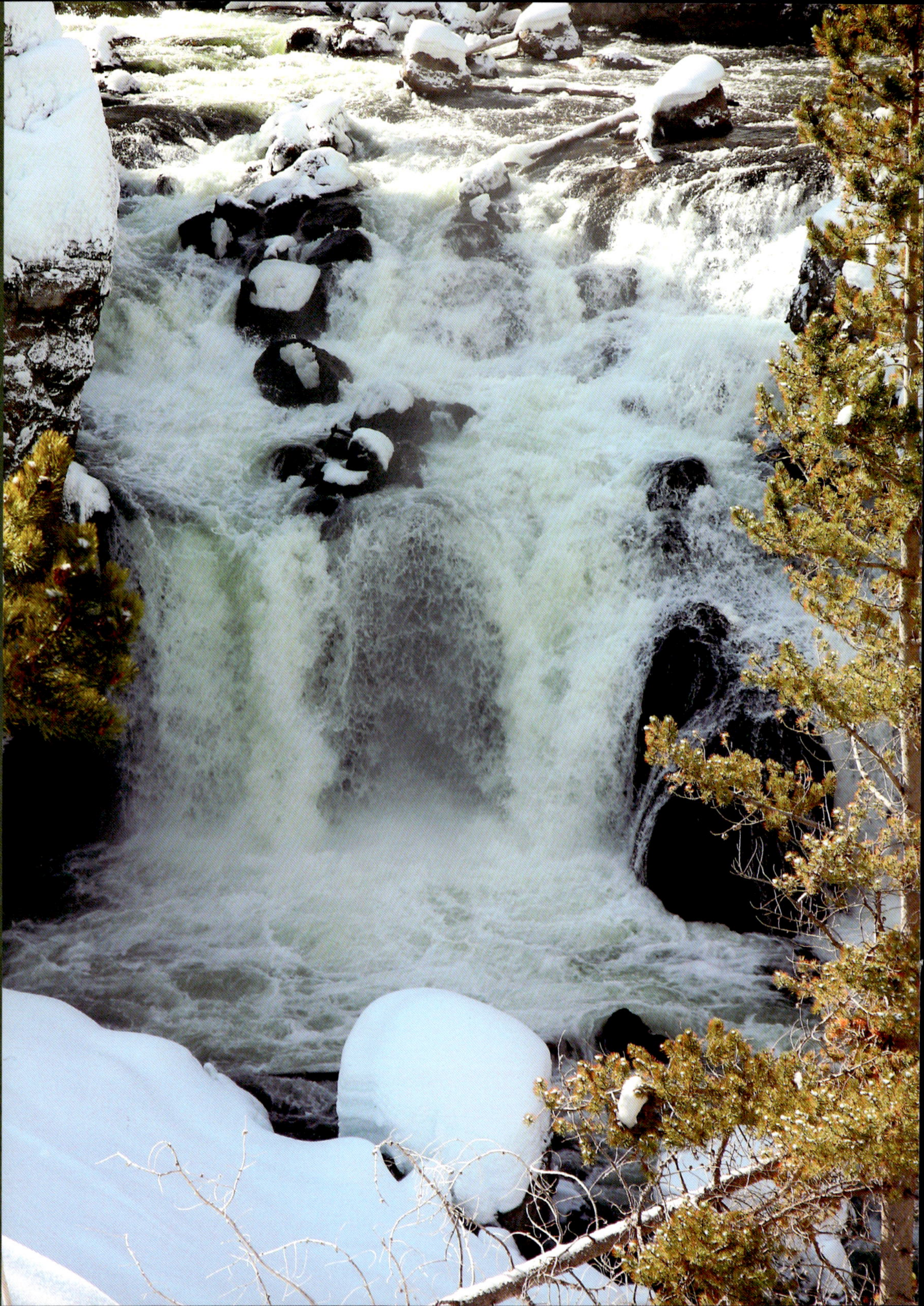

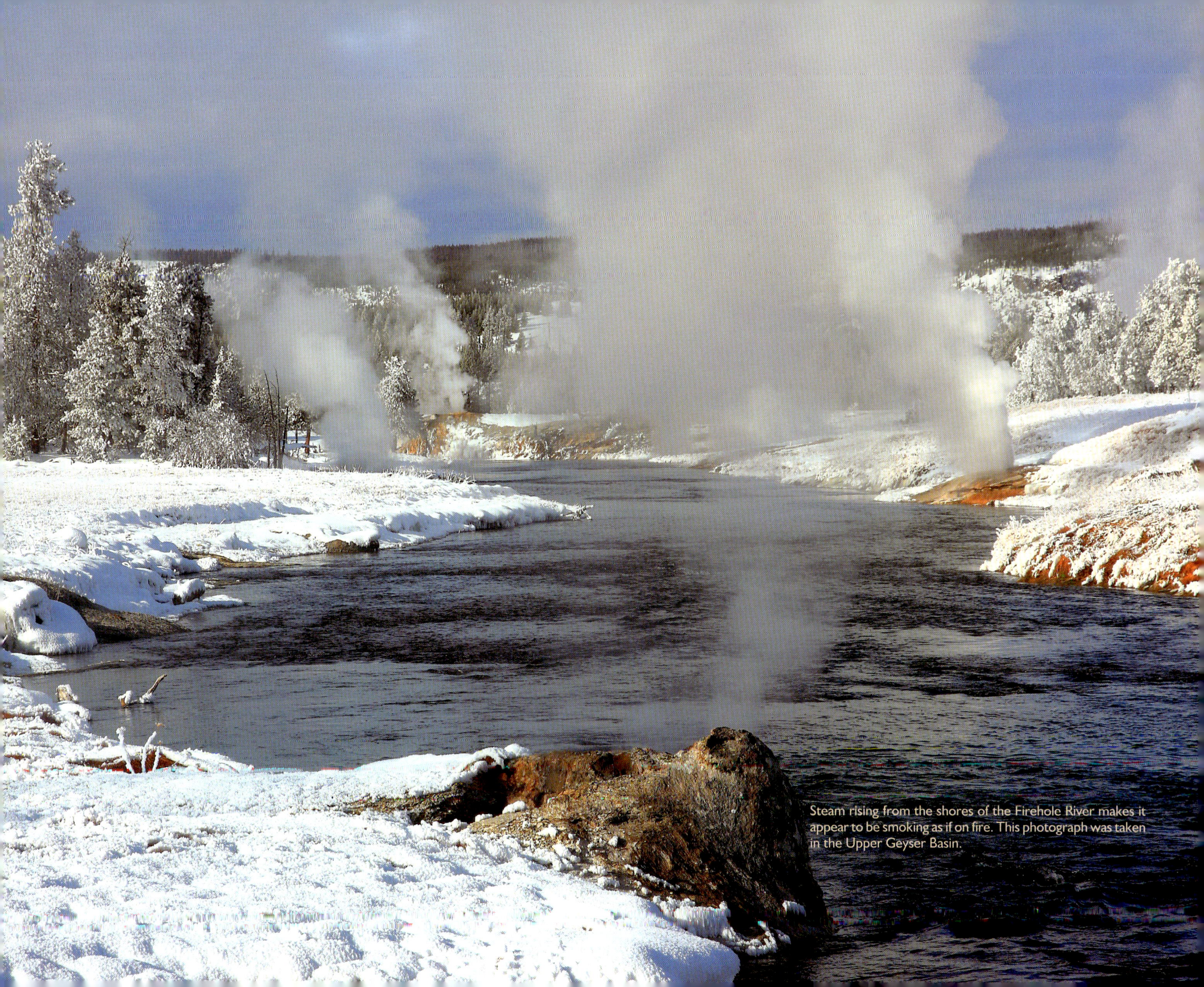

Steam rising from the shores of the Firehole River makes it appear to be smoking as if on fire. This photograph was taken in the Upper Geyser Basin.

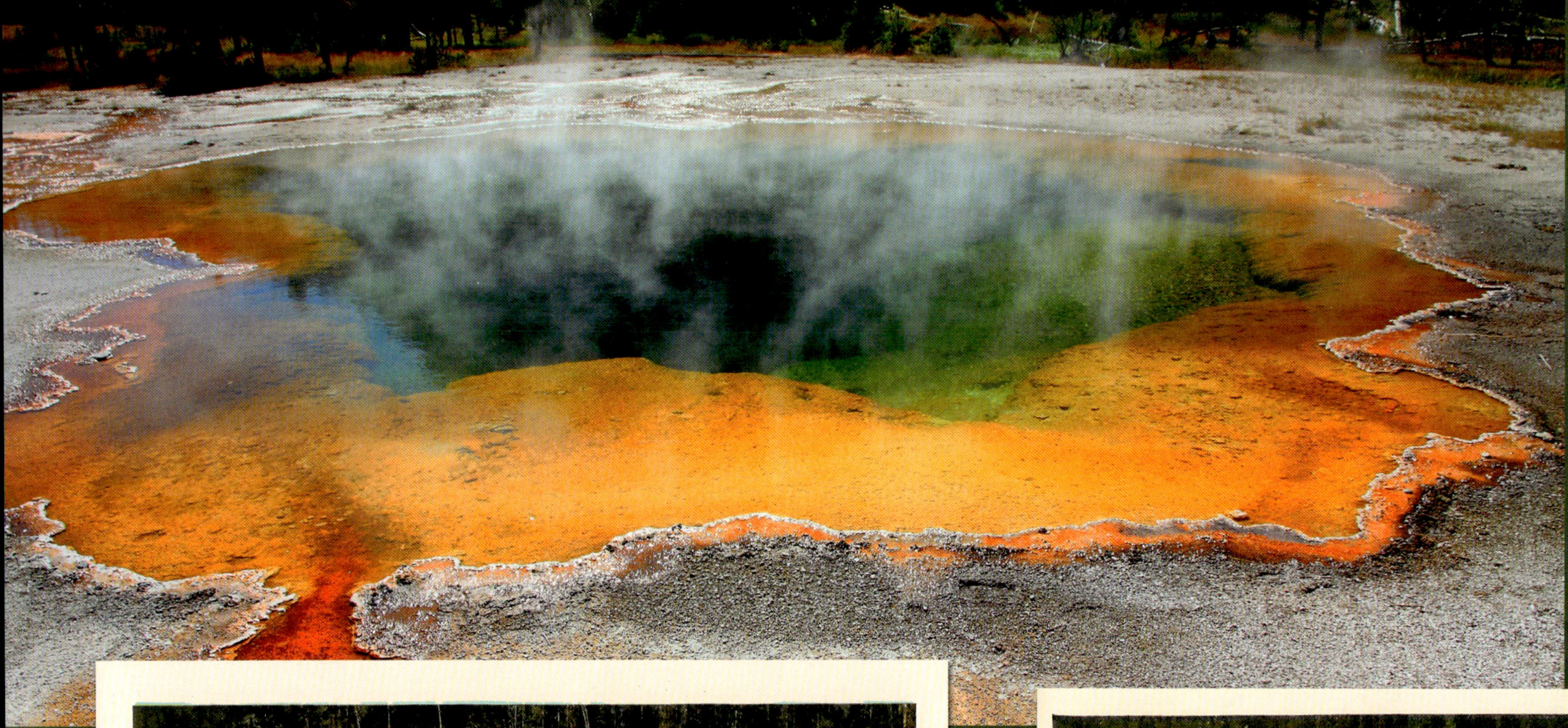

Emerald Pool is one of the main features in Black Sand Basin. It was appropriately named after its emerald green color in the pool.

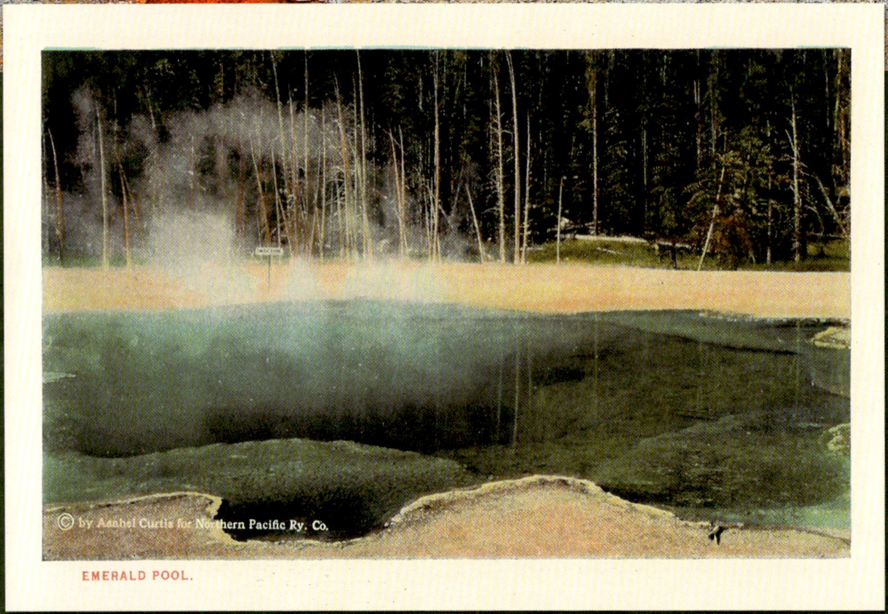

Geysers and hot springs at Black Sand Basin are located near Punch Bowl Spring and are accessed by trail or road, including the popular Emerald Pool. Postcard by Asahel Curtis for Northern Pacific Ry. Co.

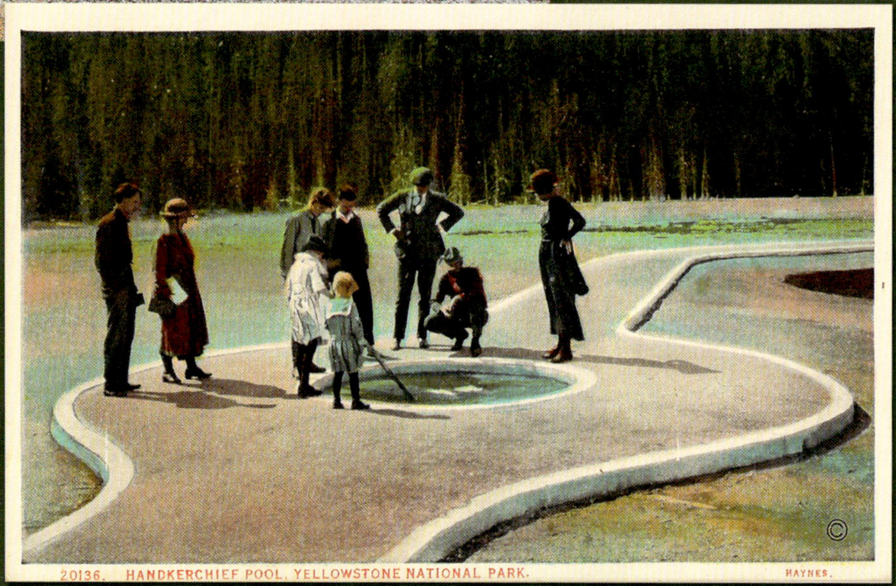

In the earlier days, the nearby Handkerchief Pool was popular due to its novelty. If a handkerchief was placed in the pool, it would be drawn downward out of sight until the upward current caught it and it was brought to the surface again after it had been "cleaned." This common practice likely damaged the pool causing the action to cease functioning as it had in the past. Placing objects into any of the park's thermal features has since become illegal. This circa 1920 postcard pictures tourists observing the handkerchief experiment. Postcard by Haynes Picture Shops, Inc.

Grand Prismatic Spring is found in the Midway Geyser Basin. It is more than three hundred feet in diameter. Postcard by J. E. Haynes, St. Paul, Minnesota.

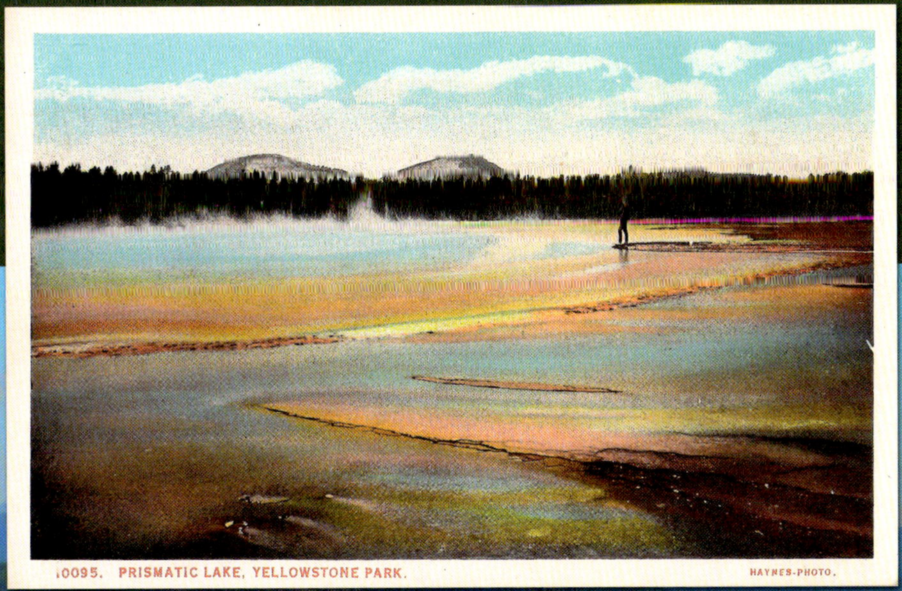

The Midway Geyser Basin is also home to Excelsior Geyser which is considered to be the largest geyser in the world. Its last major eruptions occurred in the 1880s as pictured on this J.E. Haynes postcard, with heights reaching three hundred feet.

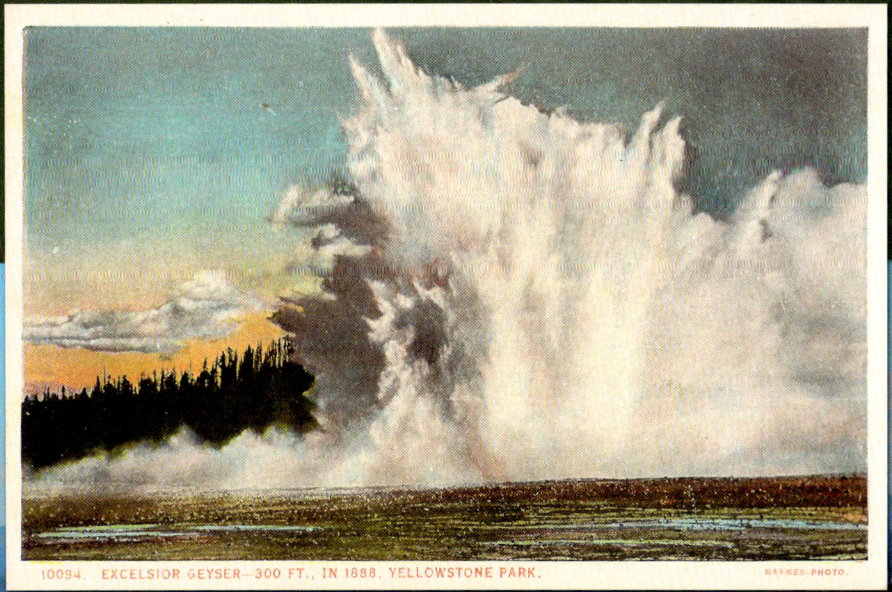

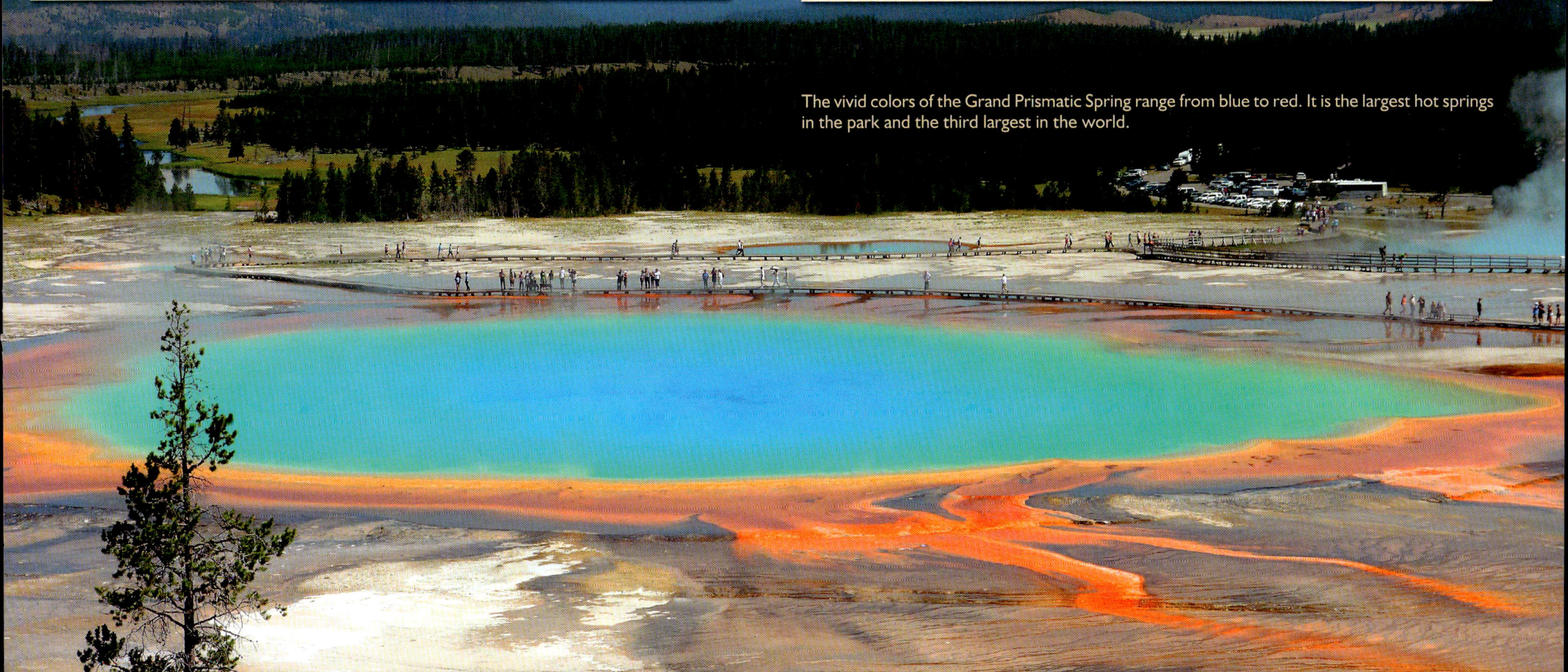

The vivid colors of the Grand Prismatic Spring range from blue to red. It is the largest hot springs in the park and the third largest in the world.

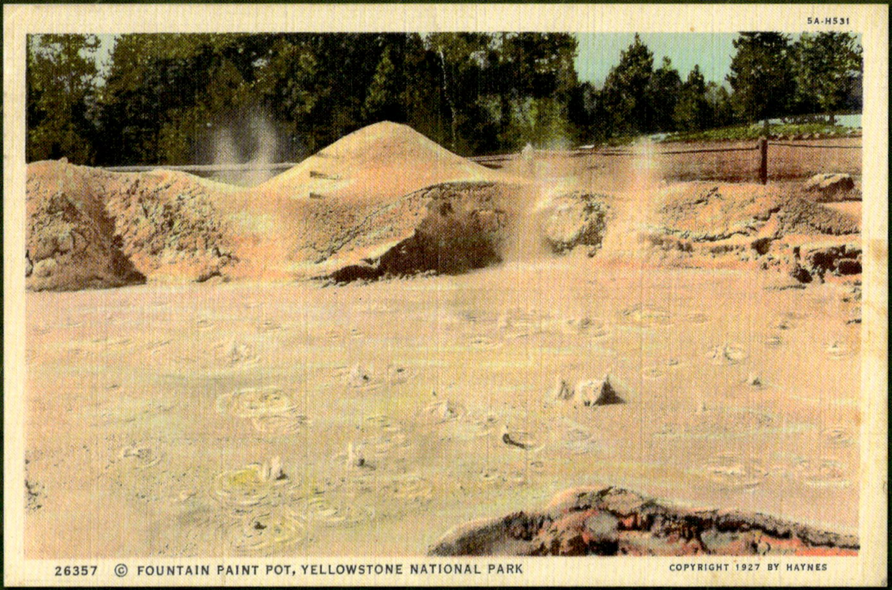

The Lower Geyser Basin area covers about eleven square miles and features the Fountain Paint Pot area. It is accessed on Grand Loop Road between Old Faithful and Madison. The Fountain Paint Pot is described on this Haynes postcard as "being a boiling cauldron of a tinted clay about 40 x 60 feet in size." The card was postmarked in 1938.

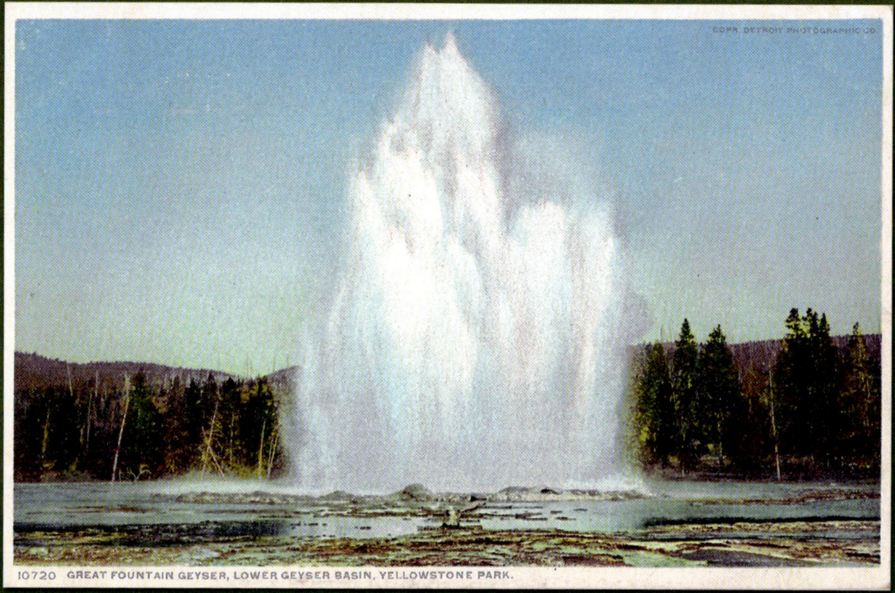

Visitors who follow Firehole Lake Drive have many more of nature's sights to enjoy, including the Great Fountain Geyser. It erupts every eight to seventeen hours in spectacular fashion as pictured in this early phostint postcard made by Detroit Publishing Co.

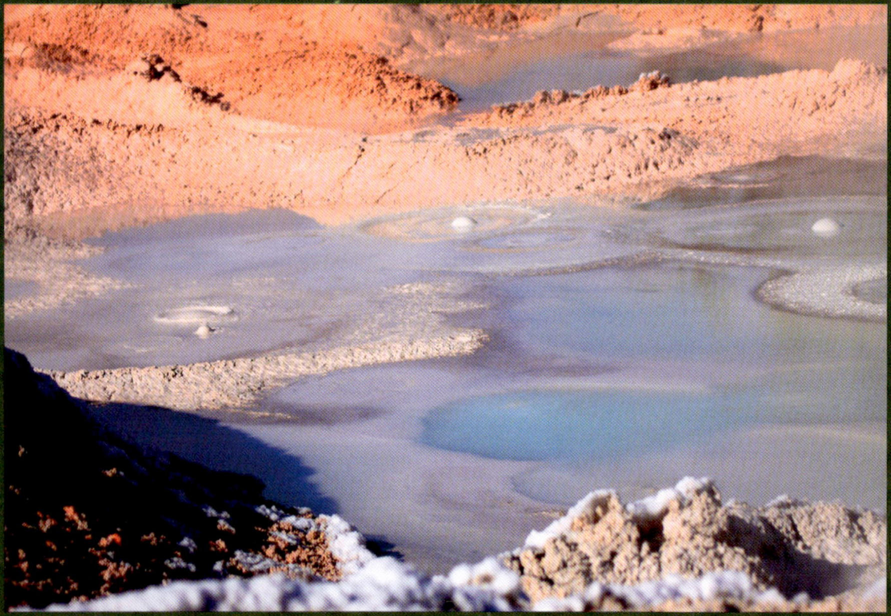

A more recent scene of the Fountain Paint Pot shows the hot mud springs. The color variation is caused by differences in oxidation of the iron in the mud.

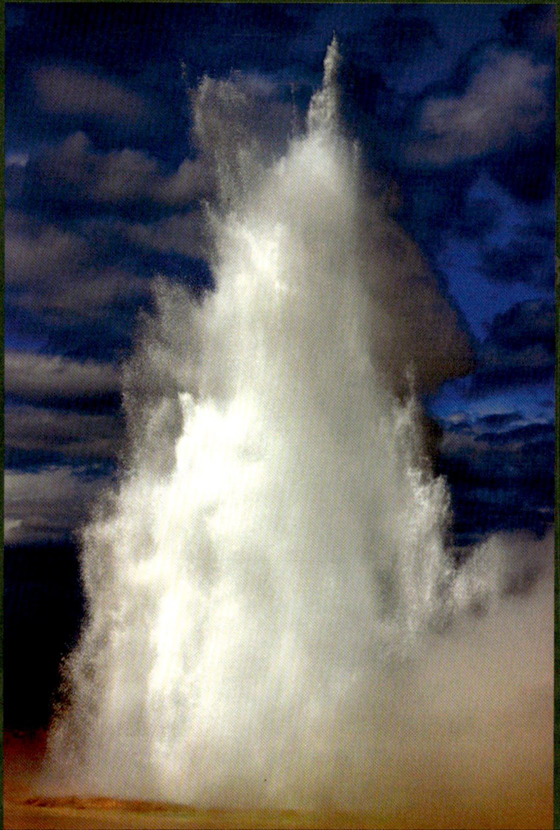

The Great Fountain Geyser is the most explosive geyser in the area with eruptions that can sometimes spew up to two hundred feet in a fountain-like manner. It is one of the few major geysers that can be viewed from the roadside on Firehole Lake Drive.

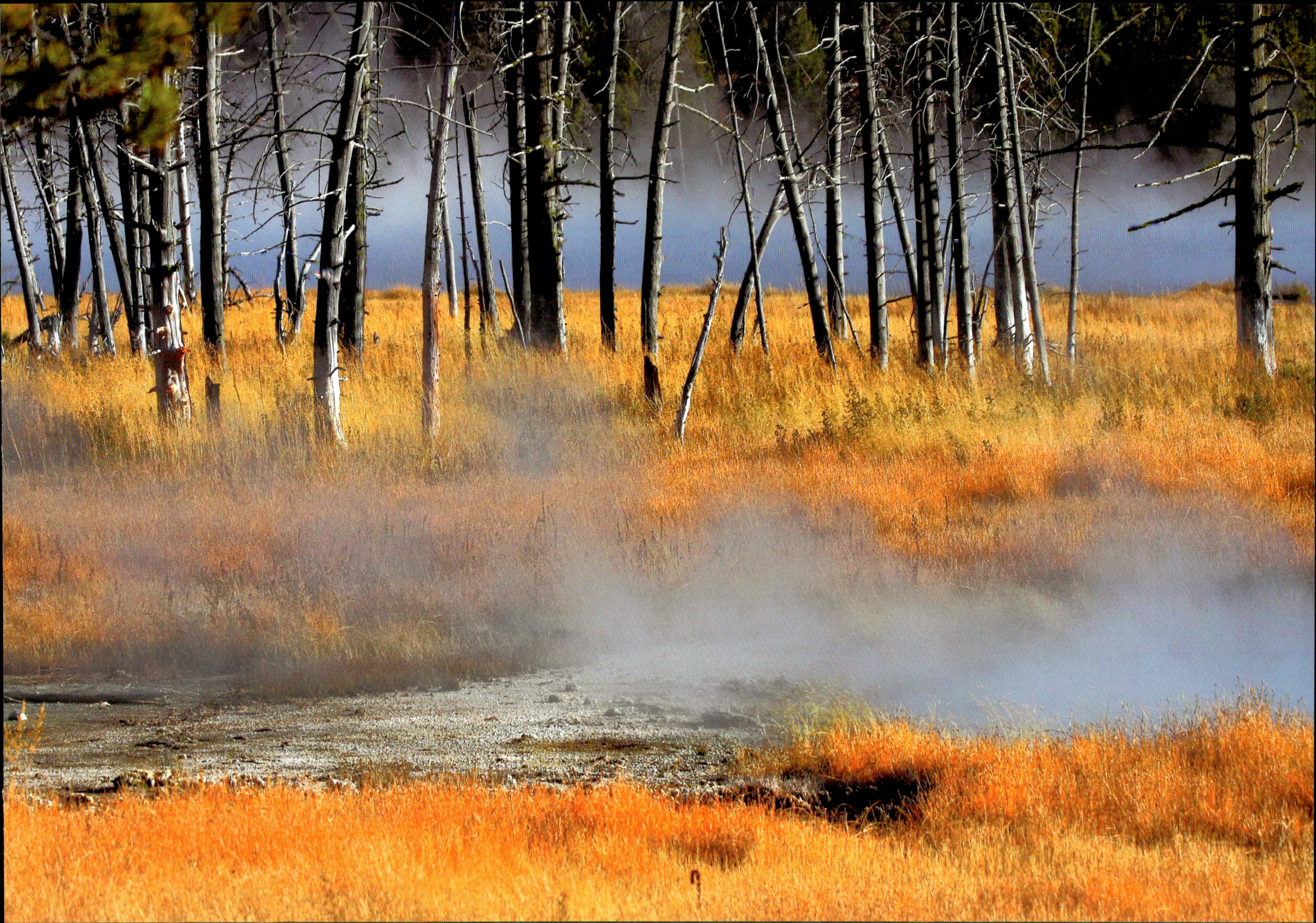

Another unusual feature viewed from Firehole Lake Drive is the Bobby Socks trees. They were named because of the whitish minerals left on the bottom of the trees. This occurs when water absorbed by the trees evaporates and leaves the sock-like effect at the bottom.

NORRIS AREA

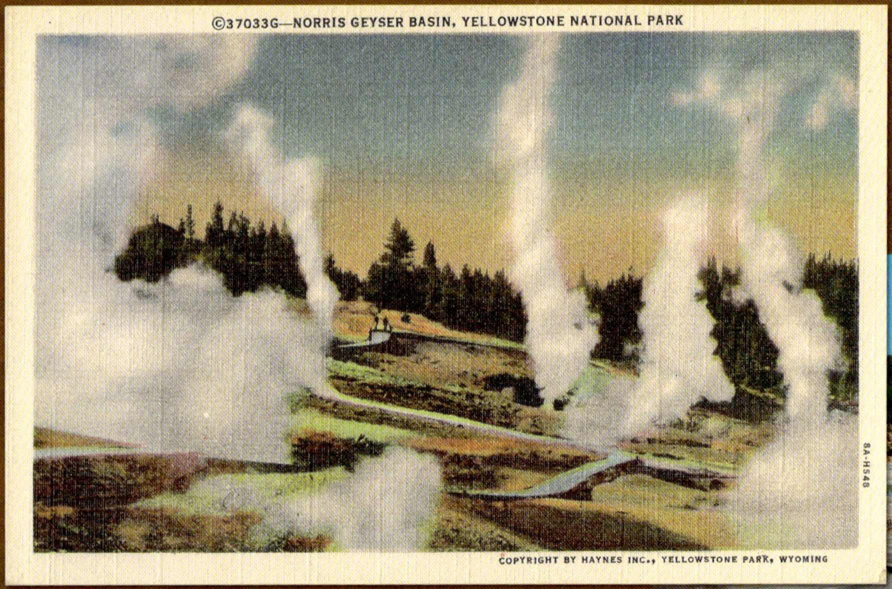

Norris Geyser Basin is home to the oldest geyser basin in the park. The area was named for Philetus Norris, the park's second superintendent. This Haynes linen postcard pictures a few of the several hundred fumaroles and small geysers in the area.

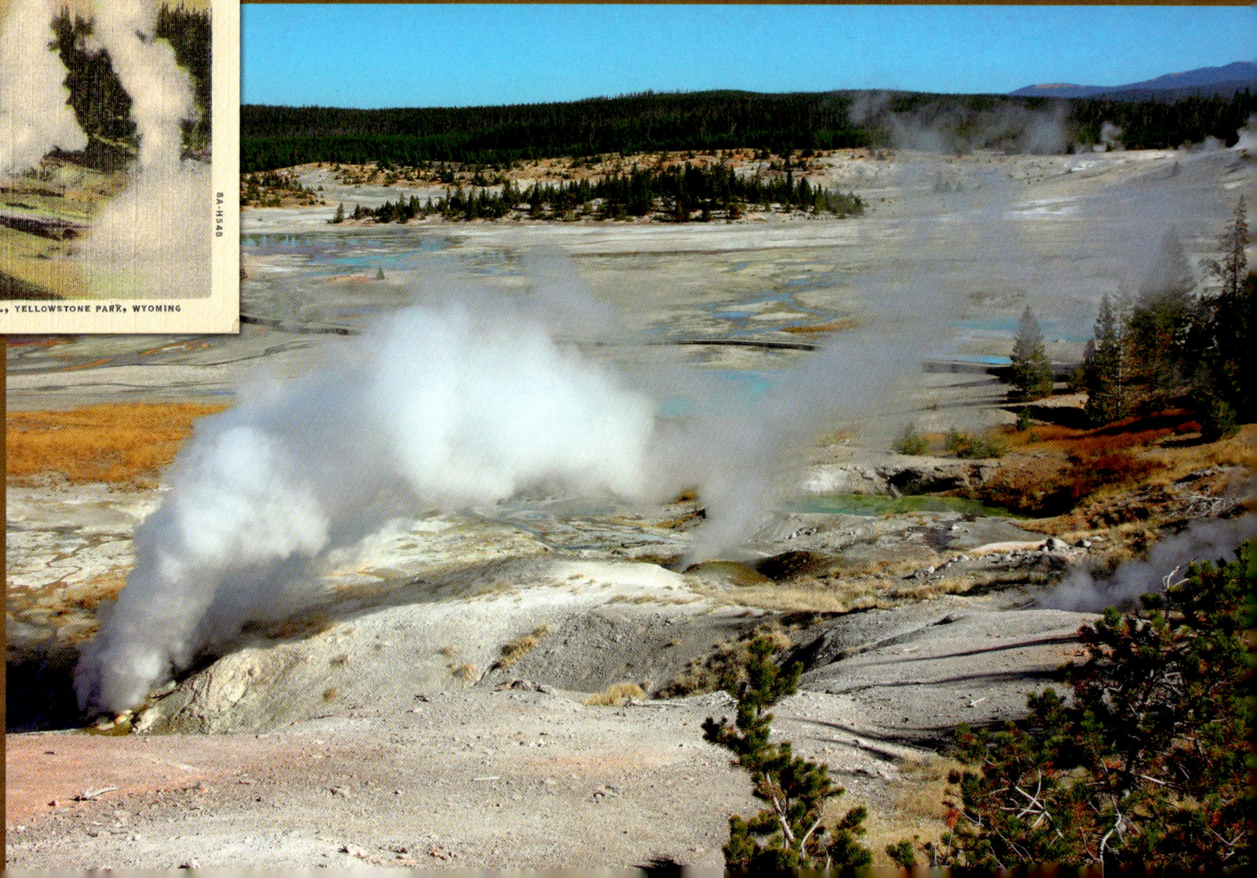

The thermal activity at Norris Geyser Basin changes unpredictably. This is the most dynamic area in the park as there are faults underground. Acid pools, such as Echinus Geyser, are also found here. Most other pools in the park are alkaline. A museum is located nearby with displays on how geysers differ from other thermal features

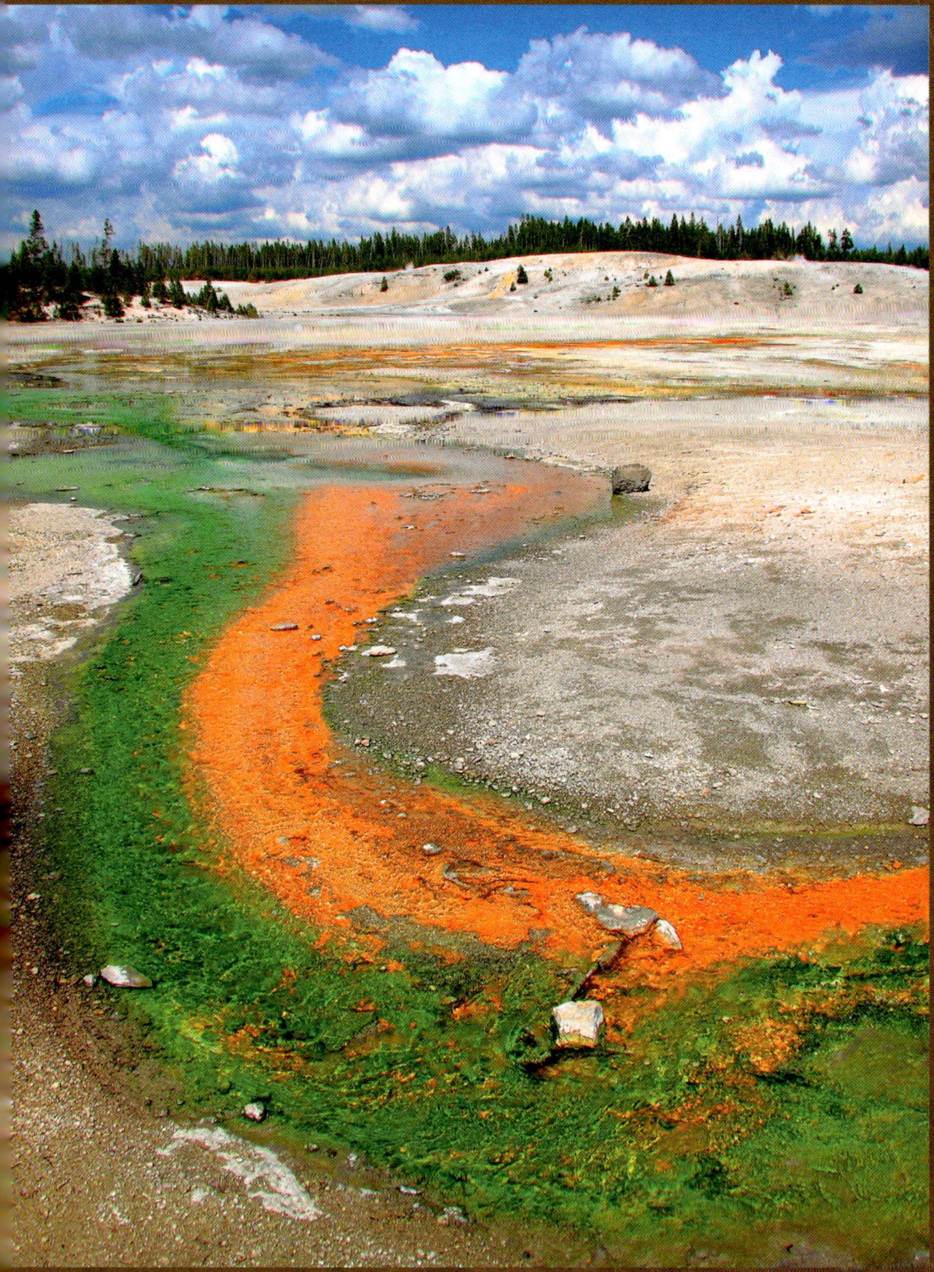

The long-held notion that no living organisms could exist in the hot pools was dispelled in 1966 with the discovery of thermophiles by Dr. Thomas Brock, a researcher from Indiana University. The microorganisms thrive in Yellowstone's most extreme thermal environments and can be seen in many thermal areas including the green and orange patterns pictured here in the Norris Geyser Basin. Thermophiles have been found to be an important component in copying the DNA sequence. A Nobel Prize was awarded to Dr. Kary Mullis in 1993 as a result of this continuing research.

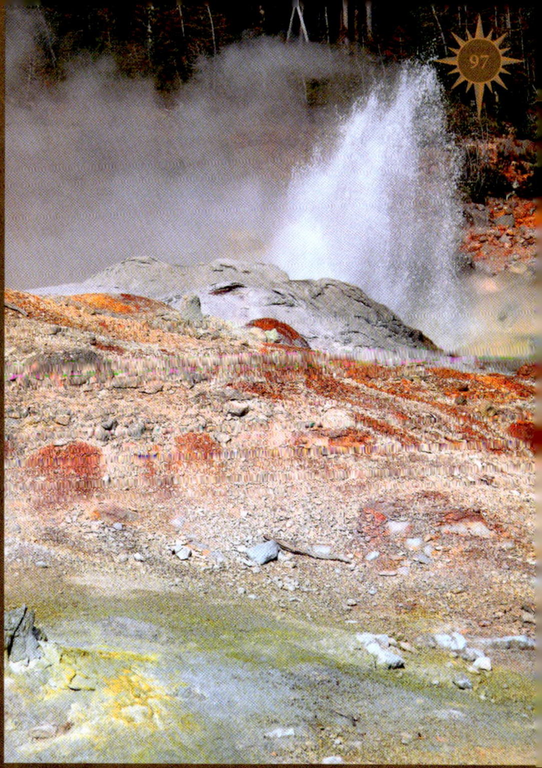

Despite its recognition as the highest of all active geysers, eruptions at Steamboat Geyser are infrequent and hard to predict. This photograph shows the bursts of hot water as seen by most people.

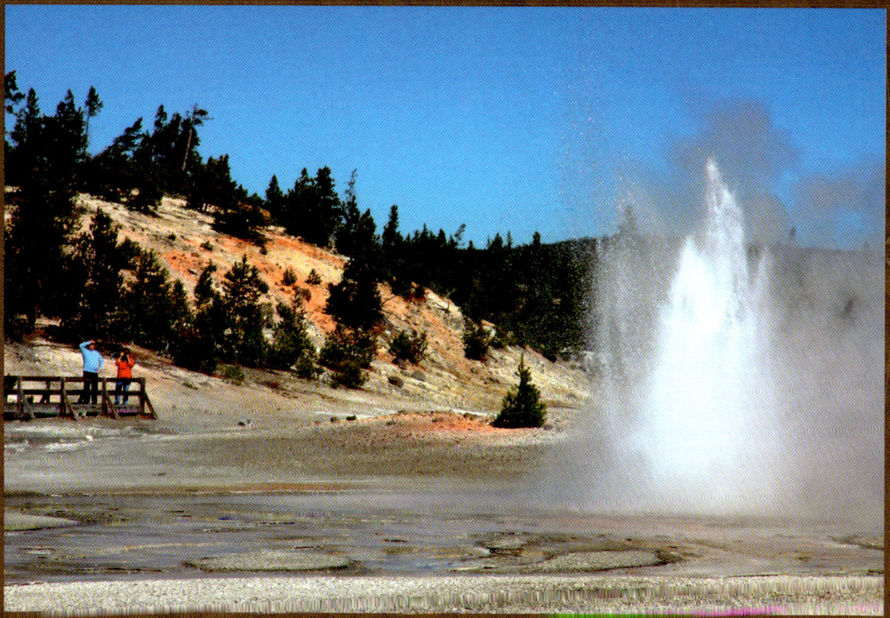

By following the green and orange pattern caused by the thermophiles, Whirligig Geyser can be found. It is among the features in the Norris Geyser Basin that erupt frequently. Due to the geological instability, eruptions of geysers in this area are usually unpredictable.

MAMMOTH AREA

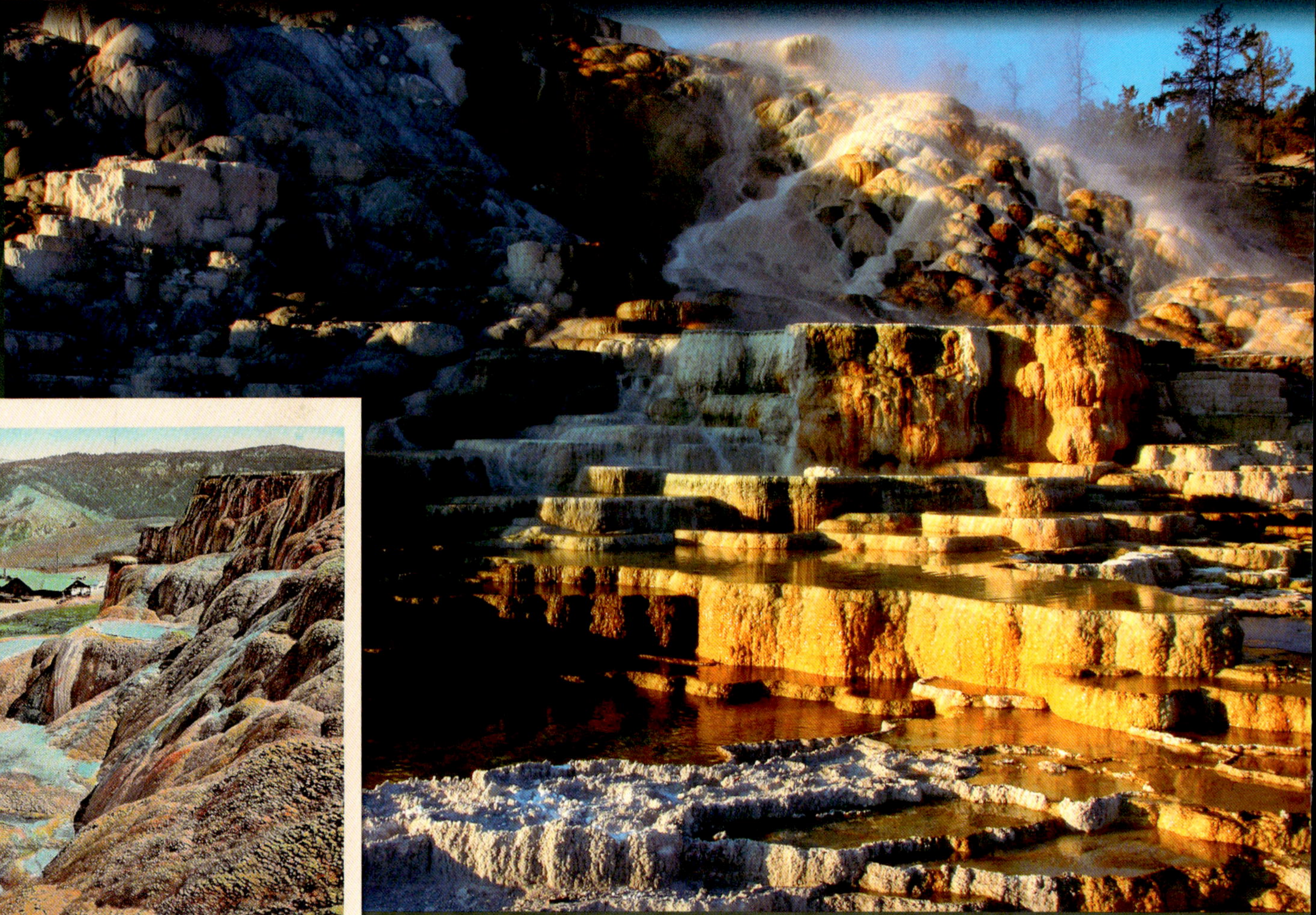

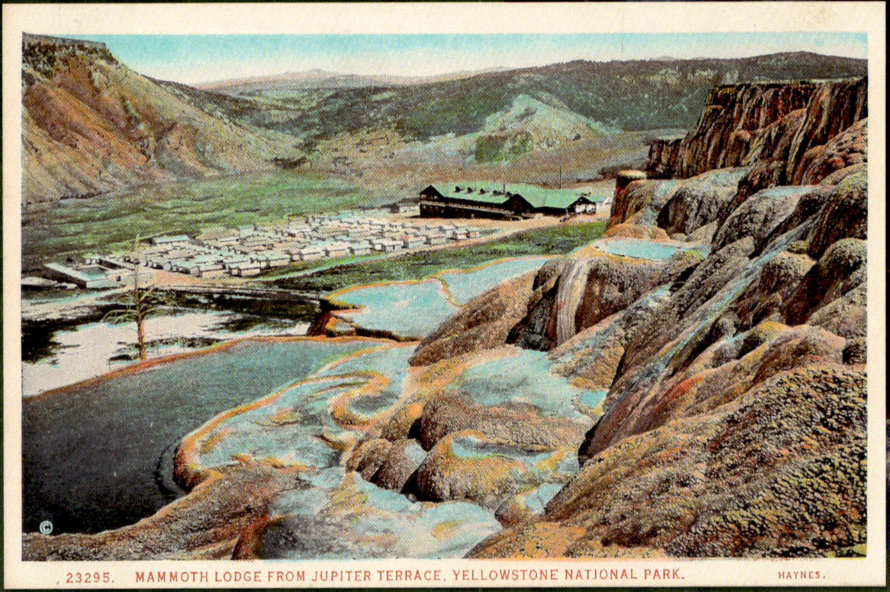

Visitors have been drawn to Mammoth since the park's earliest days. The first hotel was built here along with Fort Yellowstone. This postcard shows the proximity of the Mammoth Lodge and cabins to the travertine terraces. Today, the area includes lodging, a post office, general store, chapel, clinic, visitor center, food service, and park headquarters. Postcard by Haynes Picture Shops, Inc.

Fascinating geological formations of various shapes and sizes can be found at Mammoth Hot Springs near the North Entrance. The terraces are made of calcium carbonate and are formed as the hot springs trickle through them. With water flowing from Palette Spring, this photograph gives the area a mystical look and feel.

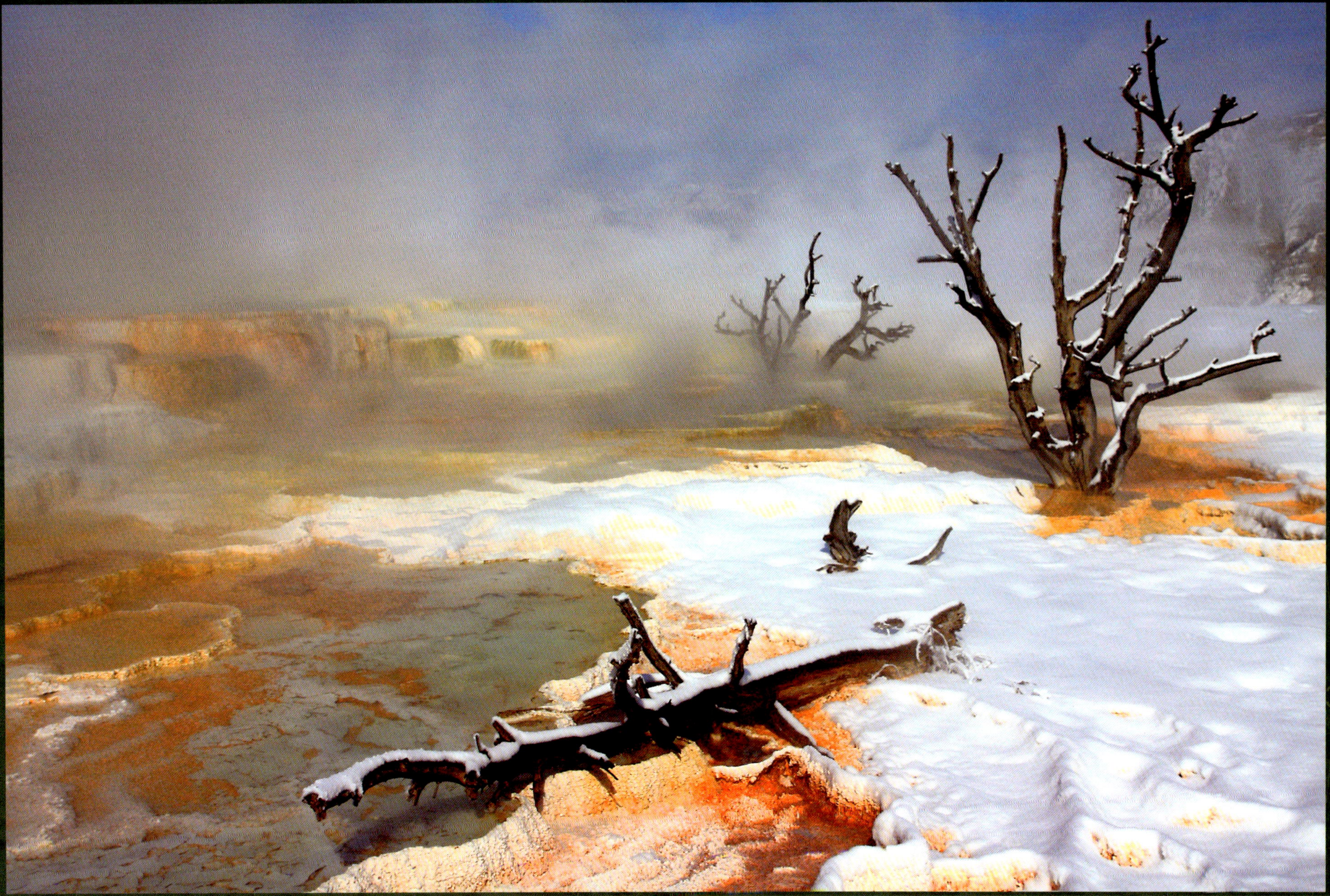

The beauty of Mammoth's surroundings is captured following an autumn snow storm. The combination of terrace, hot water, snow, steam, and dead trees creates a surreal feeling of heaven on earth.

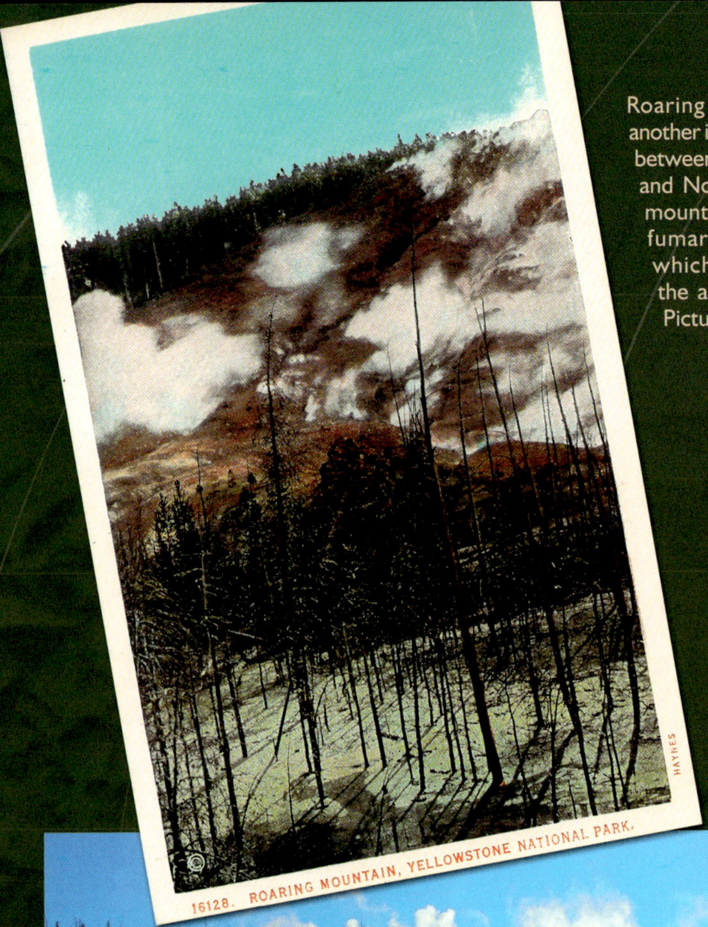

Roaring Mountain offers yet another interesting stop. Located between Mammoth Hot Springs and Norris Geyser Basin, the mountain contains countless fumaroles, or vents, from which steam escapes into the air. Postcard by Haynes Picture Shops, Inc.

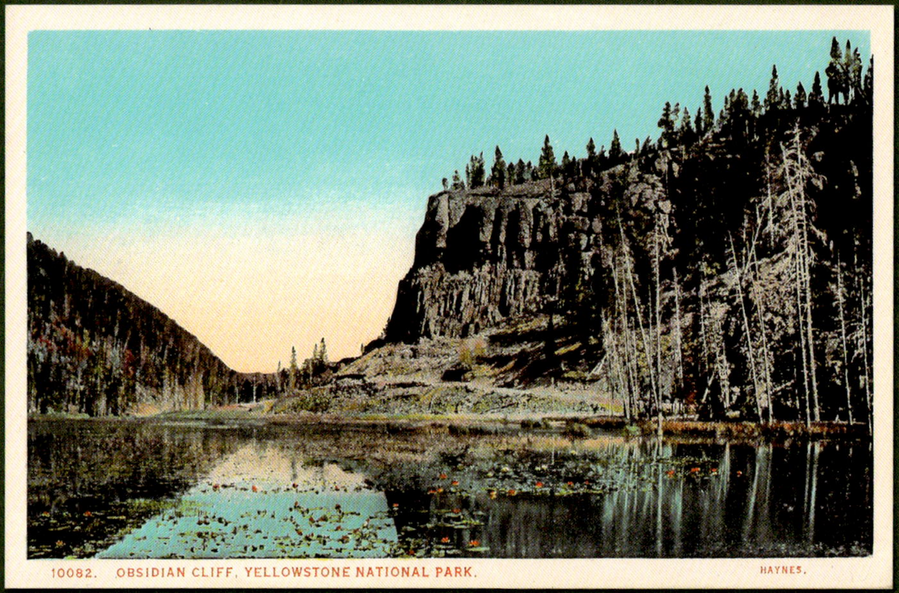

Obsidian Cliff can be found south of Mammoth Hot Springs at the northern end of Beaver Lake. In the early days, Native Americans came to this area to find volcanic glass for arrowhead material, according to information contained on this postcard by Haynes Picture Shops, Inc.

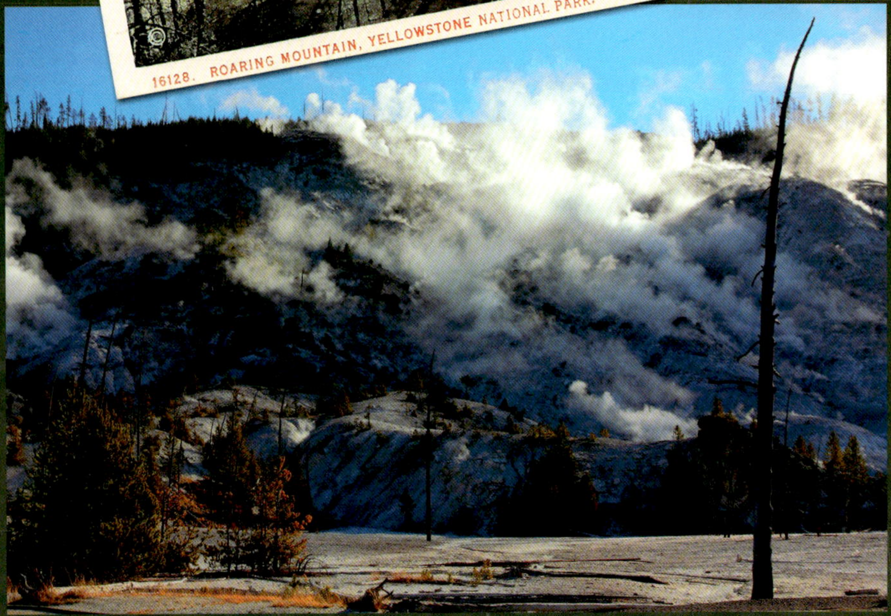

Roaring Mountain was named in the early 1900s for the sound of the steam escaping from the vents.

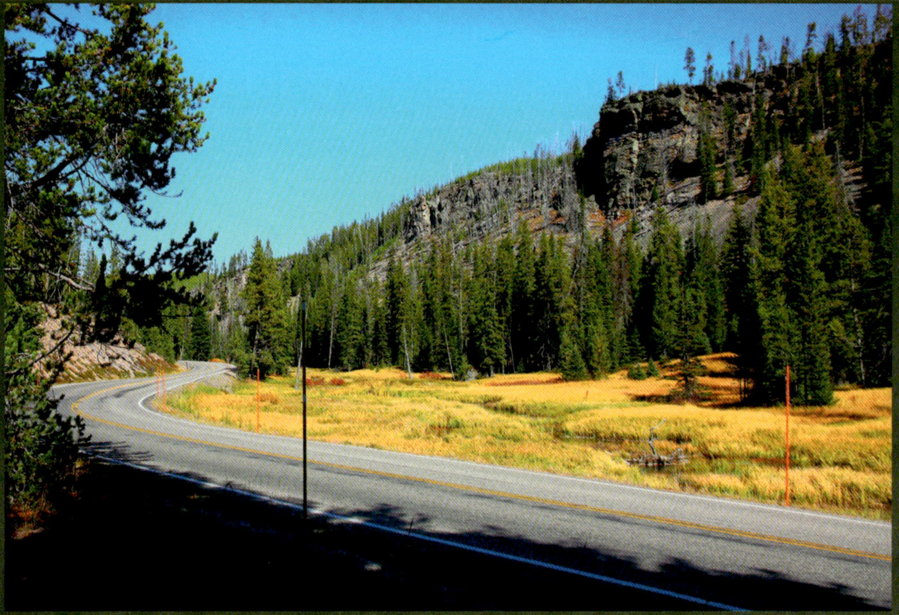

Obsidian Cliff is now a National Historic Landmark. Native Americans were known to use obsidian as knives and tips for spears and arrows. The obsidian in Yellowstone was used in trading as far east as Ohio.

TOWER-ROOSEVELT AREA

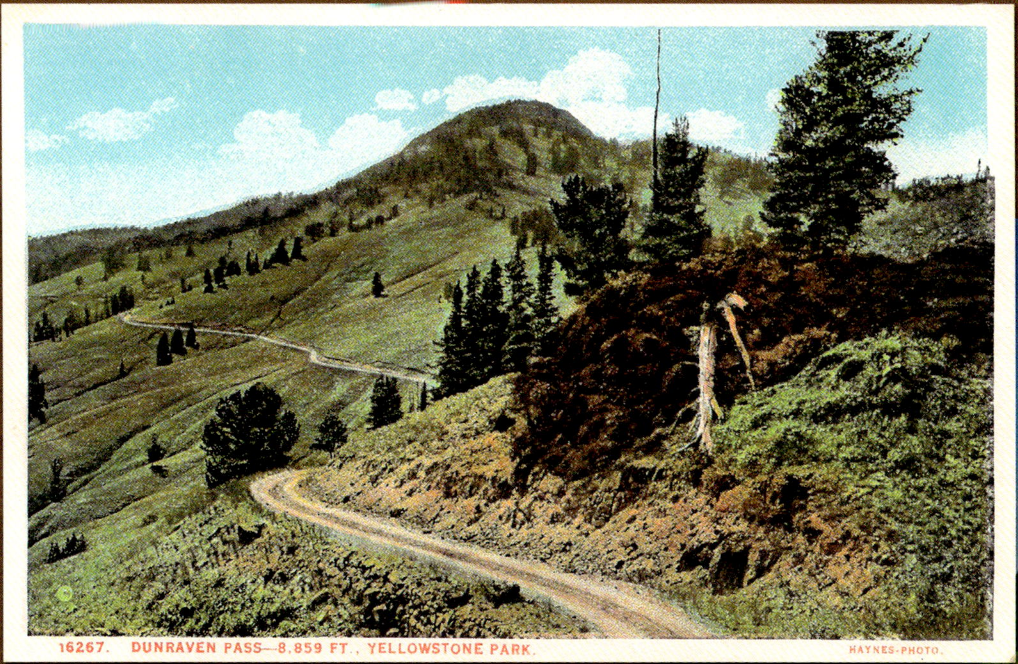

Dunraven Pass, with an elevation of nearly 8,900 feet, is located between the Canyon and Tower-Roosevelt areas on the Grand Loop Road. The pass is the highest elevation road inside the park and was named for the Earl of Dunraven who made trips to the area in the early days and published his observations about its beauty. Postcard by J. E. Haynes, St. Paul, Minnesota.

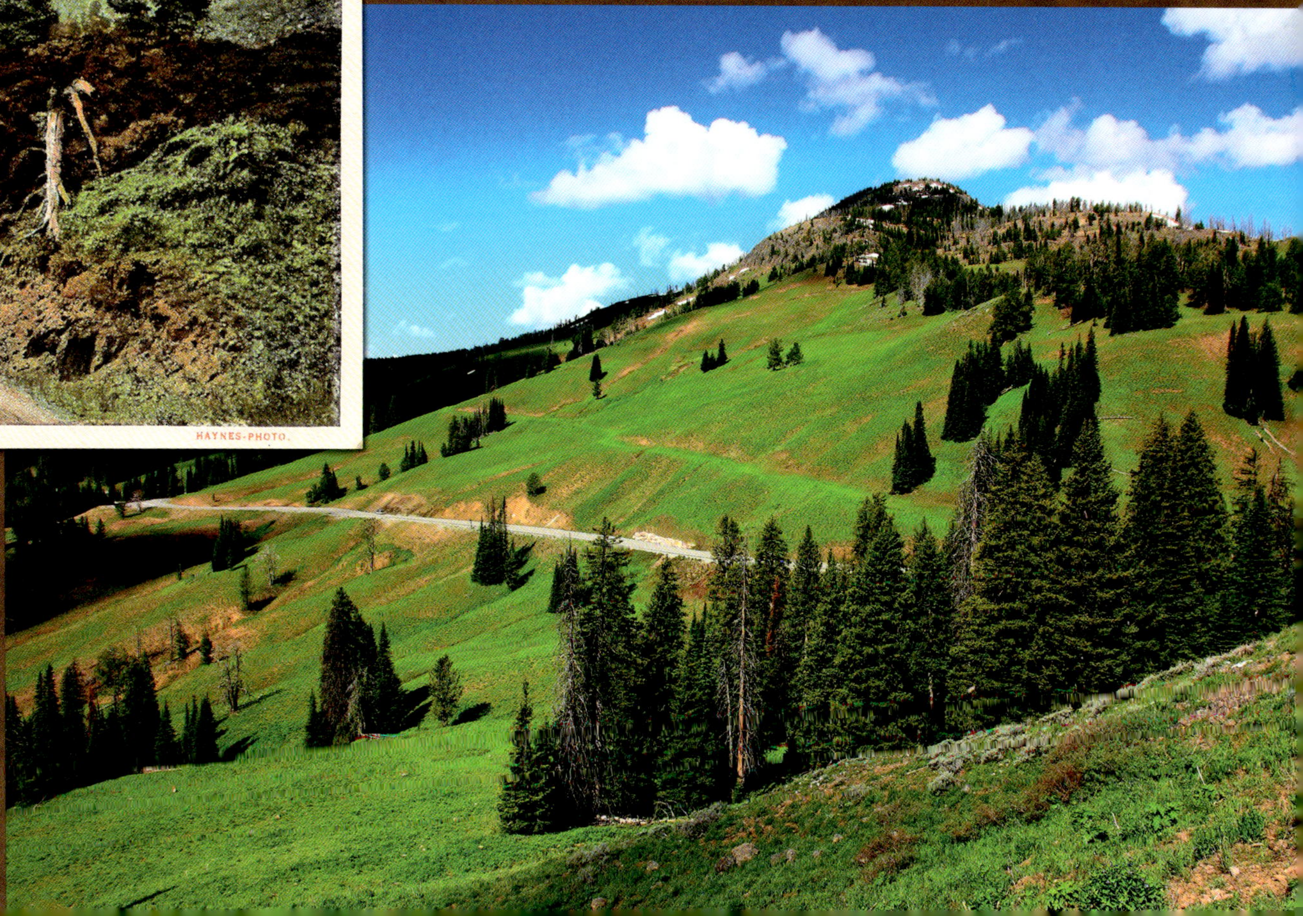

On a clear day like this one, views of the Dunraven Pass area are best seen from the early stages of a hike on the Mount Washburn Trail.

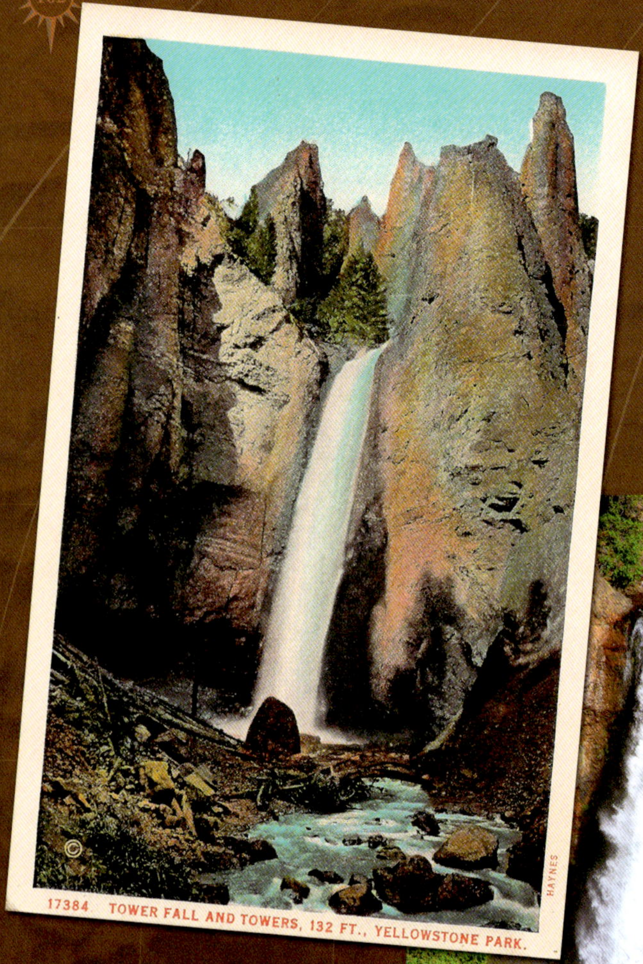

Another popular sight is Tower Fall, located near Tower Junction. The waterfall is 132 feet high and is framed by the towering volcanic formations above it. This was the setting for the famous painting by artist Thomas Moran who played a vital role in creation of the park. Postcard by Haynes Picture Shops, Inc.

Also in this area is the Petrified Tree which can be seen a short distance from the loop road. It is protected by fencing to prevent souvenir-taking. Haynes postcard.

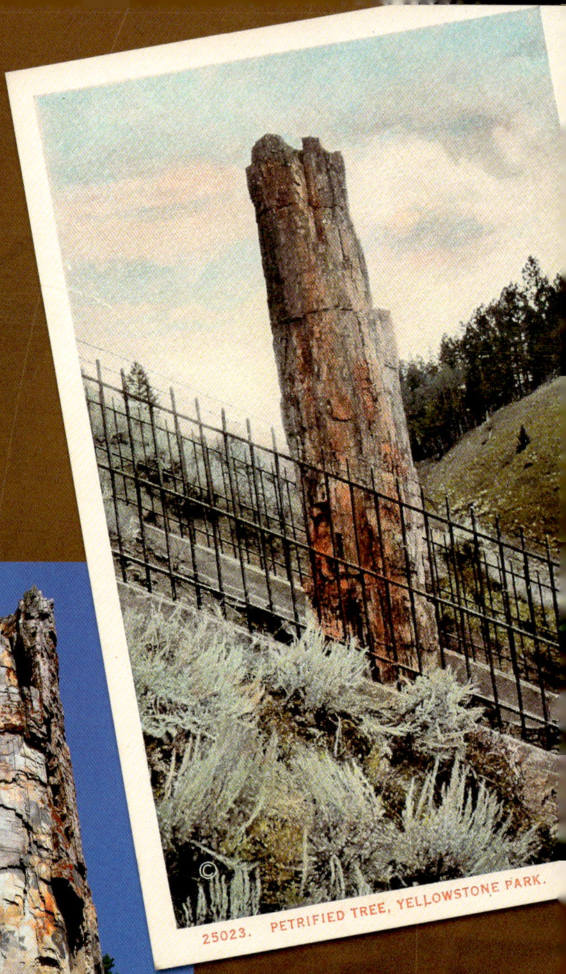

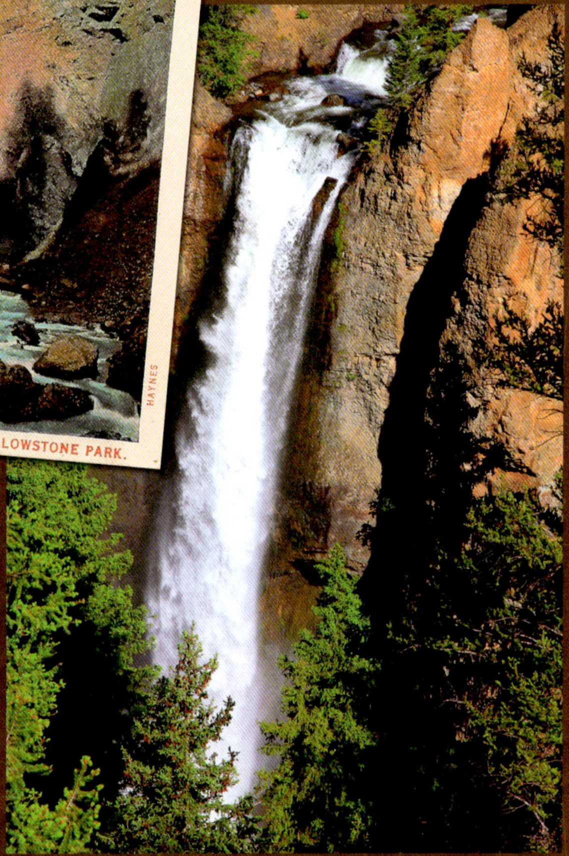

Tower Fall as pictured from the overlook. A half-mile trail to the base of the waterfall offers a more imposing view. The waterfall is also a popular sight in the winter for cross-country skiers and snowshoers.

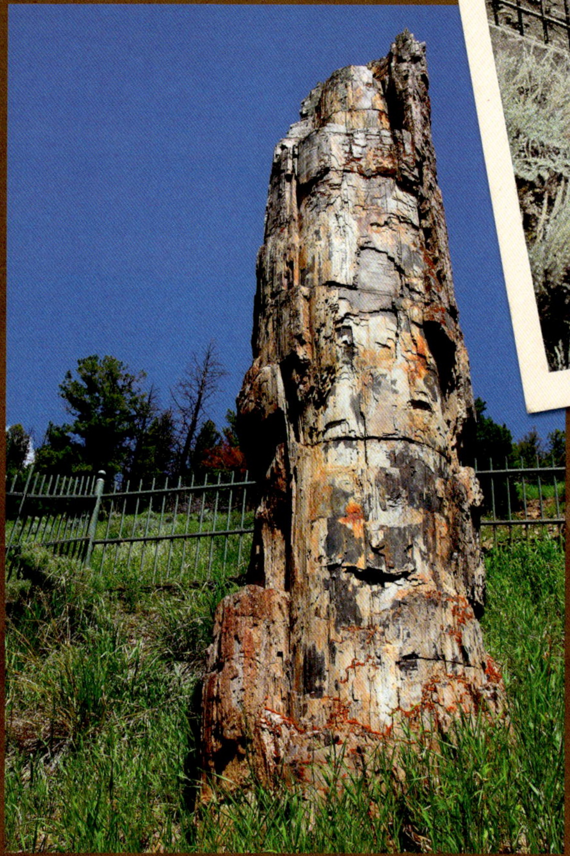

This ancient redwood is the only remaining petrified tree in the area. Two others were removed as souvenirs in earlier times.

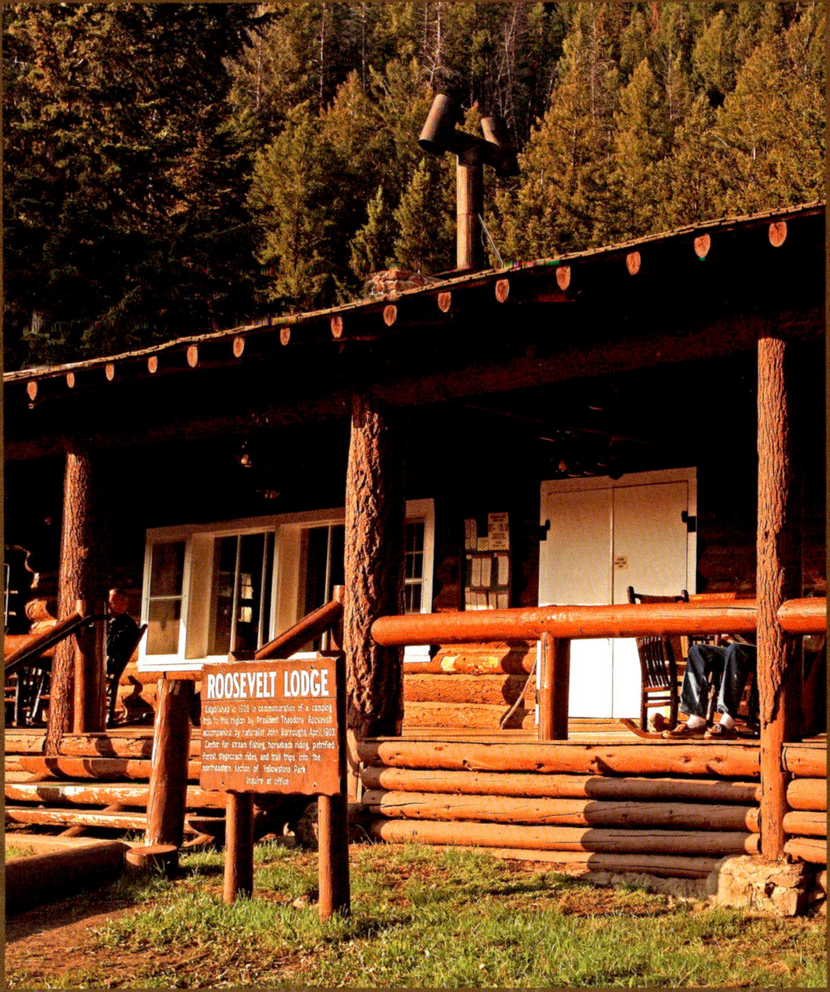

Roosevelt Lodge overlooks the Lamar River Valley. Near here, President Teddy Roosevelt camped for a month in 1903. The lodge is still in use as a dining hall and registration area for its cabins. *Courtesy of Xanterra Parks & Resorts.*

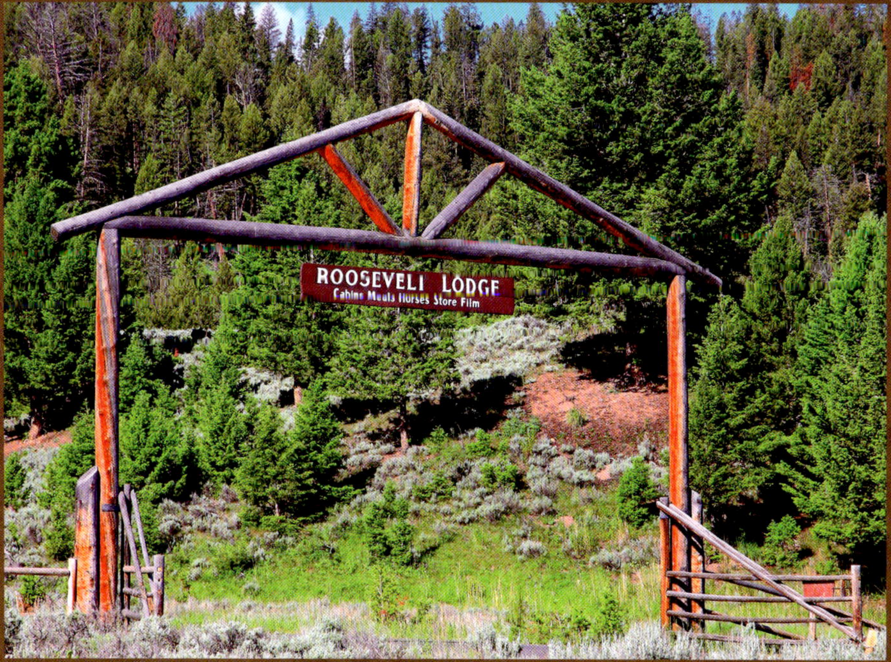

Guided trail rides, stage coach rides, as well as Old West Cookouts are available from the Roosevelt Lodge location and are provided by the park's concessionaire, Xanterra Parks & Resorts.

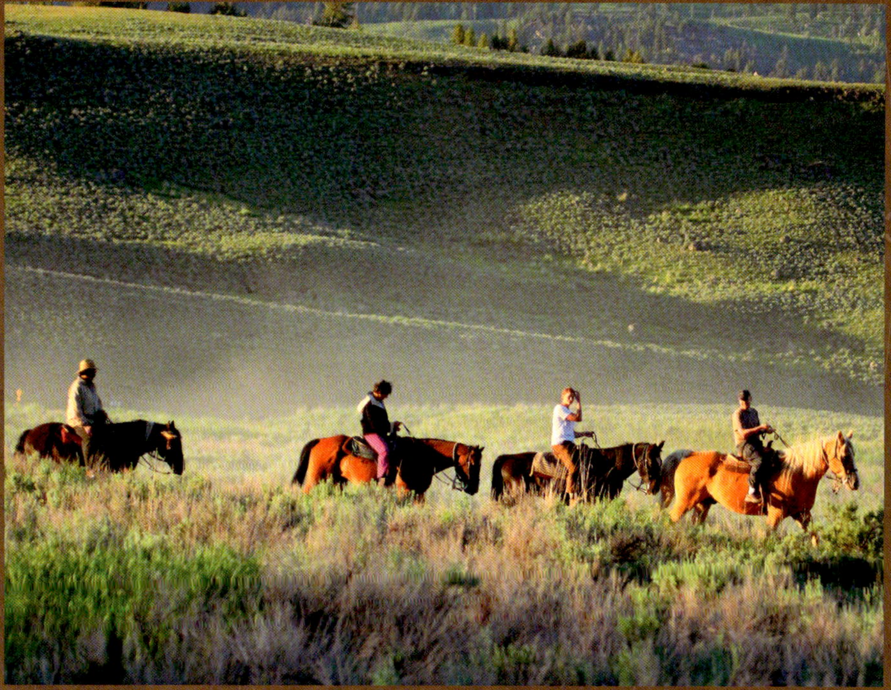

Trail rides offer a way to explore the park in a more quiet setting. In addition to the Roosevelt area, horseback riding is available in Canyon Village and Mammoth Hot Springs.

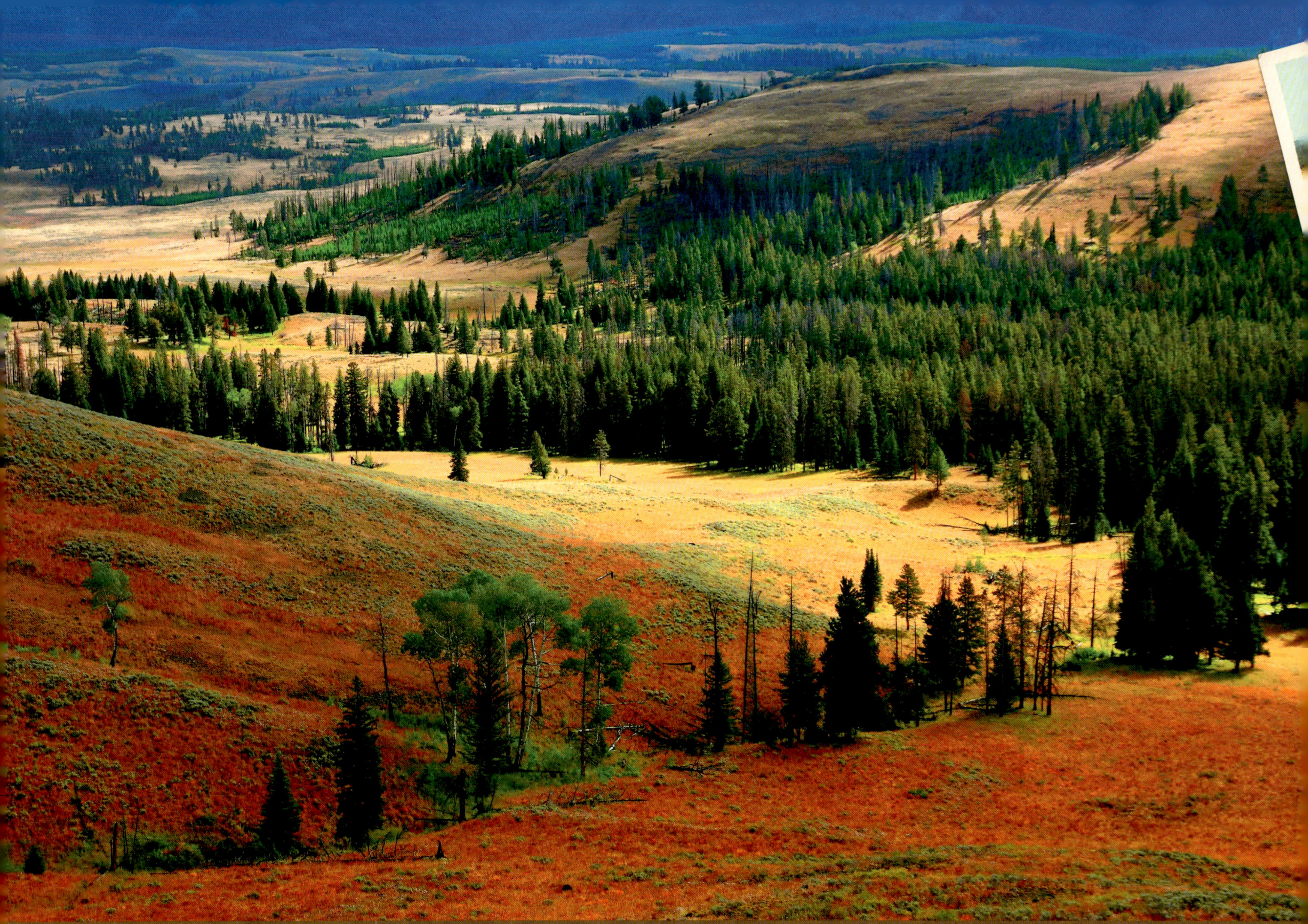

The northern part of the park near Tower Junction is especially beautiful during the fall, where visitors enjoy bird's-eye views of the open terrain from the Grand Loop Road. From this vantage point, elk and grizzly bears can oftentimes be seen in the distance.

CANYON AREA

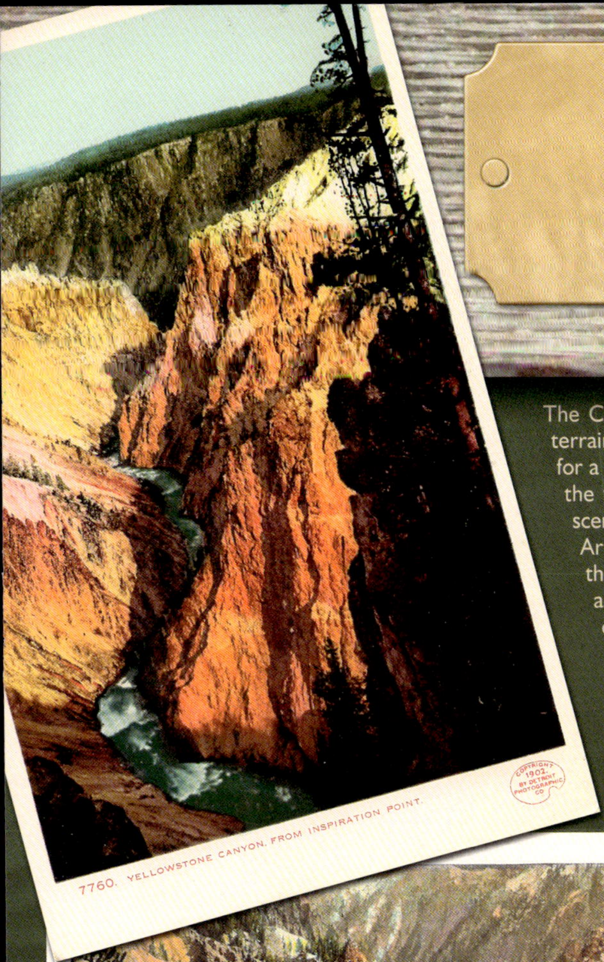

The Canyon area offers entirely different terrain where a stop at Inspiration Point for a view of the Yellowstone Canyon and the famous Lower Falls has provided a scenic wonder since the park's founding. Artist Point on the South Rim offers the classic view. Upper Falls Viewpoint and Uncle Tom's Trail are also popular on the South Rim. Inspiration Point, Grandview Point, Lookout Point, and Red Rock Point provide additional views of the canyon from the North Rim and are accessed by North Rim Drive. Postcard from 1902 by Detroit Photographic Co.

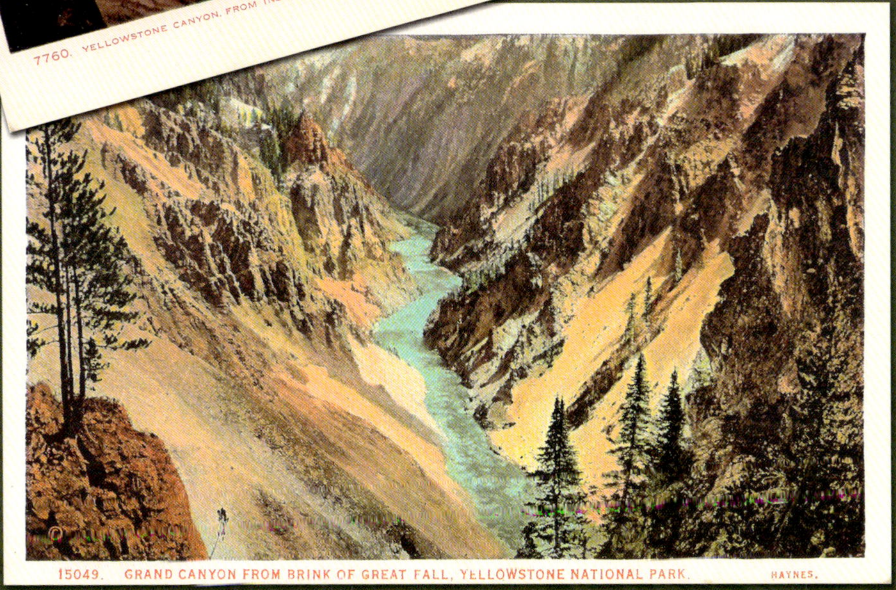

The Grand Canyon of the Yellowstone originated in the same volcanic eruption that created Yellowstone Lake. In some places it is 1,200 feet deep and 4,000 feet wide. There are three waterfalls in the canyon. Lower Falls, which was also known as Great Fall, is larger than its upstream companion, Upper Falls. Crystal Falls is located in the middle. This early postcard by Haynes Picture Shop shows the brink of Great Fall.

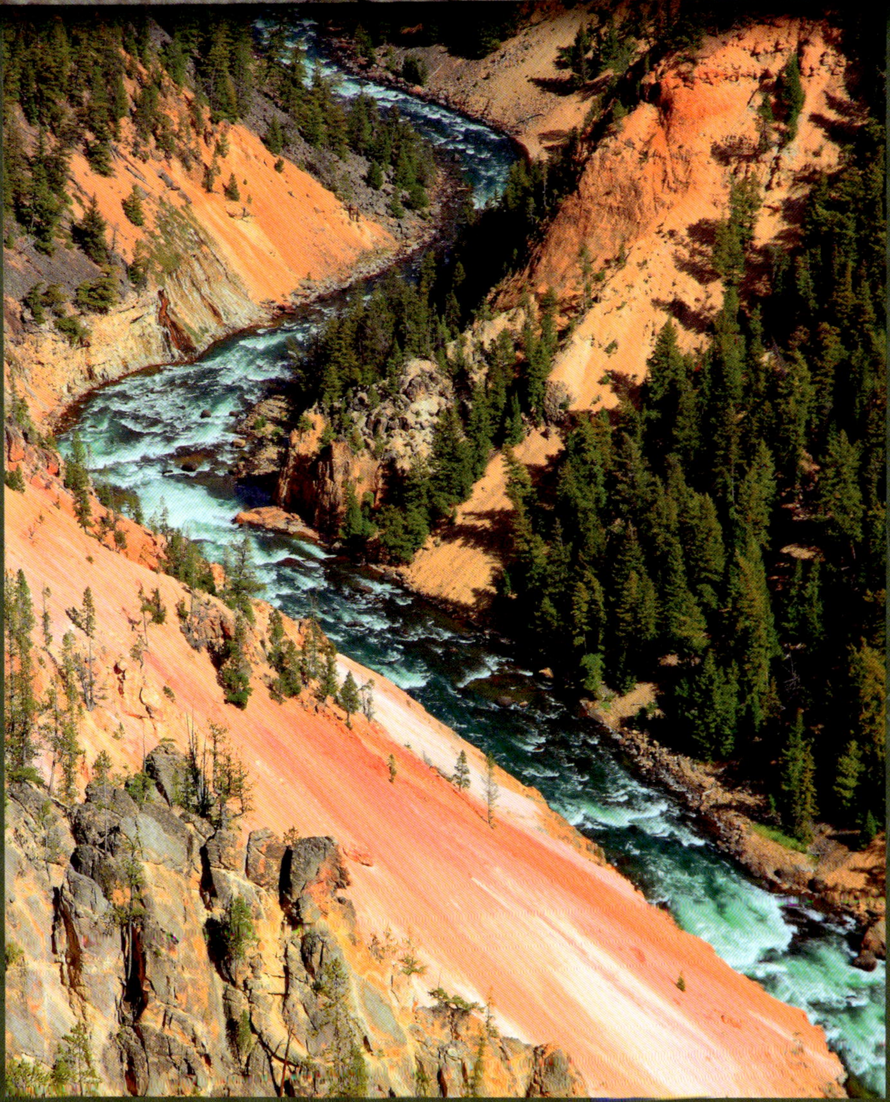

The sheer beauty and the rich colors of the Yellowstone River and the walls of the Grand Canyon come alive in this scene from Inspiration Point. The coloring of the walls is created by varying degrees of oxidation of the iron compounds within the rock.

Lower Falls (Great Fall) is one of the most photographed features in the park. This early postcard shows the enormity and surrounding beauty of the waterfall which measures 308 feet high. The picture was taken about halfway down the north wall of the gorge near Red Rock, according to information on the back of the card, "which is so close that its terrific roar adds awe to the spectacle." Postcard by Haynes Picture Shops.

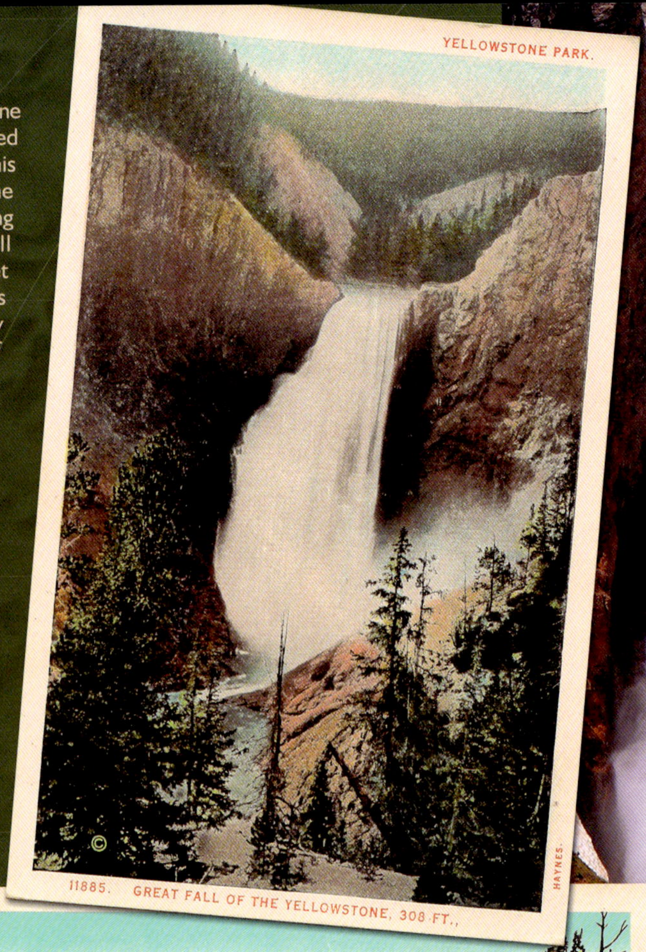

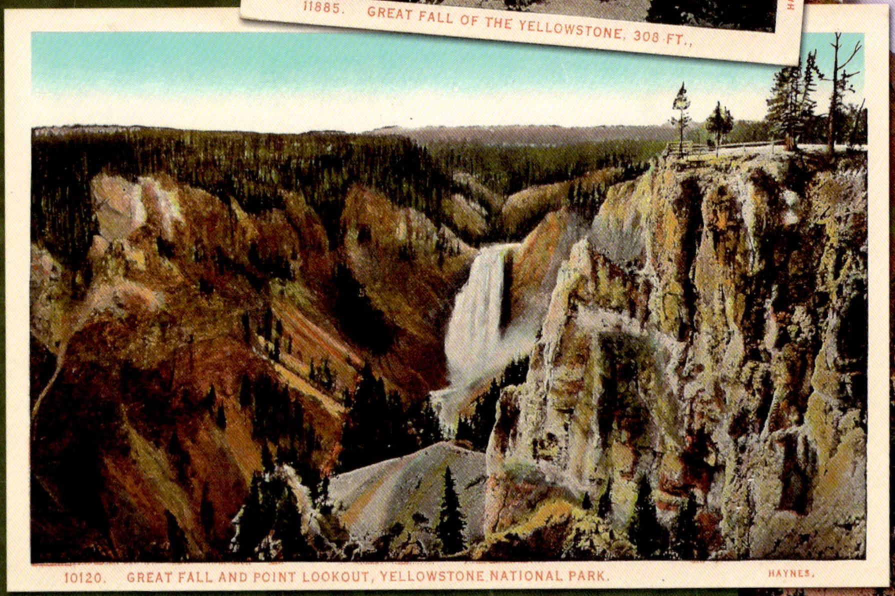

Another scene of Lower Falls is shown from Lookout Point in this early postcard by Haynes Picture Shops.

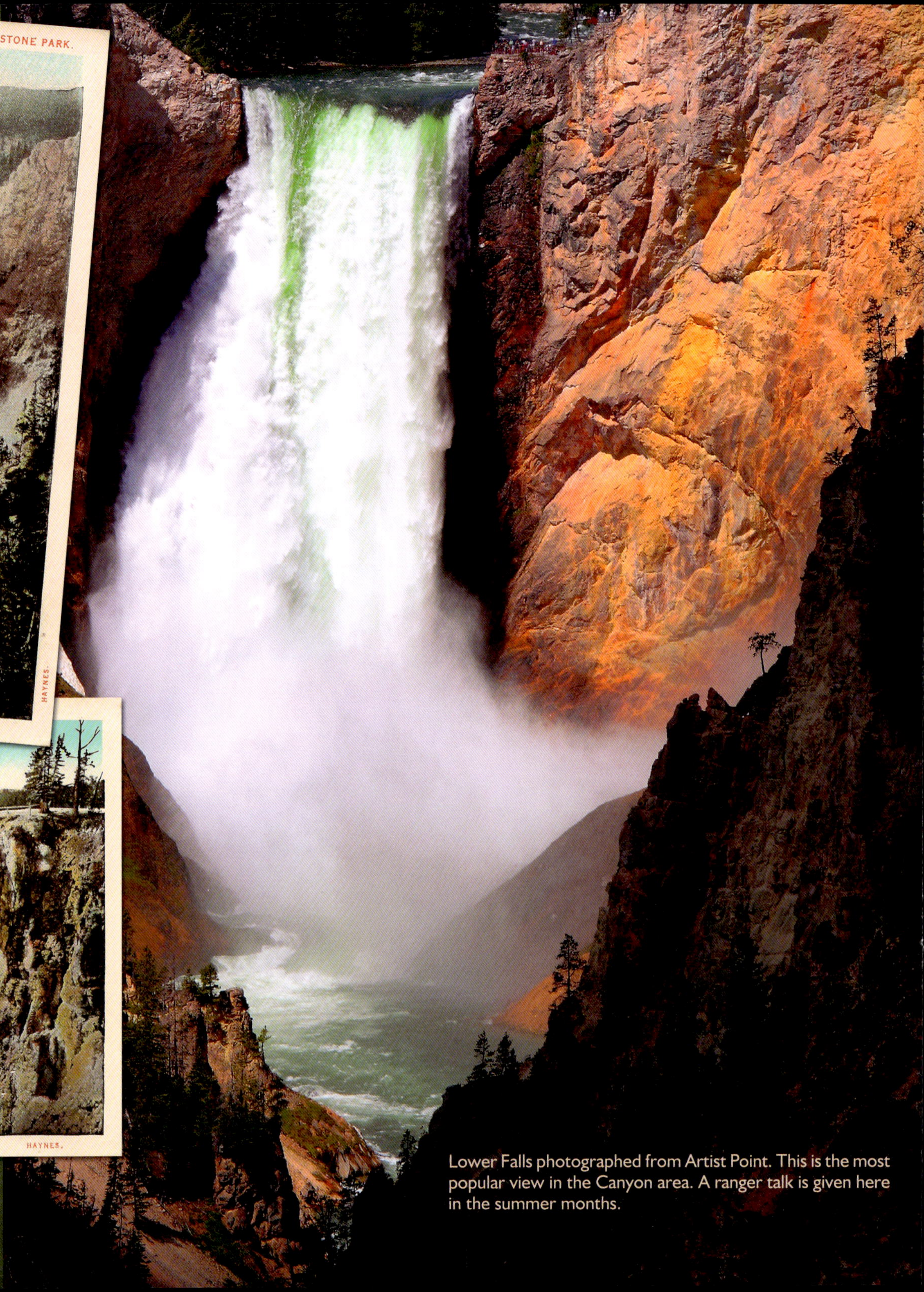

Lower Falls photographed from Artist Point. This is the most popular view in the Canyon area. A ranger talk is given here in the summer months.

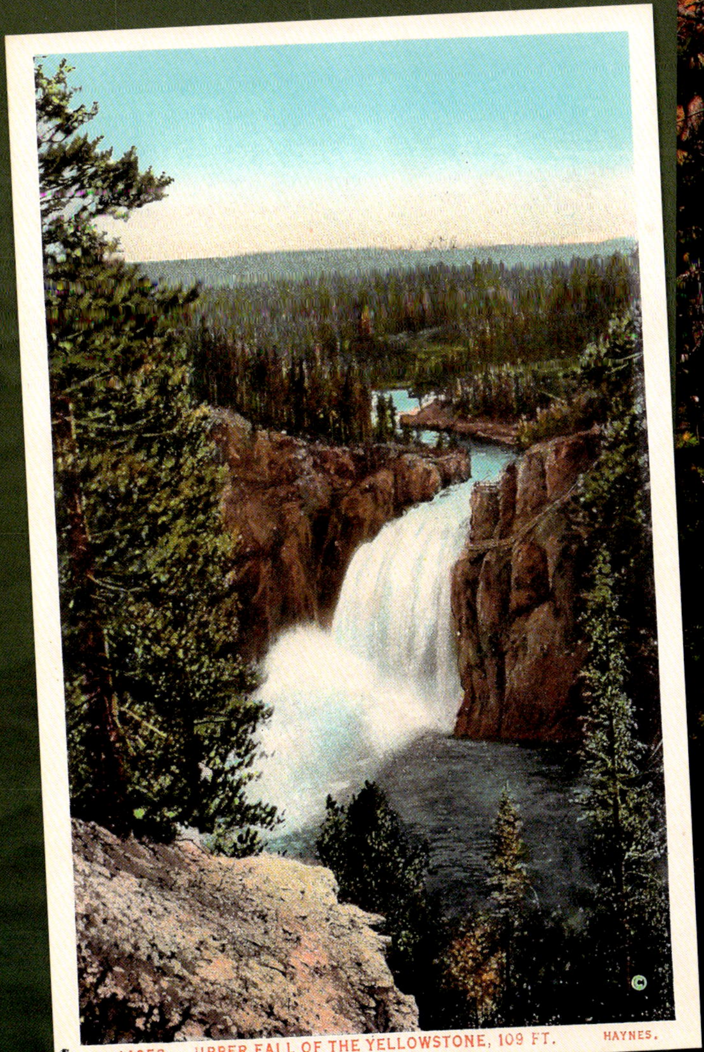

The Upper Falls is about a half-mile upstream of the Lower Falls and is 109 feet high, as pictured on this Haynes Picture Shops postcard.

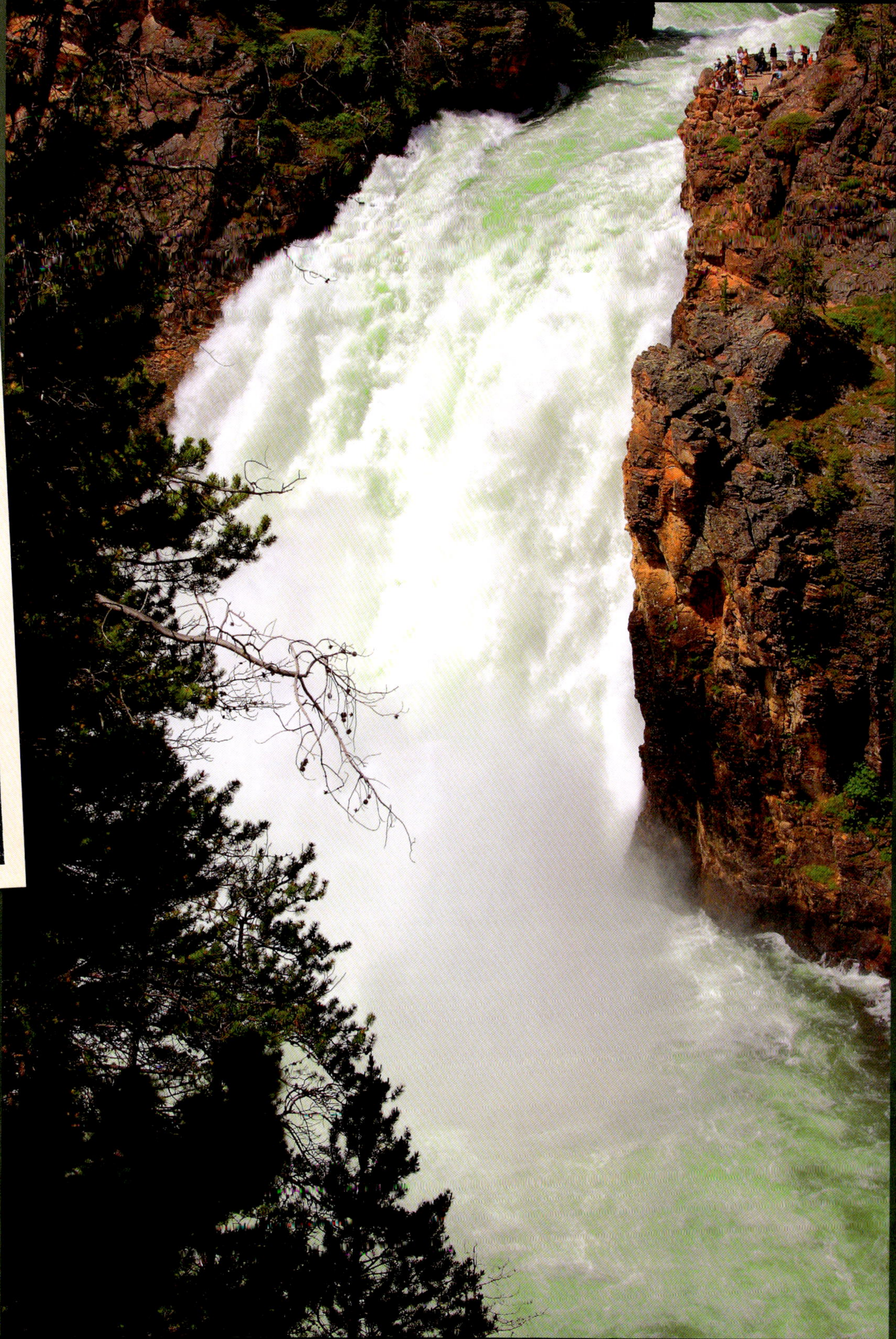

Upper Falls as seen from the Upper Falls Viewpoint. Another viewing area is the brink of the Upper Falls, where a group of visitors can be seen standing on the right.

YELLOWSTONE LAKE AREA
GRANT VILLAGE • WEST THUMB

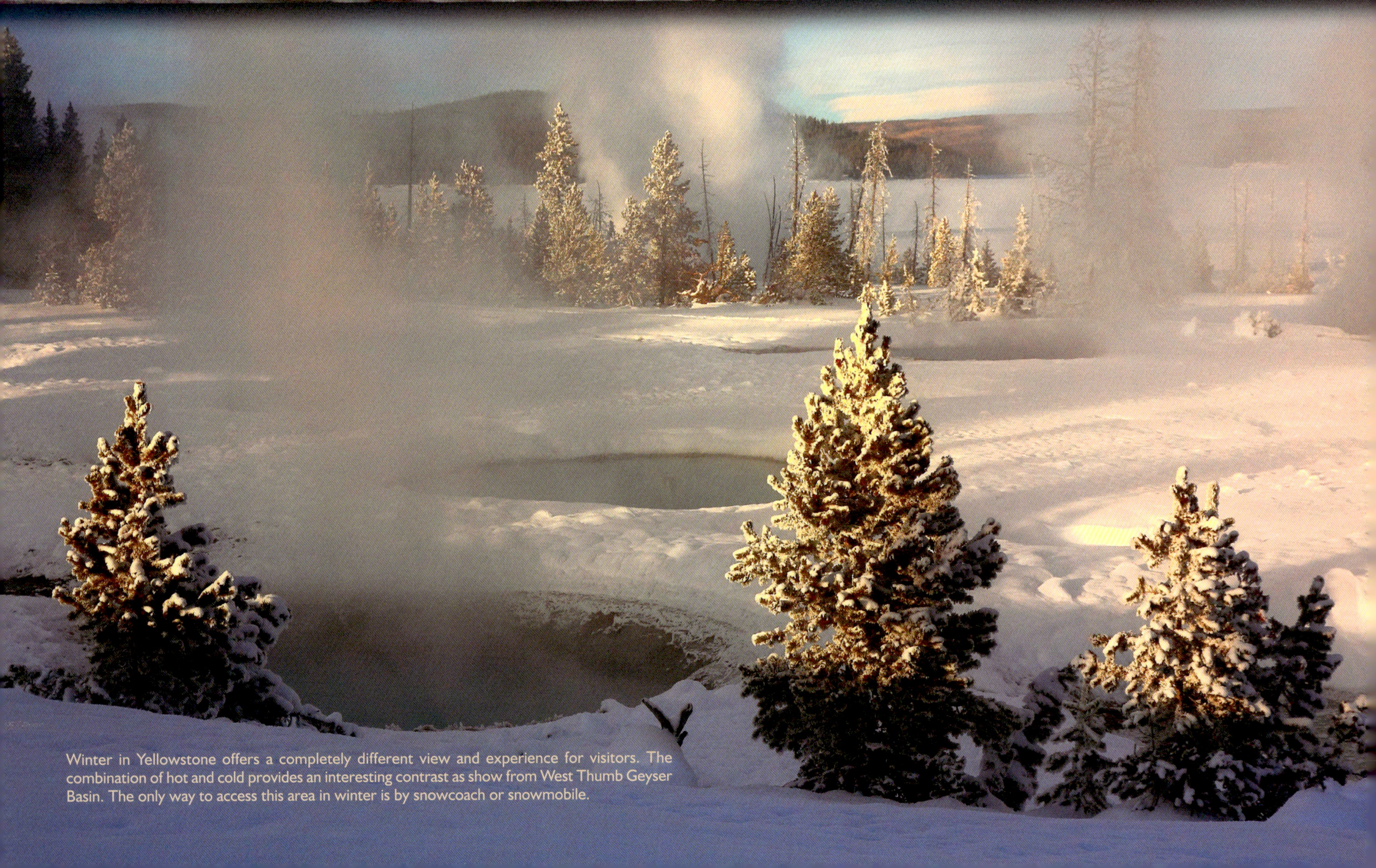

Winter in Yellowstone offers a completely different view and experience for visitors. The combination of hot and cold provides an interesting contrast as show from West Thumb Geyser Basin. The only way to access this area in winter is by snowcoach or snowmobile.

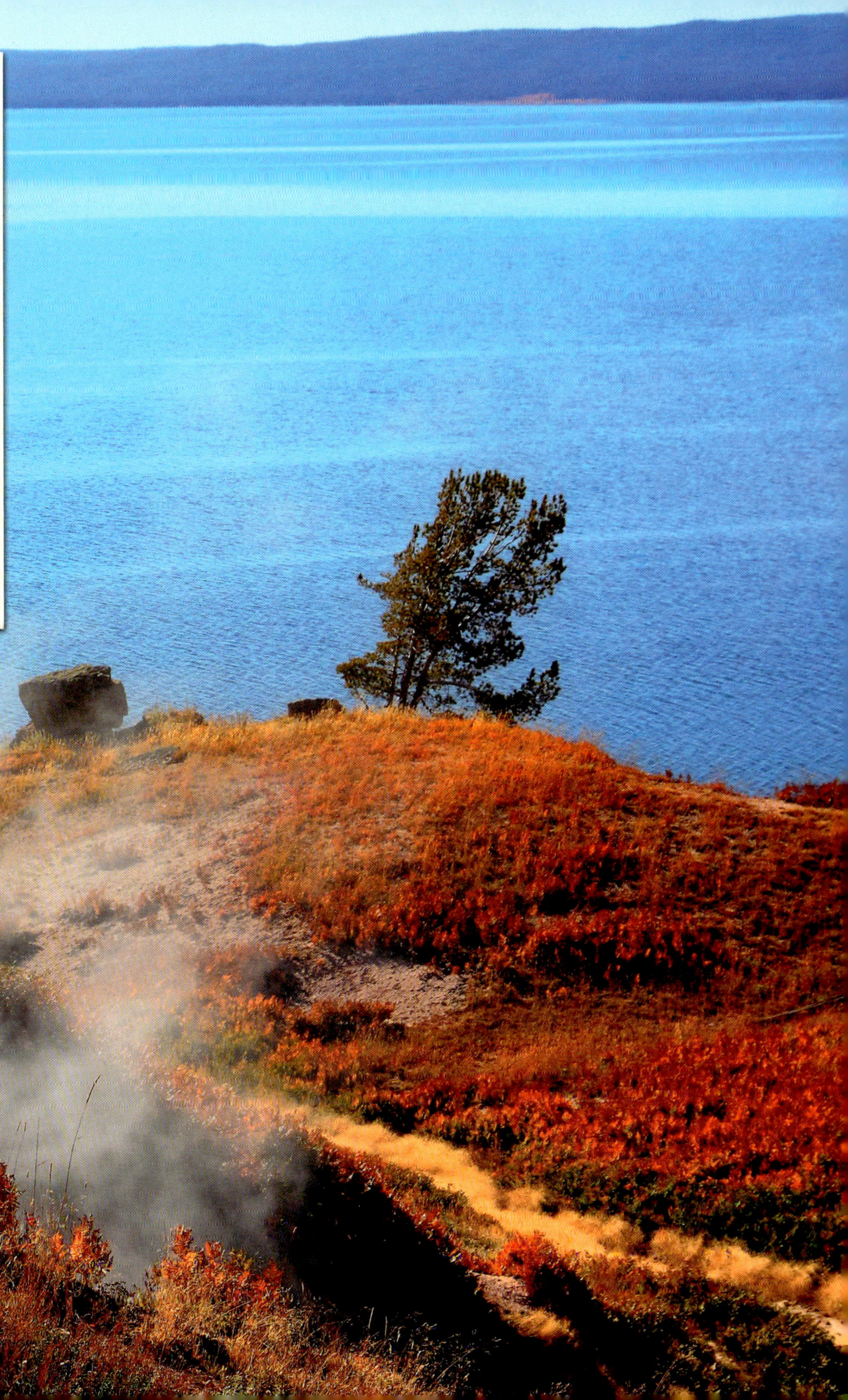

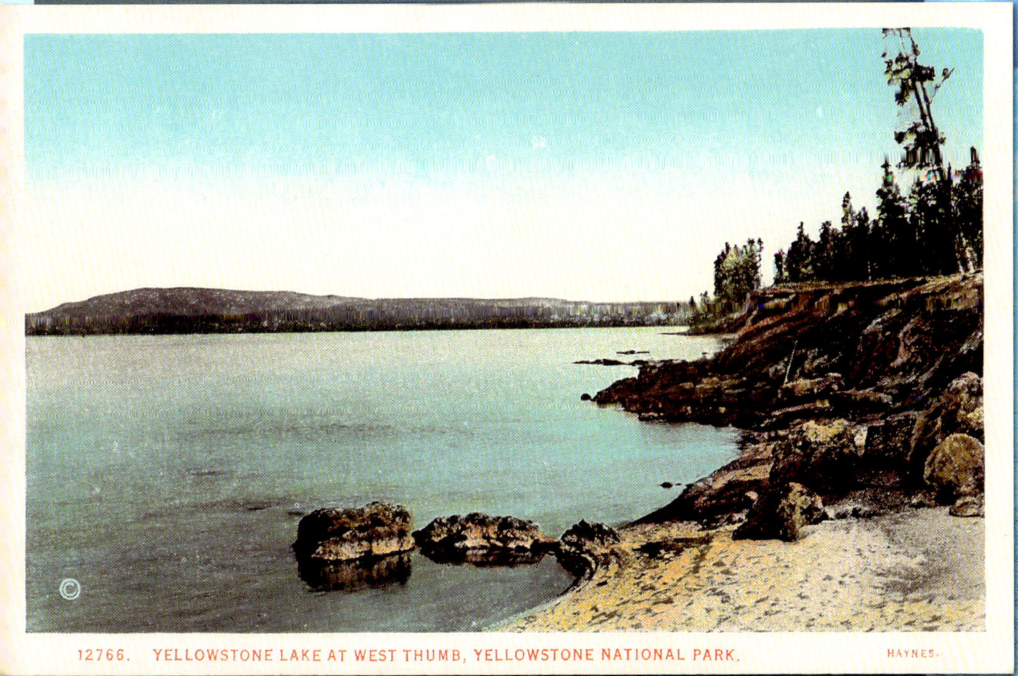

Yellowstone Lake can be accessed at West Thumb as pictured on this early postcard. A description of the area is described on the back of the card, "Near the geysers and paint pots near West Thumb Bay this beautiful picture of Yellowstone Lake was taken. With its shoreline of one hundred miles and its elevation of 7,730 feet, Yellowstone Lake is the largest lake at its elevation in North America." The lake is twenty miles long and fifteen miles wide. Recreation here includes fishing, boating, and hiking. At one time, it had the largest population of cutthroat trout in North America. Postcard by Haynes Picture Shops, Inc.

Yellowstone Lake as pictured from Steamboat Point. In addition to West Thumb, Steamboat Point is another place to see the thermal features around the lake.

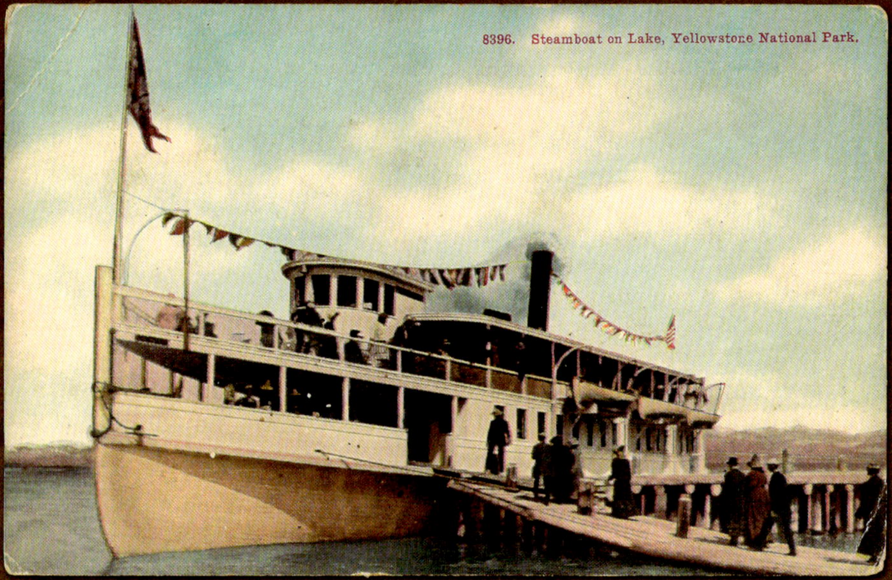

This early unmarked postcard of a steamboat on Lake Yellowstone pictures ladies in long dresses circa early 1900s. Although no name can be seen on the vessel, in earlier days, tourists could travel on a boat called *Zillah* from Thumb Bay across Lake Yellowstone to the Lake Hotel.

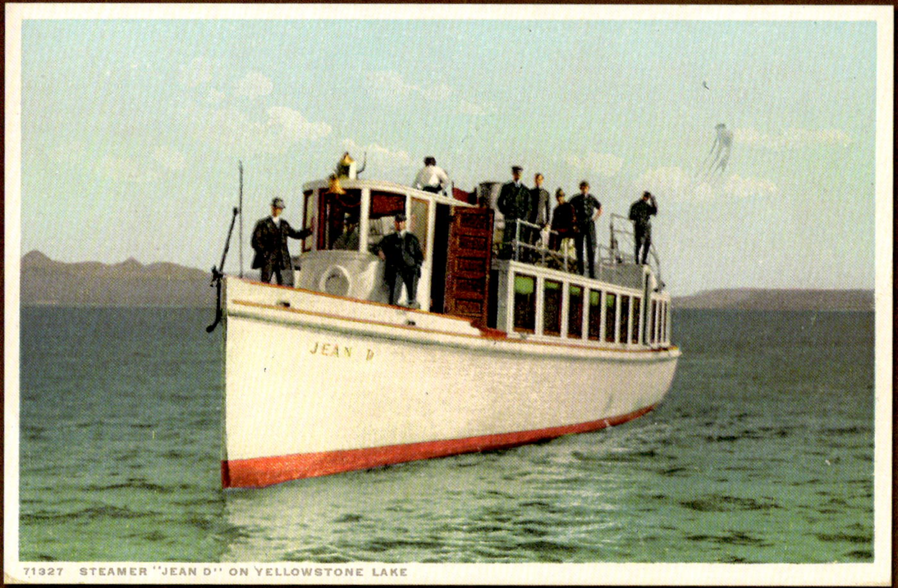

Jean D. was one of the steamers used on Yellowstone Lake to provide scenic tours as pictured on this postcard. On the back of the card is handwritten "Summer 1914" which is apparently when the visitor's trip was made. Phostint card made by Detroit Publishing Co.

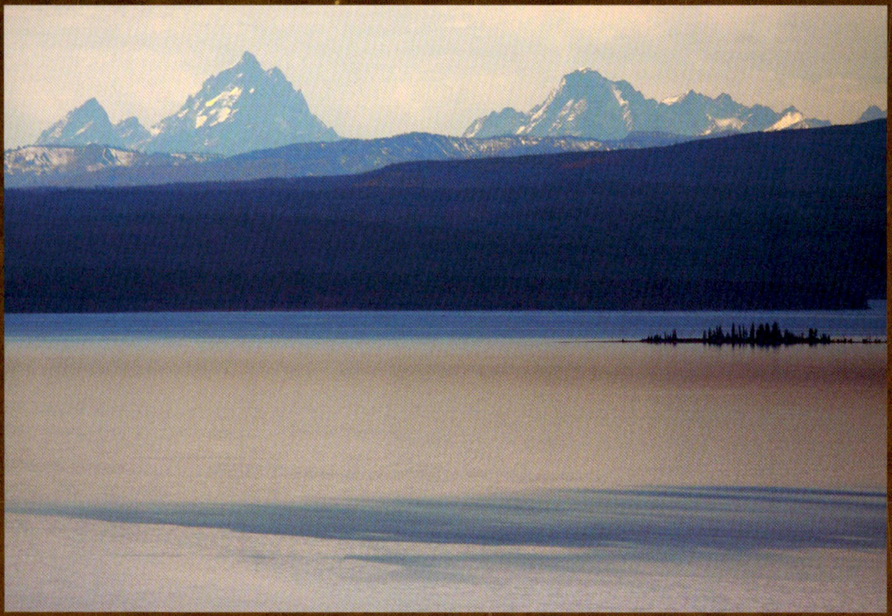

The jagged peaks of the Grand Tetons, some sixty miles away, can be seen in the distance as the calming waters of Yellowstone Lake are shown from the Lake Butte Overlook.

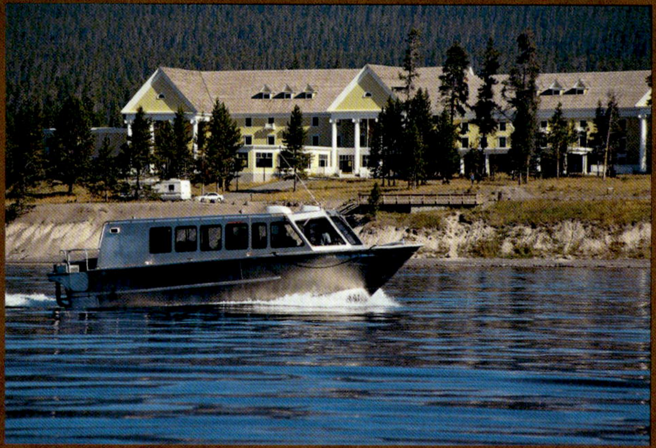

Today, visitors can enjoy tours of the lake aboard the *Lake Queen II*, which is shown passing by the Lake Hotel. The cruises are offered by the park's concessionaire. Boat rentals also are available. *Courtesy Xanterra Parks & Resorts.*

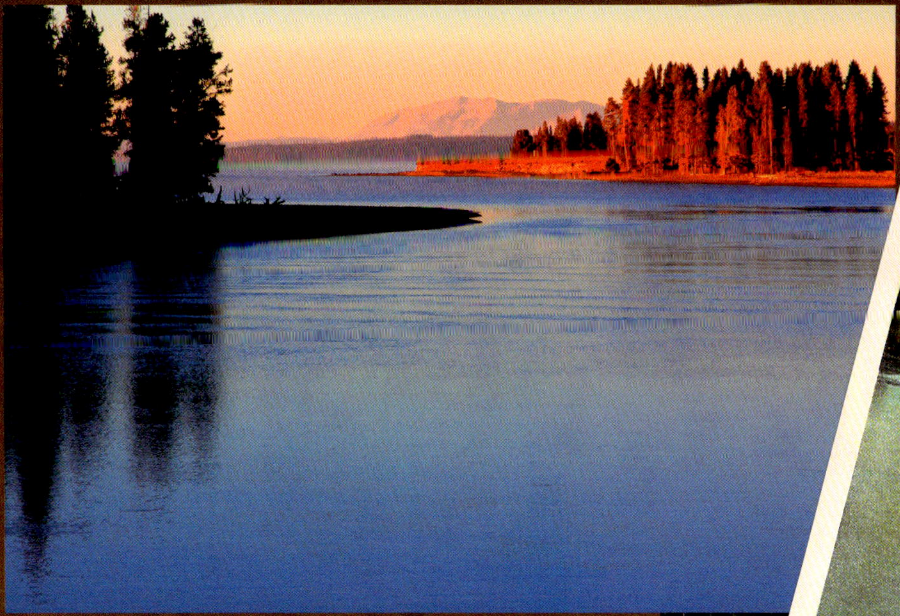

Yellowstone Lake as pictured from Fishing Bridge at sunrise. The lake has a shoreline of nearly one hundred miles and an area of about 140 square miles, with a depth around four hundred feet.

The Fishing Bridge spanned the Yellowstone River and was built in 1902. For decades, visitors were allowed to fish from the bridge as pictured on this postcard. This was the favorite fishing place for thousands of tourists who came to catch cutthroat trout. The back of the card notes the convenience of the nearby Fishing Bridge Auto Campgrounds which offered free camping. This bridge was replaced in 1937. Postcard published by J. E. Haynes.

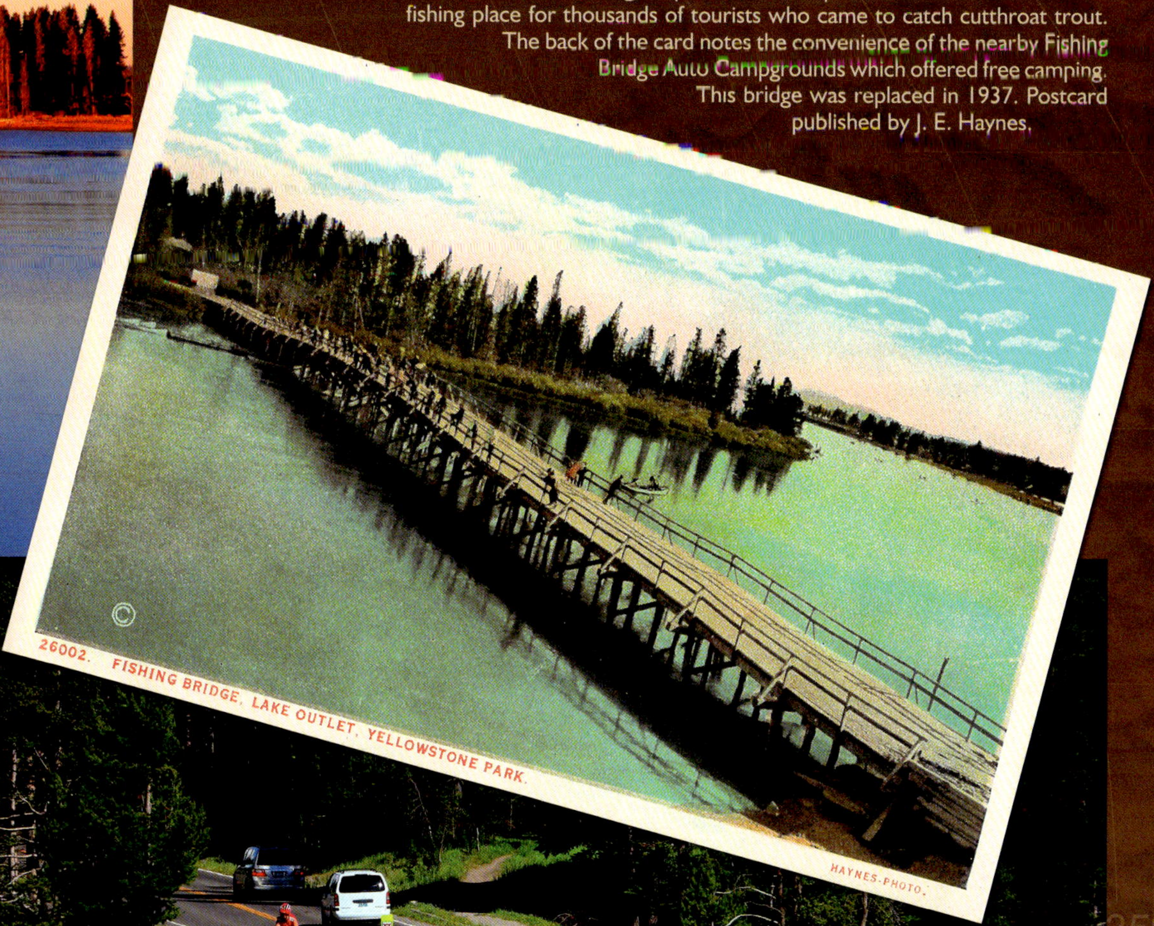

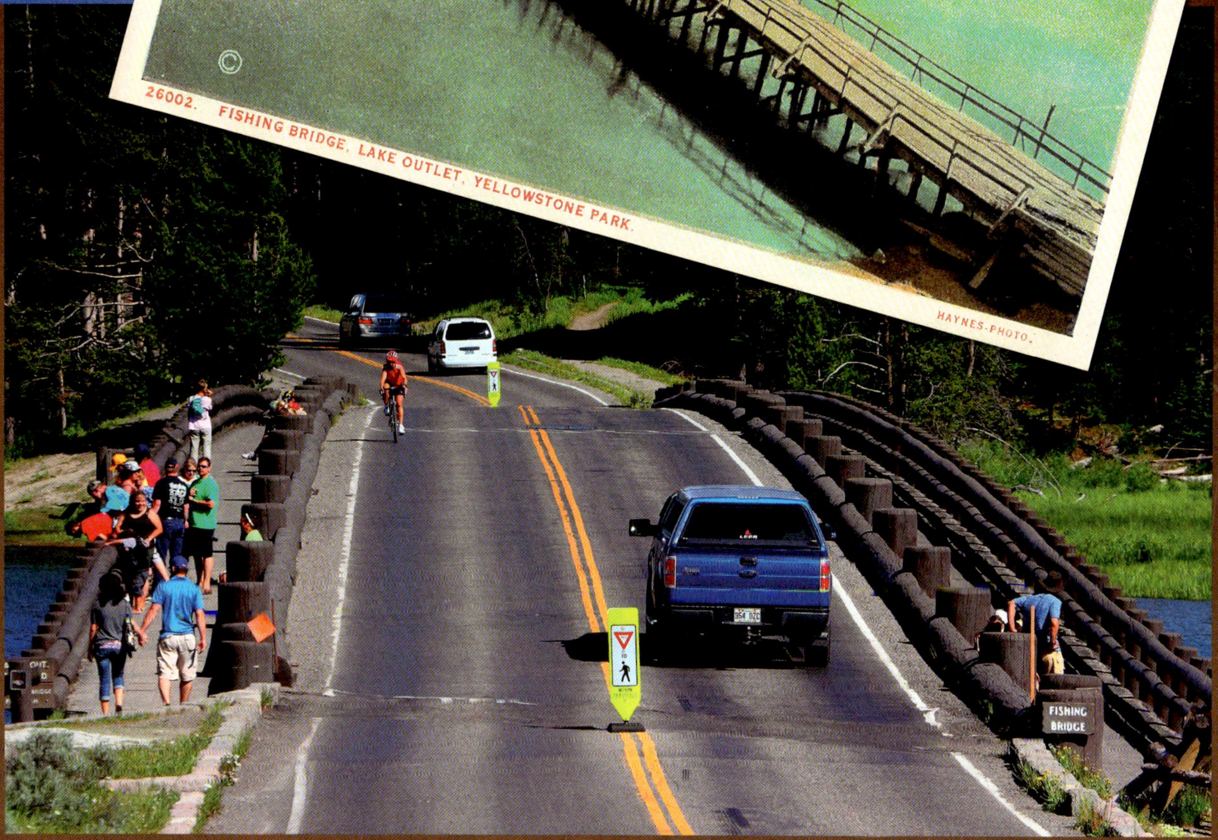

While fishing from the new bridge has been prohibited since 1973 to protect the spawning of native cutthroat trout, today's visitors can usually see pelicans and Canadian geese from this location. The Fishing Bridge Visitor Center and the Yellowstone Park General Store are also in the area.

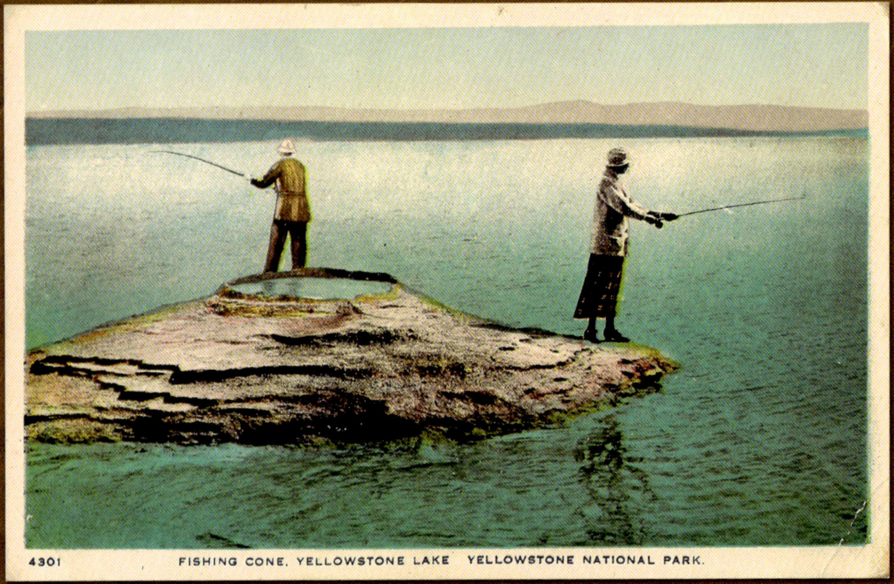

An unusual way to fish in Yellowstone Lake was from this Fishing Cone as shown on this early postcard which pictures a man and woman standing on the cone as they fish for trout. Information on the card states, "Fish Pot, part of the famous Paint Pots, is located a few feet out of the lake with a cone standing about two feet out of the water." HHT Co. postcard.

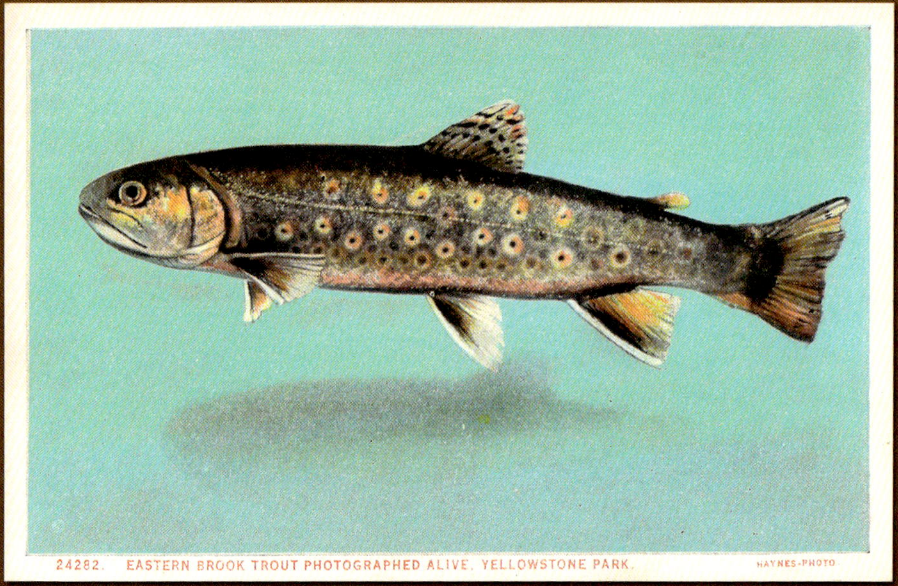

Most people fish for trout in Yellowstone Park. This early postcard pictures an Eastern brook trout. Others include rainbows, mackinaws, cutthroats, and other species of game fish, according to information on this early card. Published by J. E. Haynes.

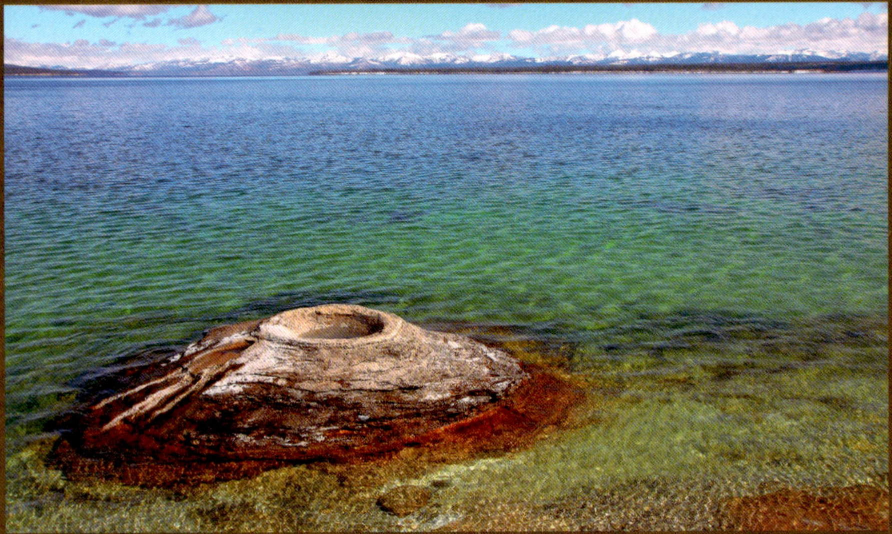

The Fishing Cone looks much as it did in its earlier years and provides a sharp contrast to the blue waters of the lake. In the early days of the park, the so called "Hook-N-Cook" activity was attempted in response to adventurer Jim Bridger's famous tall tale. Bridger boasted of catching a fish in the lake, swinging it into the hot spring and immediately cooking the fish on the hook. Regulations prohibiting such practices were implemented long ago. Visitors are also no longer allowed to stand on the cone due to safety concerns.

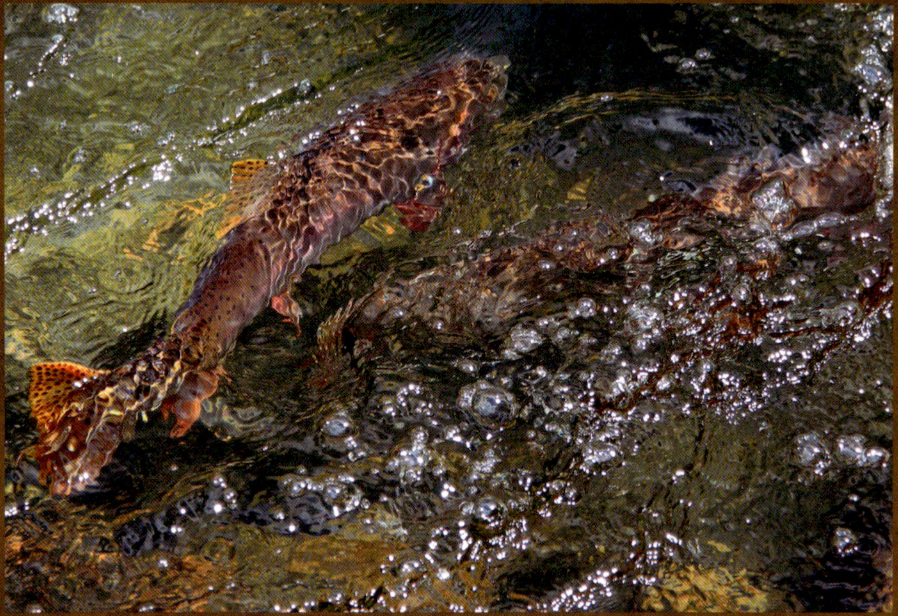

LeHardy Rapids is one of the best places to see cutthroat trout spawn. Here, trout are getting ready to jump over the rapids to their destination in Yellowstone Lake.

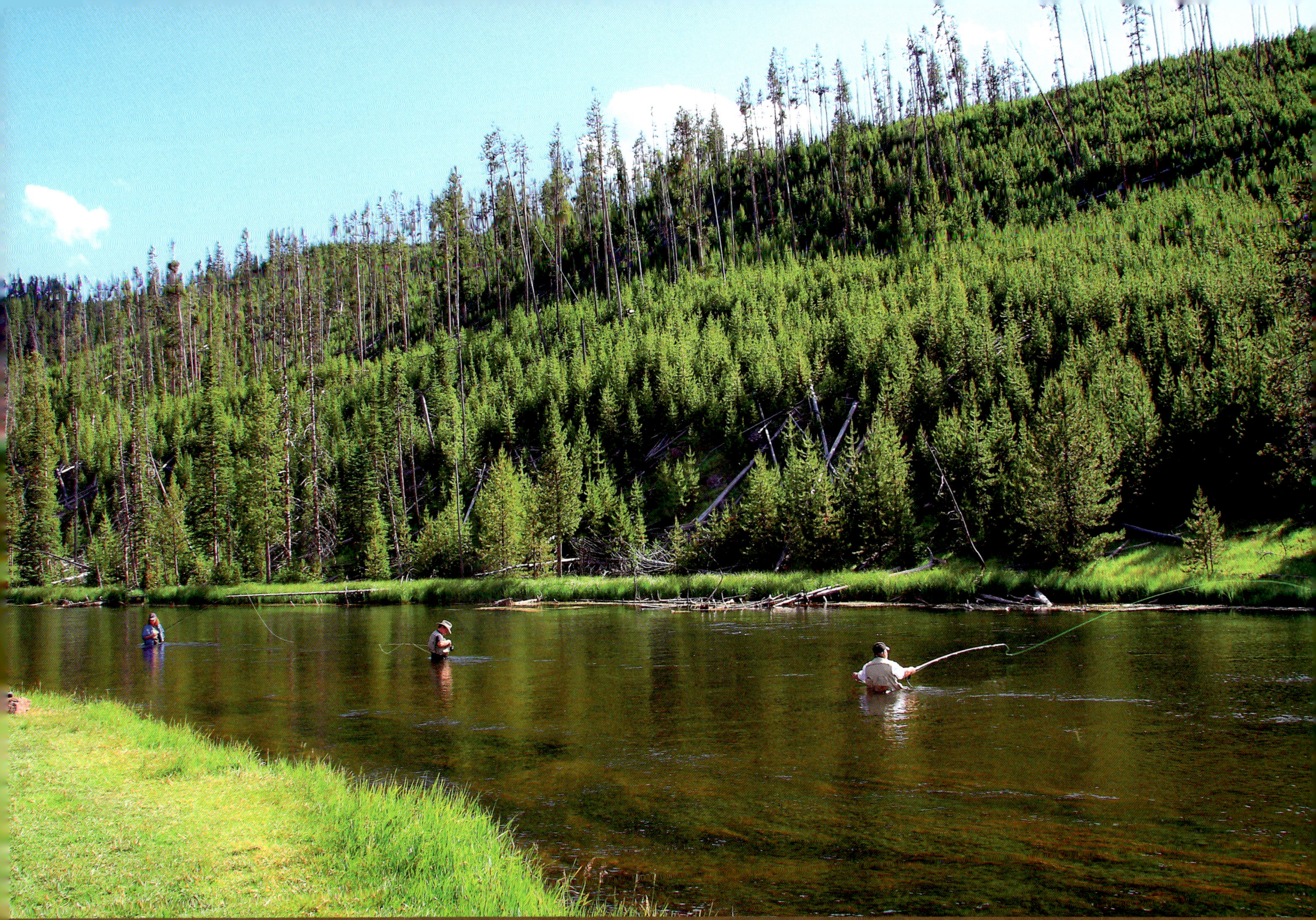

Fly fishing is also a popular activity in the park. These fishermen were photographed along Gibbon River. Catch and release policies are in place for most fish, except lake trout, an invasive species that threatens native fish. A park fishing license, available throughout the park, is required.

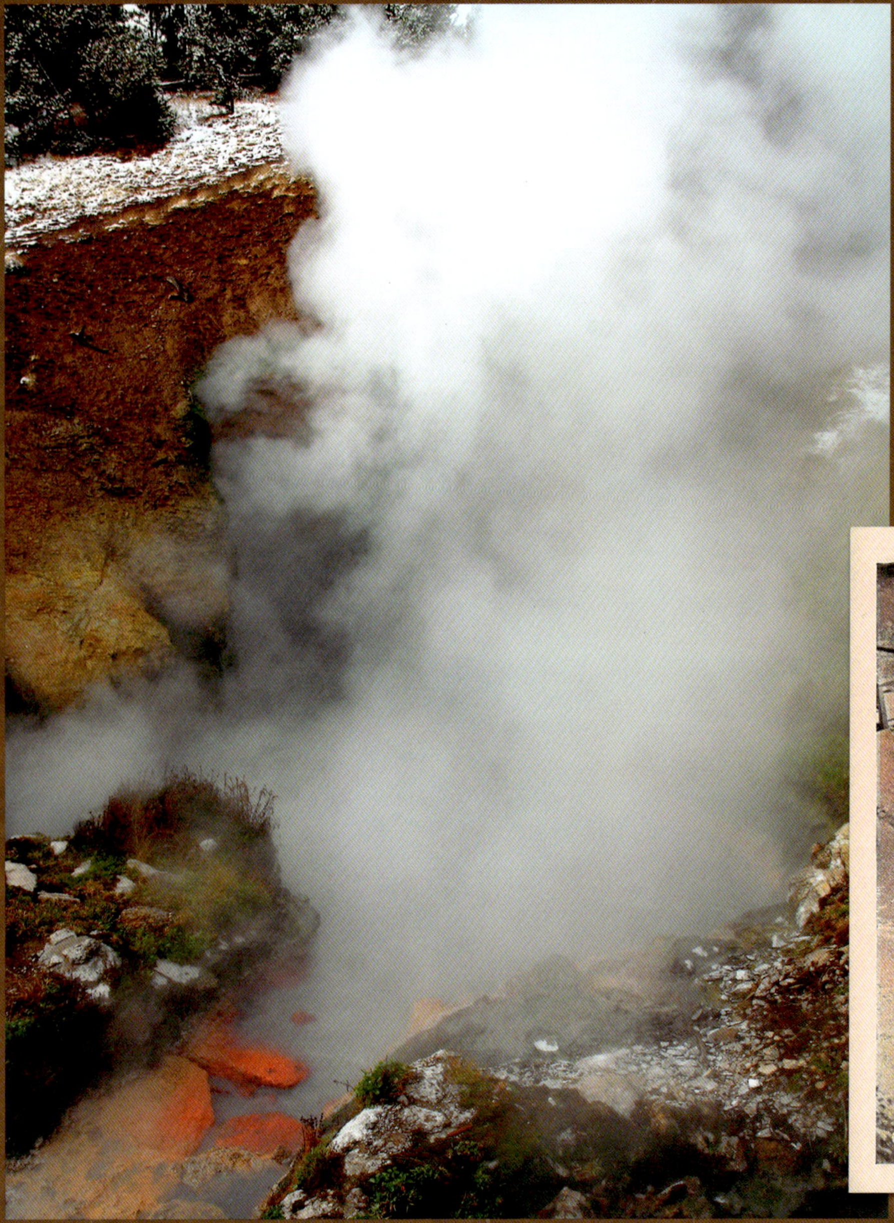

North of Yellowstone Lake is the Mud Volcano, an active thermal feature with a distinctive odor which is full of boiling mud pots. Dragon's Mouth Spring can be found here in a cave on the hillside. It was named for its tongue-like look when gases cause the water to splash back and forth.

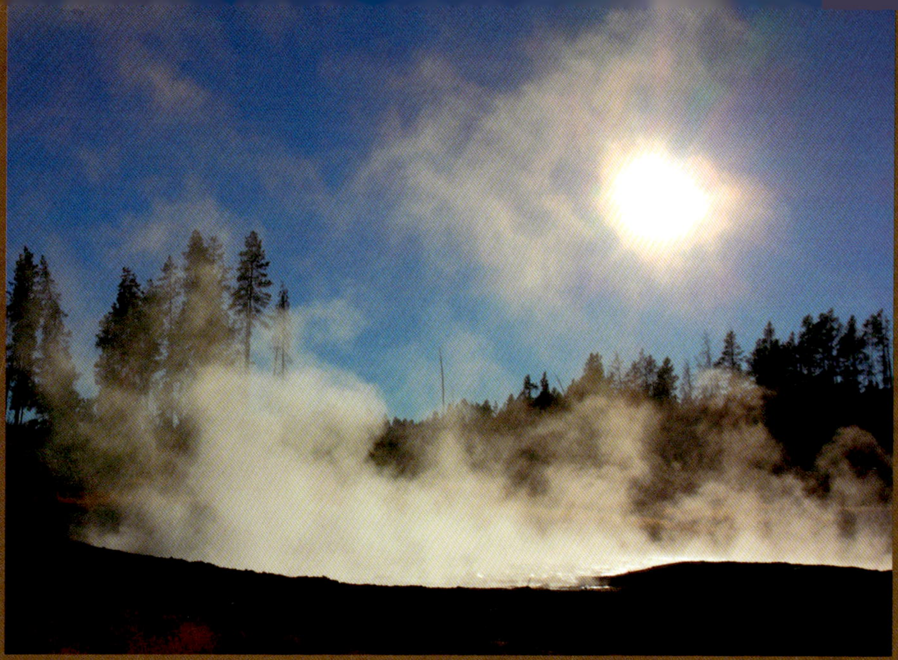

The crater of Mud Volcano is a paint pot about thirty feet in size emitting frequent bursts of steam.

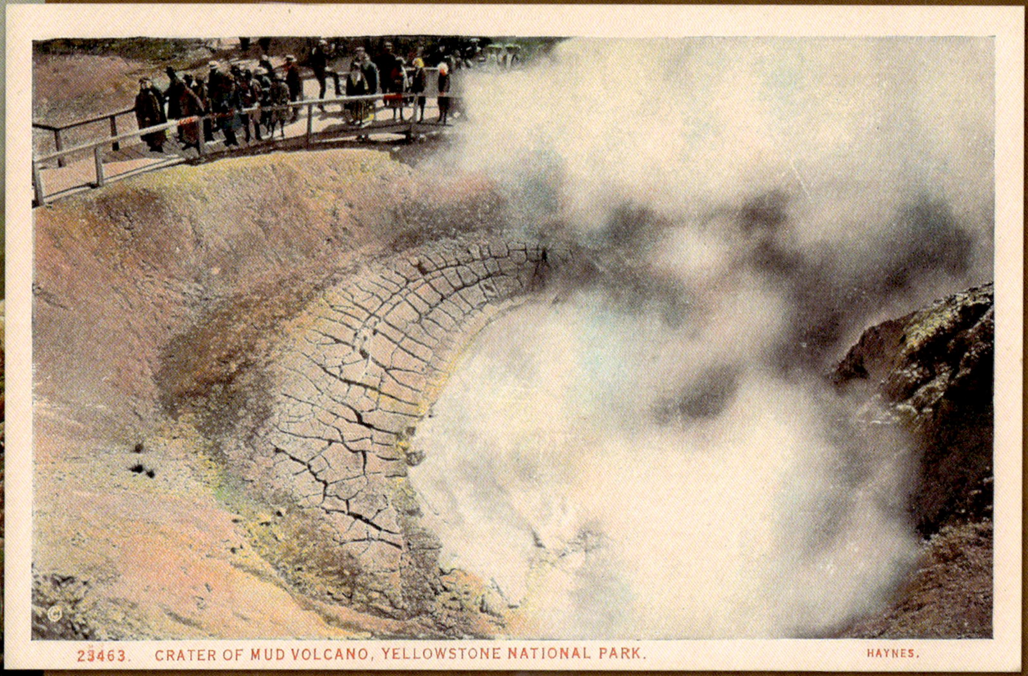

Mud Volcano was named by the 1871 Hayden Expedition when it was an active mud spring. It is no longer as active as it once was. Haynes postcard.

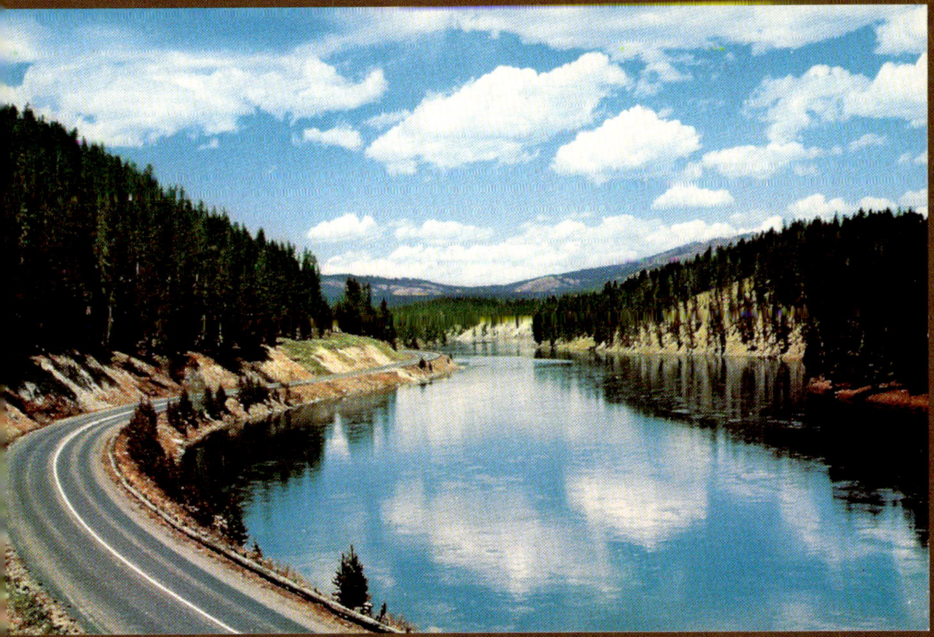

Yellowstone River is the largest and most scenic of the many streams found in the park, according to the description on the back of this postcard. The river flows along the Continental Divide and into Yellowstone Lake, then through the Hayden Valley before churning into breathtaking waterfalls at the Grand Canyon of the Yellowstone. Postcard by Intermountain Tourist Supply, Inc.

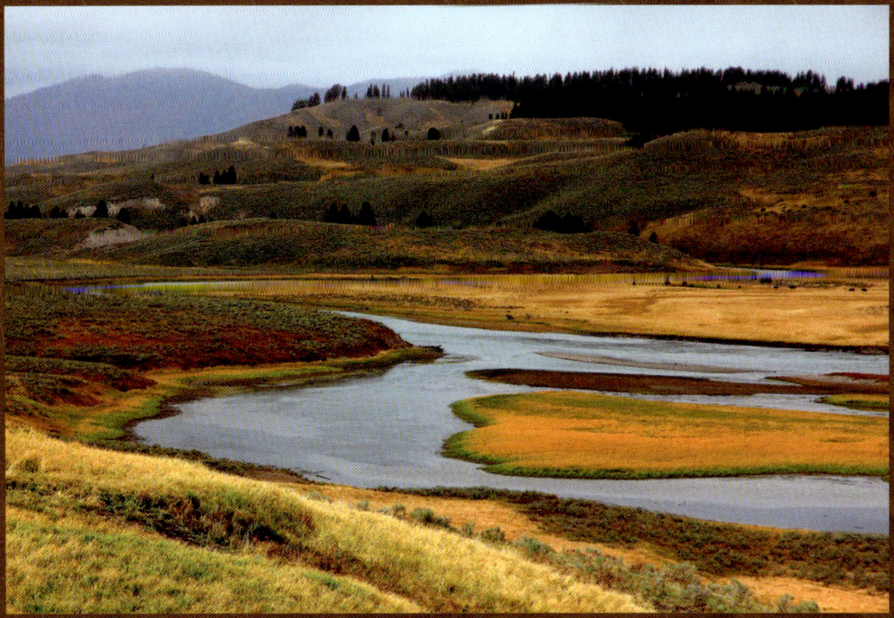

The Yellowstone River meanders peacefully through the Hayden Valley in this photograph. The water extends six hundred miles and empties into the Missouri River in North Dakota, making it the longest undammed river in the continental United States.

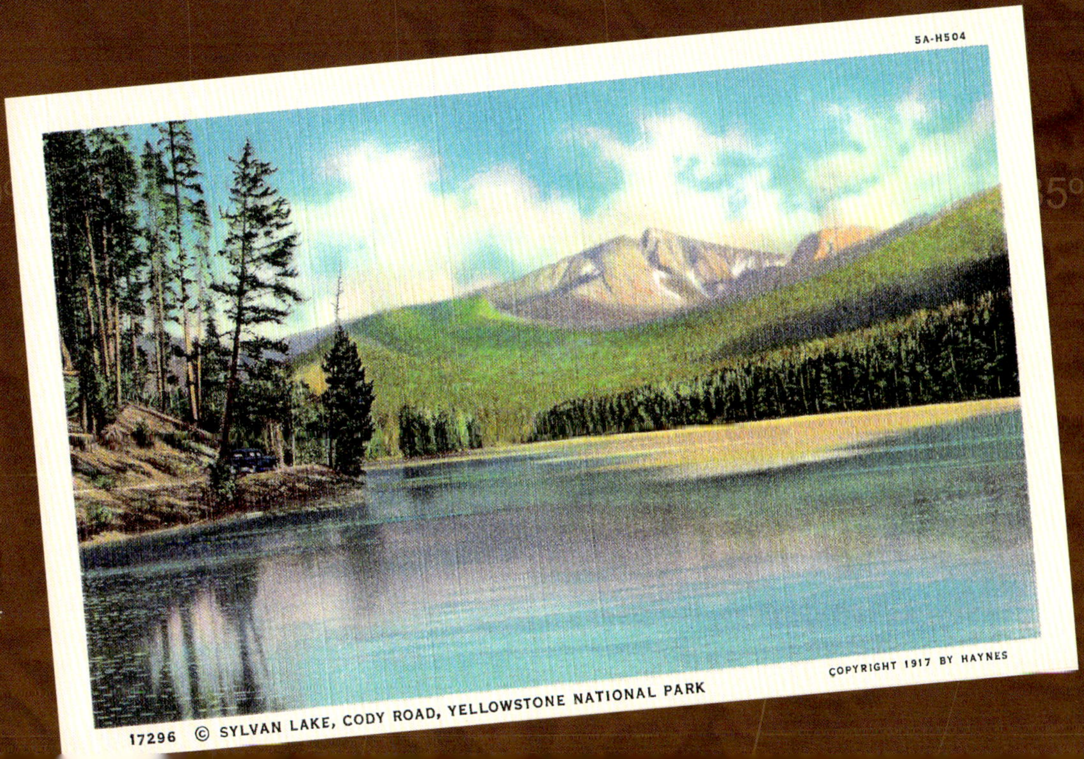

Linen postcard of Sylvan Lake and Top Notch Peak. The lake is just east of the 8,530 feet Sylvan Pass, which provides access to the park from the East Entrance. The postcard was first issued in 1917 by Haynes Picture Shops, Inc. and became one of the most popular of the entire Haynes' collection of park photographs.

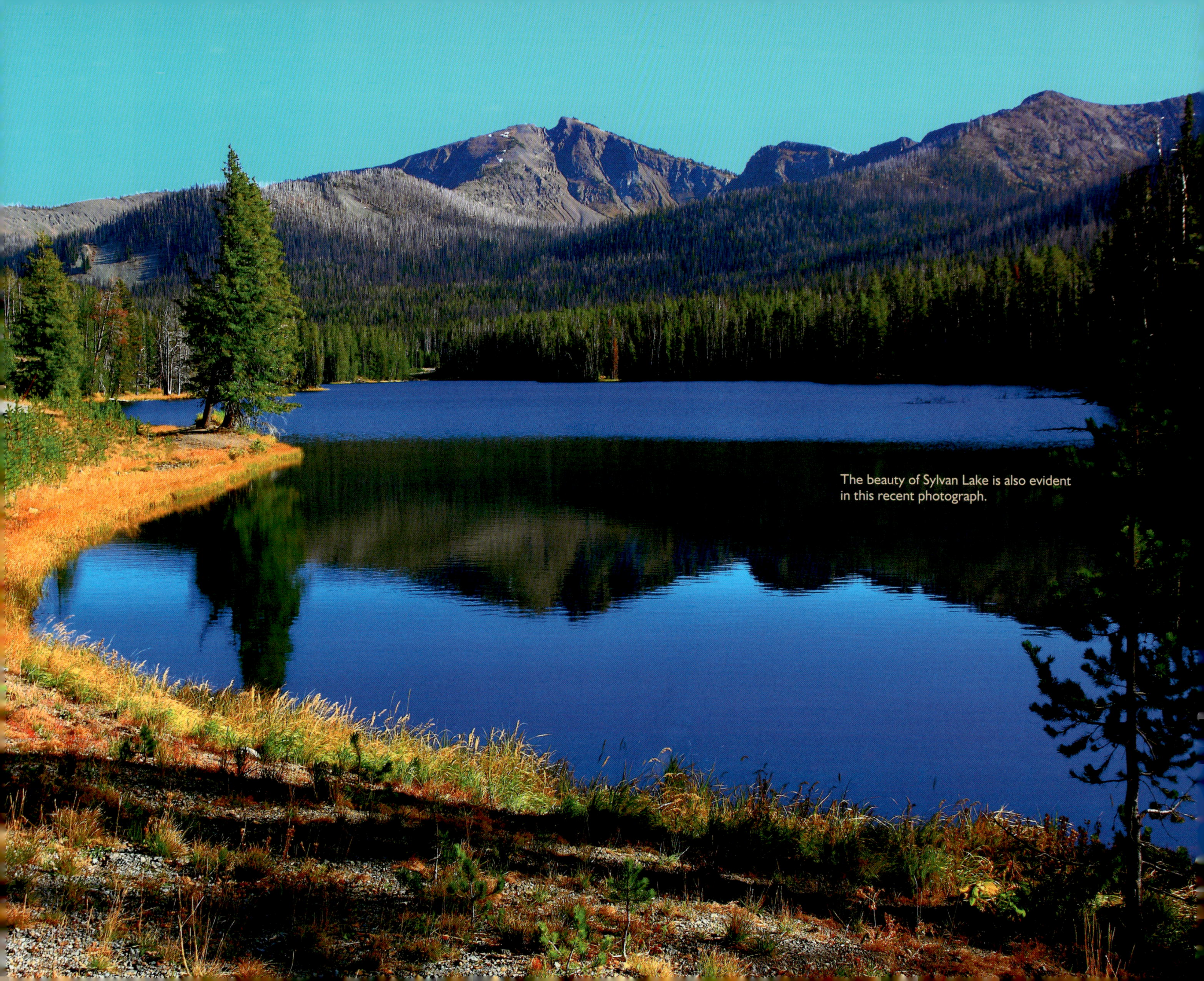

The beauty of Sylvan Lake is also evident in this recent photograph.

NATURE STRIKES

A powerful earthquake and a raging wildfire have served as recent reminders of nature's fury.

The destructive Hebgen Lake earthquake registered as much as 7.5 on the Richter scale and struck after 11 p.m. on August 17, 1959. The epicenter was at Hebgen Lake, located to the east in Montana. At nearby Yellowstone, many of the geysers and paint pots were changed by the earthquake. The Fountain Paint Pots became so active they took over a paved parking lot, while many of the geysers changed their eruption intervals and durations, with some ceasing all activity. Sadly, twenty-eight people, none within the park, were killed and many buildings and roads were damaged or destroyed throughout the region. The park's most treasured building, the Old Faithful Inn, survived, but sustained damage to its chimney as well as broken water pipes. The inn was repaired during a ten-year restoration project that began in 1979. The work would eventually cost $7.3 million. The Canyon Hotel suffered a different fate with earthquake damage accelerating decisions for its demolition.

Since its existence, the Yellowstone region has been one of the most seismically active areas in the country with earthquakes occurring as often as 1,000 to 3,000 times each year. While most are too small to be noticed, more moderate quakes can be felt during any given year.

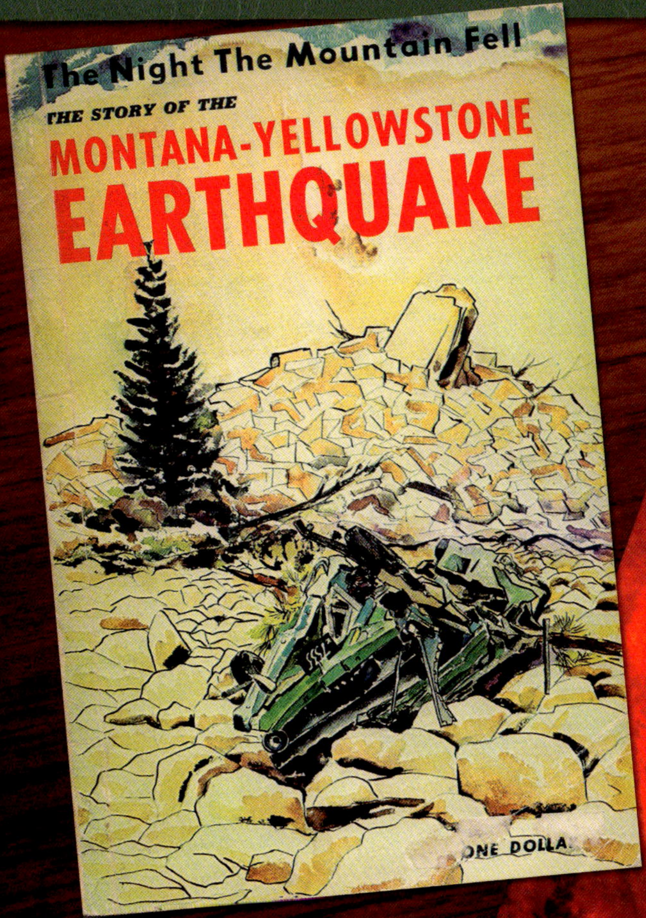

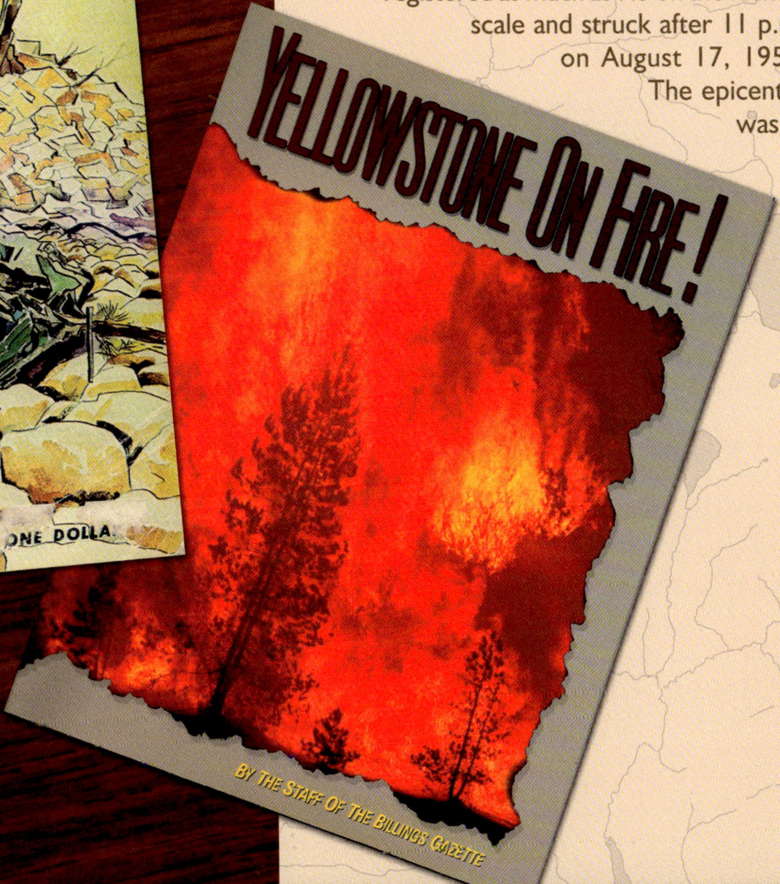

Pictured are booklets about the destructive earthquake and fire that struck Yellowstone. *The Night the Mountain Fell – The Story of the Montana-Yellowstone Earthquake* is by Edmund Christopherson and *Yellowstone on Fire!* was published by the staff of the *Billings Gazette*.

1988 WILDFIRES

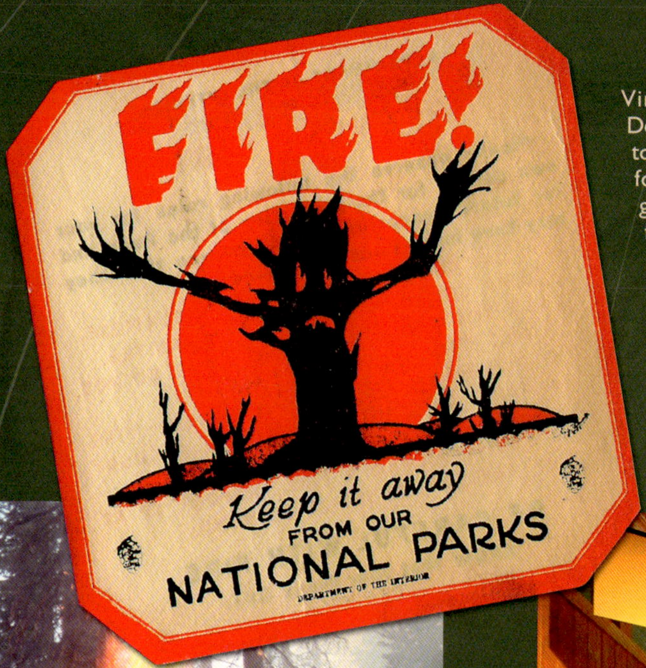

Vintage fire prevention decal issued by the Department of the Interior. The back warns visitors to be careful with campfires "for your own safety, for the protection of the Park, and for future generations of Americans that they may have forests and playgrounds."

The summer of wildfires in Yellowstone Park occurred in 1988. There were nearly 250 fires in the greater Yellowstone area from June to August of that year. Because of a National Park Service policy at the time to let nature take its course, many of the fires within the park were allowed to burn, but became uncontrollable due to wind and drought. The worst day of fires occurred on August 20th, known as Black Saturday, when the fast-burning fires doubled in size to 250,000 acres. At one point during the fires, Old Faithful Inn was threatened, but a shift in the wind and water sprayed on embers by firefighters saved the building. Nineteen other structures in the complex were destroyed. The fires were finally contained by late fall with the changing of the season. By that time, thirty-six percent of the park, or 793,000 acres, had been burned, sixty-seven structures destroyed, and campgrounds and bridges damaged. While no one in the park was killed and losses to fish and wildlife were minimal, the fires claimed the lives of two firefighters outside the park. One was killed in a plane crash while the other was hit by a falling tree. The government spent millions responding to the wildfires with air and ground support from more than 25,000 firefighters.

In the years since the fires, much of the park has been rejuvenated with trees, wildflowers, and other vegetation coming back on their own. These natural processes are being studied by researchers who are examining the long-term effects of the fire and its recovery. Nonetheless, the 1988 wildfires served as a catalyst for discussions about national wildfire suppression and today, federal fire-management policies have been modified with stricter guidelines under which naturally occurring fires are allowed to burn.

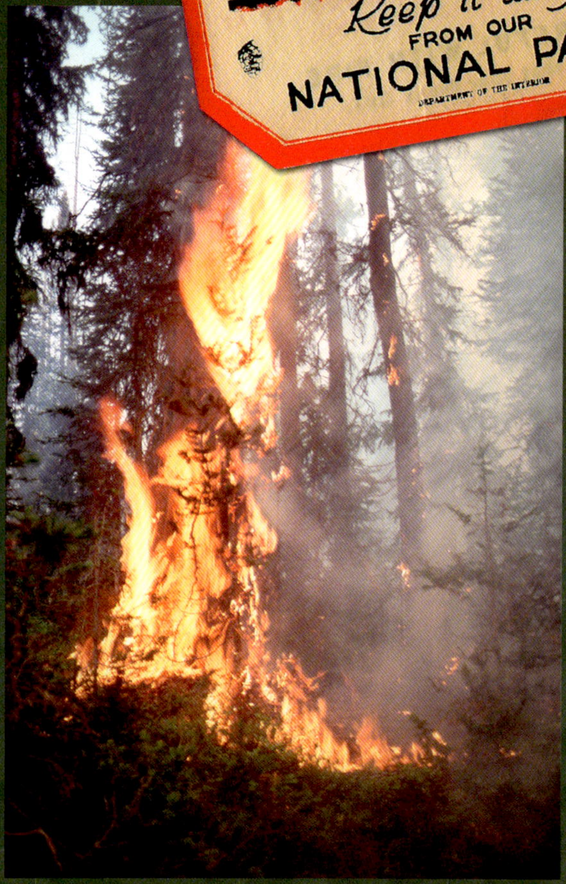

The wildfires of 1988 were the largest fires in the park's history, burning about thirty-six percent of the park's acreage and prompting a national debate about fire management policies. *National Park Service photo by Jim Peaco showing trees burning near Lewis Lake.*

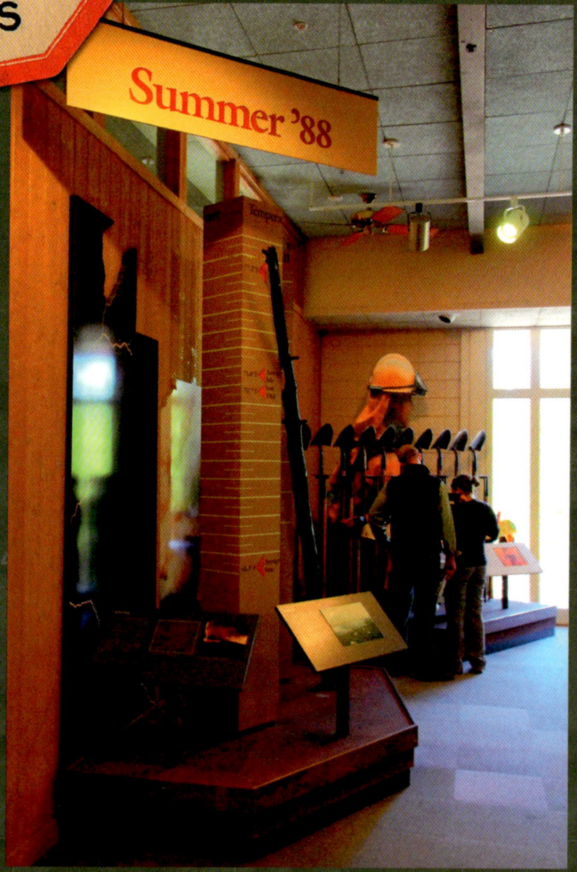

The Grant Visitor Center at West Thumb features an exhibit on the 1988 wildfires and tells the story of fire's role in the rebirth of a forest.

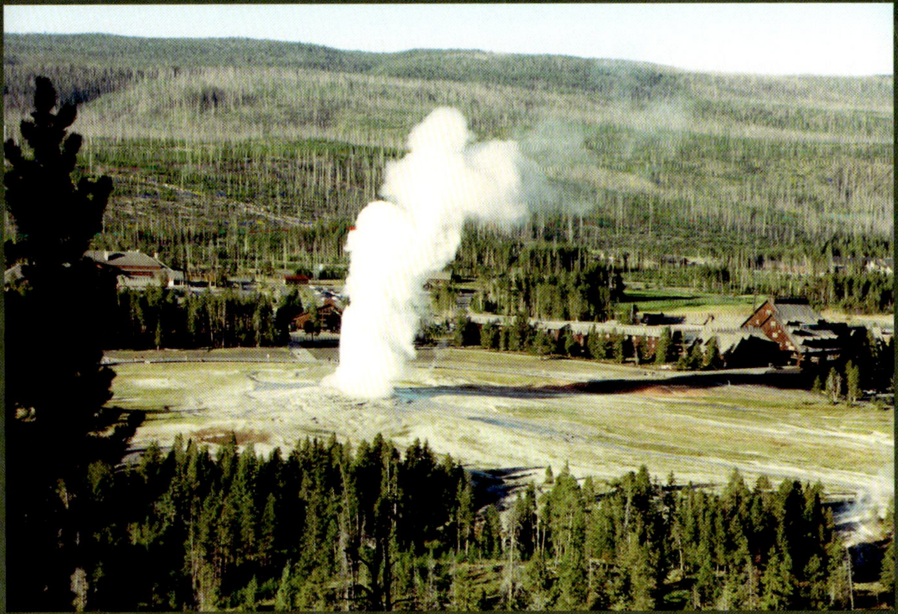

After surviving the earthquake in 1959, the Old Faithful Inn was again threatened during the summer fires of 1988. This 2004 picture shows how close the inn came to being burned. Dead trees that resemble matchsticks can still be seen on the hillside behind the inn to the right of the famous geyser. A shift in the wind and water sprayed by firefighters to douse embers on the roof saved the historic building. Nineteen other structures in the Old Faithful complex were destroyed.

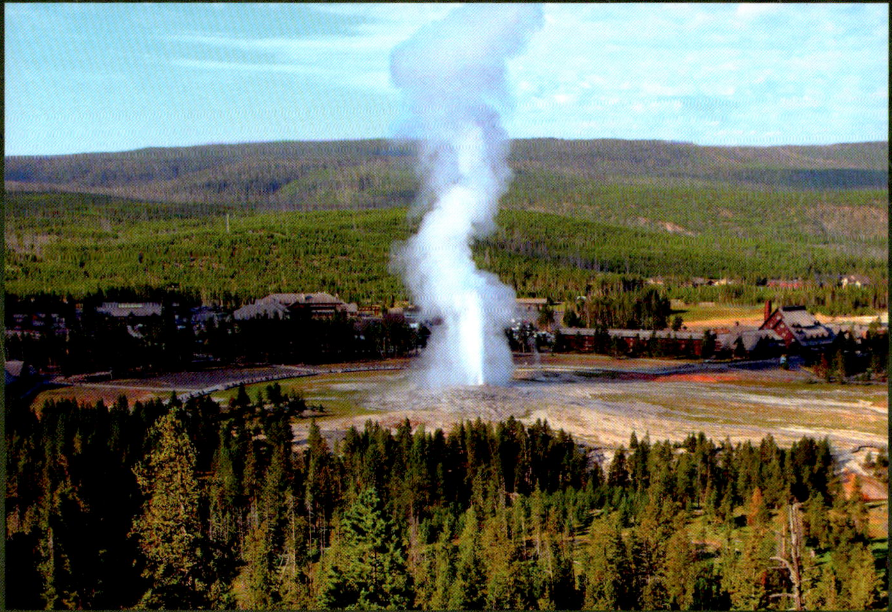

Fires are part of the natural regeneration process. Among the benefits are new plant growth and improved habitat for wildlife. This photo was taken from the Observation Point Trail in 2012 and shows significant changes in the vegetation.

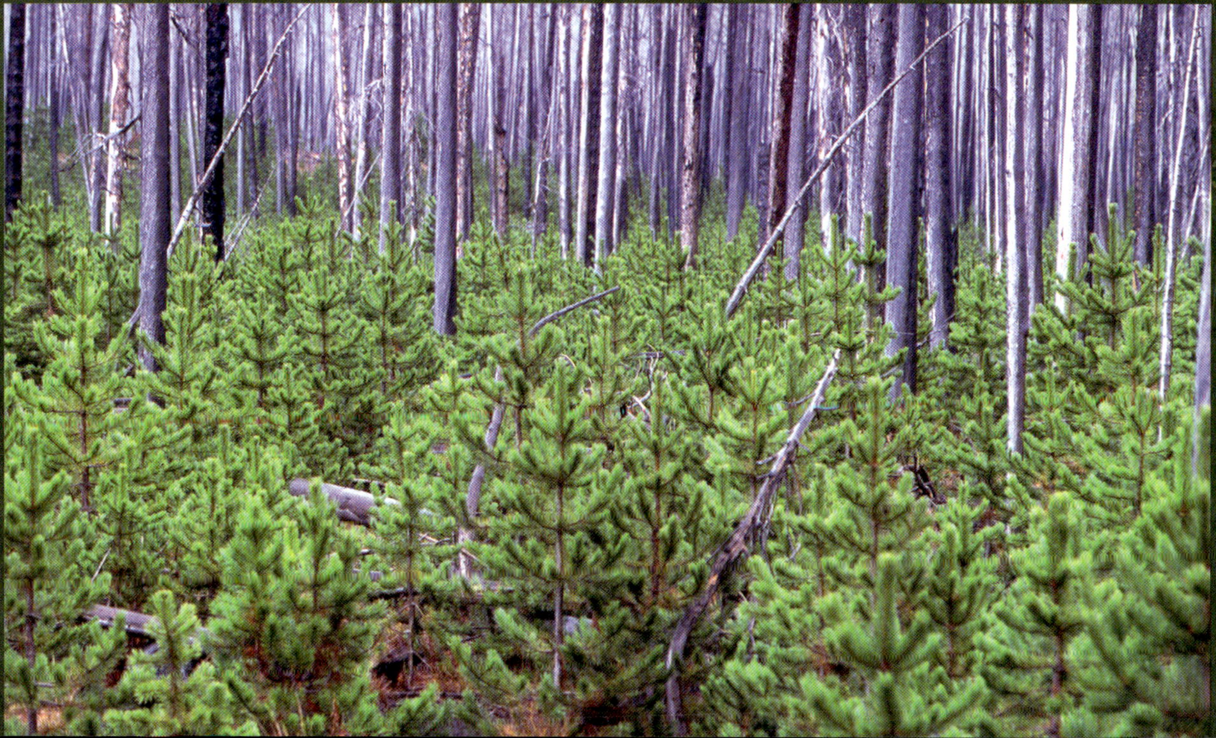

Ten years after the fires of 1988, these young lodgepole pines were photographed within a stand of dead trees to illustrate changes in the forest. *National Park Service photo by Jim Peaco.*

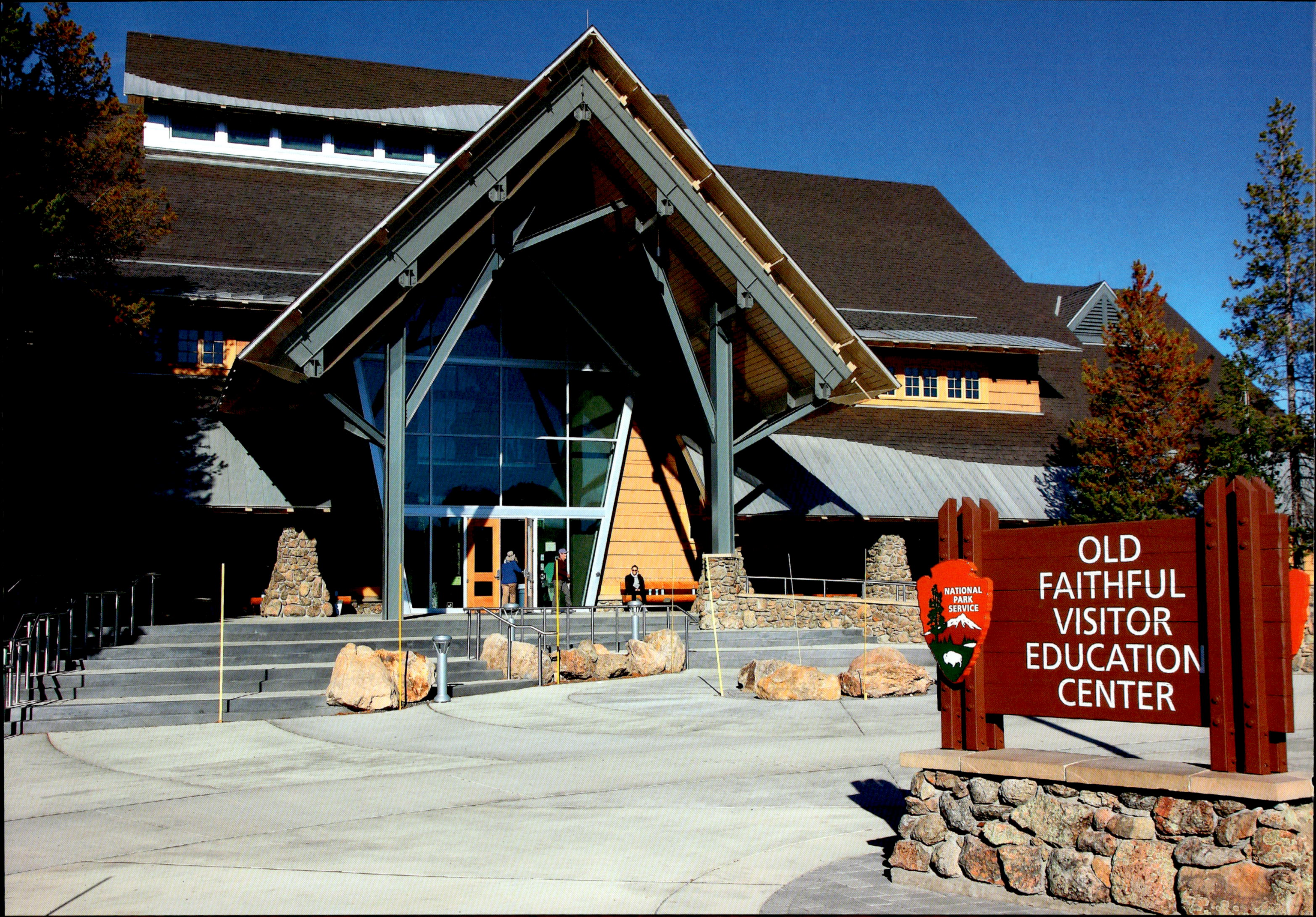

The state-of-the-art Old Faithful Visitor Education Center which opened in 2010 showcases the park's newest initiatives in helping visitors discover the international significance of Yellowstone as a living scientific laboratory and to inspire children to be future scientists and conservationists. Nearly eight years in the making, the center has been recognized for its environmentally-friendly design, use of recycled building materials, and its ongoing energy efficiencies. It is one of the most energy-efficient visitor centers within the national park system and has earned a Leadership in Energy and Environmental Design (LEED) Gold certification from the United States Green Building Council.

OUTLOOK

Yellowstone's one hundred millionth visitor was recorded in 1993 and, with annual visitation exceeding three million today, preservation and protection measures for this national treasure are essential for the park's future. As with the Mission 66 program, which implemented protections and improvements throughout the parks from 1956 to 1966 to coincide with the 50th anniversary of the National Park Service, scholars will look back upon the 100th anniversary with similar regard. Yellowstone, as the nation's flagship park, has embarked on numerous environmental initiatives to meet the centennial challenge, including pollution controls, recycling projects, use of alternative fuels, and engaging its visitors in shared environmental stewardship.

The long-term management of the park's wintertime enjoyment is also evolving, as researchers evaluate snowmobile and snowcoach capacity, air and noise quality standards, visitor access, and wildlife impacts.

Protection of the wildlife remains a fixture of the park's stewardship. Of utmost importance is monitoring the impact of wolves on the park's ecosystem following their reintroduction in 1995. Comprehensive management of the park's iconic bison is included in a wildlife health program, as is conservation of the trumpeter swans and peregrine falcons. Other programs aim to reduce the number of human-bear encounters, study disease in bighorn sheep, facilitate safe migration of the pronghorn, as well as research and restoration efforts to help ensure the survival of native fish species.

Improvements to roads and trails, as well as other man-made structures, are guided by environmental impact studies in keeping with the park's goals to protect, preserve, and enhance its natural and cultural resources.

Looking ahead to the next one hundred years, evolving management practices and assistance from the non-profit Yellowstone Park Foundation and Yellowstone Association will contribute greatly to the park's sustainability. Together, numerous fund-raising, educational, and volunteer initiatives will be used to preserve Yellowstone as a place of pilgrimage for generations of visitors to come.

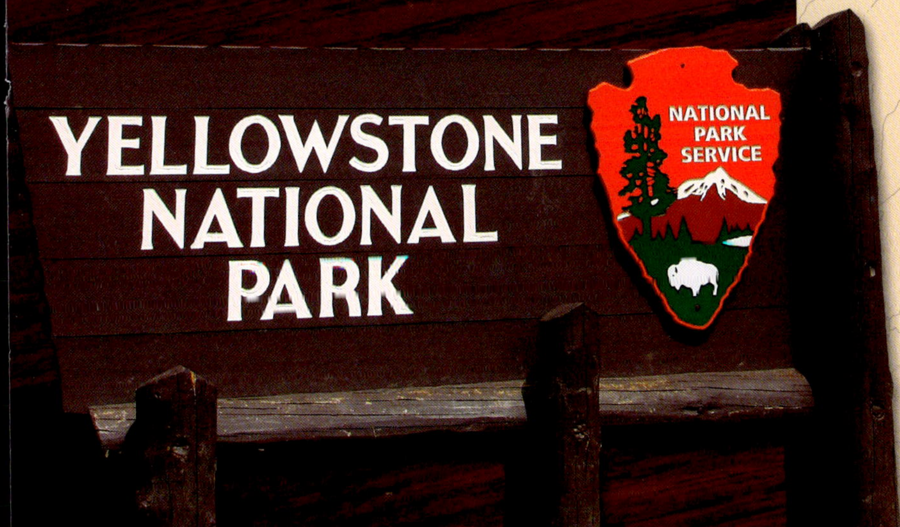

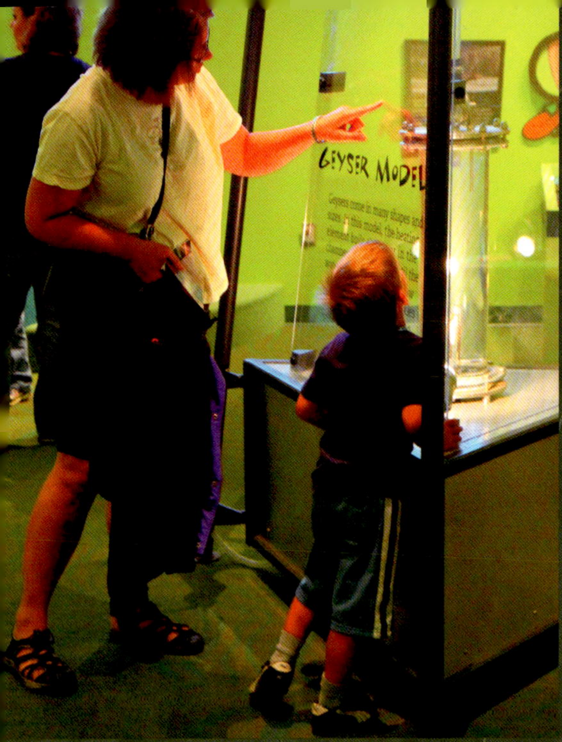

The Old Faithful Visitor Education Center offers hands-on earning experiences for visitors of all ages. Here, a child earns how a geyser works.

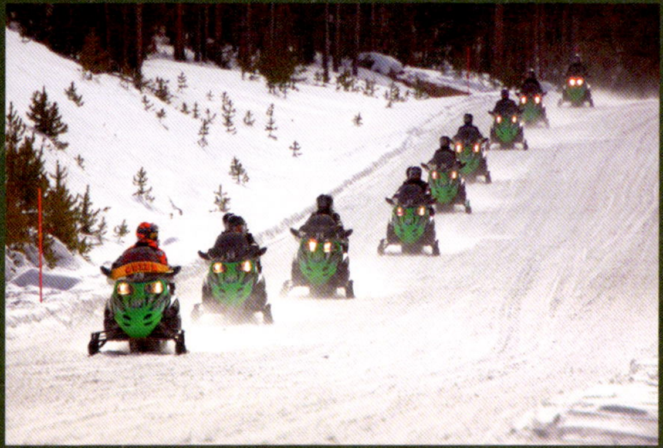

Winter visitation to Yellowstone has steadily increased since the first motorized, oversnow vehicles were introduced in the 1960s. By the 1970s, impacts from noise, pollution, crowding, and wildlife disturbances caused the park to begin regulating winter access. Those regulations are continuing to evolve. Only guided snowmobile and snowcoach tours are permitted. Park employees are the only ones allowed to travel alone.

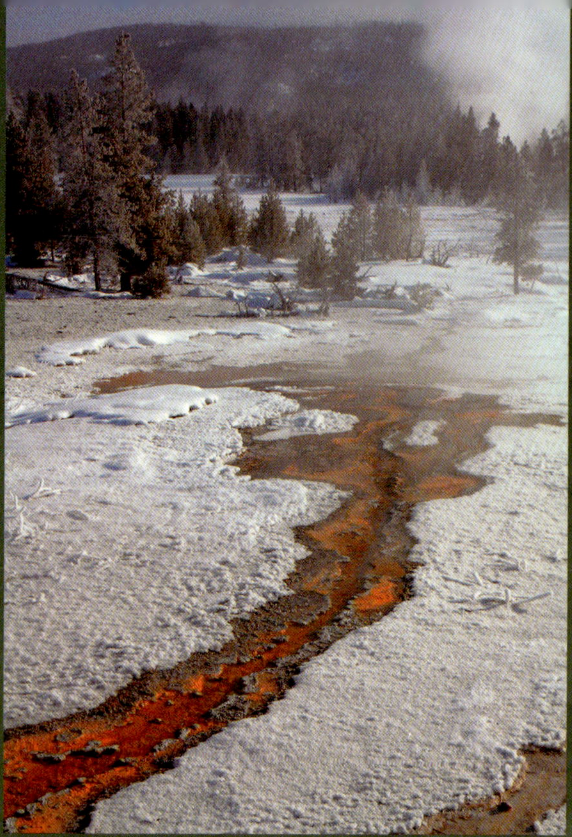

The landscape changes dramatically during a visit to Yellowstone in winter. Photographers delight in capturing images of the park's solitude, including this scene of a hot spring run-off in Upper Geyser Basin (above) and another showing Hayden Valley from a snowcoach tour. The interior of the park is usually open from mid-December to early March for the winter season.

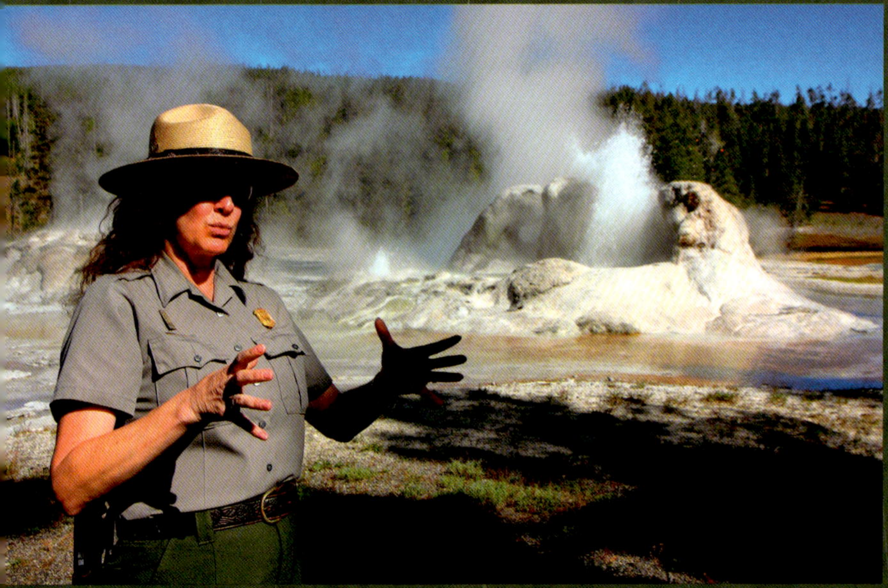

Ranger-led programs like this one at Grotto Geyser are offered throughout the park to help visitors make the most of their experience.

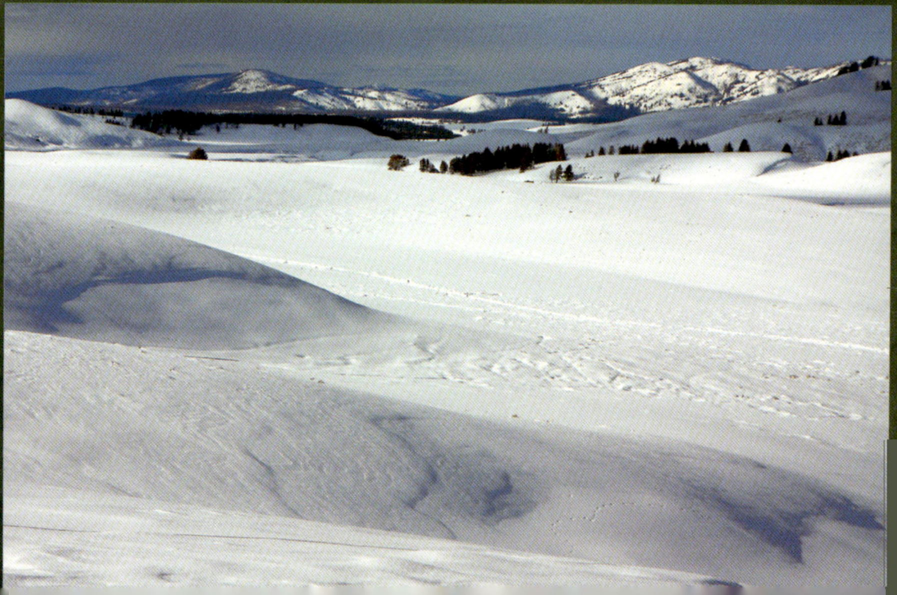

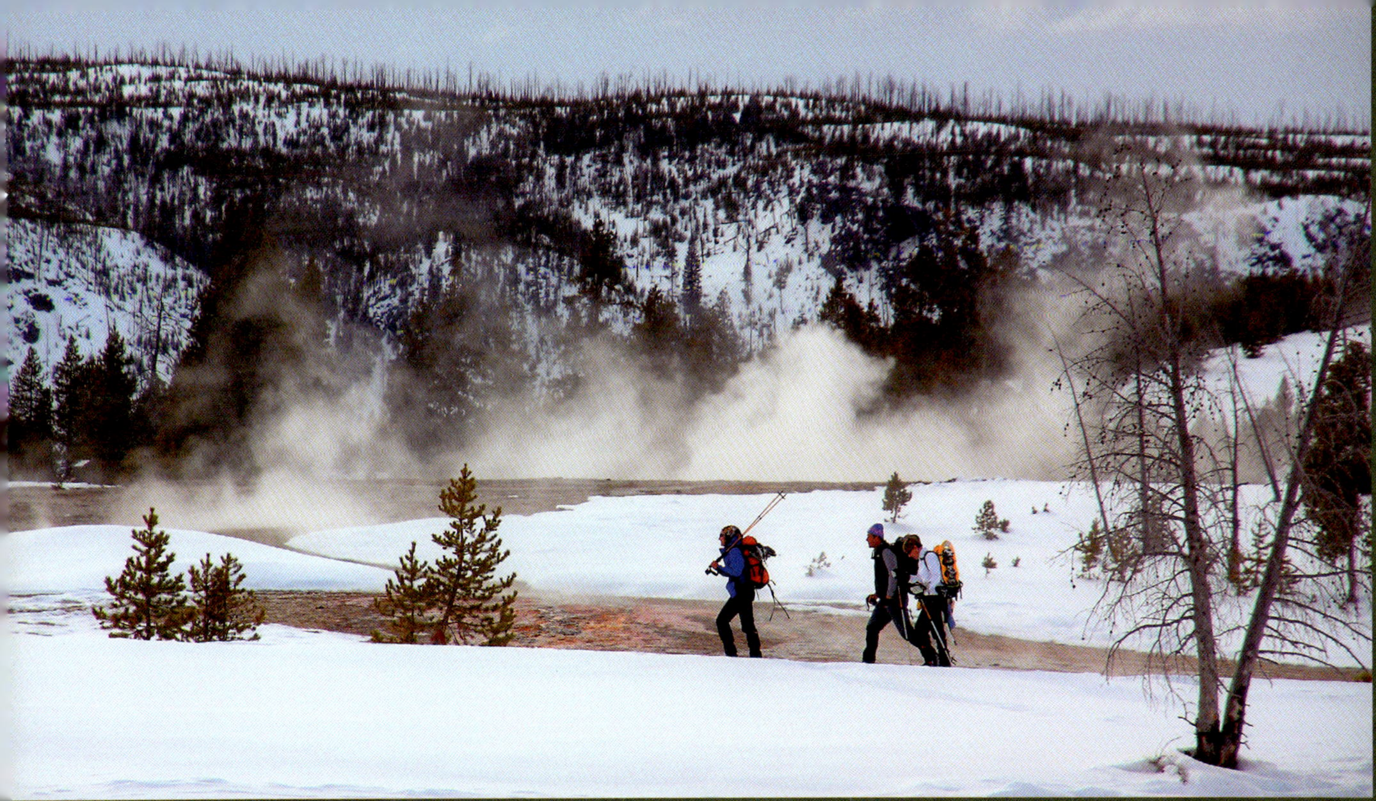

Yellowstone's winter wonderland is enjoyed by cold weather enthusiasts who take part in activities such as cross-country skiing, snowshoeing, and snowcoach tours. The park records approximately 100,000 visitors during the winter season. The Canyon and Old Faithful areas are the most popular destinations for winter visitors and can be accessed from Old Faithful Snow Lodge, Mammoth Hot Springs or from the gateway towns of West Yellowstone and Jackson.

Recognizing the growing popularity of a trip to Yellowstone during the winter, the Old Faithful Snow Lodge, the park's newest, was built in 1998 and is located in the Old Faithful area. The lodge, with its surrounding cabins, is one of only two park facilities offering winter lodging. The other is Mammoth Hot Springs Hotel. For the hearty, winter camping is available at Mammoth Hot Springs campground. A permit is required for backcountry camping.

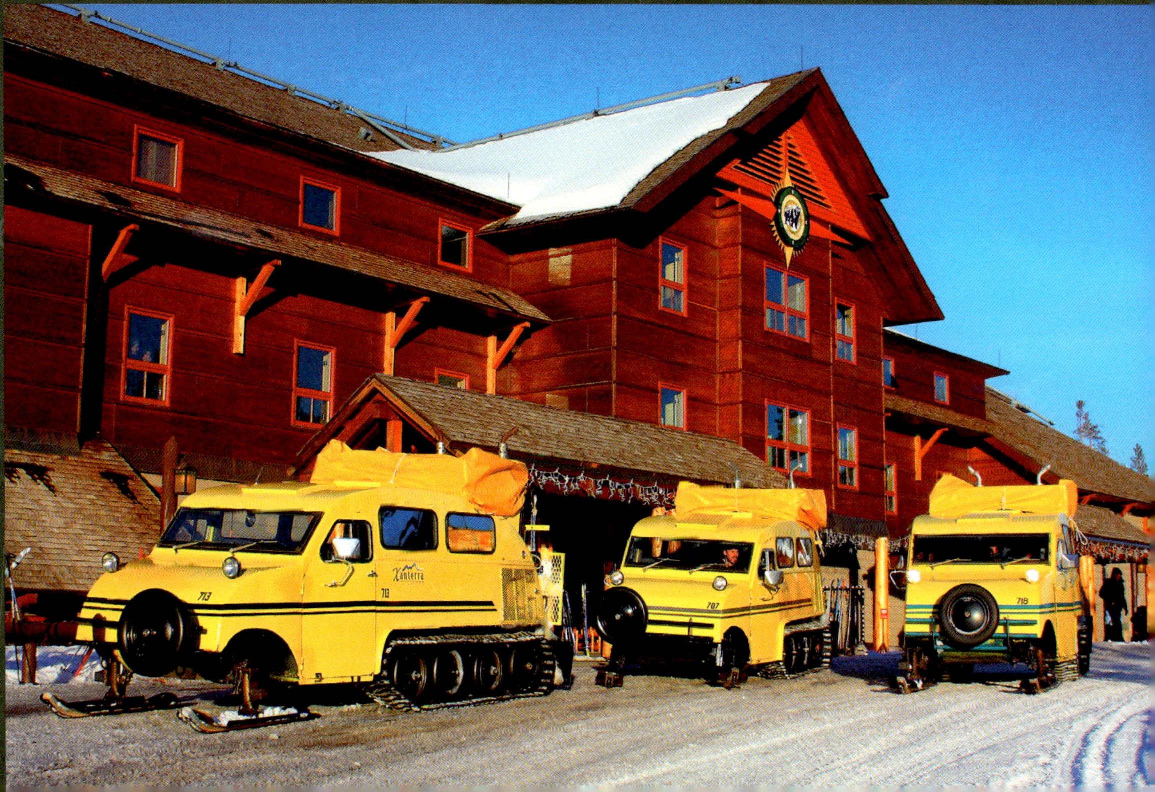

Protection of the park's wildlife is paramount to the park's ongoing stewardship. The susceptibility of bighorn sheep to disease, for example, is well documented and of concern to biologists. An outbreak of pinkeye in the 1980s caused losses in the population. The park's wildlife management programs require coordination with neighboring property owners and other federal and state agencies to address conflicting policies and goals.

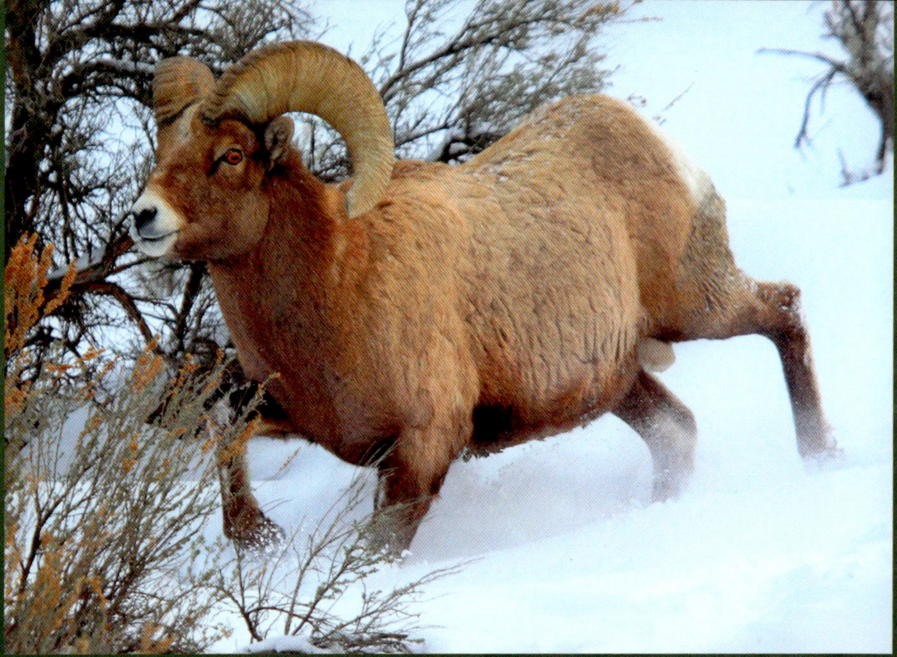

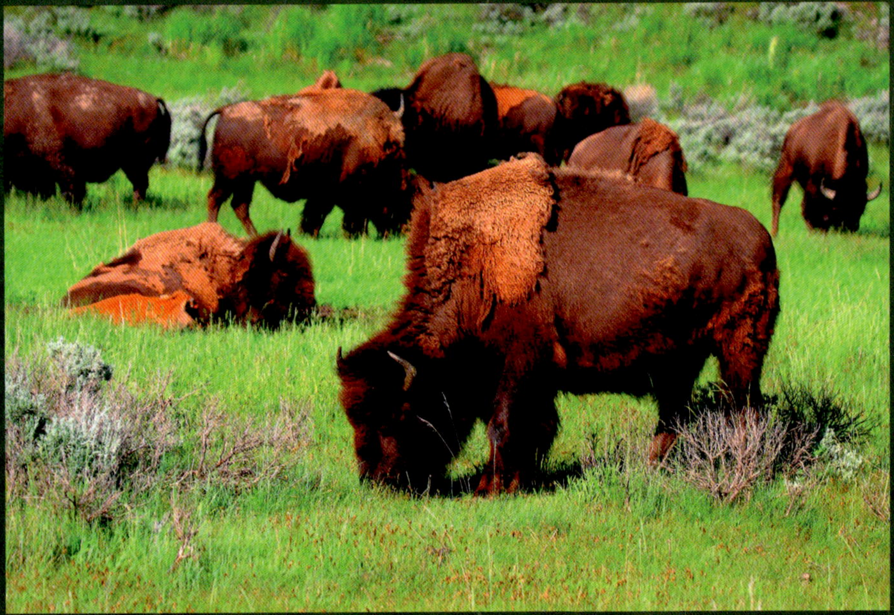

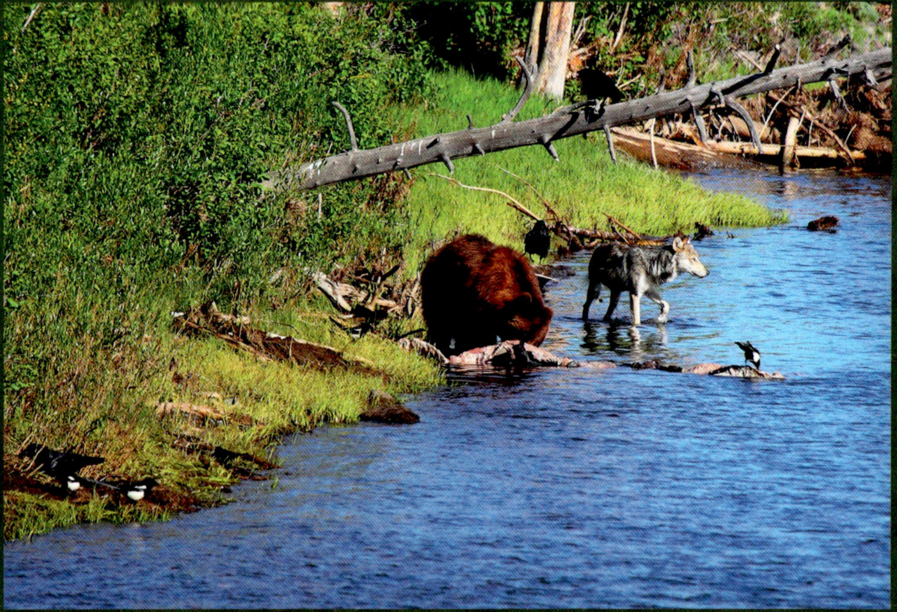

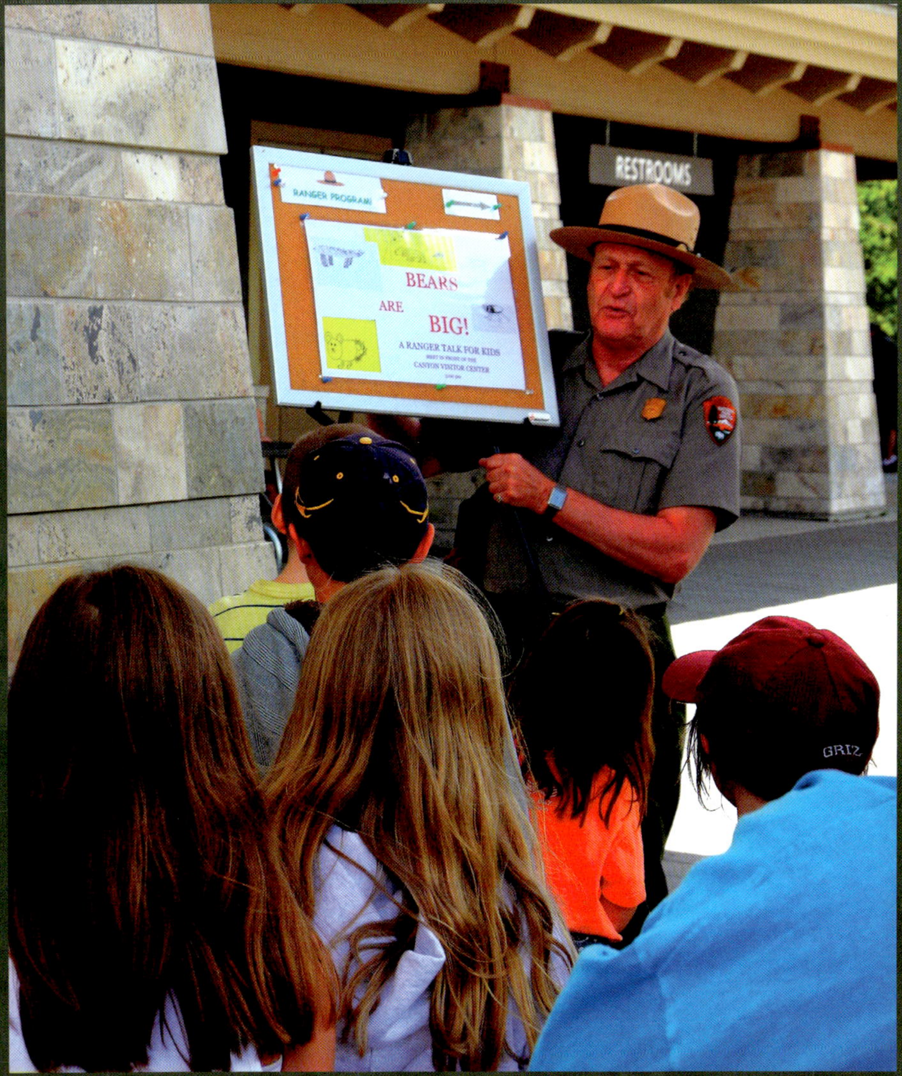

While looking to inspire the next generation of conservationists through its Junior Ranger programs and other youth-based initiatives, park facilities are also meant to honor Yellowstone's rich heritage. The Museum of the National Park Ranger is one of nine visitor centers and museums within the park. Located at the entrance to Norris Campground, the museum celebrates the history of rangers in the National Park Service, which had its roots during the park's occupation by the U.S. Army. The museum is housed in the Norris Soldier Station, built in 1908, that was once used for soldiers on patrol. The museum is open daily during the summer season and is staffed by former Park Service employees. Other visitor centers and museums include Albright Visitor Center, Canyon Visitor Education Center, Fishing Bridge Visitor Center, Grant Village Visitor Center, Madison Information Station, Norris Geyser Basin Museum and Information Station, Old Faithful Visitor Education Center, and West Thumb Information Center.

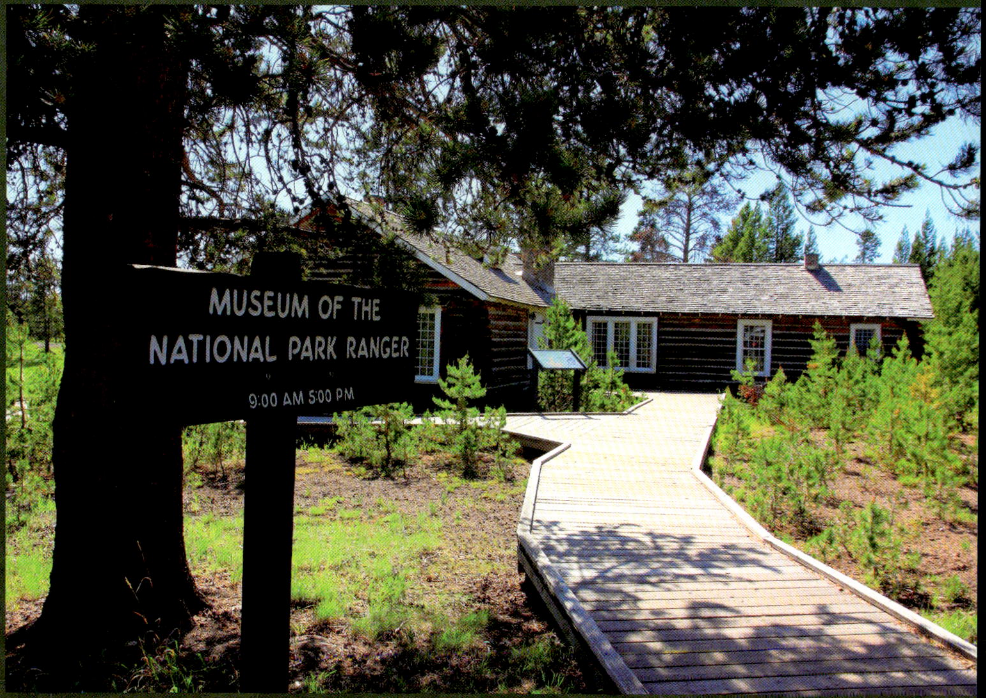

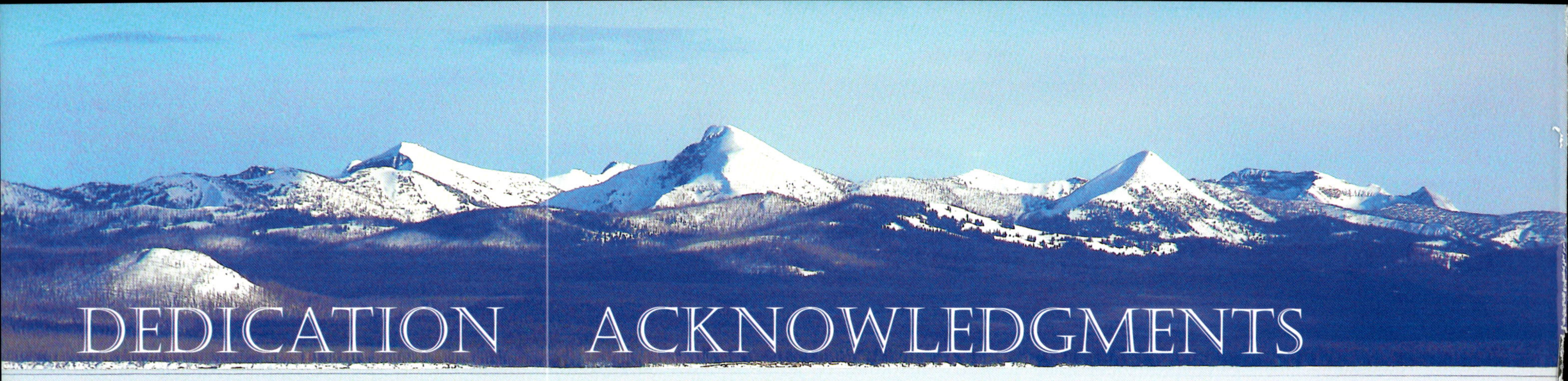

DEDICATION

This book is dedicated to our grandmothers, Ah-See Lai Chiang and Flossie Scofield, each of whom made great sacrifices during their lives so their children and grandchildren could have a better life. Ah-See, an uneducated woman, spent time helping to care for I-Ting as a young boy in Taiwan while his mother and father worked. He fondly remembers the lullabies she would sing in Japanese to comfort him and her ongoing encouragement to pursue an education. Flossie was widowed early in life and was working outside the home long before it was common for women to enter the workplace. Her success and confidence afforded numerous opportunities for travel. Always one to share her good fortune, she arranged for Suzanne, then ten years old, to accompany her on a trip to the Grand Canyon and Yosemite National Park. It was Suzanne's first cross-country trip and will forever serve as a reminder of her grandmother's lifelong generosity.

ACKNOWLEDGMENTS

We owe this book in large part to Flickr. Chiang had been posting images of his travels to the national parks on the photo-sharing site while Silverthorn was using the site to search for specific photos to complete an assignment. It was the perfect combination: I-Ting with his photography portfolio and Suzanne, the history buff, with her vast postcard collection. Together, their strengths have culminated in this book, as well as others.

There are many other people who have also helped to make this publication possible. We thank those who answered questions, helped with research, and supplied photography, including Lee and Jane Whiteley; Colleen E. Curry, Supervisory Museum Curator, Yellowstone National Park; Jim Peaco, National Park Service; Tom Mesereau, Mesereau Public Relations; Xanterra Parks & Resorts; Gardiner Chamber of Commerce, Gardiner, Montana; Yellowstone Historic Center, West Yellowstone, Montana; Charissa Reid, Headwaters of the Yellowstone B&B, Gardiner, Montana; and Union Pacific Railroad.

Thanks also to our Flickr colleague, Darlene Bushue, plus Ellen Feigin Johnson of Designs by Ellen, and Bob Jovick, ephemera collector.

Lastly, we thank Dian Zillner, Silverthorn's mother, for assisting with research, and the remainder of our families for their patience and support. Additional recognition is extended to Schiffer Publishing, Ltd. and its outstanding staff, especially Jennifer Marie Savage, our editor.

BIBLIOGRAPHY

Books

Barnes, Christine. *Great Lodges of the National Parks*. Bend, Oregon: W.W. West, Inc., 2002.

Billings Gazette. "Yellowstone on Fire." *Billings Gazette*, Billings Montana, 1989.

Bryan, T. Scott. *The Geysers of Yellowstone, 4th Edition*. Boulder, Colorado: University Press of Colorado, 2008.

Christopherson, Edmund. "The Night the Mountain Fell: The Story of the Montana-Yellowstone Earthquake." *Earthquake Press Book*. Missoula, Montana: Lawton Printing, Inc., 1960 and 1962.

Fodor's Complete Guide to the National Parks of the West. New York, New York: Fodor's Travel, a Division of Random House, Inc., 2007.

Haines, Aubrey L. *The Yellowstone Story, Volumes I and II*. Yellowstone National Park, Wyoming: Yellowstone Library and Museum Association, 1977.

Haynes, Jack E. *Haynes' Official Guide Yellowstone National Park, 27th Edition*. St. Paul, Minnesota: Published and Illustrated by F. Jay Haynes, 1913.

Peterson, Eric. *Yellowstone and Grand Teton National Parks, 5th Edition*. Hoboken, New Jersey: Wiley Publishing, Inc., 2006.

Scott, David L. and Kay W. Scott. *The Complete Guide to the National Park Lodges, 5th Edition*. Guilford, Connecticut: The Globe Pequot Press, 2006.

Whiteley, Lee. *The Yellowstone Highway: Denver to the Park, Past and Present*. Boulder, Colorado: Printed by Johnson Printing, 2001.

Brochures

Fountain Paint Pot Nature Trail Yellowstone National Park. Published by Yellowstone Library and Museum Assoc. in cooperation with the National Park Service and the U.S. Dept. of the Interior.

Guide to the Upper Geyser Basin Yellowstone National Park. Yellowstone Library and Museum Association.

Raftery, J. H. *A Miracle in Hotel Building: The Dramatic Story of the Building of the New Canyon Hotel*. Published by the Yellowstone Park Co.

Yellowstone National Park. Dept. of the Interior National Park Service, U.S. Govt. Printing Office, Washington, D.C., 1954, 1956, 1961, 1982.

Yellowstone National Park. Omaha, Nebraska.: Union Pacific System, 1928.

Yellowstone National Park. Chicago, Illinois: Wyoming-Montana-Idaho-Union Pacific System, 1920.

Yellowstone Park Hotels. Yellowstone Park, Wyoming: Yellowstone Park Hotel Co., 1931.

Yellowstone Park Hotels-Camps-Lodges-Transportation. Yellowstone Park, Wyoming: Yellowstone Park Hotel Co. and Yellowstone Park Lodge & Camp Co., circa 1930s.

Yellowstone and Teton National Parks. San Francisco, California: H. S. Crocker Co. Inc., 1954.

Newspaper Articles

"20 Years Later, Lessons from the Fire in Yellowstone." Denver, Colorado: *Denver Post*, August 31, 2008.

Brown, Matthew/Associated Press. "Bison Deal Expected to Stem Slaughter of Animals." Vail, Colorado: *Vail Daily*, April 17, 2008.

Wagner, Kyle. "Quiet, Cold, Breathtaking." Denver, Colorado: *Denver Post*, April, 13, 2008.

"Wyoming May Let Hunters Take 25 Wolves." Denver, Colorado: *Denver Post*, May 25, 2008.

Websites

Yellowstone Association:
www.yellowstoneassociation.org

Yellowstone Historic Center:
www.yellowstonehistoriccenter.org

Yellowstone National Park,
U.S. National Park Service:
www.nps.gov/yell/

Yellowstone Park Foundation:
www.ypf.org

INDEX

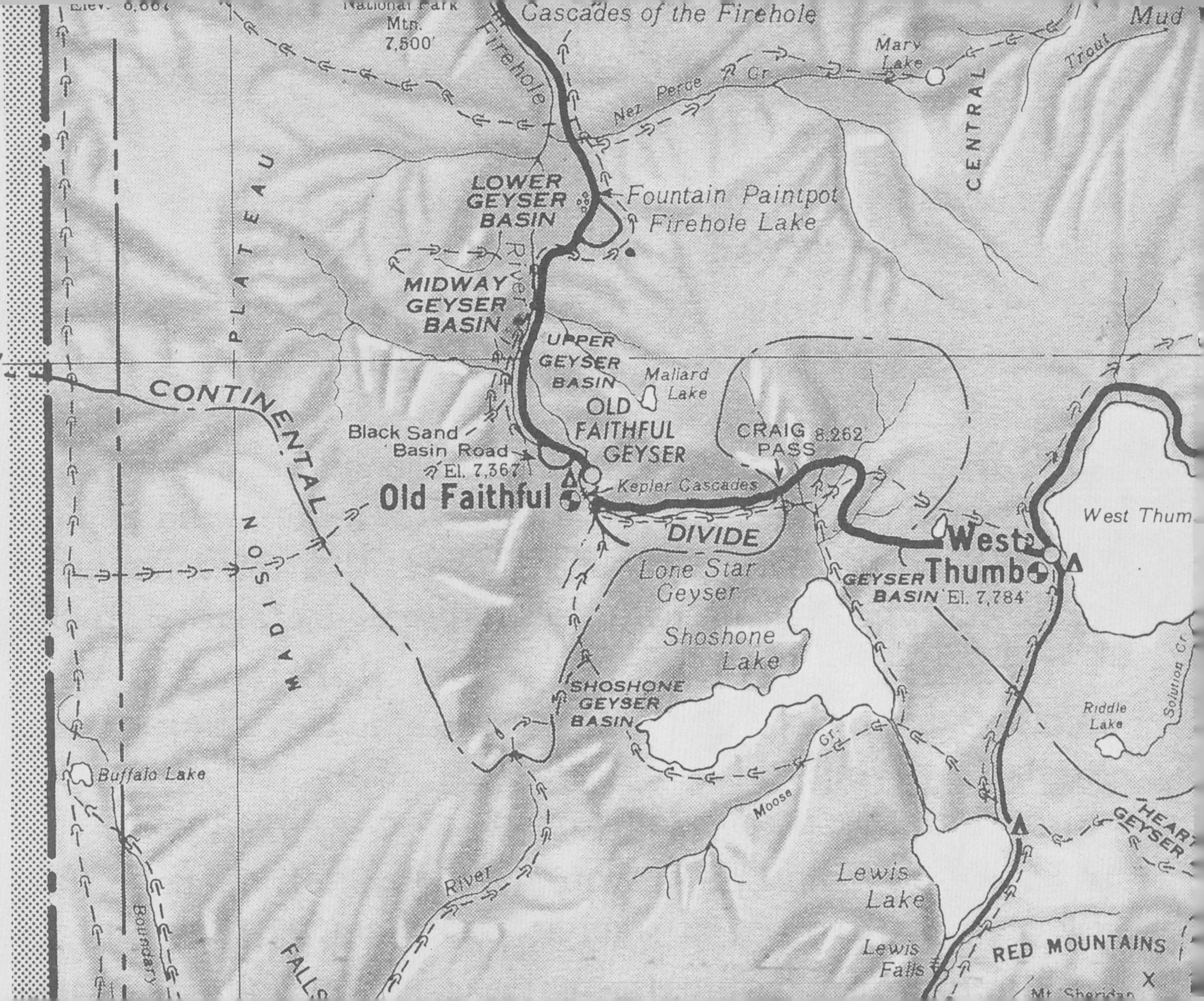
Cascades of the Firehole
Mud
Mtn.
7,500'
Mary Lake
Trout
Nez Perce Cr.
Firehole
CENTRAL
LOWER GEYSER BASIN
Fountain Paintpot
Firehole Lake
PLATEAU
River
MIDWAY GEYSER BASIN
UPPER GEYSER BASIN
Mallard Lake
30'
CONTINENTAL
OLD FAITHFUL GEYSER
Black Sand Basin Road
El. 7,367
CRAIG PASS
8,262'
Kepler Cascades
Old Faithful
DIVIDE
West Thumb
MADISON
Lone Star Geyser
GEYSER BASIN
El. 7,784'
Shoshone Lake
SHOSHONE GEYSER BASIN
Riddle Lake
Solution Cr.
Buffalo Lake
Moose
Cr.
HEART
GEYSER
Lewis Lake
River
Boundary
Lewis Falls
RED MOUNTAINS